THE American Association

A BASEBALL HISTORY 1902 — 1991

BILL O'NEAL

EAKIN PRESS ★ Austin, Texas

For Judy

A lovely Christian lady
and a delightful sister

FIRST EDITION

Published in the United States of America
By Eakin Press
A Division of Eakin Publications, Inc.
P.O. Drawer 90159 ★ Austin, TX 78709-0159

ISBN 0-89015-812-6

Library of Congress Cataloging-in-Publication Data

O'Neal, Bill, 1942–
The American Association : a baseball history, 1902–1990 / Bill O'Neal, — 1st ed.
p. cm.
Includes bibliographical references (p.) and index.
ISBN 0-89015-812-6 : $15.95
1. American Association (Baseball league) — History. I. Title.
GV875.A57054 1991
796.357'64'0973--dc20 91-24176
CIP

Contents

Foreword

Having grown up in a baseball family, it has seemed natural for me to want to spend my life around the game. Like so many others who are exposed to this sport at an early age, I have found myself fascinated by baseball's never-ending excitement and complexity. The more I learn about the game, the greater my curiosity is about its history and roots.

How has a game managed to become so inextricably and thoroughly woven into our culture and everyday routines? We take for granted the wearing of team logos on clothing, and we are stirred by movies where player heroes casually appear from out of a cornfield. How natural it seems to us that the sports sections of newspapers overflow with updates of major league transactions, and that business meetings often begin with references to some team's recent play. Our language is filled with slogans common to the players, and kids prize autographs over other things their parents can buy.

So I find nothing unusual about the fact that Bill O'Neal has dedicated a considerable part of four years compiling this eclectic history. I suspect he has a need to do it for himself, as well as wanting to help the rest of us protect our baseball heritage; I suspect we all understand.

For those of us who love baseball, the history of the American Association is a part of our inheritance. We owe a debt of gratitude to an accomplished baseball historian for compiling these facts and stories. I entrust this prized material into your hands and hope that it will linger in your memory.

BRANCH B. RICKEY
American Association President
February 1992

Acknowledgments

I owe my first debt of gratitude to Harold Cooper, a native of Columbus who attended Red Birds' games as a child, became clubhouse boy in 1935, worked in the front office for years, led the city into the International League in 1955, and eventually became the first commissioner of the Triple-A Alliance. Mr. Cooper wholeheartedly supported this project from the beginning. He paved my way with introductions to club officials, generated financial support from the league to offset my research expenses, and assisted me in numerous ways by phone and mail. His knowledge of the American Association stretches back for more than half a century, and I am deeply grateful for his invaluable assistance.

Randy Mobley, who succeeded Harold Cooper as commissioner of the Triple-A Alliance and who currently is president of the American Association, also extended gracious cooperation to me. Randy met with me after hours in his office to offer a lengthy explanation of league affairs. With great cordiality he provided me with photographs, research materials and important phone numbers, and he has responded promptly to every request for help. I am greatly appreciative of Randy's support, without which I could not have properly completed this book.

The National Baseball Hall of Fame in Cooperstown provided a large amount of materials essential to this project, and I am especially indebted to Gary Van Allen for his assistance. It has been a pleasure to work with editor Melissa Locke Roberts on five books, and as usual she suggested a number of improvements and corrections.

In Carthage I benefited from the friendship of three veterans of American Association play. Joe Vitter, a versatile St. Paul player of the 1940s, shared many lively stories with me, and his lovely wife, Eleanor, generously loaned me scrapbooks and photos. Jon

Perlman, who pitched four years for Iowa during the 1980s, shared his reflections as well as a miscellany of information on the contemporary AA. Former big league and AA catcher Jacke Davis, now coach of the Panola Pony baseball team, regaled me with stories of the 1960s.

Two colleagues and treasured friends at Panola College, librarians Mary Rose Johnson and Barbara Bell, were extremely resourceful in acquiring materials for me. Brenda Allums, head of the journalism department at Panola College, once again was kind enough to provide me with a cover photo. Another colleague and friend, math instructor Karon Ashby, was of immense aid in compiling the statistical section. Ted Leach, talented sports editor of the *Panola Watchman* in Carthage, was extremely helpful with his photographic expertise.

In Hubbard, Texas, I visited Mariana York, widow of Tony York, a gifted shortstop who played for St. Paul and Milwaukee half a century ago. Mrs. York reminisced about great players of the era and prominent figures such as Bill Veeck, then loaned me her superb collection of scrapbooks and photographs. Mrs. Vernon Washington, who recently passed away, and her daughter, Lana Foster, also shared memories, scrapbooks, and photos of the 1936 AA batting champ at the family home near Linden, Texas.

Bit McCullough, who lives in Texarkana and who was a hard-hitting AA outfielder during the 1930s, related a number of stories to me, and so did another former player, Dr. Bill Hughes, dean of students at Texarkana College. Homer Peel, a legendary minor league hitter who played for Minneapolis and Toledo in the 1930s, reminisced with me over the phone and at his home in Shreveport, Louisiana.

The only professional baseball player ever to hit more than 60 home runs in *two* seasons, Joe Hauser of Sheboygan, Wisconsin, has shared grand memories with me by correspondence and telephone on several memorable occasions. Carl Sawatski of Little Rock, who has served as president of the Texas League since 1975, was the slugging catcher for Minneapolis in 1955 when the Millers blasted 241 home runs, and he reminisced with me about that record-setting team.

Joe Ryan, the personable and progressive executive who served as president of the American Association for nearly two decades, generously granted me a lengthy and highly informative interview. Equally generous with his time and insider's knowledge of league history was A. Ray Smith, flamboyant and spectacularly successful AA club owner. As an admirer from boyhood of Yankee pitching great Allie Reynolds, who served as league president when the AA was resurrected in 1969, it was a special treat for me to talk by long distance with the "Superchief."

I was privileged to meet at a Nashville Sounds' game the superb Yankee pitching coach and former AA hurler Jim Turner, who responded to my many questions with uncanny detail. Also at Nashville I had the pleasure of interviewing Richard Sterban, the remarkable bass singer with the Oak Ridge Boys and a Sounds owner since 1978. I also was assisted by Sounds President and General Manager Larry Schmittou, Executive Vice-president George Dyce, Director of Publicity Jim Ballweg, and Secretary Jean Carney. At the Nashville Room of the Public Library of Nashville and Davidson County I received expert guidance from Mary Glenn Hearne, director, and Carol Kaplan and Laura Rehmert.

In Evansville I was aided by Carl M. Wallace, a former Triplets owner who took time from his work to tour me around Bosse Field, and who generously loaned a stranger his scrapbooks and photographs. I was treated to recollections of Swayne Field and the old Mud Hens by a good friend and accomplished Western historian, Toledo resident Robert K. DeArment.

At Cardinal Stadium in Louisville I was treated with extreme courtesy by the Redbirds' executive secretary, Mary Barney, who granted me an informative interview, then provided me with various materials and arranged for the delivery of a number of important photographs. The staff of the Louisville Public Library helped me mine the rich resources of their collections. Max Schumacher, the congenial president of the Indianapolis Indians, gave me the run of his charming ballpark and permitted me to take two books that have proven invaluable to this project.

Robin Lenhard, advertising and promotions manager of the Buffalo Bisons, guided me around magnificent Pilot Field, then entrusted me with a collection of valuable materials. Robin also arranged with caretaker John McLennan for me to tour War Memorial Stadium, and at the Buffalo Public Library Suzy Gaddio helped me explore several useful resources. In Milwaukee the research staff of the public library allowed me to examine and photocopy a number of rare and exciting items.

I am indebted to Rev. Jim Smith of Minneapolis for his enthusiastic suggestions, and for putting me in contact with Joe Hauser.

At the St. Paul Public Library the staff was extremely resourceful in helping me to locate useful materials, and across town the cordial staff of the Minnesota Historical Society made the task of exploring their extensive files unusually pleasant.

Bill Gorman, vice-president and general manager of the Omaha Royals, was most generous with his time during a doubleheader with Toledo. Bill reflected at length on conditions and events around the league, and furnished me with phone numbers which led to invaluable interviews. Staff members of Omaha's W. Dale Clark Library were helpful with my investigations, and so were staff members of the Iowa State Historical Museum in Des Moines. I am grateful to Todd Weber, director of PR and promotions for the Iowa Cubs, who provided me with useful materials when I visited Sec Taylor Stadium. Doug Ward, media relations director for the Denver Zephyrs, placed photos and other items at my disposal.

In Kansas City I received welcome assistance from staff members in the public libraries on both the Kansas and Missouri sides of the city. The staff of the Wichita Public Library likewise was cooperative and resourceful. Phillip Tolbert, public services librarian of Oklahoma City's Metropolitan Library System, provided guidance through his excellent collections, and staff members of the Tulsa Public Library offered similar assistance with their abundant resources. The preeminent expert on professional baseball in Tulsa, Wayne McCombs, generously supplied me with information and materials.

In the impressive Local History Room of the Houston Public Library, staff members facilitated my search for information and photos. Travis Dudley of the Dallas Public Library was extremely helpful in locating materials. At the Fort Worth Public Library, Max Hill enthusiastically embraced my project and directed me to numerous discoveries among the vast collections of the Local History and Genealogy Department.

My four daughters, Lynn, Shellie, Berri and Causby, ably assisted me by proofreading the manuscript and performing miscellaneous tasks during the research and writing phases. My wife, Faye, provided reliable tips on points of grammar, while allowing me to immerse myself in the history of the American Association.

BILL O'NEAL

1902–1909

Birth of the American Association

By the early years of the twentieth century a growing fascination with sports had spread throughout the United States. Football and boxing were being cleaned up and popularized, basketball had been invented in the 1890s and was spreading rapidly to colleges and high schools, and Americans were enthusiastically participating in bicycling and golf and a host of other athletic activities.

Reigning unchallenged atop the American sports world was baseball, *the* national pastime. Amateur teams were organized in every city and town, virtually all high schools and colleges had clubs, and boys played with crude bats and tattered balls on thousands of vacant lots across the land. Semipro teams abounded in rural as well as urban areas; paid professionals, usually a pitcher, catcher and perhaps a shortstop, were imported from a nearby city to play with country nines in important weekend games. Professional teams had existed for more than four decades, since the Cincinnati Red Stockings of 1869, and the National Association of Professional Base-Ball Players was organized two years later. A stronger circuit, the National League, was formed in 1876, then successfully withstood the challenges of rival "major leagues" for a quarter of a century.

The first American Association was established in 1882 to provide major league competition against the National League. Teams were located in Baltimore, Cincinnati, Louisville, Philadelphia, Pittsburgh, and St. Louis. Ticket charges ranged from 10 to 25 cents — half the National League price. Other competitive devices utilized against the National League included selling beer and liquor at the ballparks, playing games on Sundays, and hiring a staff of umpires paid by the league instead of the home clubs. Aside from defying Sunday blue laws and selling alcoholic beverages at games, the American Association had several owners who made their livings in the liquor business, and irate churchmen dubbed the new circuit the "Whiskey League." But good players were hired, the quality of AA baseball was comparable to that of the National League, and the American Association offered formidable competition for the NL, even though the senior circuit pirated several AA stars.

After the first season Abraham G. Mills, a brilliant lawyer, Civil War veteran and former professional player, became president of the National League. Mills regarded the head-to-head conflict with the American Association as suicidal, and with AA officials he hammered out a National Agreement by which all organized major and minor leagues would honor player contracts. Like the AA, the National League hired a staff of umpires. The NL also transferred weak franchises from Troy and Worcester to New York and Philadelphia. Interleague peace brought prosperity to both the American Association and the National League in 1884. But the next season a new circuit, the Union Association, was organized to fight the "outrageous" player limits. The UA went after players from the AA and the NL — which contributed to a common cash pool to provide bonuses to would-be defectors to the UA. But there was a total of 34 major league teams — 13 in the AA, 13 in the UA, and eight in the NL — in 1884, many in duplicate markets, and the Union Association failed financially after one season.

The American Association and the National League existed peacefully until 1890, when the pinchpenny policies of club owners resulted in the formation of the Players' League. The three leagues combined for 25 teams — nine in the AA, and eight apiece in the PL and NL — and 1890 was hard on each circuit. The Players' League disbanded after a single season, but the two surviving circuits squabbled greedily over the athletes from the PL. After the 1891 season the American Association tried to raid NL players, but the National League countered by luring away four key AA franchises. After 10 years (1882–1891), the American Association folded, and the National League reigned as the sole major league until 1901, when there was a new challenge from the American League.

The American League developed from the most successful minor league of the 1890s, the Western League. Ban Johnson, a preacher's son and former sports editor of the Cincinnati *Commercial Gazette,* took over the Western League in 1894 with visions of upgrading the circuit to major league status. Johnson attracted club owners in key cities, top players were acquired, the circuit was renamed the American League in 1900, and in 1901 equality with the National League was declared (indeed, 60 percent of the 1901 American Leaguers had played earlier as National Leaguers). In searching for talent, Johnson's league increasingly had ignored the National Agreement. Under the threat of the upstart league the National League announced in August 1901 its decision to scrap the agreement which had established the sanctity of player contracts and territorial rights. Now the best players owned by minor league clubs could be added to National or American league rosters without compensation.

The aggressive, energetic new president of the Western League, Thomas J. Hickey, immediately fired off telegrams to presidents of the other minor leagues, calling for an emergency meeting on Thursday, September 5, 1901, in Chicago. Hickey and six other league presidents met and organized the National Association for Professional Baseball Leagues, a name which has endured to the present. Any minor league which belonged to the National Association was included in "Organized Baseball," and any non-member would be an "outlaw" league. Hickey declined the presidency of the National Association because he was deeply involved in forming a new circuit — the American Association.

The next month another organizational meeting was held in New York City, and by the opening of the 1902 season 15 circuits had joined the National Association. Ironically, Tom Hickey's newly organized American Association was *not* one of the member leagues. Hickey had resigned from the Western League and organized the American Association with teams in Columbus, Indianapolis, Kansas City, Louisville*, Milwaukee, Minneapolis, St. Paul, and Toledo. These were prosperous cities which had deep baseball traditions, but the Western League protested to the National Association that the American Association had invaded its territory. Kansas City and St. Paul had indeed fielded teams in the Western League the previous year, while in 1902 there would be WL clubs in Kansas City and Milwaukee. The National Association upheld the complaint, and for the first two years of its existence the American Association would be considered an outlaw league.

Unfazed, Hickey set up a 140-game schedule, calling for the eight teams to play each opponent 10 times at home and 10 times on the road. The season was scheduled to run from Wednesday, April 23, through Monday, September 22. Opening day brought parades and ballpark ceremonies featuring political celebrities. In Louisville, for example, a half-holiday was declared so that citizens could view the parade, scheduled to leave the Galt House at 1:30 and climax at Eclipse Park by game time at 3:00. A crowd of 6,000 witnessed Louisville's first AA game, but the Colonels were trounced by Kansas City, 16–6.

Despite predictions that the American Association would be a "Fourth of July league," the full schedule was played out to a scintillating finish. Louisville led the circuit throughout most of the season. The Colonels paced the league in most offensive categories, including team batting average (.293), stolen bases (253), and runs scored (an average of 6.4 per game). First baseman John Ganzel (.370 with 135 runs scored in 138 games) was the batting champ, and other key run producers were shortstop Lee Tannehill (.324), an outfielder-pitcher named Kerwin (.318 with 114 runs, as well as a 9–7 record from the mound), and catcher Pop Shriver (.315). The magnificent pitching staff was anchored by Ed Dunkle (30–10), lefthander Pat Flaherty (26–16), and John Coons (24–10).

But Indianapolis also boasted a superb mound corps: southpaws Win Kellum (25–10) and Frank Killen (16–6), and righthanders Tom Williams (24–12) and Jack Sutthoff (24–13). The Indians finally moved into a first-place tie with the Colonels on

* Omaha was one of the eight cities that formed the AA in the fall of 1901, but owners decided that the Nebraska city was so distant that travel expenses would be excessive. Louisville was lined up early in 1902, and Omaha remained in the Western League.

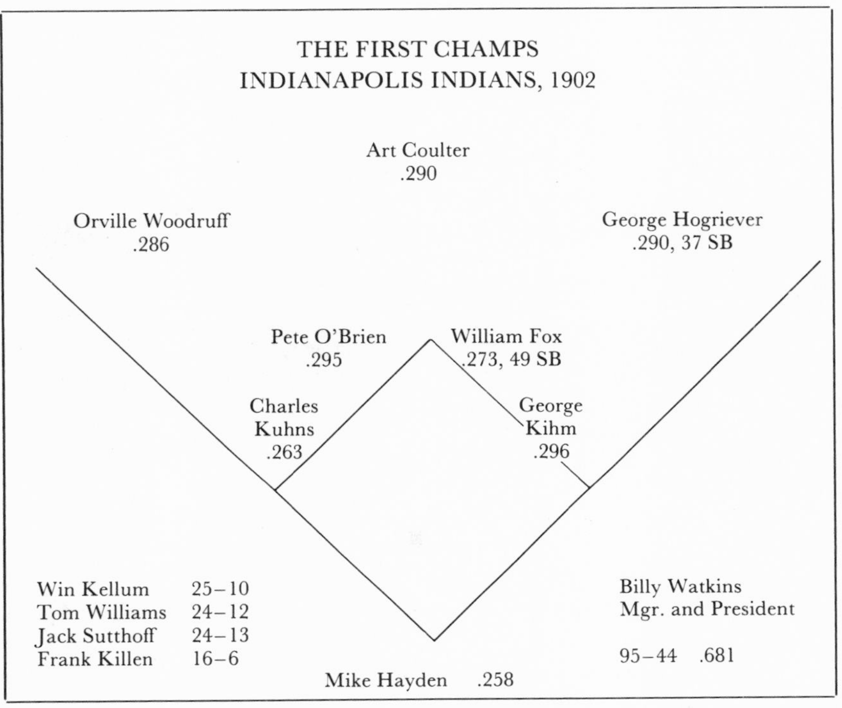

September 6, and the two teams remained even until the last day of the season, Monday, September 22. Louisville won a doubleheader over Minneapolis, but Indianapolis took *three* games from St. Paul — the scheduled doubleheader, plus a rainout that had been postponed.

The league's inaugural season had been an artistic triumph, and as "kranks" (a term rapidly being replaced by "fans") filed into plank ballparks throughout the AA, club owners enjoyed satisfactory financial success. The game that proved so popular with the sporting public of the American Association cities was played by men who, for the most part, were poorly educated and often from rural origins. They dressed in baggy uniforms of heavy flannel, swung thick bats designed to make contact (rather than produce power drives) with the decidedly unlively balls of the era, and wore flimsy little gloves with no padding. Playing surfaces often were rough and unmanicured, and fielding was so uncertain that

The grandstand at Columbus' Neil Park was built in 1900 and substantially renovated in 1904. Replaced by baseball's first concrete-and-steel stadium in 1909, this structure was dismantled and rebuilt into bleachers that could seat 5,000 fans.

— Courtesy Columbus Clippers

fielding performance columns were printed beside hitting columns in all published box scores.

During the first season of AA play, Charles Ferguson, a St. Paul pitcher (21–10), and Toledo catcher John Kleinow (.298) established all-time league records for errors at their positions (16 and 44). Within the next decade similar records had been set at all other positions — most notably in 1905, when Milwaukee shortstop Clyde Robinson was charged with 99 miscues. An occasional obstacle to fielding might be stray gloves scattered around the field: At the end of each inning, fielders customarily dropped their gloves as they headed for the dugout, then picked them up again when they next took up their positions.

Rosters were small, numbering only 15 in the early seasons, then gradually expanding through the years to more than 20. The first AA teams carried five pitchers, two catchers, one regular at each of the other seven positions, and a utility player. The manager on most clubs customarily doubled as a player, and pitchers, when not on the mound, filled in as outfielders — or even infielders — as needed.

American Association clubs, like almost all minor league operations during the first two or three decades of the twentieth century, were independently owned with no ties to major league teams. Owners, therefore, were free to acquire and retain the best players that could be found. A great many AA players had spent considerable time in the big leagues, and these experienced, mature athletes proved to be outstanding performers for Indianapolis or Kansas City or St. Paul. Such players, frequently paid as much in the AA as they could earn from tight-fisted big league owners, would become fixtures for years at first base or shortstop or in left field. The familiarity of fans with "their" players bred close loyalties for the local franchise, and even when players were traded around the league knowledgeable spectators still enjoyed the exploits of favorite visiting athletes.

Pitchers were expected to work the entire game, and sometimes a hurler would pitch both ends of a doubleheader. Relief pitching was confined to infrequent mop-up appearances, but when a crucial late-inning situation demanded emergency pitching, the team's best starter usually was called in from the bullpen. Some clubs used just a three-man rotation, producing high totals for complete games, innings pitched and decisions among durable starters. In 1902 Louisville and Indianapolis each boasted three 20-game winners. In 1904, the first year in which inning and game totals were recorded by the AA, 30 of the top 31 pitchers in the league had a decision in *every* game they worked. There were seven 20-game winners and six 20-game losers, including Cliff Curtis of Milwaukee (24–20) and Wish Eagan of Louisville (20–20). Nine pitchers worked more than 300 innings in 1904 and 1905, and 12 in 1906. The game was dominated by pitching, and hurlers were allowed to doctor the ball with tobacco juice, slippery elm, or almost any other substance that would produce elusive movement. It was customary to issue only three baseballs to umpires at the start of each game. Fans were expected to toss foul balls back onto the field, and by the late innings the balls were scuffed and discolored and hard to hit.

Under these conditions strategy demanded the hit-and-run, sacrifice bunting and base stealing. During the league's first season, stolen base totals per team ranged from 104 to 253; in 1903 from 105 to 267; in 1906 from 148 to 215; in 1907 from 149 to 223; in 1908 from 152 to 230; in 1910 from 165 to 267; in 1912 from 132 to 292. Except for the war-shortened 1918 season, it was 1921 be-

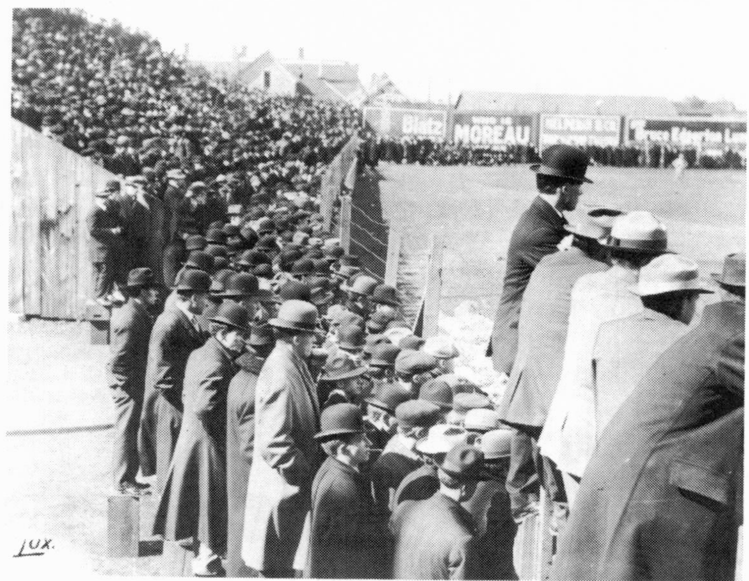

An overflow crowd at Minneapolis' Nicollet Park on a crisp afternoon in 1904. No one was ever turned away—fans were placed behind roped-off areas in the outfield and down the foul lines.

— Courtesy Minnesota Historical Society

fore a single team (Minneapolis with 82 thefts) failed to steal at least 100 bases.

Before the advent of night ball in the 1930s, games were started at 3:00 or 3:30, so that businessmen could leave work early and play hooky at the ballpark. In Minneapolis and St. Paul doubleheaders were arranged so that a morning game would be played in one city and an afternoon game in the other; doubleheaders between the Twin City rivals always were scheduled for opening day, the Fourth of July, and Labor Day. When a ballpark filled up, no one was turned away; fans stood alongside the foul lines and, when the overflow was sufficient, behind roped-off areas in front of the outfield fences.

At the start of each game the umpire would announce through a megaphone the opposing batteries to the crowd. In the early years only one umpire was used at a game; when a runner reached base the ump would come out from behind the catcher and call balls and strikes from behind the pitcher. Umpires were expected to keep the game moving so that the ninth inning could be completed before darkness fell. Pitchers and catchers did not stall between pitches, there was little substitution to slow the action, and games regularly were finished in an hour and a half to two hours. In 1904 30-year-old Bill Klem umpired so impressively in the American Association that he was offered employment in both major leagues. While in the AA, Klem introduced the practice of drawing a line in the dirt with his toe plate to ward off angry players and managers. The authoritarian, combative Klem spent the rest of his career in the National League, became renowned as a caller of balls and strikes, and was voted into the Hall of Fame in 1953.

The second AA pennant race was won by St. Paul, which led the league in team hitting, stolen bases, fielding and double plays. Player-manager Mike Kelley (.309) again was the Saints' first baseman (in 1902, at 26, he was the youngest manager in the league, and he would be associated with the AA for 40 years). The rest of the infield consisted of Miller Huggins at second (.308, 48 SB), shortstop Germany Schaefer (.306), and third-sacker Ed Wheeler (.293). The outfield was even more productive: batting champ Phil Geier (.362), run leader Spike Shannon (.308, 132 R, 41 SB), and Jim Jackson (.307, 42 SB). The best pitchers were Charles Chech (24–9), George Ferguson (19–10), and Joe Stewart (16–10).

Other fine pitchers in 1903 included victory and percentage leader Tom Walker (26–7) and Wish Eagan (24–16) of Louisville, strikeout king Claude Elliott (24–10 with 226 Ks) and Bill McGill (19–5) of Milwaukee, and Win Kellum (23–10) of Indianapolis. Kansas City infielder Mike Grady (.335, 16 HR) led the league in homers and finished second in hitting. Other strong performances were recorded by Louisville player-manager "Derby Day" Bill Clymer (.350) and veteran Indianapolis outfielder George Hogriever (.330).

After the season, St. Paul owner George Lennon profited from the sale of several stars to National League teams: Phil Geier and Joe Stewart went to Boston, Spike Shannon would play in St. Louis, and Miller Huggins donned a Cincinnati uniform. But Mike Kelley (.298) kept his team in the 1904 race with solid work from returning veterans Ed Wheeler (.296), George Ferguson (14–8), victory leader Charles Chech (27–8), and Jim Jackson (.335, 13 HR, 59 SB), who won the home run and stolen base titles. Columbus, however, seized first place behind the pitching of John Malar-

St. Paul Saints, 1903 champs. Top row, L to R: Eddie Wheeler (.298, 3B), AA run leader Spike Shannon (.308 — CF), Ted Corbett (P), Charles Chech (24–9, and the 1904 victory leader at 27–8), Jenny Hurley (C), George Ferguson (19–10), batting champ Phil Geier (.362). Middle row, L to R: Jack Sullivan (C), player-manager Mike Kelley (.309 — 1B), Germany Schaefer (.306 — SS), Bill Davis (P). Bottom row, L to R: Elmer Pierce (C), Miller Huggins (.308 — 2B), Jake Volz (P), Art Marcan (IF), Jimmy Jackson (.307 — OF), who led the 1904 AA in homers and stolen bases (.335, 13 HR, 59 SB). Many of these players returned to lead the Saints to another flag in 1904.

— Courtesy Minnesota Historical Society

key (24–9) and threatened to run away with the pennant, before slumping badly at midseason. Milwaukee fielded a strong contender which featured newly acquired shortstop Germany Schaefer (.356, 48 SB), spitballing righthander Elmer Stricklett (20–11), strikeout leader Clifton Curtis (24–20, 210 Ks), and hitting king George Stone, who recorded the highest batting average (.405) in the history of the American Association. Stone is the only regular ever to hit .400 during a season of AA play.

But the AA schedule had been expanded from 140 to 154 games, and when Columbus faltered, Kelley's Saints surged into first place and won their second consecutive pennant by an eight-game margin. Fans then turned out to enjoy a five-hour spectacle in which the Saints donned burlesque costumes and later split the

The Tenth Man

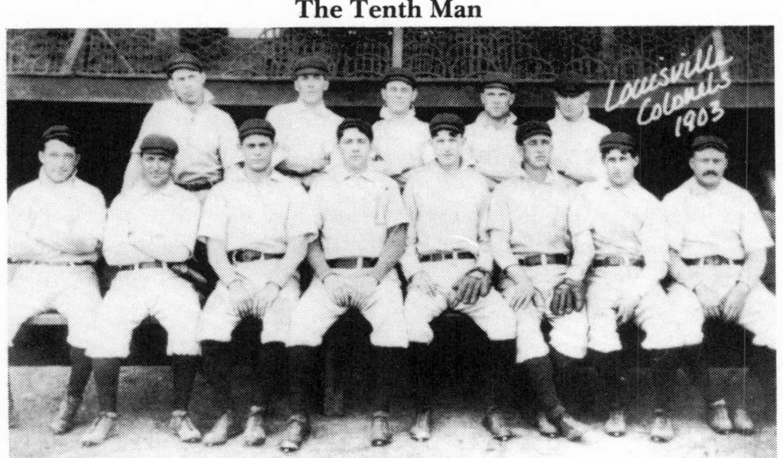

Louisville Colonels, 1903.

— Courtesy Louisville Redbirds

On opening day of 1903 an overflow crowd jammed into Louisville's Eclipse Park to cheer the Colonels and taunt the visiting Indianapolis Indians. When the grandstand and bleachers were filled, fans were placed — as customary — along the foul lines and against the outfield fence.

But Colonels' fans had little to enjoy until the last inning. The Indians jumped out to an early lead, and entering the bottom of the ninth the Colonels trailed, 2–0. Louisville pitching ace Tom Walker reached, however, and when outfielder Fred Odwell came to bat he represented the tying run. Odwell lofted a fly to deep right field, but George Hogriever seemed to have a bead on it — until a tall fan standing against the fence shied his derby at the ball. The derby missed, but so did Hogriever!

The ball landed among several Colonels' partisans and Odwell began to sprint around the bases. Hogriever shouldered his way through the spectators toward the ball. Suddenly, a local real estate agent slugged him in the nose. As Hogriever staggered back, a Louisville physician swung wildly at him and a popular politician landed a kick. Walker scored easily and, before the beleaguered Hogriever could retrieve the ball, Odwell crossed home plate to tie the score. In the tenth inning the fans helped out again, and Louisville won, 4–2!

gate receipts as a bonus. Then the Saints played a best-two-of-three series with the Eastern League (later called the International League) champions, losing to Buffalo two games to one in the forerunner of the Little World Series. But George Lennon again sold his best players — Charles Chech went to Cincinnati and Jim Jackson to Cleveland — and Mike Kelley could not bring the Saints back in 1905. St. Paul suffered the first of five straight losing seasons in 1905, finished last in 1907 and 1908, and would not return to the AA throne room for 15 seasons. Toledo finished in the cellar during the first three AA seasons, and in 1904 became the first team to lose 100 games (42–109).

W. H. Watkins, owner-manager of Indianapolis, had guided the Indians to the first AA pennant in 1902. After the Indians dropped to fourth place in 1903, Watkins purchased Minneapolis in 1904 and managed the Millers for two seasons. But during these same two seasons he retained ownership of the Indianapolis franchise, and also in 1904 and 1905 George Tebeau owned both Kansas City and Louisville. Tebeau called upon his fellow owners for help in August 1905, after his Louisville players, riding prominently through the streets of Kansas City toward a game with the Blues, were struck by a trolley car. No one was killed, but several players were sidelined for the season, and rival owners generously supplied Louisville with enough athletes to complete the schedule.

Most of the ballparks around the American Association had been built around the turn of the century, and each facility featured wooden grandstands and bleachers, as well as plank outfield fences. But in 1905 Columbus moved into baseball's first concrete-and-steel stadium. Neil Park was completely renovated at a cost of $23,000: The diamond was shifted from a northwest to a northeast alignment; the old wooden grandstand was razed and the lumber was used to build bleachers which could accommodate 5,000; and a concrete, double-decked, 6,000-seat grandstand was erected. The major leagues would not enjoy a concrete-and-steel stadium until Forbes Field opened in Pittsburgh in 1909.

The Senators responded to their impressive new ballpark by reeling off three consecutive pennants. "Derby Day" Bill Clymer had been lured away from Louisville for the 1904 season. Clymer's first Columbus team finished second, and by the next season his Senators had been fine-tuned into a superb dead-ball-era machine, with emphasis on fielding, pitching and base-running.

Minneapolis Millers, 1905. Team captain Billy Fox is seated second from left.
— Courtesy Minnesota Historical Society

The Senators led the American Association in fielding in 1905 and 1906, and missed in 1907 by merely one percentage point. Clymer's club stole more bases than any other team in 1905, finished with the second-highest total the next year, and provided the league pitching leader in victories in each of the championship seasons.

Fans responded in record numbers to the combination of pennant-winning baseball and a state-of-the-art stadium. In 1907, the third consecutive championship year, attendance soared to 316,980 — even though the population of Columbus was just 125,000. Columbus was the smallest city in the American Association, but led the league in attendance for eight years in a row.

The 1905 Senators became the first AA team to win 100 or more games (102–53) and made a shambles of the race. A trio of righthanders, Gus Dorner (29–8), strikeout king Heinie Berger (25–14), and Bucky Veil (21–12) provided overwhelming pitching, while the offense was sparked by outfielders Ollie Pickering (.326) and Bunk Congalton (.314). Shortstop Rudy Hulswitt, second baseman Zeke Wrigley, and first sacker Dummy Kihm formed the nucleus of an excellent defense during the dynasty years, and

Mike Kelley vs. the American Association

Mike Kelley, player-manager of St. Paul, had led the Saints to back-to-back pennants in 1903 and 1904. But late in the 1905 season Kelley and Saints' owner George Lennon clashed, and in December Kelley, backed financially by several local businessmen, moved across the Mississippi River to become president and general manager of the Minneapolis Millers.

Kelley's contract, however, already had been sold to the St. Louis Browns by Lennon. With the cooperation of other owners who wanted Kelley out of the American Association, Lennon appealed to the National Association office that Kelley now was the property of the Browns. Minneapolis opened the 1905 season on Wednesday, April 18, in Louisville, but the National Association ordered Kelley to stay off the field and out of the dugout. The next day, however, Kelley joined his team in the dugout, and when he refused to leave the bench, umpire Brick Owens forfeited the game.

Soon the National Association ruled that Kelley could assume his managerial duties, but in June, Mike again became the center of controversy when he accused umpires Brick Owens and Steve Kane of tipping off Louisville batters to the signs between his pitcher and catcher. AA President Joseph D. O'Brien suspended Kelley and the two umpires pending an investigation, but Kelley soon withdrew his charges. On July 18 the Millers, riding a 10-game winning streak, opened a four-game series at home with the first-place Columbus Senators. Brick Owens was umpiring, and he called a close play at the plate in the eighth against the Millers. The game went into extra innings, and when the Millers lost in the 12th, hundreds of Minneapolis fans surged onto the field in pursuit of Owens. The umpire dashed beneath the stands and police tried to escort him away, but they were surrounded by a threatening mob. Suddenly, a prominent and imposing Minnesota citizen, Pudge Heffelfinger, a former All-American guard at Yale, took charge of Owens and led him through the crowd, although rocks and other missiles were thrown.

The next day a diehard Miller fan stood outside Nicollet Park, passing out eggs from a crate. The stands filled with surly fans, and Minneapolis police advised Owens not to come onto the field. But Owens stepped behind the plate, called one pitch — then was pelted with a barrage of eggs. Owens fled for cover and ordered the game forfeited. Columbus swept the four-game series and went on

(continued)

to win the pennant. A week after the riot of July 18, charges were filed by Kelley that Owens had placed a bet on the game with local gamblers. League directors exonerated Owens of the charges and, on August 12, Kelley was suspended indefinitely, along with several Miller players who had been involved in the riot.

In the meantime, during a June 30 doubleheader in Indianapolis, fans at Washington Park began shouting threats against umpire Brick Owens for favoritism toward Louisville. Two bottles were hurled at Owens from the grandstand in the bottom of the ninth inning of the second game, then fans jumped onto the field and began throwing stones. Two fans were arrested, but Indianapolis businessmen petitioned the league president to keep Owens out of their city, and O'Brien complied.

After Kelley's departure from Minneapolis, second baseman Billy Fox, the team captain, managed the Millers through the rest of the schedule. In 1907 Kelley signed to manage Des Moines of the Western League, but he left the team after 20 games. The following year he managed Toronto of the International League until July 21. American Association directors voted to reinstate Kelley, and he resumed his managerial post at St. Paul on August 8, 1908. He stayed at the Saints' helm through 1923, with the exception of 1913, which he spent as manager at Indianapolis. In addition to the 1903 and 1904 titles, Kelley won flags in 1919, 1920, 1922 and 1923. After the 1923 season, Kelley again moved across the river, buying the Minneapolis franchise and retaining control until 1946. Kelley managed the Millers through 1931, spending 28 of his 30 years as a minor league manager in the American Association.

Kihm also added a steady bat to the lineup (.285 in 1905, .278 in 1906, .288 in 1907).

At the other end of the league in 1905, Kansas City displaced Toledo in the cellar (45–102) and established an all-time league record with 17 consecutive losses. The Blues set a far more desirable record on June 14, 1905, becoming the only team in AA history to turn *two* triple plays in a single game. St. Paul outfielder Charles "Eagle Eye" Hemphill was the offensive star of 1905, leading the league in hits, total bases, and batting average (.364).

Gus Dorner and Bunk Congalton were sold to Cincinnati and Cleveland for 1906, and two other Columbus starters also were peddled. But most of the roster remained intact, and after a slow start the Senators caught fire. Heinie Berger again led the league in strikeouts (264) as well as victories (28–13) and innings pitched

Milwaukee Score Card cover, 1905.

— Courtesy Milwaukee Public Library

(371). Bucky Veil (17–11) returned to the pitching staff, while the most potent newcomers were big league veterans Patsy Flaherty (23–9) and Chick Robertaille (17–16). Ollie Pickering (.317) returned to lead the offense, along with fellow outfielder Bill Hinchman (.314). The Little World Series had not been played in 1905, but in 1906 Columbus took on Buffalo, losing to the Eastern League champs, three games to two. Another loss that season, a 5–0 decision on August 10 against Kansas City and righthander Henry "Ducky" Swann, had historic significance: the first no-hitter in AA history.

After two magnificent seasons, Berger was purchased by Cleveland, along with Hinchman, and Pickering was bought by the St. Louis Browns, while Flaherty went up to Boston's National League club. But Clymer rebuilt his team again. Shortstop Rudy Hulswitt enjoyed his best year at the plate (.296), and Chick Robertaille improved his performance (21–14). Southpaw George Upp

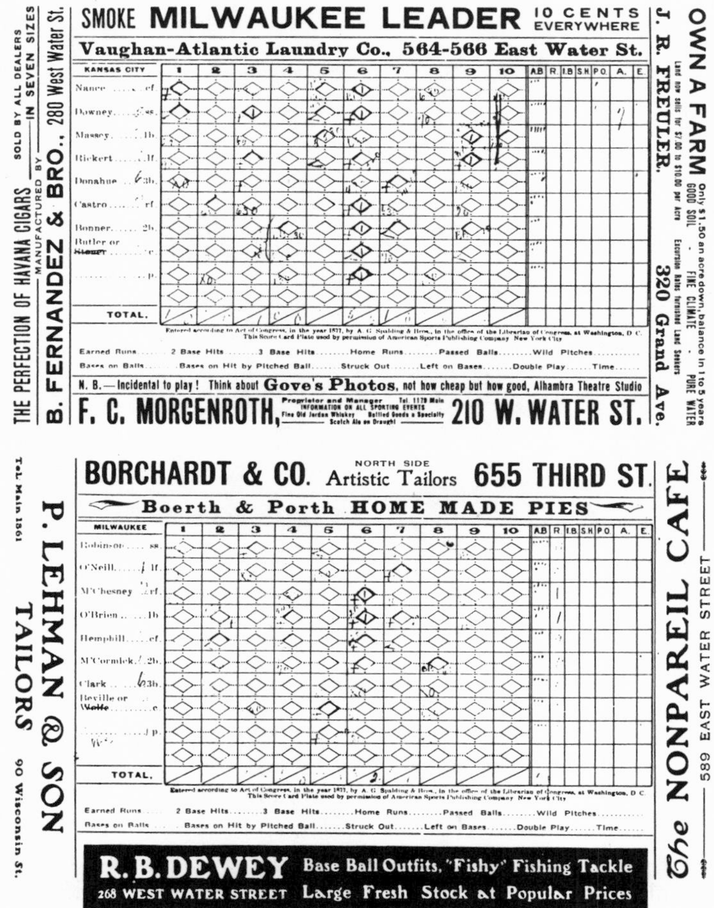

Early score cards included printed lineups for both teams.
— Courtesy Milwaukee Public Library

led the AA in wins (27–10), while outfielder Doc Gessler (.325) was another outstanding newcomer (newcomer to Columbus — he already had logged four seasons in the big leagues). The Senators edged Toledo for a third straight pennant but dropped the Little World Series to Toronto, four games to one. The American Association had lost all three postseason encounters with the Eastern League champs, and the Little World Series would not be resumed for a decade.

Once again the best Columbus regulars were sold to major

Milwaukee's Athletic Park from the faraway reaches of center field.
— Courtesy Milwaukee Public Library

league clubs, and Clymer's 1908 rebuilding job could boost the Senators only to third place. Toledo and Minneapolis were contenders throughout the season, Louisville finished a close second, and, after the tightest race in the seven years of AA play, Indianapolis won its second pennant. The Indians' offense was triggered by batting champ John Hayden (.316), player-manager C. C. Carr (.301 — only two other regulars in the entire league hit above .300), and stolen base leader Otto Williams (.252, 38 SB). The home run title was split by Minneapolis outfielder Buck Freeman (.218 with 10 homers in 92 games), who recorded his second consecutive championship, and Indianapolis catcher Bert James (.273 with 10 homers in 88 games), who would win a total of three home run crowns.

But 1908 was a pitchers' year. Louisville had three 20-game winners: southpaw Ambrose Puttman (26–12), who had won the strikeout crown the previous year with a 21–20 record; lefty John Halla (23–16); and Babe Adams (22–12). Lou Durham, who hurled for both Indianapolis and Louisville during the season, pitched and won *five* doubleheaders and compiled the year's best winning percentage (19–7). Only one no-hitter had been pitched

Big-league veteran Billy Fox, who played second base for Indianapolis in 1902 and 1903 and for Minneapolis in 1904, 1905, and 1906. He was the stolen base champ in 1903, and in 1906 he managed the Millers while Mike Kelley was under suspension. The thick-handled bat and choked grip were hallmarks of the dead-ball era.

— Courtesy Minnesota Historical Society

during the league's first six years, but in 1908 a record seven no-hitters were recorded. The season's best performance was turned in by a future Hall of Famer, 18-year-old southpaw Rube Marquard, who twirled a no-hitter and led the AA in victories, strikeouts, and innings (28–19, 367 IP, 250 K).

Not a single no-hitter was made in 1909, but AA pitchers turned in an astounding 159 shutouts, a mark which would never be matched. The season leader in shutouts and almost every other pitching category was Stoney McGlynn, a 37-year-old righthander whose three-year totals in other leagues from 1904 to 1906 had been 30–11, 28–16 and 43–13 (with 511 innings in 64 games!). The iron-armed McGlynn went to Milwaukee in 1909 after two years with the St. Louis Cardinals (he led the 1907 National League in innings, losses, and walks). McGlynn established all-time AA records in 1909 with 446 innings (yielding only 304 hits) and 14 shutouts, and he also paced the league in games (64), strikeouts (183), hits, runs, and wins *and* losses (27–21).

Other strong pitching performances around the league were

Minneapolis Millers, 1908. Owner-manager Mike Cantillon (coat and tie) had purchased the club after the 1906 season for $27,500. Lou Fiene (bottom right) went 20–13 in 1908, while Tip O'Neill (bottom left) was the 1909 batting champ.
— Courtesy Minnesota Historical Society

turned in by Fred Olmstead (24–12 with nine shutouts) and southpaw "Young Cy" Young (23–18) of Minneapolis. On July 13 at Nicollet Park, Young spun a four-hitter and hit a home run to win the opening game of a doubleheader against Milwaukee, 1–0. Manager Jimmy Collins decided to let Young pitch the second game, and the lefthander did not allow a hit until the ninth inning, finishing with a one-hit, 5–0 victory and a double shutout.

With 159 shutouts and general dominance by pitchers, team batting averages (ranging from .230 to .247) and home run totals (10 to 26) were anemic. Not a single regular hit .300 in 1909. Bert James again was the home run leader (.274 with merely seven homers) and Minneapolis outfielder Mike O'Neill became the only man ever to win the AA batting crown with an average below .300 (.296).

The 1909 flag chase was even closer than in the previous season, with Milwaukee, Minneapolis, Louisville, and Indianapolis battling for the lead throughout the year. By August it seemed that Milwaukee or Minneapolis would win, but both teams faltered in the final week of the season. Louisville put on a late surge and took

Louisville Colonels of 1909 in their dugout at Eclipse Park.
— Courtesy Louisville Redbirds

over first place on the next-to-last day of the schedule. Louisville had won its first AA flag (93–75, .554), but last-place Kansas City (71–93, .432) was only 122 percentage points behind.

With eight competitive teams and a second consecutive air-tight pennant race, the American Association was building a base of stable prosperity on high quality baseball. "In point of fast ball and close race the 1908 season was the best in the history of this league, which is almost of major league calibre," commented *The Reach Official American League Guide.* The 1909 season was even better, and the *Guide* again lauded "the high class of ball" and the "general good order on the field and a remarkable absence of contention among the magnates." Because of these favorable conditions, "attendance exceeded even the liberal total of the preceding year," which enabled "every club" to clear "more or less profit." After just eight years the American Association was firmly established as one of the top minor leagues in the country.

The Millers host the archrival Saints at Nicollet Park in 1909. Note the umpire's outside chest protector.

— Courtesy Minnesota Historical Society

1910–1919

Decade of Challenge

The American Association entered the second decade of the twentieth century with eight prosperous clubs and a solid brand of baseball played by former major leaguers, top-notch career minor leaguers, and gifted athletes who would rise from the AA to the big leagues. Beginning in 1910 the league assigned two umpires to every game, which decidedly improved the quality of officiating and control of players. Throughout the decade the AA refined the dead-ball style of play emphasizing strong pitching, bunting, the hit-and-run, and base stealing. But while baseball still was entrenched as America's favorite sport, during the next ten years the American Association would face challenges posed by the Federal League, the AA's first franchise shift, and the First World War.

The first three pennants of the decade were won by the league's second great dynasty, Mike Cantillon's Minneapolis Millers. Cantillon had been building a powerhouse bv paying good salaries to players with substantial major league experience. In 1910 he signed his brother to manage the Millers, and Joe would produce four pennants in six seasons. Joe Cantillon had been a popular second baseman in San Francisco, a Western League umpire, a highly perceptive scout (credited with discovering future Hall of Fame pitchers Walter Johnson, Rube Waddell, and Amos Rusie), and manager of the Washington Senators.

The club he guided in Minneapolis led the league in hitting in 1910, 1911 and 1912 and established the all-time AA record for stolen bases in 1912 (292). The pitching staff produced the victory leader in each championship season — "Long Tom" Hughes (31–12 in 1910), Roy Patterson (24–10 the next year), and Fred Olmstead (28–10). The club also touted stolen base champs Dave Altizer (65 thefts in 1910 and 68 in 1912) and Warren Gill (55 steals in 1911). The offensive star of 1910 and 1911 was left fielder Gavvy Cravath, who led the league both years in batting, doubles, and homers (.326, 41 2B, 14 HR, and .363, 53 2B, 29 HR).

Cravath was purchased in 1911 by the Philadelphia Phillies, while 10-year big leaguer Hughes went back to the Washington Senators after setting the all-time AA record for victories. But Mike Cantillon managed to keep most of his players in Minneapolis during all three championship seasons, a stability that was characteristic of the independent minor league operations of the era, and that certainly was a major factor in maintaining a dynasty. Eight players were regulars during each of the pennant-winning years:

> "Daredevel Dave" Altizer — a six-year big-league veteran who led the AA in runs and stolen bases and set the league sacrifice record (61) in 1910, played 37 games with Cincinnati in 1911 before returning to hit .335 for the Millers, then again was the stolen base champ in 1912.
>
> Jimmy Williams — a veteran of 11 major league seasons who hit well for the Miller dynasty (.315, .332 and .296); as second baseman Williams and shortstop Altizer provided a reliable double-play combination.
>
> Roy Patterson — a seven-year big league vet, the righthander was a 20-game winner for each of the pennant-winners (21–12, 24–10 and 21–9).
>
> Otis Clymer — a five-year major leaguer, the fleet, lefthanded batter (.308 with 38 steals, .342 and 51 SB, .307 and 61 SB) led the AA in runs scored in 1911 and 1912, and set a record for the period with a 28-game hitting streak in 1911.
>
> Claude Rossman — the five-year big league veteran was a left-handed outfielder and a fine batter (.278, .356 and .322).
>
> Doc Gill — the first baseman won his second AA stolen base title for the Millers in 1911.
>
> Hobe Ferris — the nine-year major league veteran enjoyed his

St. Paul, 1911. Manager Mike Kelley is dressed in suit and tie, while the Saints are uniformed in lace-up jerseys and stylish caps.

— Courtesy Minnesota Historical Society

best season as the Miller third sacker in 1911 (.303).

Yip Owens — the light-hitting catcher had logged two seasons in the big leagues and kept the Minneapolis clubhouse loose with his sense of humor and practical jokes.

The 1911 and 1912 Minneapolis clubs showcased future Hall of Famer Rube Waddell, who came to the AA at the age of 34. The eccentric lefthander worked in 54 games in 1911, and his victory total (20–17) included a doubleheader sweep over Louisville with a three-hitter and a one-hitter. Waddell was effective in 33 games in 1912 (12–6), but his career ended the following year in the Northern League, and he died in 1914.

In 1910, 1911 and 1912 the Millers dominated the AA with 107, 99 and 105 victories. Elsewhere around the league, fans enjoyed the 1910 performances of Toledo outfielder Dave Hickman (.317) and Chink Yingling (22–9), Kansas City righthanders Dusty Rhoades (21–15) and Chick Brandom (20–15), Columbus ace Glenn Liebhart (23–16), and Milwaukee workhorse Stoney McGlynn, who led the league in games and innings for the second

"Just spit tobacco juice on it!"

Johnny Hughes was typical of the competent career minor leaguer who formed the roster nucleus of circuits like the American Association. Hughes (his real name was Mulgrew) was a 5′5½″, 145-pound catcher who never even had a cup of coffee in the big leagues. When he was 19 his right thumb was smashed by a foul tip early in a game. Hughes spit tobacco juice on the shattered digit, stayed in the game, and for the final six innings threw with his *left* hand!

In 1907, when he was 25, Hughes worked his way up to the AA, catching 89 games (.221) for the Louisville Colonels. The next year (81 games, .237), he caught Jesse Stovall's no-hitter, and in 1909 (108 games, .214) he was a good field — a no-hit backstop for the AA champions. He enjoyed his best offensive season for Louisville in 1910 (108 games, .283), and his second-best the next year (110 games, .254).

Milwaukee was trying to build a championship club and purchased the veteran catcher for $1,000 in 1912. Hughes responded with his best offensive performance (.296 in 81 games), and he caught a second no-hitter, from Ed Hovlik. The Brewers won back-to-back pennants in 1913 and 1914 with Hughes as the regular catcher (143 games, .257, and 151 games, .268). But the next year Hughes slumped badly (.214 in 67 games), and after nine unspectacular seasons he was dealt out of the American Association. When his playing days ended he made his home in Milwaukee, where he died at the age of 63 in 1947.

year in a row (16–21 in 63 games and 392 innings). In 1911 the 39-year-old McGlynn had his last good year (22–15 in 55 games), although his final season of pro ball, in the Rio Grande Valley League, came three years later.

Other AA stars of 1911 included Kansas City first baseman-outfielder Ham Hyatt (.326 with a league-leading 159 runs) and pitchers Nick Maddox (22–13) and Dusty Rhoades (20–16); infielder George Perring (.321) and outfielder Bunk Congalton (.315) of Columbus; and Louisville first baseman-outfielder Moose Grimshaw (.363 in 97 games). In 1912 the batting champ was St. Paul shortstop-outfielder Art Butler (.329), while Kansas City catcher Bert James (.286 with 10 homers in 91 games) won his third home run crown. Blues righthander "Big Bill" Powell was the strikeout leader (27–12 with 174 Ks), eight-year American League veteran

OFFICIAL SCHEDULE OF AMERICAN ASSOCIATION OF PROFESSIONAL BASE BALL CLUBS, 1911

CLUB	At Columbus	At Toledo	At Indianapolis	At Louisville	At Milwaukee	At Kansas City	At Minneapolis	At St. Paul
Columbus	WIS. LAKES	May 15 16 17 July 15 16 17 Sept. 4 4 5 Sept. 30 Oct. 1 1	May 9 10 11 July 9 10 11 Aug. 16 17 18 Sept. 12 13 14	May 12 13 14 July 12 13 14 Aug. 13 14 15 Sept. 6 7 8	April 25 26 27 June 17 18 19 July 25 26 27 Sept. 22 23 24	April 28 29 30 June 14 15 16 July 22 23 24 Sept. 25 26 26	May 2 3 4 June 11 12 13 July 31 Aug. 1 2 Sept. 16 17 17	May 5 6 7 June 8 9 10 July 28 29 30 Sept. 18 19 20
Toledo	June 4 5 6 July 6 7 8 Aug. 10 11 12 Sept. 9 10 11	ICE AND	May 12 13 14 July 18 19 20 Aug. 13 14 15 Sept. 6 7 8	May 9 10 11 July 4 4 5 Aug. 16 17 18 Sept. 1 2 3	May 5 6 7 June 8 9 10 July 28 29 30 Sept. 18 19 20	May 1 2 3 4 June 11 12 13 July 31 Aug. 1 2 Sept. 16 17	April 25 26 27 June 17 18 19 July 25 26 27 Sept. 22 23 24	April 28 29 30 June 15 16 July 22 23 24 Sept. 25 26 26 27
Indianapolis ...	June 1 2 3 July 4 4 5 Aug. 7 8 9 Sept. 1 2 3	May 29 30 30 31 July 12 13 14 Aug. 4 5 6 Sept. 28 29	CARTAGE CO.	June 4 5 6 July 6 7 8 Aug. 10 11 12 Sept. 9 10 11	May 1 2 3 4 June 11 12 13 July 31 Aug. 1 2 Sept. 16 17	May 5 6 7 June 8 9 10 July 28 29 30 Sept. 18 19 20	April 28 29 30 June 14 15 16 July 22 23 24 Sept. 25 26 27	April 25 26 27 June 17 18 19 July 25 26 27 Sept. 22 23 24
Louisville	May 29 30 30 31 July 18 19 20 Aug. 4 5 6 Sept. 28 29	June 1 2 3 July 9 10 11 Aug. 7 8 9 Sept. 12 13 14	May 15 16 17 July 15 16 17 Sept. 4 4 5 Sept. 30 Oct. 1 1	Gen. Offices	April 28 29 30 June 14 15 16 July 22 23 24 Sept. 25 26 26	April 25 26 27 June 17 18 19 July 25 26 Sept. 21 22 23 24	May 5 6 7 June 8 9 10 July 28 29 30 Sept. 18 19 20	May 1 2 3 4 June 11 12 13 July 31 Aug. 1 2 Sept. 16 17
Milwaukee	April 18 19 20 May 21 22 23 June 30 July 1 2 Aug. 28 29 30	April 21 22 23 May 18 19 20 June 27 28 29 Aug. 25 26 27	April 12 13 14 May 27 28 June 24 25 26 Aug. 22 23 24 24	April 15 16 17 May 24 25 26 June 21 22 23 Aug. 19 20 21	Second Floor	May 30 30 31 July 4 4 5 Sept. 1 2 3 Sept. 27 28 29	May 11 12 13 July 10 11 12 Aug. 11 12 13 Sept. 6 7 8	May 9 10 July 7 8 9 Aug. 7 8 9 10 Sept. 9 10 11
Kansas City....	April 21 22 23 May 24 25 26 June 24 25 26 Aug. 22 23 24	April 18 19 20 May 27 28 June 21 22 23 Aug. 19 20 20 21	April 15 16 17 May 18 19 20 June 30 July 1 2 Aug. 28 29 30	April 12 13 14 May 21 22 23 June 27 28 29 Aug. 25 26 27	May 14 15 16 July 19 20 21 Aug. 4 5 6 Sept. 4 4 5	Wells Building	May 9 10 July 7 8 9 Aug. 7 8 9 10 Sept. 9 10 11	May 11 12 13 June 10 11 12 Aug. 11 12 13 Sept. 6 7 8
Minneapolis ...	April 15 16 17 May 18 19 20 June 27 28 29 Aug. 25 26 27	April 12 13 14 May 21 22 23 June 30 July 1 2 Aug. 28 29 30	April 21 22 23 May 24 25 26 June 21 22 23 Aug. 19 20 21	April 18 19 20 May 27 28 June 24 25 26 Aug. 22 23 24 24	June 1 2 3 July 16 17 18 Aug. 16 17 18 Sept. 12 13 14	June 4 5 6 July 13 14 15 Aug. 14 15 Sept. 30 30 Oct. 1 1	PHONE	May 8 15 May 30 pm., 31 July 4 am., 20 21 Aug. 4 6 Sept. 1 2, 4 am.
St. Paul.........	April 12 13 14 May 27 28 June 21 22 23 Aug. 19 20 20 21	April 15 16 17 May 24 25 26 June 24 25 26 Aug. 22 23 24	April 18 19 20 May 21 22 23 June 27 28 29 Aug. 25 26 27	April 21 22 23 May 18 19 20 June 30 July 1 2 Aug. 28 29 30	June 4 5 6 July 13 14 15 Aug. 14 15 31 Sept. 30 Oct. 1 1	June 1 2 3 July 16 17 18 Aug. 16 17 18 Sept. 12 13 14	May 14 16 May 30, a. m. July 4 pm 5 6 19 Aug. 3 5 Sept. 3, 4 pm. 28	MAIN 3300

1911 schedule.

— Courtesy Milwaukee Public Library

Cy Falkenberg posted a record for Toledo (25–8) that returned him to the big leagues, and dependable Dusty Rhoades again was a 20-game winner for Kansas City (21–15).

In 1913 the Milwaukee Brewers, a team which had never won an American Association pennant, bolted to the league lead behind player-manager Harry Clark (.286), who had manned third base since 1904. Clark's talented pitching staff included victory leader Cy Slapnicka (25–14), Ralph Cutting (21–19), "Young Cy" Young (15–10), Tom Dougherty (14–9), who had pitched for the Brewers for a decade, and Ed Hovlik (11–9). First baseman Tom Jones (.272) had spent eight seasons in the American League, while hard-hitting outfielder Larry Chappelle (.349 in 85 games) qualified for the batting title before being sold to the Chicago White Sox. The offensive gap was partially filled by outfielders Newt Randall (.288) and Larry Gilbert (.282 with 10 homers and 43 steals). After Chappelle departed, the Brewers faltered and Minneapolis surged into the lead, threatening to seize a fourth consecutive flag behind outfielder Claude Rossman (.302) and first baseman Jim Delahanty (.297). But the Brewers rallied during the final two weeks of the season, winning 100 games and the championship.

The Brewers successfully defended their title in 1914. Larry Gilbert and shortstop Lena Blackburne went up to the big leagues, but otherwise player-manager Harry Clark (.301 with a league-

The 1913 opener at Louisville's Eclipse Park.
— Courtesy Louisville Redbirds

leading 143 walks) returned his championship roster intact, including his entire starting mound corps. Slapnicka (8–9) and Cutting (9–8) sagged badly, but the slack was amply taken up by Ed Hovlik (24–14 and a league-leading 2.54 ERA), "Young Cy" Young (20–16), veteran Tom Dougherty (14–4), and newly acquired Jim Shackleford (11–2). Second baseman Phil Lewis (.295) raised his batting average 45 points, and the revamped outfield was superb: returnee Newt Randall (.321), Milwaukee native Oscar Felsch (.304 with a league-leading 19 HRs), and newcomer John Beall (.312).

In other AA action, Louisville righthander Grover Cleveland Lowdermilk (18–16 with 254 Ks in 284 IP) won his second consecutive strikeout crown (he was 20–14 with 197 Ks in 51 games in 1913). Lowdermilk pitched sporadically with six major league clubs from 1909 through 1920, but he would become the only hurler to collect three American Association strikeout titles. The 1914 victory leaders were righthanders Bert Gallia of Kansas City (26–12 with a 2.65 ERA in 51 games) and Louisville's Jake Northrup (26–10), who would go on to win more games than any other pitcher in American Association history. The offensive star of 1914

Opening day at Eclipse Park, 1913. Paying customers were never turned away. Any hit that went into the overflow crowd behind the rope was a ground-rule double.

— Courtesy Louisville Redbirds

The 39-inning Game

On April 25, 1913, Indianapolis and Minneapolis squared off in the 14th game of the young season. In the sixth inning, with the score tied, 1–1, the contest was called because of rain and rescheduled as part of a June 15 doubleheader. Minneapolis won the June 15 opener, 2–0, but after nine innings, with the score even at 6–6, smoke from nearby factories and locomotives reduced visibility, and the game again was rescheduled, this time as the second contest of an August 7 doubleheader.

On August 7 the Indians won the lidbuster, 7–4, but the second game once more deadlocked, finally being called because of darkness after 13 innings with the score 2–2. The teams tried again the next day. The Indians once more won the opener, 4–1, but the Millers finally found their offense in the oft-postponed second game, trouncing the Tribe, 11–1. It had taken a record total of 39 innings for Indianapolis and Minneapolis to determine the outcome of Game 14.

was Columbus player-manager Bill Hinchman, who led the league in batting average (.366), runs scored (139), hits (227), doubles (57), triples (21), and total bases (353).

In 1913 the Federal League began posing problems for the American Association. As baseball increased in popularity, John T. Powers of Chicago organized the Federal League as a minor circuit with hopes of soon competing with the American and National leagues. The Federal League of 1913 had clubs in Cleveland, Chicago, Pittsburgh, St. Louis, Covington, and Indianapolis. The Indianapolis Hoosiers played at Riverside Beach Park in the northwestern part of the city and ran away with the pennant. Covington, a suburb of Cincinnati, lost its franchise during the season, and the team finished the year in Kansas City, playing in Association Park on alternate dates from the Blues.

Now established in several solid cities, league backers poured money into the venture to upgrade ballparks and raid major league rosters of top talent. Hoping to duplicate Ban Johnson's success with the American League, the Federal League aggressively opened play in 1914 with eight "major league" franchises in Indianapolis, Kansas City, Baltimore, Brooklyn, Buffalo, Chicago, Pittsburgh, and St. Louis. The Indiananolis Hoosiers, again winners of the Federal League pennant, and the sixth-place Kansas City Packers provided formidable competition for the American Association Indians and Blues. Both Kansas City clubs finished sixth in their respective leagues, while the Indians took third in the AA.

Although there were severe financial losses throughout the Federal League in 1914, the primary investors were seasoned entrepeneurs who anticipated initial setbacks as a necessary prelude to eventual profits. For 1915 it was decided to place a franchise in the greater New York area, and the championship Indianapolis club was transplanted to Newark. In 1915, therefore, the AA would face Federal League competition only in Kansas City, where the Blues finished fifth against the fourth-place Packers. But the novelty that had interested fans in 1914 was past, and the Federal League again suffered serious losses despite an airtight pennant race. After the 1915 season, antitrust suits against organized baseball were dropped in exchange for financial compensation from the American and National leagues. A costly failure, the Federal League experiment ended in 1915.

The All-time AA Victory Leader

Jake Northrup did not enter professional baseball until he was 21, catching on with Trenton of the Class B Tri-State League in 1909. A 5′11″, 170-pound righthander, Northrup had two mediocre seasons, then led the circuit in victories while posting a brilliant record for Reading in 1911 (27–4). Northrup moved up to Louisville of the American Association in 1912, and pitched in every subsequent season in the AA until he retired in 1925. Following a superb performance during the abbreviated 1918 season, he was purchased by Boston of the National League, posting a 5–1 record during the remainder of the year. But he went 1–5 in 1919, and by mid-season he was back in the American Association.

In 14 AA seasons Northrup pitched for Louisville, Indianapolis, Milwaukee and Columbus, and he was a 20-game winner four times. Although he seldom led the league in seasonal pitching categories, because of his consistency and durability he established lifetime records for the American Association in victories (222), innings (3,516), strikeouts (1,176), and losses (189). Northrup died where he was born, in Monroeton, Pennsylvania, in 1945 at the age of 57.

Year	Club	G	IP	W	L	H	BB	SO	ERA
1912	Louisville	36	221	12	15	215	68	91	—
1913	Louisville	48	268	17	10	232	61	118	—
1914	Louisville	46	329	26*	10	329	87	114	3.18
1915	Louisville	48	335	25	15	308	98	97	2.82
1916	Louisville	34	222	16	13	194	49	81	3.08
1917	Indianapolis	31	253	20	10	241	68	110	2.53
1918	Indianapolis	18	161	13	3	141	34	36	1.95
	Boston	7	40	5	1	26	3	4	1.35
1919	Boston	11	37	1	5	43	10	9	4.62
	Milwaukee	25	164	10	11	194	32	65	3.84
1920	Milwaukee	39	339*	20	17	372*	48	127	3.53
1921	Columbus	40	276	16	16	332	62	85	4.40
1922	Columbus	39	256	11	19	293	73	66	3.87
1923	Columbus	40	249	15	13	280	77	70	4.34
1924	Columbus	38	227	13	18	279	65	62	4.52
1925	Columbus	35	216	8	19	275	70	54	5.00
	AA	517	3516	222	189	3684	885	1176	3.58

One result of the Federal League was the move of the Toledo franchise to Cleveland. Coal baron Charles W. Somers was a baseball enthusiast who had provided crucial financial support to the fledgling American League and whose Cleveland club was a bellwether of the circuit. Through the years Somers owned a number of minor league teams, including the Toledo Mud Hens. With only a two-hour train journey separating Toledo and Cleveland, Somers readily brought up Mud Hens who could help the Naps, and just as readily sent to Toledo big leaguers whose performances were sagging. There was a constant shuttle of players back and forth from the American Association team to its major league parent club — a practice which would become common in future decades.

In 1912 the United States League had been organized as an "outlaw" major league to challenge the American and National leagues. Cleveland was one of the cities in which a competing franchise was placed, and even though the USL folded in June, the Federal League of 1913 located one of its minor league clubs in Cleveland. When plans were laid to upgrade the circuit to major league status, Somers determined to avert further competition in Cleveland. League Park, which Somers had renovated and expanded in 1910, was the only facility in Cleveland suitable for minor league ball, and the owner of the Naps decided to offer local fans a professional game every day of the season.

The only franchise move during the first 51 years of the American Association was the transfer of Toledo to Cleveland in 1914, and the subsequent return of the Mud Hens after the Federal League disbanded in December 1915. For two seasons Cleveland's double-decked, concrete League Park hosted American Association teams while the Naps were on the road. The Cleveland club finished fifth in the AA in 1914 and seventh the following year, while the Naps were last in 1914 and next-to-last in 1915. And baseball fans accustomed to major league quality at least could see various former Naps in the lineup when the American Association played in League Park.

Now there was not even a train ride between the AA and AL teams, and Somers shuttled players more freely than ever. Jay Kirke, for example, was a fine first baseman and outfielder who split the season between the two clubs in both 1914 (.349 in 74 AA games, .273 in 67 AL games) and 1915 (.286 in 68 AA games, .310 in 87 AL games). In 1914 Jack Lelivelt played first base for the minor league club (.295 in 92 games) and outfield for the Naps (.328 in 32 games). Lefty James pitched 19 AA games in 1914 (9–6) and made 11 AL appearances (0–3); Al Collamore worked in 21 games for the Naps in 1914 (3–7), but was more successful in nine AA starts (5–4); in 1915 Buck Brenton pitched 28 AA games (11–

11) and 11 AL games (2–3). Numerous other players filled in a gap in the Naps' lineup occasioned by injuries, while big leaguers were sent down to help during important AA series. It was a unique situation in the history of organized baseball, but in 1916 Swayne Field again would host the Toledo Mud Hens and the other seven teams of the American Association.

Like the Federal League, the American Association offered fans a scintillating pennant chase in 1915. Milwaukee, which had won the flag the last two seasons, was challenged by Indianapolis, Louisville, and Kansas City. By midseason, however, Mike Kelley had piloted St. Paul into first place, and after the Fourth of July doubleheaders Minneapolis rose from the second division to challenge for the lead. The Millers reeled off 18 consecutive victories, finally moved into first place on September 2, then fought off archrival St. Paul to win their fourth pennant since 1910.

The Millers led the AA in batting average (.282), runs, hits, doubles and total bases with a lineup featuring outfielders Henri Rondeau (.333) and 38-year-old Dave Altizer (.302 with a league-leading 118 runs), infielder-outfielder Jay Cashion (.327), and catcher Patsy Gharrity (.308). Righthander Mutt Williams paced the league in wins, games, complete games and innings (29–16 with 32 CG in 64 games and 441 IP), while southpaw Chink Yingling (19–13 with a 2.17 ERA) won the league's second ERA title (Lefty James of Cleveland was awarded the first ERA crown in 1914, even though he worked just 134 innings in 19 games). Another lefty, fireballer Harry Harper, twirled a no-hitter against St. Paul in March, then set an AA record by walking 20 Saints in just eight innings of a July game. Harper walked 127 batters in 154 innings, but he struck out 148 and allowed just 99 hits (his won-loss record was a mediocre 7–9). But the Washington Senators looked at the no-hitter and the strikeout numbers and traded righthander "Bird Dog" Hopper to the Millers for Harper. Hopper proved to be the key to the Minneapolis pennant drive, posting a brilliant record (18–3 in 22 games) and leading the league in winning percentage. Louisville southpaw Dave Danforth (12–8), a fastballer who would win back-to-back strikeout crowns in 1920 and 1921, whiffed 18 Kansas City hitters on September 12, 1915, to set a league record that would last for 35 years.

St. Paul was led in 1915 by "Sea Lion" Hall (24–10), who won a record-setting 16 consecutive games, and lefthanded strikeout leader Robert Steele (20–16 with 183 Ks). Kansas City boasted the best two hitters of 1915: batting champ Jack Lelivelt (.346 with a league-leading 41 doubles) and outfielder Bash Compton (.343 with nine homers), who had won the 1914 stolen base title. Compton also tied for the 1915 home run lead, along with St. Paul outfielder Joe Riggert (.282, nine HR), who won outright homer crowns in 1913 (.293, 12 HR) and in war-shortened 1918 (.325, six HR). Indianapolis outfielder Joe Kelly (.300 with 61 steals) claimed the 1915 stolen base crown.

The 1916 theft champ was America's most famous athlete, football and track star Jim Thorpe. After dominating the 1912 Olympics, Thorpe played three seasons with John McGraw's New York Giants. His batting average was weak, and he spent 1916 with Milwaukee (.274 with 48 steals), winning the stolen base title and playing well enough to return to the Giants. Following three more years in the National League and one in the International League, the 35-year-old Thorpe played for the Toledo Mud Hens in 1921 (.358 with 34 steals and 112 RBIs). He divided 1922 between the Pacific Coast League (.308) and the Eastern League (.344) before retiring with a .320 average in 704 minor league games.

"Derby Day" Bill Clymer, who had left Columbus after the 1909 season, returned to the American Association in 1916 and promptly guided Louisville to the Colonels' second AA pennant, despite a constantly shifting roster. When newly acquired first baseman Clarence "Big Boy" Kraft failed to produce at the plate, he was traded to Milwaukee for Jay Kirke (.303), a six-year big league veteran who became the only Colonel regular to hit above .277. Seven players were interchanged in the outfield, but the light-hitting infield led the league in fielding. Jake Northrup, a big winner the previous two years (26–10 in 1914 and 25–15 in 1915), tailed off in 1916 (16–13), and Clymer's only reliable pitcher throughout the season was John Middleton (21–9). Clymer masterfully juggled pitching and hitting combinations and won 101 games.

Minneapolis lefty Chink Yingling had another fine season (24–13) in 1916, pacing the AA in victories, while the Indianapolis staff produced the ERA, percentage, and strikeout leaders in right-handers Paul Carter (15–4, .789, 1.65 ERA) and Cy Falkenburg (19–14, 178 K). Kansas City outfielder Beals Becker, who had just completed an eight-year National League career, exploded onto the

Jay Kirke

— Courtesy Louisville Redbirds

In 1906, 17-year-old Jay Kirke began his pro career as a shortstop in the Hudson River League, although eventually he would play every position except pitcher and catcher. Kirke was a six-footer, weighed 195 pounds, and batted from the left side. A fine hitter (.301 in 320 major league games, .316 in 2,617 minor league contests), Kirke moved up to the National League with Boston in 1911. But in 1913 Kirke got off to a weak start and went down to Toledo, where he became the regular first baseman (.320).

For 12 consecutive seasons he would hold down first for six different American Association clubs. When the Toledo franchise was moved to Cleveland for 1914 and 1915, Kirke alternated between the AA team (.349 and .286) and the AL Naps (.273 and .310). Early in 1916, Kirke was traded from Milwaukee to Louisville, and he was the top hitter (.303 with a league-leading 40 doubles) for the pennant-winning Colonels. He played in Louisville for seven years, winning the batting title in the championship season of 1921 and establishing the all-time AA record for hits (.386, 282 hits, 125 R, 43 2B, 17 3B, 21 HR, 157 RBI). Kirke again led the league in hits the next season (.355 with 282 hits and 123 RBIs).

In 1923 he was bought by Indianapolis, but after a disap-

(continued)

pointing season (.250) he went to Minneapolis and again hit well (.326 in 1924). Nevertheless, Kirke now was 36, and he went down to the Texas League in 1925 (.322) and 1926 (.333). In 1927 he played for Decatur of the Three-I League (.306), then retired. But after six years he made a single-season comeback with Opelousas of the Evangeline League, hitting .281 at the age of 47. Kirke lived until he was 80, dying in 1968 in New Orleans.

American Association scene by winning back-to-back batting championships and home run crowns in 1916 (.343, 15 HR) and 1917 (.323, 15 HR).

Another star of 1917 was Columbus righthander Grover Cleveland Lowdermilk, who recorded the first pitcher's Triple Crown in AA history (25–14, 250 K, 1.70 ERA), although Louisville righthander Dixie Davis matched his victory total (25–11). Minneapolis outfielder Dave Altizer at the age of 40 missed the batting title by one point (.322).

T. M. Chivington of Chicago, president of the AA since 1910, retired after seven years of strong leadership. The new president was Thomas Jefferson Hickey, who had founded the league and served as president in 1902 and 1903, and who would remain as president through 1934. For 1917 the American Association and the International League planned a 44-game interleague series — anticipating the Triple-A Alliance by more than seven decades! The AA and IL each intended to stage a 112-game schedule, then commence interleague play on August 5. But war had broken out in Europe in 1914, and on April 4, 1917, a week before opening day in the AA, the United States Congress ratified President Woodrow Wilson's declaration of war. The American Association decided to pull out of the interleague schedule and resume a 154-game season, although the AA and IL once more set up a Little World Series between the two league champs.

The pennant race again was a dandy. Louisville, St. Paul, Columbus, and Indianapolis battled throughout the season, and at the end of the schedule just six games separated the top four teams. Indianapolis kept a precarious hold on first place throughout 1917, but the Indians had to down Milwaukee on the last day of the season, using a triple play to help clinch the pennant. The Indians finished next-to-last in team hitting (.251), but in the style of deadball play led the league in fielding and fewest errors while featuring

INTER-LEAGUE SERIES.

AT HOME

AUGUST			
NEWARK	6	7	7
PROVIDENCE	8	9	9
RICHMOND	11	11	*12
BALTIMORE	13	14	15
BUFFALO	17	18	*19
ROCHESTER	20	21	22
TORONTO	24	25	*26
MONTREAL	27	28	29

ABROAD

AUGUST			
PROVIDENCE			31

SEPTEMBER			
PROVIDENCE		1	*2
NEWARK	**3	**3	4
RICHMOND	5	6	7
BALTIMORE	8	8	10
ROCHESTER	11	12	13
BUFFALO	14	15	16
MONTREAL	17	18	19
TORONTO	20	21	22

* Indicates Sunday dates.
** Indicates holiday dates.

Proposed interleague schedule between AA and IL teams as printed in 1917 Milwaukee program. The plan preceded the Triple-A Alliance by more than 70 years, but was thwarted by U.S. entry into World War I.

— Courtesy Milwaukee Public Library

pitchers such as Dana Fillingim (20–9), Jake Northrup (20–10), and the reliable Cy Falkenburg (11–6 with a 1.99 ERA in 20 games), who spent half of the season with the Philadelphia Athletics. In postseason play the Indians downed Toronto, four games to one — the first time in four tries that the American Association champ had won the Little World Series.

As the 1918 season approached, wartime travel restrictions and the entry of many players into military service prompted the AA to reduce its schedule to 140 games and postpone the opening date to May 1. In 1914, 42 minor leagues had opened the season, but in 1918 the AA was one of just nine circuits to attempt play. Throughout the league the price of grandstand seats was raised to 60 cents and bleacher seats to 30 cents, with several cents per ticket to be applied to the federal war tax. But in the spring of 1918, Secretary of War Newton Baker issued a "work or fight" order, which mandated that draft-age men engaged in nonessential work — such as professional baseball — would become subject to the draft. The American and National leagues played out an abbreviated season and, with special permission from the government, conducted the World Series. But of the nine minor league circuits, only the International League could complete its schedule.

On July 21, 1918, President Hickey convened a special meeting of the owners in Chicago. Bowing to the difficulties of maintaining rosters and arranging travel, the league adopted the following resolution:

The First "Night" Game

The distractions of war, as well as the soaring popularity of moving pictures and other popular amusements, caused attendance to plummet throughout organized baseball. With the adoption of Daylight Savings Time, various club owners realized that a game could be started as late as 7:00 P.M. and completed in natural light, hopefully with improved attendance from off-duty workers.

In the American Association, the first "night" game was staged in Minneapolis at 7:00 P.M. on Friday, May 24, 1918. A season-high "crowd" of 1,200 gathered at Nicollet Park to view the contest, and other late games also had encouraging effects upon attendance. In June, Columbus manager Joe Tinker refused to let his team take the field because of poor light, but umpires forfeited the game to the Millers. Although the early end of the season halted the experiment, owners would remember the possibilities of late starting times during the Great Depression.

Resolved, That on account of the war "work-or-fight" order issued by Secretary Baker, the 1918 playing schedule of the American Association of Professional Base Ball Clubs is hereby suspended for the balance of the 1918 season and all ball clubs disbanded after July 21, 1918. This action is taken by the Association to conform to the wishes of the Government.

Each team had played from 73 to 77 games. Kansas City had the best record (44–30) and was awarded its first AA pennant. With less than half of a regular schedule having been played, 1918 statistics include such irregularities as the decade's highest average by a batting champ (.374, by Milwaukee first baseman Doc Johnston in just 31 games and 115 at-bats) and the lowest winning ERA (1.50, by righthanders George Merritt of St. Paul, 6–3 in 10 games, and Gene Dale of Indianapolis, 2–3 in nine games). Three players tied for the stolen base title with 20 thefts each: St. Paul outfielder Joe Riggert (.325 with a league-leading six homers), St. Paul second baseman-outfielder Art Butler (.235), and Louisville outfielder Bob Bescher (.257).

Kansas City's champions were led by outfielder Wilbur Good (.321) and righthander Charles "Babe" Adams (14–3), who would log a total of 19 seasons in the National League. Cuban righthander Dolf Luque pitched well enough for Louisville (11–2) to launch a 20-year National League career, while other impressive hurlers

"Oh, say can you see . . ."

The national anthem has been played or sung regularly at the start of major league games since the Second World War. But during the First World War, management of the Columbus Senators decided to play "The Star-Spangled Banner" to open each game of the 1918 season (Columbus fans were proud that a native son, catcher Hank Gowdy of the Boston Braves, had been the first big leaguer to enlist for service in the Great War). Although wartime conditions caused American Association play to cease prematurely in July, the Senators resumed the performance of the national anthem in 1919 and never stopped, surely influencing other teams and leagues to adopt this patriotic custom.

At Columbus on opening day of 1918 it was decided to honor manager-president Joe Tinker, shortstop of the famous "Tinker-to-Evers-to-Chance" double-play combination. Marching bands led an automobile parade to Neil Park, and dignitaries included Ohio Governor James M. Cox. It was necessary to accommodate an overflow crowd of 18,000 (Neil Park seated 11,000) by roping off the outfield and infield. At the conclusion of impressive pre-game ceremonies, the throng stood and, accompanied by the Fort Hayes drum and bugle corps, sang the national anthem.

"Play ball!" shouted the umpire, and the crowd sat down in unison. But the sudden stress caused the wooden bleachers to break apart with a loud crack. Spectators were hurled to the ground from heights as great as 30 feet.

Several physicians who were present hurried toward the left field line and quickly had the injured placed in orderly rows on the field. Ambulances soon arrived but could not enter the park because of a traffic jam in the streets. Alertly, Wally Gerber and Ray Demmitt seized their bats and led other Senator players in an assault on the center field fence. Within moments a section of the plank wall had been battered down, and ambulances sped to the rescue. No one suffered serious injuries, Neil Park was repaired, and Senators games continued to be introduced by the national anthem.

were righthanders Sea Lion Hall of St. Paul (15–8) and Indianapolis ace Jake Northrup (13–3). The best player of 1918, however, was Milwaukee lefthander Dickie Kerr, who led the league in victories and strikeouts (17–7, 99 K) while working in 28 of the Brewers' 73 games and accounting for nearly half of their 38 wins.

The war ended in November 1918, prompting the American

Association to resume a 154-game schedule. Sensing that an increase in offense would boost attendance, AA owners joined a growing movement to legislate in favor of hitters by voting to abolish "freak delivery by pitchers." The league also decided to create a players' pool by taking one cent from each paid admission during the season. By the end of the year over $10,000 had been accumulated. The pool was distributed among the players on a prorated basis — members of the pennant-winners received the largest amount, while the last-place club got nothing.

Mike Kelley led St. Paul to the first of two back-to-back championships in 1919. The four-man rotation was a primary strength of the club: Richard Niehaus (23–13), Rusty Griner (21–14), Howard Merritt (19–9), and Sea Lion Hall (17–13). The offense was sparked by home run leader Elmer Miller (.314 with 15 homers), catcher Bubbles Hargrave (.303 with 11 homers), and first sacker Leo Dressen (.272 with 46 steals), who won his second stolen base title (he had recorded 55 thefts in 1917).

The batting champ was Louisville outfielder Tim Hendryx (.368). Batting averages began to climb, as indicated by the performances of KC outfielders Wilbur Good (.349) and Beals Becker (.332 with 14 homers), Indianapolis shortstop Ollie O'Mara (.340), and Minneapolis catcher Frank Owens. A total of 20 position players hit over .300. Indianapolis southpaw Teller Cavet (28–16 with a 2.26 ERA in 60 games) paced the league in victories and games, while Louisville workhorse Dixie Davis was the leader in strikeouts, innings, walks and losses (22–20, 372 IP, 165 K, 161 W, 2.42 ERA). Kansas City righthander Jesse Haines posted the league's best winning percentage (21–5, .808, 2.12 ERA), then went up to St. Louis and 18 years on the Cardinals' pitching staff. Louisville southpaw Tom Long (23–13) and Lefty George of Columbus (20–15) were among ten 20-game winners in 1919. On the final day of the season Columbus and Toledo, both mired in the second division, raced through nine innings in 53 minutes — the shortest game in AA history.

After winning the pennant, the Saints traveled by rail to Los Angeles to play a best five-of-nine series with the Vernon Tigers, champs of the Pacific Coast League. The Saints having led the AA in stolen bases (216), Vernon watered the field to slow their fleet opponents. The Tigers also used an ineligible player, then edged the Saints, five games to four. The series was covered in the na-

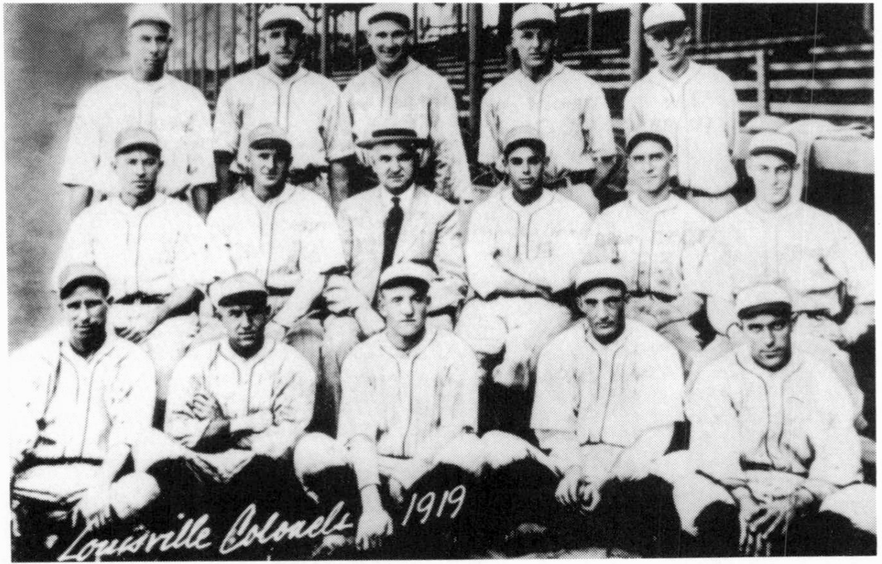

Louisville Colonels, 1919. The batting champ was Tim Hendryx (middle row, extreme left). Player-manager Joe McCarthy is seated next to him. The owner, Colonel William Knebelkamp, is in a coat and tie. Other stars on the middle row, left to right, are Merito Acosta, Bruno Betzel and Bill Meyer. On the bottom row Tom Long (middle) went 22–13, and Dixie Davis (second from right) led the AA in strikeouts and losses at 22–20. On the top row Ben Tincup (extreme left) won 180 games in 13 seasons in Louisville, and hitting star Jay Kirke stands at his side.

— Courtesy Louisville Redbirds

tional press and the Saints won widespread praise, but in the future the AA would concentrate upon the Little World Series for post-season play.

Fourteen minor leagues, up from nine in 1918, played organized baseball in 1919. Developments during the 1920s, the famous Golden Age of Sports in America, worked to popularize baseball, and by 1925 there were 25 minor leagues in operation. Since 1913 the American Association had successfully dealt with problems stemming from the Federal League and the Great War, emerging from this period stronger than ever. Firmly established as a showcase of future and former major league players, the American Association entered the 1920s as one of baseball's finest minor leagues.

1920–1929

An American Association Golden Age

In 1919 Boston Red Sox pitcher-outfielder Babe Ruth electrified the baseball world by setting a major league record with 29 home runs. Purchased by the New York Yankees during the off-season, Ruth hammered an incredible 54 home runs in 1920, 59 the following year, and 60 in 1927. Baseball experienced a revolution during the 1920s every bit as extreme as the social and cultural revolution of the Jazz Age. The dominant style of play in the American Association as well as in other leagues during the first two decades of the twentieth century was "inside baseball," which emphasized pitching, stolen bases, the hit-and-run play, and sacrifice bunting.

These low-scoring tactics became obsolete during the 1920s as a barrage of home runs excited fans and brought record crowds into ballparks across the country. The all-time AA home run record prior to 1920 was 19, stroked by Milwaukee outfielder Happy Felsch in 1914. But in 1920 Kansas City first baseman Bunny Brief hit 23 homers, followed by 42 in 1921 and 40 the next year. Before 1920 the highest team total of home runs was 68, garnered by Minneapolis in 1911, but in 1921 the Millers hit 120, while run totals and ERAs also exploded. Individual and team records continued to swell in ensuing years, and so did attendance. By 1921 a record 1.5 million fans filed into American Association ballparks, and such

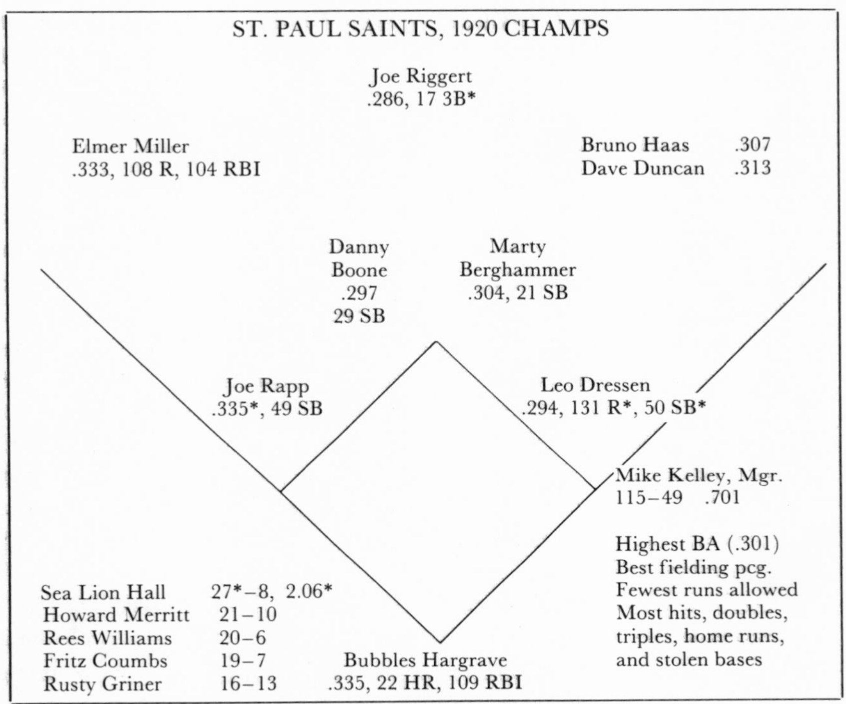

enthusiasm would prevail throughout the 1920s.

The first pennant "race" of the decade was completely dominated by St. Paul. Mike Kelley brought back most of the players from the 1919 championship club, while owner John W. Norton picked up several new athletes with talent and experience. The AA had voted to expand the schedule from 154 to 168 games, and the Saints won their first eight games en route to a total of 115 victories, the all-time league mark. Second-place Louisville won 88 games, giving the Saints a record 28½-game margin, while Kansas City brought up the cellar at 60–106. Kansas City outfielder Wilbur "Lefty" Good, an 11-year big league veteran, enjoyed a fine season (.334, 110 R, 109 RBI), and so did Toledo righthander John Middleton (26–14).

But 1920 belonged to the Saints. The experienced defense posted the league's best fielding percentage, while the pitching staff yielded the fewest runs for the second year in a row. Sea Lion Hall led the league in victories and ERA (27–8, 2.06) and twirled his second AA no-hitter, while Howard Merritt (21–10), Steamboat Williams (20–6), and lefty Fritz Coumbe (19–7) were nearly as hard to beat. The mound corps worked with an awesome offense which paced the league in hitting (.301 — second-place Minneapolis batted .280), runs (961 — 142 more than second-place Toledo), base hits, doubles, triples, homers, total bases, and, for the second consecutive season, stolen bases. First sacker Leo Dressen won his third stolen base championship in four years and led the AA in runs scored (.294, 50 SB, 131 R). The batting champ was third baseman Joe Rapp (.3351 with 49 SB in 155 games), but catcher Bubbles Hargrave came within a fraction of a percentage point of matching him (.3347, 22 HR, 109 RBI), and outfielder Elmer Miller was right behind (.333, 108 R, 104 RBI).

Since there would be no postseason playoff with the PCL champs in 1920, it was decided to resume the Little World Series. The Series had been played just four times, in 1904, 1906, 1907 and 1917, but it would be conducted without interruption from 1920 through 1963. Powerful St. Paul was confident of winning, even though Baltimore had recorded its second consecutive International League pennant with a higher winning percentage (110–43, .719) than the Saints (115–49, .701). Jack Dunn's Orioles won the last 25 games of 1920 and would become the greatest dynasty in baseball history (seven consecutive pennants from 1919 through 1925, and each IL champ won 100 games or more). The Orioles dumped the Saints, five games to one, putting the only blemish on an otherwise brilliant season for St. Paul. The final game was played at Lexington Park, a one-run decision against the Saints; shortstop Danny Boone hurled his glove into the grandstand to protest an umpire's call, fans nearly rioted in frustration against the men in blue, and a St. Paul headline the next morning blasted complaints against "Umpiracy."

In 1920 Bunny Brief won the first of his record-setting five AA home run championships. Born Antonio Bordetski in 1892, the right-handed outfielder-first baseman began his professional career at the age of 17. Bunny Brief played with the St. Louis Browns in 1912 and 1913, but went to Kansas City in 1913 and earned another shot at the big leagues with his first full AA season in 1914. Bunny started 1915 with the White Sox but finished the year with Salt Lake City of the Pacific Coast League, then won the PCL home run championship in 1916 — his third minor league home run title. The next season Bunny had a final big league trial with Pittsburgh but was sent down to Louisville late in the year (his lifetime batting average in 183 big league games was a paltry .223, as opposed to a .331 career mark in 2,426 minor league contests). Bunny would spend the rest of his career in the American Association, hammering AA pitchers for more than a decade. In addition to his five home run titles, he won four consecutive RBI championships, skipped a year, then won another, and his 1921 total of 191 set the all-time AA RBI mark. He also led the league twice in runs scored and once in doubles, and established career American Association records for home runs (276), doubles (458), runs scored (1,342), hits (2,196), and RBIs (more than 1,451 — RBI totals were not kept during Bunny's first year in the AA).

Bunny Brief in the American Association:

Year	Club	G	AB	R	H	2B	3B	HR	RBI	PCG.
1913	Kansas City	37	120	7	29	3	2	0	—	.225
1914	Kansas City	169	645	117	205	51	16	12	123	.318
1917	Louisville	48	156	23	45	8	2	1	19	.288
1918	Kansas City	74	260	32	68	6	2	4	36	.261
1919	Kansas City	152	564	89	183	30	11	13	101	.324
1920	Kansas City	165	615	99	196	41	9	23*	120*	.319
1921	Kansas City	164	615	166*	222	51*	11	42*	191*	.361
1922	Kansas City	139	519	133	176	40	7	40*	151*	.339
1923	Kansas City	166	640	161*	230	47	15	29	164*	.359
1924	Kansas City	159	601	106	203	58	12	17	104	.338
1925	Milwaukee	167	618	134	221	45	13	37*	175*	.358
1926	Milwaukee	161	583	130	205	38	10	26*	122	.352
1927	Milwaukee	126	432	89	133	27	4	14	86	.308
1928	Milwaukee	90	259	56	80	12	3	18	59	.309

A record level of slugging came from Minneapolis in 1921, as the Millers became the first AA club to hit more than 100 home runs (120) behind outfielders Reb Russell (.368, 33 HR, 132 RBI) and Rip Wade (.327, 31 HR, 126 RBI). Kansas City also broke the 100 barrier (112) behind home run-RBI champ Bunny Brief (.361, 42 HR, 191 RBI) and outfielders Lefty Good (.349, 23 HR, 157 RBI) and Dutch Zwilling (.325, 23 HR, 120 RBI). Indianapolis outfielder Ralph Shinner raised his batting average exactly 100 points and led his team in doubles, triples, and home runs (.347, 50 2B, a league-leading 26 3B, 13 HR, 94 RBI).

As hitters began to swing for the fences, stolen base totals declined, but not in 1921. Indianapolis third baseman Doug Baird (.310) set a league record with 72 thefts. Power hitter Ralph Shinner added 52 to the Indians' league-leading total of 222. Shinner and Baird were bought at the end of the season by the New York Giants, whose manager, John J. McGraw, stubbornly clung to the "inside baseball" methods which he had popularized with the Baltimore Orioles of the 1890s and with his championship New York clubs.

But the high-scoring trend of the future was unmistakable in the American Association. Kansas City won seven out of eight team batting titles from 1916 through 1923. The first three of these titles, however, were won with team averages of .268, .265 and .267, and the best mark of 1909 was Columbus' .247. But in 1920 St. Paul matched Minneapolis' old league record of .301 in 1911, and in 1921 Kansas City hit .313, followed by .315 averages in each of the next two seasons, a league standard that was matched by Toledo in 1930. During the first 18 seasons of AA play, 1902–1919, only one team hit over .300; during the next 18 seasons, 1920–1937, in just two years, 1924 (when Milwaukee led the league at .299) and 1935 (Columbus, also .299) did the AA fail to produce at least one club that hit over .300. Run totals soared accordingly, from 700 or 800 in a typical pre-1920 season to Kansas City's 1,148 in 1921. Hard-hitting Minneapolis was not shut out a single time during the 1921 season, and played 238 games without a shutout from September 1920 until June 1922.

Pitching performances, of course, suffered under the onslaught of free-swinging power hitters and a livelier ball. There had been 22 no-hitters in the AA prior to 1920, and three more followed during the 1920 season. But there was only one no-hitter during the next season, none in 1922, 1923, 1924 and 1925, one in 1926, then not another until 1932. In 1921, however, Columbus southpaw Dave Danforth hurled his way back into the big leagues with a magnificent season, leading the AA in victories, ERA and, for the second year in a row, strikeouts (25–16, 204 Ks, 2.66 ERA). Danforth's claim to the league's second pitcher's Triple Crown was blurred by Kansas City righthander Gus Bono, who tied for the most wins (25–11). Pug Cavet of Indianapolis pitched the most innings (23–16, 331 IP), the Saints' Sea Lion Hall worked in the most games (20–14 in 54 G), while Ernie Koob (22–9 in 50 G) and Ben Tincup (9–0 as a pitcher, he also was an outfielder and hit .284 in 102

In 1921 Louisville hit .308 as manager Joe McCarthy led the Colonels to the AA pennant.

— Courtesy Louisville Redbirds

games) were especially effective for the eventual pennant-winners.

Louisville, with a fine offense (.308 with 1,042 runs) and the best fielding team in the league, seized first place by June. Manager Joe McCarthy had a lineup that bristled with .300 hitters: batting champ Jay Kirke (.386, 21 HR, 157 RBI), who established an all-time AA record with 282 hits; catcher Bill Meyer (.312); third baseman Joe Schepner (.317 with 109 RBI); second sacker Bruno Betzel (.313); and outfielders Merito Acosta (.350 with 135 R), Rube Ellis (.336 with 100 RBIs) and Roy Massey (.316 with 134 R). Minneapolis (.308 as a team) provided the strongest challenge, with a remarkable performance from first baseman Bill Conroy (.310), who struck out merely four times in 562 at-bats. But Louisville outdistanced the Millers by six and a half games to win the pennant (98–70), then defeated favored Baltimore (119–47), five games to three, in the Little World Series.

St. Paul, winner of two consecutive pennants, sagged to sixth place in 1921 because many stars had been sold to major league clubs. Owner John Norton and manager Mike Kelley skillfully developed young players and rejuvenated former big leaguers, then arranged profitable sales. In 10 years — 1914 to 1924 — as owner of the Millers, Norton brought in nearly half a million dollars and numerous traded players, while spending little more than $100,000 on these transactions. But because they were such expert judges of talent, Norton and Kelley could rebuild quickly and by 1922 they

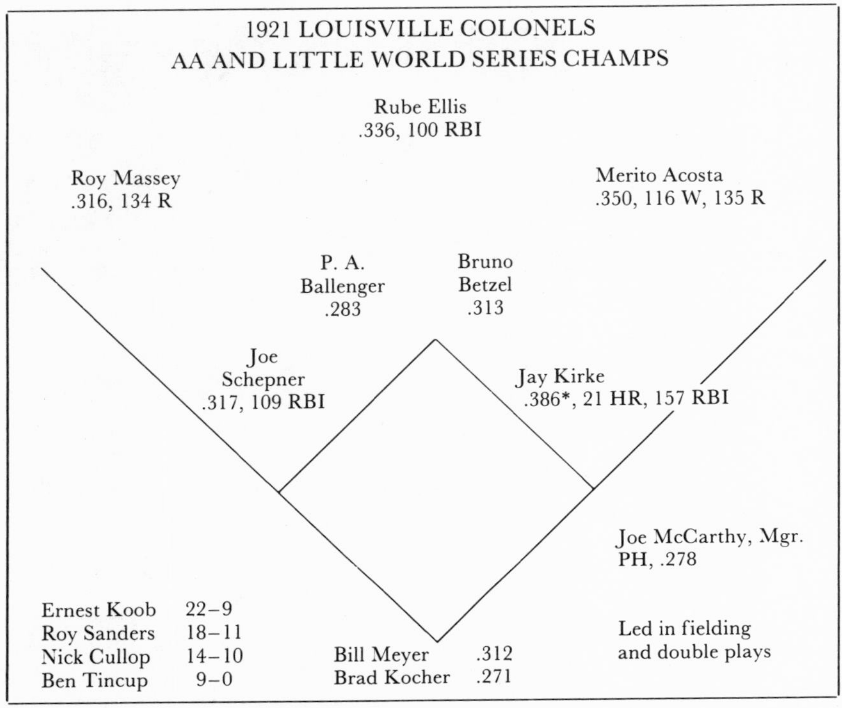

had assembled another championship team.

The 1922 Saints featured a pitching staff built around Sea Lion Hall (22–8), Rube Benton (22–11), and Tom Sheehan (26–12, 3.01 ERA), who led the AA in victories and ERA. The offense boasted no significant individual or team titles, except the stolen base championship (161), but overall the lineup was studded with such dangerous hitters as first baseman-outfielder Tim Hendryx (.341), outfielders Bruno Haas (.331) and Joe Riggert (.316), and future big league standout Charlie Dressen (.304). After early season success by Indianapolis, the Saints easily (107–60) collected their third pennant in four years, outdistancing second-place Minneapolis by 15 games, but again falling to Baltimore in the Little World Series.

During the season, Columbus shortstop Charley Pechous pulled off the only unassisted triple play in AA history against Minneapolis, but the emphasis throughout the season was on hitting. For the third consecutive year, Bunny Brief of Kansas City won

Saints righthander Tom Sheehan led the AA in victories and ERA in 1922 (26–12) and 1923 (31–9).

— Courtesy Louisville Redbirds

both the home run and RBI crowns (.339, 40 HR, 151 RBI), while Milwaukee catcher Glenn Myatt was the batting champ (.370). Jay Kirke of Louisville had another fine year (.355, 123 RBI), and so did Lefty Good of Kansas City (.352), along with a great many other hitters — 42 position players batted over .300, including 20 who hit .330 or better.

The hitting barrage continued the next year, as 47 regulars batted .300 or better, and titlist William Lamar of Toledo blasted out a .391 average. Future Hall of Famers Earle Combs (.380 with a league-leading 241 hits for Louisville) and Bill Terry (.377 and the best fielder in the league as Toledo's first baseman) used spectacular seasons to vault themselves into the major leagues.

Mike Kelley again made a run at the throne room behind a superb pitching staff that featured four 20-game winners: Tom Sheehan tied the league record for most victories and repeated as ERA champ (31–9, 2.90); the strikeout champ was Cliff Markle (25–12, 184 Ks); Sea Lion Hall performed brilliantly at the age of 38, recording his fourth consecutive 20-win season (24–13) and posting the club's highest batting average (.308 — third baseman Charlie Dressen hit .304); and Howard Merritt once more won 20

Future Hall of Fame catcher Al Simmons broke in with Milwaukee in 1922, played with the Brewers part of the next season, then went up to the big leagues for 21 years.
— Author's collection

games for the Saints (20–11). Outstanding pitching propelled St. Paul to the all-time franchise victory total (111–57), but the Saints were nosed out for the flag by an even better performance by Kansas City (112–54). St. Paul became the first team in AA history to record 100 victories and *not* win the pennant; the only other club with this frustrating distinction was the 1929 Saints (102–64), again losers to a superior Kansas City team (111–56).

Kansas City led the 1923 AA in batting by 20 points (.315) and was the only team to hit more than 88 homers (109). Bunny Brief led this devastating attack by winning his fourth consecutive RBI title and by scoring the most runs and drawing the most walks (.359, 29 HR, 164 RBI, 161 R, 101 W). Player-manager Lefty Good led by example (.350, 136 R, 91 RBI), and he was impressively followed by outfielder Dud Branom (.348), catcher William Skiff (.335), and shortstop Buckshot Wright (.313). Righthander Jimmy Zinn led the pitching staff (27–6 with a league-leading .818 winning percentage) and hit superbly for a hurler (.354 — he averaged .301 over a long career).

Righthander Wayland Dean pitched well enough for Louisville (21–8) to earn a big league berth, while Millers outfielder

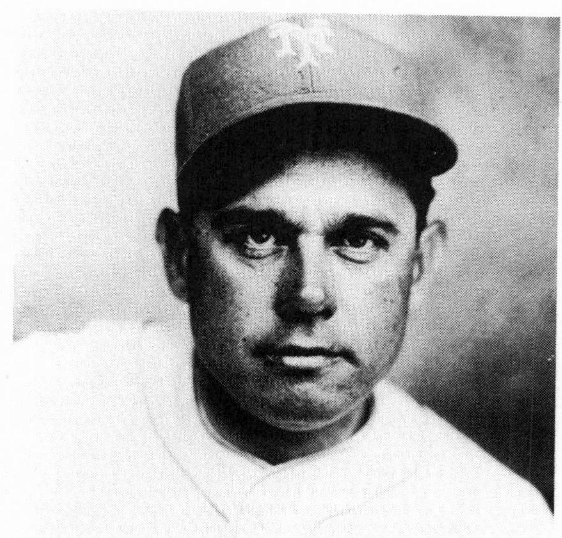

Bill Terry played first base for Toledo in 1922 (.336) and 1923 (.377), then went on to a Hall of Fame career with the New York Giants.

Author's collection

Carlton East (.375, 31 HR, 151 RBI) broke Bunny Brief's stranglehold on the home run title, and Milwaukee shortstop James Cooney (.308, 60 SB) won the stolen base crown. But the pennant race belonged to defending champ St. Paul and to Kansas City, which could boast only of a flag won during the war-shortened 1918 season.

The Saints and Blues outdistanced the rest of the league, but went into the season-ending doubleheaders with either team the possible winner. St. Paul split a pair with third-place Louisville, while KC came through with two victories over hapless Toledo (54–114). The Blues' momentum carried over into the Little World Series, which also came down to the final game. Kansas City climaxed an outstanding season by defeating perennial International League champ, Baltimore, five games to four.

After the season the 29 corporate owners of Minneapolis sold the Millers to Mike Kelley, who moved across the river from St. Paul to take over Minneapolis for the second time. Pongo Joe Cantillon, field general of the Millers since 1910, resigned, and Kelley assumed the managerial reins of his club. St. Paul catcher Nick Allen, who had logged six years in the big leagues, was appointed

Lefthanded outfielder Earle Combs entered pro ball with Louisville in 1922 (.344) and 1923 (.380), then spent 12 seasons with the Yankees and was voted into the Hall of Fame in 1970.

— Courtesy Louisville Redbirds

manager of the Saints. Allen handled the roster artfully, blending returnees such as Cliff Markle (19–9), Howard Merritt (19–17), RBI leader Charlie Dressen (.351, 18 HR, 151 RBI), Sea Cap Christensen (.314, 145 R), Joe Riggert (.294) and Bruno Haas (.293), with newcomers Anthony Faeth (15–4) and Johnny Neun, a hard-hitting first baseman who led the league in stolen bases (.353, 136 R, 55 SB). The Saints posted the best fielding percentage in the league, stole the most bases (223), and permitted the fewest runs.

Kansas City's lineup was decimated by sales to big league clubs, and the defending champs plunged to last place. Joe McCarthy produced another contender at Louisville behind the Colonels' *only* AA home run champ, Elmer Smith (.334 with 28 homers), along with shortstop Red Shannon (.340), outfielder Ty Tyson (.331), and Ben Tincup (24–17). Indianapolis manager Donie Bush made a run at the pennant with veteran southpaw Jesse Petty, who won the ERA and victory titles (29–8, 2.83), and iron man catcher Ernie Krueger (.339, 17 HR, 128 RBI), who caught 160 games and pinch hit in four others.

Bill Burwell

Bill Burwell was a 5′11, 175-pound righthander who pitched three years of minor league ball before entering the army for service in France during World War I. In combat a German machine gun bullet ripped away part of the index finger of his pitching hand. Surgeons had to remove a portion of the splintered bone, leaving the finger at a right angle and threatening Burwell's pitching career.

But when he recovered, he found that his breaking pitch was noticeably improved. "I discovered later," reflected Burwell, "that I had found a method of putting a spin on the ball with the new grip which produces a sharp, breaking curve."

Resuming his baseball career, Burwell pitched with the St. Louis Browns in 1920 and 1921 before making his first appearance in the American Association with Columbus in 1923 (14–23 to lead the league in losses). The next year he was acquired by Indianapolis, winning 175 games in 12 seasons. He paced the AA in innings pitched in 1923, and in victories and ERA in 1925. His best seasons came in 1925 (24–9) and 1926 (21–14). Burwell finally went down to Terre Haute of the Three-I League in 1935, then returned to the American Association in 1936 as a pitching coach for Minneapolis. In 1937 he was reactivated at the age of 42 and went 4–0 in 10 games with the Millers.

The next season he finished his playing career with Crookston of the Northern League but soon returned to the AA as a manager. He managed Louisville from 1940 through 1943 and Indianapolis in 1945 and 1946, winning the playoffs in 1940 and reaching the finals in 1941 and 1946. He coached with the Boston Red Sox in 1944 and with the Pittsburgh Pirates in 1947 and 1948 and from 1958 through 1962. He died in 1973 at the age of 78. Burwell served as a player, coach, and manager in the American Association for 22 years, recording a 193–163 record as an AA pitcher.

The Colonels, Indians, and Saints battled for the flag throughout the season, but St. Paul finally emerged on top, winning their fourth championship in six years. The Saints had lost the Little World Series to Jack Dunn's Baltimore dynasty in 1920 and 1922 with more talented clubs than the 1924 aggregation (96–70, .578), and St. Paul was given little chance to beat the Orioles (117–48, .709) in the best five-of-nine series. In the opener, Orioles ace Lefty Grove (27–6) whiffed 11 Saints, and in the fourth game he struck

An enthusiastic crowd on the field at Nicollet Park at a Millers game, ca. 1923.
— Courtesy Minnesota Historical Society

out the side after St. Paul loaded the bases with no outs. After five games the Saints had recorded just one victory, although the third game was a 13-inning, 6–6 deadlock. St. Paul won the sixth game but lost the next contest, and Baltimore needed only one more victory. But the Saints squeezed out a 3–2 win in the eighth game, then beat Grove to tie the series. Saints southpaw Paul Fittery (16–10 during the season) won the deciding contest, then proclaimed in a jubilant dressing room: "Pick out a star on this club. You can't do it. There's 22 of them."

The winners' share amounted to $796 per man (the Orioles took home $531 apiece), and owner John Norton happily handed an additional $100 to each player. Then the Saints boarded a westbound train to take on Seattle, champions of the Pacific Coast League. The American Association had agreed to another postseason series with the PCL winners. The Coast League played the longest schedule in organized baseball (200 games in 1924) and considered their circuit markedly superior to any other minor league. But after the opener was postponed by rain, St. Paul stunned Seattle, 12–4. Rain settled in for the next two days, and it was decided to cancel the remainder of the series. The Saints col-

How to Pilfer a Slugger

In 1925 Hack Wilson, a stocky, 25-year-old outfielder for the New York Giants, slumped badly at the plate (.239 in 62 games) and was sent down on option to the Toledo Mud Hens. Wilson recovered his batting eye (.343 in 55 games), but the Mud Hens finished a dismal sixth (77–90) and manager Jimmy Burke was fired. Although John J. McGraw, who had a financial interest in the Mud Hens, fully intended to recall Wilson to the Giants, someone forgot to list his name with the league office. Aware of this oversight, Burke somewhat vindictively tipped off Joe McCarthy.

McCarthy had managed Louisville to the 1925 American Association pennant, then was named field general of the Chicago Cubs. He notified Cubs president William Veeck (father of Bill Veeck, who would make an impact on the AA in the 1940s as owner-president of Milwaukee) and Chicago drafted Hack Wilson from the list of available players. McGraw protested that he was being cheated out of a player on a technicality, but the move was legal and Wilson stayed with the Cubs, winning four National League home run crowns in the next five seasons.

lected another $175 apiece, then finally took off their uniforms until spring training.

John Norton, who had specialized in selling players after successful seasons, sold his club after a highly successful 10-year reign in St. Paul. With Norton and Mike Kelley and the usual number of star players gone, the 1925 Saints sagged to third place, and did not return to the throne room until 1931. Donie Bush again brought Indianapolis into second place behind the efforts of ERA and victory leader Bill Burwell (24–9, 2.73). Bunny Brief celebrated his first season in Milwaukee by winning the combined home run-RBI titles for the fourth time since 1920 (.358, 37 HR, 175 RBI), while Columbus outfielder Eddie Murphy, an 11-year veteran of the American League, seized the batting championship with a spectacular performance (.397).

Louisville had assembled a club that would rule the American Association for two years. Joe McCarthy led the 1925 Colonels (106–61) to a 13½-game victory margin, then left for a Hall of Fame career as a big league manager. Catcher Bill Meyer took over as manager and produced an equally powerful team (105–62). Five righthanders handled most of the pitching in both seasons:

Flag-raising ceremonies on opening day at Nicollet Park, ca. 1925.
— Courtesy Minnesota Historical Society

An umpire throwing out the first ball on opening day at Nicollet Park, ca. 1925.
— Courtesy Minnesota Historical Society

A run crosses the plate on opening day at Nicollet Park, ca. 1925.
— Courtesy Minnesota Historical Society

Nick Cullop (22–8 and 20–8), Joe DeBerry (20–8 and 17–13), Ed Holley (20–7 in 1925), Ben Tincup (18–7 in 1926), and Joe Dawson (17–7 in 1926). Other two-year regulars included Meyer (.287 and .306), outfielders Joe Guyon (.363 and .343) and John Anderson (.314 and .310), second baseman Bruno Betzel (.312 and .322), and first sacker Hooks Cotter (.326 and .273). Single season standouts were outfielder Ty Tyson (.352) in 1925 and, the next year, catcher Al DeVormer (.368) and outfielders Rube Ellis (.352) and Earl Webb (.333). The only disappointments were Little World Series losses to Baltimore and Toronto.

St. Paul righthander George Pipgras led the 1926 AA in victories (and losses), innings pitched and strikeouts (22–19), then resumed a 12-year career in the American League. Bunny Brief won his fifth home run crown since 1920 (.352, 26 HR, 122 RBI), and his Milwaukee teammate, outfielder Lance Richbourg, scored the most runs, stole the most bases, and hit the most triples (.346, 151 R, 48 SB, 28 3B). Brief and Richbourg sparked the Brewers to an all-time league record of 21 consecutive victories, recorded from May 25 through June 16. At the opposite scale of performance was last-place Columbus, which committed a record 12 errors in one

Casey Stengel became player-manager at Toledo in 1926. The colorful ex-big leaguer led the Mud Hens to their first AA pennant the next year.

— Courtesy Louisville Redbirds

game and compiled the all-time AA mark for losses (39–125, .238).

In 1926 Casey Stengel became player-manager of the Toledo Mud Hens. The colorful Stengel had spent 13 years as a National League outfielder, then was sent by the Boston Braves early in the 1925 season to run their Worcester farm club in the Eastern League. As player-manager-president Stengel hit well and led the team from the cellar to third place, then was offered the Toledo job. Toledo did not want to have to pay Boston for Stengel's contract, so *President* Stengel released himself as a player, fired himself as manager, then resigned as president and joined the Mud Hens.

Toledo was partially owned by and was a farm club of the New York Giants, and Stengel had played in two World Series for John J. McGraw's team. During his six years with Toledo, Stengel utilized a steady stream of players sent down from the Giants or acquired from other big league clubs. The 37-year-old Stengel played well (.328 in 88 games); outfielder Bevo LeBourveau, a veteran of four years in the National League, won the 1926 AA batting crown (.385, 17 HR, 117 RBI); righthander Ernest Maun became the ERA champ (2.71) after coming down from the Phillies; and 38-year-old Bobby Veach, who had just completed 14 seasons in the

The Mud Hens finally brought an AA flag to Toledo in 1927.
— Courtesy Toledo Mud Hens

American League (.310 lifetime), began three explosive years with the Mud Hens (.362, 113 R, 105 RBI).

By 1927 Stengel was ready for a championship drive. Veach won the RBI crown (.363 with 145 RBI), and plenty of other offense (the team hit .312) was generated by outfielders Bevo LeBourveau (.346) and Joe Kelly (.328), first baseman Roy Grimes (.368 with 122 RBIs), catcher John Heving (.356), second sacker Fred Maguire (.326), and former National League outfield star Irish Meusel (.354).

The Mud Hens were challenged by Milwaukee, which led the AA in batting (.313) behind shortstop Harry Rinconda (.353, with a league-leading 255 hits and 57 doubles), outfielder-pitcher Oswald Orwoll (.370 in 99 games, and 17–6 from the left side of the mound), outfielder Frank Wilson (.337), second sacker Fred Lear (.330), and a host of other .300-plus hitters who made life easier for righthanders Claude Jonnard (22–14) and Joe Eddelman (21–10). Kansas City had an even better one-two mound combination, with victory leader Tom Sheehan (26–13) and ERA champ Jimmy Zinn (24–12, .308). Hitting star Joe Hauser (.353, 20 HR, 134 RBI, and a league-leading 26 triples) sparked an excellent offense (.310 as a team with a league-leading 127 triples), and the Blues also made a run for the pennant.

Indianapolis outfielder Reb Russell, a former big league pitcher, won the batting championship (.385), but the Indians had a losing record. Minneapolis led the AA in home runs, Miller shortstop Frank Emmet hit the most homers and scored the most runs (.330, 32 HR, 116 RBI, 154 R), and righthander Pat Malone won the strikeout crown (20–18, 214 Ks), but the team finished in the second division. Columbus again finished last (60–108), even though catcher Richard Ferrell tied a league record by striking out merely four times during the season (Ferrell, however, played in just 104 games, while Bill Conroy was in 149 games in 1921 when he set the mark).

The pennant race, then, was a three-way battle all season between Toledo, Kansas City, and Milwaukee. Late in the year the Mud Hens apparently were knocked out of contention by the Blues and Millers. While his team was losing a Labor Day decision to Columbus, Casey Stengel angrily incited the home fans over a close call at first base. Hundreds of spectators climbed out of the stands to pursue the umpire into the dugout, where he was rescued by police. AA President Tim Hickey suspended Stengel, but the Mud Hens came back to life. Stengel's team rallied for 10 victories in a row to win Toledo's first pennant on the last day of the season, while KC and Milwaukee tied for second place. The Mud Hens' momentum carried over to the Little World Series, where they triumphed over Buffalo, five games to one.

The next year 40-year-old Bobby Veach won the batting crown (.382) and Casey Stengel played effectively in 26 games, usually as a pinch hitter (.328 with 12 RBIs in only 32 at-bats), but the Mud Hens dropped out of contention early. So did Kansas City, despite the efforts of Jimmy Zinn (23–13), who was promoted to Cleveland. Milwaukee produced a third-place team built around the pitching of victory leader James Wingard (24–10) and strikeout king Claude Jonnard (20–11, 150 Ks). Mike Kelley guided Minneapolis into first place late in the year, utilizing the brilliant pitching of Ad Liska (20–4) and the hitting of home run champ Spencer Harris (.327 with 32 homers), outfielder-first baseman Ernie Orsatti, who narrowly missed the batting title (.381), and 40-year-old outfielder Zack Wheat (.309 in 82 games), in his last year

The Minneapolis Millers pose before a gathering crowd at Nicollet Park on April 26, 1926.

— Courtesy Minnesota Historical Society

of pro ball after a 19-year big league career that would place him in the Hall of Fame.

Minneapolis battled for the pennant throughout the year against Indianapolis, which had been rejuvenated by a wealthy, enthusiastic new owner, Jim Perry. Third baseman Fred Haney (.334, 43 SB) won the stolen base crown, outfielders Adam Comorsky (.357 in 89 games), Herman Layne (.347), Wid Matthews (.323) and Reb Russell (.311) also provided offensive help, and righthander Steve Swetonic (20–8) led a solid pitching staff. The Indians held first place during most of June, July and August, sagged to second place late in August and during the first half of September, then won the flag with a strong stretch drive. In the Little World Series the Indians dumped the Rochester Red Wings, 5–1–1, winning the final three games before cheering crowds at Washington Park. Perry honored his club with a dinner, proudly presenting each player with a gold watch charm. The four-cornered charms had a small diamond set in each corner, a gold Indian head above crossed bats in the center, the inscription "American Association Champions 1928," and each player's name. Tragically, Perry was killed in a plane crash during the middle of the following season, but his brother Norman would guide the Indians for the next 13 years.

In 1929 Kansas City stormed back into the throne room (111–56). Manager Dutch Zwilling enjoyed a deep mound corps that included Marlon Thomas (18–11), Robert Murray (17–8), Tom Sheehan (16–11, and .341 at the plate), Lynn Nelson (15–6), Cy Warmoth (14–4), and Clyde Day (12–5). The explosive batting order featured catchers John Peters (.320) and Tom Angley (.389 in 76 games), outfielders Denver Grigsby (.345), Fred Nicholson (.344), Robert Seeds (.342) and Ollie Tucker (.336), first baseman Joe Kuhel (.325 with a league-leading 26 triples), and infielder Harry Riconda (.320). The Blues won the season series with every AA rival, then outlasted Rochester in the Little World Series, five games to four.

St. Paul catcher-manager Bubbles Hargrave nearly won the batting title (.369 in 104 games) and brought the Saints into the runner-up slot. It was the second time in the decade that St. Paul won over 100 games only to be denied the pennant, but Hargrave was consoled by being brought up as a player to the New York Yankees. St. Paul led the league in hitting (.306) behind home run-RBI champ Dusty Cooke (.358, 33 HR, 148 RBI, 153 R), run leader William Chapman (.336, 31 HR, 162 R), infielder William Rogell (.336, 134 R), and first baseman Oscar Roettger (.326). The pitching staff showcased ERA titlist Archie Campbell (15–3, 2.79), victory leader Americo Polli (22–9), and National League veteran Huck Betts (21–13).

Toledo outfielder Art Ruble qualified for the first of two consecutive batting crowns (.376), although the Mud Hens dropped to the cellar. Casey Stengel, frustrated by his team's poor performance, fought a fan in the grandstand before a game in May, participated in a brawl during a Fourth of July contest with St. Paul, and three days later rushed from the dugout to grapple with Columbus third baseman Lute Boone. Boone enjoyed a good season for the Senators, and so did future big league star Tony Cuccinello (.358, 33 HR, 56 2B, 227 H), the AA leader in hits and doubles.

By the end of the 1929 season the New York stock market had crashed and the United States soon would be in the throes of the Great Depression, with profound effects upon professional baseball as well as every other aspect of American society. During the 1920s, American sports had enjoyed a well-publicized Golden Age that

Five members of the Millers in their flannel pinstripes on April 26, 1926.
— Courtesy Minnesota Historical Society

The Fight

No sports rivalry was more bitterly contested over a longer period than the baseball competition between Minneapolis and St. Paul. Many a brawl erupted through the years, but the most explosive donnybrook occurred at Nicollet Park during the morning game of a Fourth of July doubleheader in 1929.

In the third inning, Saints righthander Huck Betts fired a beanball at Hughie McMullen. McMullen dropped to the dirt, brushed himself off, and a few pitches later grounded to first. Betts covered the bag, but was intentionally spiked by McMullen as he sped past. Betts angrily threw the ball at the back of McMullen's head. The ball missed, but first base coach Sammy Bohne, a utility player, rushed Betts and launched a series of punches.

Both dugouts emptied and the teams grappled around the pitcher's mound. Eventually a dozen policemen managed to quell the epic melee, which was remembered in awe by spectators and players as "The Fight."

had touched the American Association. The style of play in the AA, as well as throughout the rest of organized baseball, changed direction in a high-scoring, power-hitting, fast-paced manner that excited fans and produced record crowds and revenues. Despite unprecedented batting feats, there were numerous outstanding pitching performances during the decade, and the AA continued to star gifted athletes who would become (or who had been) major league stalwarts. St. Paul and Louisville won three pennants apiece, Kansas City produced two magnificent championship clubs, and Toledo won its first flag, while the league did not experience a single franchise shift. The prosperity and popularity of the 1920s would help the American Association respond to the problems of the coming decade.

1930–1939

Buddy, can you spare a dime — for a bleacher seat?

By the time the baseball season of 1930 opened, the United States was several months into the Great Depression. Minor league baseball was staggered by the economic chaos of the 1930s: 25 leagues completed the 1929 season, but the number dropped to 21 in 1930, then to just 16 the following year. Club owners fought for solvency with such innovations as night games and the Shaughnessy playoff system. The American Association was at the forefront of these developments, and weathered the Depression decade with greater stability than any other minor league.

At the National Association winter meeting in 1929, Lee Keyser announced that his Des Moines Demons of the Class A Western League would play regularly under artificial lights during the 1930 season. Keyser invested $19,000 in a lighting system and looked forward to the distinction of becoming the first club in organized baseball to stage a night game. But Des Moines opened on the road in 1930, and Independence, Kansas, of the Class C Western Association, hastily rigged temporary arclights and staged a night game against Muskogee on April 28. Four nights later Des Moines played its first game under the lights, and within the next several weeks other clubs in other leagues followed suit, posting impressive attendance results.

In the American Association, Indianapolis owner Norman Perry installed six steel towers around Washington Park. On Monday, June 9, 1930, 75 million candle power illuminated the field as the Indians were edged by St. Paul 1–0, in the first night game in AA history. Baseball Commissioner Kenesaw Mountain Landis was present, along with AA President Thomas J. Hickey, the presidents of the National Association, the St. Louis Cardinals, and the Cincinnati Reds, and 5,000 excited fans. Indianapolis was the only AA team to set up a lighting system in 1930, but the last-place Indians were surprisingly successful at the box office. Despite the Depression, Perry announced construction of a $350,000 stadium, and the Indians played their first game in the 14,500-seat facility on September 5, 1931.

Landis and Hickey again were present, this time in Columbus, when 15,000-seat Red Bird Stadium was opened to a sellout crowd on June 3, 1932. Like Perry Stadium in Indianapolis, the new home of the Red Birds boasted high-level lighting, and within the next few years every team in the AA would host night games. Players would complain that irregular playing schedules negatively affected their performances, and that fastball pitchers held an advantage over batters under the lights. Red Bird righthander Paul Dean, for example, had only a suggestion of a curve but a major league fastball (until hampered by injuries), and he won back-to-back strikeout crowns in 1932 and 1933. But the vastly greater potential pool of fans for night games, plus the appeal of attending games at night to escape summer heat, made under-the-lights baseball inevitable for all AA teams. Minneapolis in 1937 became the league's final city to install a lighting system. In 1932 only 14 minor leagues tried to operate, and throughout the Depression minor league clubs and entire circuits folded. But the American Association maintained its customary eight clubs without change throughout the Depression, a solidity decisively influenced by night baseball.

Louisville won the first pennant race of the decade in a season noted for remarkable offensive production. Not a club batted under .300 in 1930. Team averages ranged from .300 for Indianapolis to Toledo's .315, while 60 position players hit more than .300. Among the most spectacular hitters of 1930 were Robert Fenner (.391 in 98 games), Bruno Haas (.374 in 82 games) and George Davis (.366) of St. Paul; Charles High (.382 with 25 homers in 104 games) and

The 1930 Minneapolis Millers in their dugout at Nicollet Park on a warm August day. The Millers hit .312 during a season in which every AA team averaged .300 or better.

— Courtesy Minnesota Historical Society

Spencer Harris (.363 in 93 games) of Minneapolis; and Butch Simons (.371 with a league-leading 248 hits and 49 doubles), Herman Layne (.333 with a league-leading 40 steals and 19 triples), and Joe Kuhel of Kansas City (.372 in 93 games).

Even more impressive was Minneapolis outfielder Nick Cullop. "Tomato Face" Cullop began his career in 1920 as a 19-year-old righthanded pitcher, and he played in three games with Minneapolis. He was such a strong hitter that he frequently was played in the field, and after three years he became a full-time position player. His prowess with a bat carried him to stints with New York, Washington and Cleveland in the American League, and Brooklyn and Cincinnati in the National League. But he could hit only .249 against big league pitching, and he spent most of his 25-year career in the minors. Cullop became the all-time minor league RBI leader (1856, with a .312 lifetime average), and he also belted 420 homers. He played with St. Paul in 1926 (.314 with 22 homers), provided the biggest bat in Columbus from 1932 through 1936, then returned to Columbus as a highly successful player-manager in 1943.

During a 25-year playing career, Nick Cullop spent 10 seasons with three AA clubs. The all-time minor league RBI leader, his finest year was with Minneapolis in 1930 (.359, 54 HR, 152 RBI), following devastating personal tragedies during the off-season.

— Courtesy Mariana York

But his best year came in 1930, even though both of his children had died tragically in the off-season and his wife had suffered a nervous breakdown. Cullop was beaned early in the season, and managed just one homer in his first 28 games. Suddenly, however, he overcame every adversity and went on a home run binge unprecedented in AA history. Bunny Brief had crashed 42 homers in 1921 and 40 the next year, and was the only man to hit 40 home runs in the first three decades of the American Association. But in 1930 Cullop led the league in homers, RBIs and runs (.359, 54 HR, 152 RBI, 150 R), setting a home run record that would not be broken — for three years!

Again in 1931 there were 60 position players who hit .300 or better. Kansas City outfielder Gus Dugas hit *much* better (.419), but he only posted 327 at-bats in 93 games. Art Shires played 157 games for Milwaukee (.385), while other standout hitters included Tom Angley of Columbus (.375), Bevo LeBourveau, who played for both Toledo and Columbus during the season (.375), future Hall of Famer Billy Herman of Louisville (.350), and home run and

Future Hall of Famer Billy Herman played with Louisville from 1928 through 1931. After batting .350 for the Colonels in 1931, the second baseman went up to the Cubs. He returned to the AA in 1948 as player-manager of the Millers, hitting .451 in 31 at-bats.

— Courtesy Louisville Redbirds

RBI champ Cliff Crawford of Columbus (.374, 28 HR, 154 RBI). Joel Hunt, an All-American footballer for Texas A&M, played respectably (.278) in the Columbus outfield.

St. Paul (104–63) rolled to the pennant with a 14-game margin over second-place Kansas City. Righthanders Huck Betts (22–13) and Slim Harriss (20–11), and southpaw Russ Van Atta (13–5) were the Saints' best pitchers. It was an easy club to pitch for, leading the league in team hitting (.311), homers (167), doubles and fielding. Second baseman Jack Saltzgaver was the stolen base champ (.340, 19 HR, 26 SB), while first sacker Oscar Roettger (.357, 15 HR), outfielders George Davis (.343, 26 HR), Ben Paschal (.336, 14 HR) and Harold Anderson (.314, 23 HR), and shortstop Joe Morrissey (.331, 22 HR) formed the nucleus of an explosive batting order.

Although many of St. Paul's best players moved up in 1932, causing the club to drop to seventh place, Russ Van Atta posted another fine season (22–17). Cliff Crawford again swung a powerful bat for Columbus (.369, 30 HR, 140 RBI), and so did outfield-

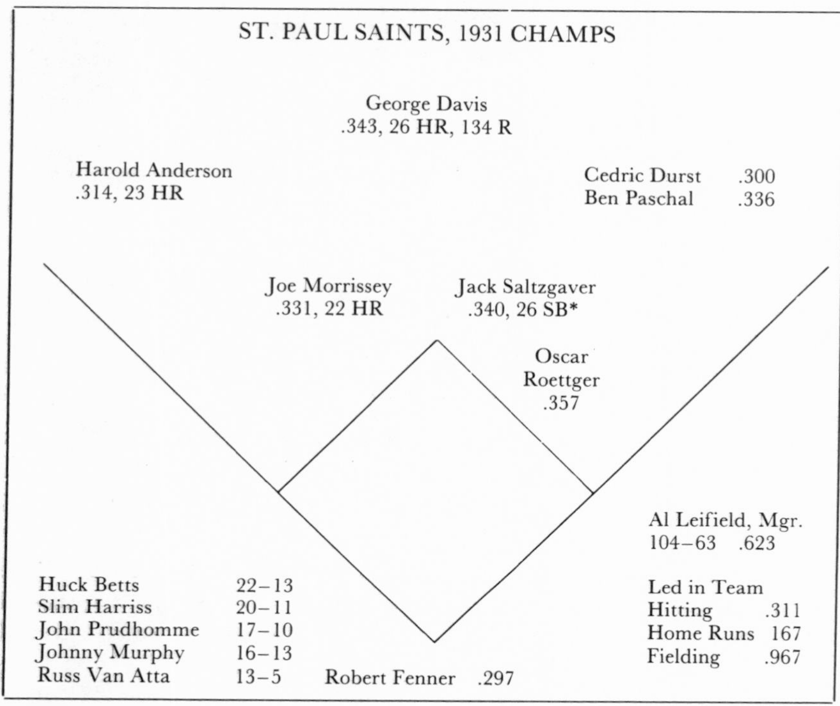

ers Evar Swanson (.375, 131 RBI, and a league-leading 45 steals) and Nick Cullop (.348, 26 HR). The Red Birds also showcased 18-year-old Paul Dean, brother of Cardinals star Dizzy Dean. Paul pitched the first no-hitter in the AA since 1926, and despite his record (7–16) he became the youngest pitcher ever to win the strikeout crown. LeRoy Parmalee pitched 18 games for the Red Birds and established an AA record for winning percentage (14–1, .933).

But Minneapolis, with a short right-field fence (279 feet down the line, 328 feet in the right-center power alley) at Nicollet Park, loaded up with lefthanded sluggers and dominated the American Association. The pennant-winners blasted a league-leading 188 homers — 149 at Nicollet. On Wednesday, July 20, the Millers scored a record-setting 40 runs during a doubleheader with Louisville, and established another mark with 32 hits in one game. Three days earlier the Millers lost a 20–22 slugfest with Indianapolis, setting an AA record for the highest run total in a single game.

Minneapolis outfielder Art Ruble won the batting crown with

the same average he had posted while winning the title with Toledo in 1929 (.376, 29 HR, 141 RBI). Outfielder Joe Mowry led the league in hits and set the all-time record for runs (.348, 175 R, 257 H). Catcher Paul Richards split the season between Brooklyn and Minneapolis (.361, 16 HR, 69 RBI in just 78 games), and utility man Harry Rice found plenty of playing time because of his explosive bat (.345 in 117 games). The home run champ was first baseman Joe Hauser (.303, 49 HR, 129 RBI), who had electrified the baseball world in 1930 by blasting 63 homers for Baltimore of the International League.

Hauser electrified the baseball world again in 1933. He hit his first home run on April 27 against Toledo, added three more the next day, then continued his record-breaking assault on AA pitching with devastating regularity. There were 13 homers in May, 15 in June, and 20 in July. Nick Cullop's record of 54 fell on August 13, then a week later Joe Hauser became the only player in professional baseball history to hit 60 home runs *twice*. During the last week of the season, Unser Choe hit seven home runs from Monday to Saturday (the Sunday finale was rained out) to finish with 69 — 50 of which came at Nicollet Park. During Hauser's unforgettable 1933 performance he led the league in RBIs and runs and set the all-time AA home run record (.332, 69 HR, 153 R, 182 RBI).

Despite Hauser's superb season, Minneapolis finished a distant second (15 games) to Columbus. Talented young Paul Dean recorded a pitcher's Triple Crown (22–7, 222 K, 3.15 ERA), fellow righthander Bill Lee rang up the second highest victory total in the league (21–9), and Lefty Heise led the AA in winning percentage (17–5). Nick Cullop (.313, 28 HR, 143 RBI) and infielder-outfielder John Rothrock (.347) were mainstays of the Red Bird batting order. At midseason the Cardinals' farm club underwent a major personnel shuffle and lost eight consecutive games, but the Red Birds regrouped and during a long home stand clinched the flag by winning 25 of 27 games.

Prior to the start of the season, Columbus President Lee MacPhail persuaded the league to adopt two innovative proposals. A player pool would be distributed among members of the top five clubs in bonuses of $800, $600, $400, $200 and $100, with an additional $200 to members of the championship club — if the champs won the Junior World Series (the AA had not beaten the IL winners since 1929). The 168-game schedule, in effect since 1920, was

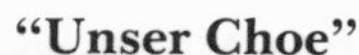

"Unser Choe"

Unser Choe Hauser, one of the greatest sluggers in minor league history, is the only man ever to hit more than 60 homers twice.

— Courtesy Joe Hauser

Joe Hauser, the only player ever to hit more than 60 home runs in two different seasons, was born on January 12, 1899, in Milwaukee. One of seven children of a German Catholic family, Joe attended parochial school for six years, then quit the classroom to go to work. But Joe continued to play baseball, proving almost unbeatable on the sandlots of Milwaukee as a southpaw hurler. At the age of 18 he was paid $12 a game to pitch semipro ball, then Connie Mack brought him to spring training in 1918 with the A's in Jacksonville, Florida. Mack released him, but Milwaukee brought him to their spring training camp in Beloit, then farmed him out to Providence in the Eastern League. He learned to bat from in front of the plate, before a curve could break, and became an impressive hitter. Soon Hauser was switched to the outfield, and as an everyday player he led the league in triples and homers in 1919.

Promoted to Milwaukee in 1920, he was converted to first base the next season. When opposing fans razzed Hauser, Milwaukee supporters began to chant, *"Unser Choe"* (German for "Our

(continued)

Joe''), and Hauser acquired his favorite nickname. Following a fine sophomore year in the American Association (.316, 20 HR, 116 RBI), Hauser was purchased by Connie Mack. He became a solid performer for the A's (1923 — .323, 1924 — .307, 1925 — .288 with 27 homers and 115 RBIs). But just before the 1925 season, Hauser shattered his kneecap during a spring exhibition game with the crosstown Phillies. Hauser's roommate, Jimmie Foxx, took over first base for the A's, and in 1927 Hauser found himself back in the American Association with Kansas City (.353, 20 HR, 134 RBIs, and a league-leading 22 triples). Hauser blasted the first two home runs ever hit over Kansas City's distant right-field wall — 450 feet away and 60 feet high.

Promoted again to the big leagues in 1928, by late in the next season Unser Choe was returned to Milwaukee. But he spent 1930 and 1931 with Baltimore, leading the International League in homers both years. The right-field fence in Baltimore was inviting, and Hauser took full advantage, especially in 1930 (.313, 63 HR, 175 RBI, and 173 R).

Hauser moved to Minneapolis in 1932, promptly nailing down another home run crown (.303, 49 HR, 129 RBI) in the friendly environs of Nicollet Park (right field loomed just 279 feet away), even though he missed the last 39 games of the season. But citing Depression conditions, Millers owner Mike Kelley slashed Hauser's monthly salary from $1,200 in 1932 to $400 in 1933. Hauser shrugged it off and recorded his fourth consecutive home run crown (.332, 69 HR — 50 at Nicollet Park — and a league-leading 182 RBIs and 153 runs). Only Joe Bauman, playing in the Class C Longhorn League in 1954 (.400, 72 HR, 224 RBI), ever hit more home runs during a season of organized baseball.

In 1934 Hauser seemed headed for another 60-plus home run year — .348 with 33 homers and 88 RBIs after just 82 games. But on July 30, 1934, he injured his good knee while playing in Kansas City, and was out for the year. He managed to drive in 101 runs in 1935, and he hit 33 homers in 1936. But both years his batting average was in the .260s, and he retired at the age of 37.

Then he agreed to serve as player-manager of a Sheboygan semipro club, and after three seasons he returned to organized baseball with Sheboygan's entry in the Class D Wisconsin State League. He spent three more years with the team, hitting .302 at the age of 43 before the league suspended play in 1942. For decades Unser Choe operated a sporting goods store in Sheboygan, where he lives today at the age of 91.

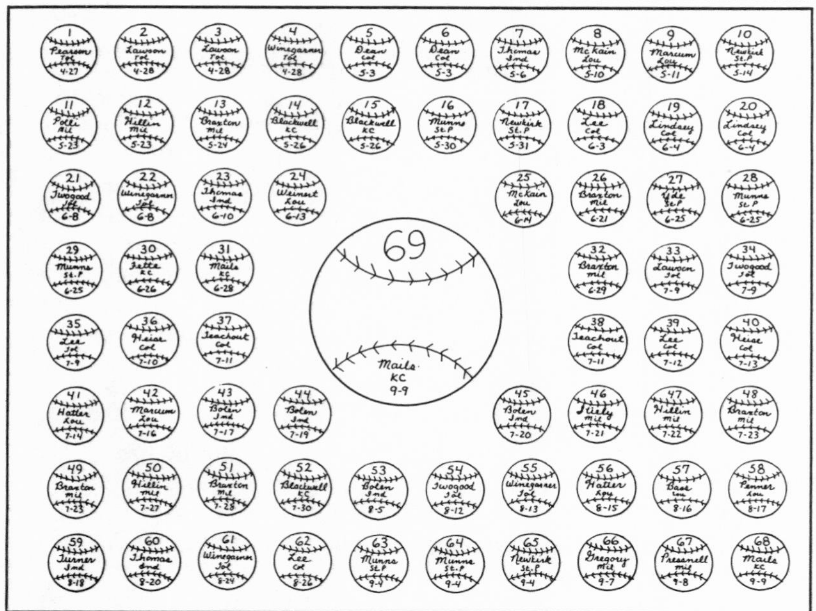

Chart detailing Joe Hauser's 69 homers in 1933.

— Courtesy Joe Hauser

reduced to 154 games. Columbus, Toledo, Louisville, and Indianapolis would comprise an Eastern division, while Minneapolis, St. Paul, Milwaukee, and Kansas City would make up the Western group. (The Eastern and Western division format was dropped after two seasons but was permanently resurrected decades later.)

The top team from the East would meet the best from the West for the right to play in the Junior World Series (the name of the postseason classic had changed from Little World Series to Junior World Series in 1932). The powerful Red Birds beat Minneapolis, of the Western Division, four games to two, then defeated Buffalo in the Junior World Series, five games to three. MacPhail's bonus system had worked to the greatest advantage of his victorious Red Birds.

Although Paul Dean and other 1933 stars went up to St. Louis, the Cardinals' farm system produced such other fine players as outfielders Terry Moore (.328) and Eugene Moore (.341 in 85 games), second baseman Charles Wilson (.325), and shortstop Billy Meyers (.313). Reliable Nick Cullop (.303, 27 HR, 130 RBI) provided the power, and player-manager Ray Blades led the "Bladesmen" to the best record in the East.

The best record in the league was compiled by Minneapolis. The Millers led the league in hitting (.308) and, as usual, home runs (176). Joe Hauser took aim for another 60-homer season — until he wrecked a knee in July (.348, 33 HR, 88 RBI in just 82 games). Slugger Spence Harris, who was a Miller outfielder from 1928 through 1937, moved over to first and led the league in runs (.322, 138 R, 100 RBI). Other offensive standouts were workhorse catcher Pinky Hargrave (.356 in 147 games) and outfielder Ab Wright (.353, 29 HR, 131 RBI). Buzz Arlett, a 35-year-old switch-hitter who was one of the greatest minor league sluggers of all time (.341 lifetime with 432 homers, the second highest total in history), was brought up late in May from Birmingham. Although Arlett logged just 116 games, it was enough to win the AA home run crown (.319, 41 HR, 132 RBI). Righthander Wally Tauscher led the league in victories and winning percentage (21–7 in 50 games), and 39-year-old southpaw Jesse Petty was right behind (19–7). On June 19, Louisville lefty Archie McKain (11–11) struck out 18 St. Paul batters to equal Dave Danforth's 1915 record.

The major leagues had created a sensation with the first All-Star Game in 1933. The American Association tried the innovation in 1934, arranging for the team that was in first place at midseason to host an All-Star squad composed of the best players from the other seven clubs. With Joe Hauser still in the lineup (two homers and six RBIs), the Millers dumped the All-Stars, 13–6. Manager Donie Bush kept the Millers in first place through the end of the season, but again lost the playoff to Columbus. After five games the Millers were ahead in the series, three games to two. In the sixth game the Millers took a 6–2 lead into the bottom of the ninth, but with only two outs left, the Red Birds staged a five-run rally to win, 7–6. Columbus then won the deciding game handily to take the series, four games to three.

There was widespread consternation that the team with the best record did not go to the Junior World Series, and the division and playoff scheme was dropped for 1935. The AA would find it necessary to adopt a more extensive playoff series within another year, but there would always be resentment when the first-place team was eliminated in postseason play. Columbus, however, again won the Junior World Series for the AA, beating Toronto five games to four. After seven games the Red Birds were ahead, four games to three. Believing that the players were dragging out the se-

Spence Harris

In 1928 Minneapolis acquired a speedy, 28-year-old outfielder from Shreveport of the Texas League. Spence Harris was a native of Duluth who had spent two years with the White Sox and five other seasons in the minors. Harris made a spectacular debut in the American Association, leading the league in homers, doubles, total bases and runs (.327, 32 HR, 127 RBI, 41 2B, 133 R). After another fine season in 1929 (.340, 100 RBI, 139 R) he went back to the American League, but he was a disappointment both with Washington (.214) and Philadelphia (.184).

Harris returned to Minneapolis in time to play 93 games of the 1930 schedule (.363). The next year he again led the league in runs (.347, 108 RBI, 156 R), a feat he repeated in 1934. The left-handed Harris for years was the league's finest center fielder, although he sometimes filled in at first base. His batting averages from 1932 through 1937 were .352, .355, .322, .337, .301 and .326. In 10 seasons with the Millers, Harris always hit above .300, and he knocked in 100 or more runs six times, even though he frequently batted leadoff.

Now in his late thirties, Harris moved in 1938 to the Pacific Coast League, where the balmy climate often put new life into aging muscles. He played pro ball until he was 48, retiring with a .318 lifetime average and the all-time career minor league leader in total bases, runs (2,287), hits (3,617) and doubles (743). Harris returned to his home state, dying in Minneapolis in 1982.

ries, a doubleheader was scheduled to finish the last two contests in one day. Toronto won the first game, but Columbus prevailed in the nightcap. Irked over certain aspects of the series and unable to come to an agreement with the International League, the AA decided not to participate in the Junior World Series. For 1935, therefore, the American Association would play a 154-game schedule to a straight championship, with no postseason play.

At the end of the 1934 season Thomas J. Hickey, who had served as president of the American Association for almost 20 years (1902–1903 and 1917–1934), announced his retirement. Hickey had founded the AA, he had maintained the circuit's remarkable stability during the worst years of the Depression, and league directors gratefully voted him a pension. Although 73 years of age, Hickey long remained a vigorous man and eagerly attended AA games, ceremonies, and banquets until well into his nineties. He died in 1956, just short of his ninety-fifth birthday.

But conditions still were difficult around the league, and the immediate future required a gifted promoter. George M. "Red" Trautman had played football, basketball, and baseball (as pitcher) at Ohio State, and after a stint at high school coaching he returned to his alma mater as varsity basketball coach. Soon he moved up to assistant athletic director, where his promotional expertise produced a noticeable increase in attendance at athletic events. The previous year Trautman had served as president of the Columbus Red Birds. When he was elected to succeed Hickey, Trautman moved the league offices from Chicago to Columbus and launched an intensive publicity campaign. Trautman provided the AA with dynamic leadership for 11 years, until he was appointed general manager of the Detroit Tigers (a year later he was elected president of the National Association).

In 1935, with Donie Bush still at the helm (he had won pennants in 1932 and 1934, the only years he had managed the Millers), Minneapolis was expected to repeat as champions. Although the club was aging, several key players returned, and 36-year-old Joe Hauser was back to provide power (.262, 23 HR, 101 RBI in 131 games). But in spring training, slugger Buzz Arlett suffered a torn ring finger on his left hand and part of the digit was amputated (he still played impressively in 122 games — .360, 25 HR, 101 RBI). Third baseman Babe Ganzel (.294 in 71 games) ran into a clothesline and damaged an eye, then sprained an ankle as he stepped off a train. Outfielder-infielder Dutch Holland was beaned in spring training, then suffered a broken jaw when he was beaned again in Milwaukee (.309 with 20 homers in 118 games). Spence Harris chipped a bone in his ankle (.337 in 127 games), pitcher Ray Kolp wrenched a leg while shagging flies in the outfield (11–9), and righthander Wally Tauscher missed several weeks with a sore shoulder but still won more games than any pitcher in the club (18–9). Hard-hitting catcher Pinky Hargrave twice suffered broken fingers and was out of action the final two months of the season (.242 in 65 games). But outfielder Johnny "Patcheye" Gill won the home run and RBI titles (.361, 43 HR, 154 RBI), and Bush somehow steered his patchwork lineup to the pennant by a five-game margin. Nicollet Park was the site of the second AA All-Star Game, and for the second year in a row the battered Millers defeated the Stars.

The All-Star shortstop was Eddie Marshall of Milwaukee (.290), who set a league record by hitting safely in 43 consecutive games. Dale Alexander, the All-Star first baseman from Kansas City, on June 14 became the first AA player to hit four home runs in a single game — which proved to be one-fourth of his season total (.358 with 16 homers). All-Star outfielder Johnny Cooney of Indianapolis won the batting crown (.371), and All-Star third baseman Fred Haney of Toledo was the stolen base champ (.321 with 29 thefts), a title he first won in 1928 while playing with Indianapolis.

On the All-Star pitching staff was St. Paul curveballer Monty Stratton (17–9), who soon would enjoy success with the White Sox. When he was 26, Stratton had to have his leg amputated following a hunting accident, but the Texan later made a courageous comeback as a minor league pitcher. Louisville righthander Jack Tising was the strikeout leader (13–15, 230 K), an honor he would repeat in 1937. On September 7 Milwaukee righthander Americo Polli (13–12) pitched a 10-inning, 2–0 no-hitter over St. Paul. It would be the last no-hitter in the AA for eight years.

In order to stimulate attendance in 1936, President Trautman led the AA in resuming the Junior World Series and in adopting the Shaughnessy Playoff Plan. Frank "Shag" Shaughnessy spent his life as a professional baseball player and manager and club official and, for a quarter of a century, president of the International League. While serving as general manager of Montreal during the Depression, he came up with a postseason playoff scheme that would encourage attendance even when a team dominated a pennant race. Under the Shaughnessy Playoffs, the top four teams would qualify for postseason play. The first-place team would play a series against the fourth-place club, while the second- and third-place teams conducted a simultaneous series. The winners of these two series then would play a championship finale, usually a best four-of-seven series. There would be fan interest, therefore, even in the race for fourth place.

The device caused a marked attendance rise in the AA in 1936. Because of lingering dismay over the 1934 postseason defeat of first-place Minneapolis, it was decided that the team with the best season's record would be declared the pennant-winner, while the playoff victor would be awarded a Governors' Cup and would represent the AA in the Junior World Series. The AA playoffs usually would pit the first-place team against the third, and the second ver-

Hall of Fame righthander Burleigh Grimes managed Louisville in 1936.
— Courtesy Minnesota Historical Society

sus the third in the opening series.

Columbus, Minneapolis, and Indianapolis conducted a spirited battle for the fourth-place playoff slot. The Red Birds were led by home run and RBI champ "Long Tom" Winsett, only the third man in AA history to hit 50 homers (.354, 50 HR, 154 RBI), by ERA leader Bill McGee (13–8, 2.93), and by catcher Mickey Owen (.336), who went on to a 13-year big league career. Minneapolis, the perennial home run leader, belted 212 homers as a team behind outfielder-third baseman Earl Browne (.328, 35 HR, 126 RBI), outfielder Fabian Gaffke (.342, 25 HR, 132 RBI), and 37-year-old Joe Hauser (.268, 34 HR, 87 RBI), in his final AA season. But it was Indianapolis that made it to the playoffs, behind the hitting of outfielders Ox Eckhardt (.353) and Fred Berger (.323), first baseman Dick Siebert (.330), and catcher John Riddle (.325).

Just half a game separated second-place St. Paul from Kansas City in third. The Saints boasted batting champ Vernon Washington (.390 in 73 games after coming down from the White Sox), victory leader Lou Fette (25–8, and .314 at the plate), and outfielder Henry Steinbacher (.353), who threatened Eddie Marshall's new record with a 37-game hitting streak. The Saints won 16 games in a

Lefthanded slugger Vern Washington moved down from the White Sox in 1936 in time to win the batting title for St. Paul (.390 in 73 games). Washington averaged .347 in the minors, including four seasons in the AA.

— Courtesy Mrs. Vern Washington

row at one point, but later an 11-game losing streak probably cost them the pennant. Kansas City had a solid pitching staff, while the offense again was led by first sacker Dale Alexander (.315 with 100 RBIs) and outfielder Bit McCulloch (.299 with a league-leading 24 triples).

But the best team in the league was Milwaukee, which won its first pennant in 22 years by a solid six-game margin. The offense was built around powerful first baseman Rudy York (.334, 119 R, 24 2B, 21 3B, 37 HR, 148 RBI), catcher George Detore (.330), outfielders Tedd Gullic (.329 with 22 homers), Chet Laabs (.324, 42 HR, 151 RBI) and Frenchy Uhalt (.322 with a league-leading 36 stolen bases), and third baseman Lin Storti (.307, 31 HR, 108 RBI). The reliable pitching rotation — Forest Pressnell (19–9), Joe Heving (19–12), Luke Hamlin (19–14), and strikeout champ Clyde Hatter (16–6, 190 K) — worked every game in postseason play, and won all but two.

In the opening round of playoffs, Indianapolis beat St. Paul while Milwaukee swept four in a row from Kansas City. The Brewers then won the first Governors' Cup from Indianapolis, four

Minneapolis player signing autographs, ca. 1938.
— Courtesy Minnesota Historical Society

games to one. In the Junior World Series, Buffalo managed a 2–1 win over Joe Heving, but the Brewers took the other five games handily. Al Sothoron was resoundingly voted *The Sporting News* Minor League Manager of the Year.

The promotions and playoff excitement of 1936 produced the "first prosperous season" of the 1930s, with Milwaukee enjoying special success. The next year there was a tight pennant race and another lively postseason, and for the first time night ball was played in every city. In 1937 attendance reached 1,425,000, nearly double the anemic totals of 1933.

Several Milwaukee players went up after the 1936 triumph and, predictably, the Brewers dropped to fourth place, despite the efforts of returnees Tedd Gullic (.321, 26 HR, 138 RBI), Forest Pressnell (18–12), and Lin Storti (.308, 25 HR, 125 RBI), who set a record for third basemen with 49 consecutive errorless games.

Minneapolis returned to the playoff picture by leading the AA in hitting (.308) and homers (170). Infielder Roy Pfleger was the home run champ (.326 with 29 HRs and 121 RBIs in just 126 games), shortstop Ralph Kress was the RBI titlist (.334, 27 HR, 157 RBI), and outfielders Allen Cooke (.345, 18 HR, 114 RBI) and

Carl Reynolds (.355, 17 HR, 110 RBI), and second sacker Andy Cohen (.320) were among several other Millers who swung heavy bats. Toledo missed the pennant by just one game. The second-place Mud Hens starred noted big-league outfielder Babe Herman (.348 in 85 games), switch-hitter Roy Cullenbine (.308, 20 HR, 109 RBI), and outfielders Ed Coleman (.308, 25 HR, 123 RBI) and Chester Morgan (.308).

Before the season, Columbus was picked for another second-division finish. But 21-year-old outfielder Enos "Country" Slaughter became the first first-year player to win a batting crown, and he also led the league in runs and hits (.382, 26 HR, 147 R, 245 H, 122 RBI). Outfielder Johnny Rizzo was almost as spectacular (.358, 21 HR, 117 R, 123 RBI), and the third outfielder, lefthanded Lynn King (.302 with 28 steals), won the first of two consecutive stolen base crowns. Bill McGee recorded his second ERA title in a row and led the league in winning percentage (17–7, 2.97), while southpaw Max Macon posted the most victories (21–12).

Manager Burt Shotton guided the Red Birds into first place in time to host the All-Star Game on June 27. The largest crowd to view an All-Star Game (12,269) turned out to watch the Red Birds drop the Stars, 7–4. In the four-year history of the game the Stars had won only in 1936. The Red Birds held on to finish first, then beat Minneapolis in the playoff opener, while Milwaukee defeated Toledo. Columbus outlasted Minneapolis to win the Governors' Cup, but injuries led to a narrow defeat, four games to three, at the hands of Newark in the Junior World Series.

In 1938 dominant players won both a pitcher's and a hitter's Triple Crown. At the age of 31 righthander Whitlow Wyatt had bounced up and down from the minors to the American League, spending all or part of nine seasons in the AL, but producing only a 23–38 record. He had a blazing fastball but a poor curve. Then with Columbus, Wyatt was taught a changeup to complement his speed, and he responded by leading the AA in victories, strikeouts, ERA (23–7, 208 K, 2.37), winning percentage, complete games (26 in 32 starts), and innings pitched (254). Wyatt's magnificent performance sent him to Brooklyn, where he enjoyed five successful years with the Dodgers.

Even more spectacular was 19-year-old Ted Williams. The tall, skinny, lefthanded slugger had grown up in balmy San Diego, playing baseball daily and signing out of high school with the

At the age of 19, Ted Williams donned a Minneapolis uniform and slugged his way to the 1938 Triple Crown.

— Courtesy Minnesota Historical Society

Padres of the Pacific Coast League. After two seasons in the PCL (.271 and .291) he came to Minneapolis with a swing so impressive that even when he took batting practice members of both teams would stop to watch him hit. Nicollet Park, with its short right-field fence, was made to order for Williams, and the Red Sox wanted him to work under Donie Bush. Bush had played 16 years in the American League and had managed three big league clubs, but the immature, hot-tempered Williams infuriated him. "I had gotten into some rotten habits," admitted Williams. Bored by fielding, he sometimes turned his back to home plate and tossed rocks at the right-field fence. Supposedly, Bush told club owner Mike Kelley, "It's Williams or me, one has to go," and Kelley presumably offered regrets at the manager's planned departure. But when Williams threatened to go home, Bush coolly offered to arrange transportation — and Ted promptly unpacked. Williams ceaselessly practiced batting, learned to use a lighter bat as the season wore on, and terrorized AA pitchers. He went hitless in his first 16 turns at bat on the road, but he cracked a home run in his initial appearance at Nicollet Park, then went on to lead the league in batting, runs, homers, RBIs (.366, 43 HR, 130 R, 142 RBI), walks, and

The 1938 Millers. Righthander Wally Tauscher (top row, second from left, standing next to Ted Williams) pitched for 13 seasons in the AA.
— Courtesy Minnesota Historical Society

total bases. Williams started for the Red Sox the next season and hit .406 two years later.

Despite the presence of Williams, Minneapolis failed to make the playoffs. Indianapolis, led by righthander Vance Page (15–5), infielder Steve Mesner (.331), outfielder Glenn Chapman (.308 with 103 RBIs), and third baseman Buck Fausett (.339), surged into first place and defeated the All-Stars, 6–3, before 12,277 fans. But the Indians faltered after the All-Star Game and barely managed a fourth-place playoff berth.

Milwaukee led the AA in homers (163) and finished third behind Tedd Gullie (.313, 28 HR, 107 RBI), Minor Heath (.294 with 32 homers), and Lin Storti (.265 with 21 homers in just 112 games). Outfielder Joe Gallagher (.343, 24 HR, 119 RBI) led Kansas City to second place. Manager Bill Meyer stressed pitching and defense and baserunning; the Blues paced the AA in stolen bases and fielding, and the mound staff gave up the fewest runs.

St. Paul gathered momentum in the second half of the season and climbed to the top of the standings. Righthanders Vic Frasier (17–7) and Art Herring (16–6) were the best pitchers, and the offense was triggered by second baseman Al Bejma (.326, 25 HR, 114 RBI) and outfielder Bit McCulloch (.301 with a league-leading 41 doubles). St. Paul reached the playoff finals hampered by injuries, and Kansas City came from behind in the final two games to win the Governors' Cup, four games to three. The Blues then went on to take Newark in the Junior World Series, again by a four to three margin.

Kansas City had become a farm club of the New York Yankees in 1937, and the Yankees promptly cut down the impossible outfield distances at renamed Ruppert Stadium. The Governors' Cup and Junior World Series triumph of 1938 reflected the infusion of promising players from the Yankee farm system, and for the next decade and a half the Blues would be a major factor in the championship picture. Manager Bill Meyer, building on the success of 1938, proceeded to field two consecutive first-place clubs.

Characteristically, both of these teams led the AA in stolen bases and ERA. The infield was solid during both seasons, with talented Billy Hitchcock at third, leadoff batter Johnny Sturm (.309 in 1939) at first, and a brilliant double-play combination in second baseman Gerry Priddy (.333, 24 HR, 107 RBI) and shortstop Phil Rizzuto (.316 with 33 SB). Outfielder Vince DiMaggio, who would be sold to Cincinnati at the end of the 1939 season, won the home run and RBI crowns (.290, 46 HR, 136 RBI). The top three ERA leaders of 1939 headed the pitching staff: Marv Breuer (17–6, 2.28), Tom Reis (17–4, 2.30), and John Babich (17–6, 2.55). The first-place Blues hosted the All-Star Game, which was delayed a day by rain. But a record crowd of 16,521 was rewarded with a slugfest, won by the All-Stars, 19–7. The Blues stormed on to set the all-time record for victories in a 154-game season (107–47).

Minneapolis came in second (99–55) behind victory leader Herb Hash (22–6) and a Murderers' Row that blasted 217 homers: outfielders Ab Wright (.337, 21 HR, 134 RBI), James Wasdell (.323, 29 HR, 90 RBI in just 102 games), and Harvey Walker (.304, 24 HR, and a league-leading 145 runs), and first baseman Phil Weintraub (.331, 33 HR, 126 RBI). Indianapolis outfielder Milt Galatzer (.325) and Myron McCormick (.318), along with catcher Bill Baker (.338), led the Indians into third place.

Louisville stumbled along in the second division through most of the season, although their flashy young shortstop, Pee Wee Reese (.279 with 35 steals), won the stolen base title. The Colonels led the league in fielding, while catcher Ed Madjeski (.313) and outfielder Chet Morgan added offensive punch. Donie Bush had

In 1938, 18-year-old Pee Wee Reese became Louisville's shortstop, and in 1939 he led the AA in triples and putouts while sparking the Colonels to the playoff title.

— Courtesy Louisville Redbirds

left Minneapolis to become president, manager, and part owner of the Colonels. But Bush fell ill, and his assistant, longtime AA pitcher Bill Burwell, took control of the club and, with strong fan support for a losing team (75–78), guided the Colonels to fourth place late in the season.

Louisville then surprised powerful Minneapolis, four games to one, in the playoff opener, while Indianapolis upset Kansas City by the same margin. In the finals the upstart Colonels beat Indianapolis in five games to win the Governors' Cup. The Junior World Series opened in Rochester, and the Colonels downed the Red Wings in the first two games. Rochester evened the series by winning the first two contests at Parkway Field, but the scrappy Colonels won their last home game. Back at Red Wing Stadium, Rochester again evened the series with a victory in the sixth game. The seventh and deciding contest was knotted, 3–3, at the end of nine innings, but the Colonels exploded for four runs in the 11th to win, 7–3, and put a proper finish to their 1939 Cinderella story.

The American Association champions had won five of the last

National Association Day

Legend insisted that Abner Doubleday invented baseball in 1839 in Cooperstown, New York (a belief no longer shared by sports historians), and in 1939 a number of promotional activities were staged in the major and minor leagues to celebrate baseball's "centennial." As a part of "National Association Day," scheduled for Sunday, July 9 in Cooperstown, an all-star game was staged, showcasing a player from each of the 41 minor leagues. But no American Association club wanted to send a key player in the midst of a pennant race.

There proved to be a perfect solution. Joe Hauser had retired from organized baseball after the 1936 season. The slugging first baseman had played for three AA clubs and had spent nine years in the league between 1920 and 1936. Now 40, Unser Choe lived in Sheboygan. Hauser was asked to represent the American Association in the National Association Day game, and he happily agreed to travel to Cooperstown. Hauser played six innings and went two for three, ripping a home run and a double, along with a screaming line drive that was speared by the second baseman. No league had a more famous or suitable representative than the AA's Unser Choe.

six Junior World Series. The prestige of the league had never been higher, while night baseball and a postseason playoff system had helped the clubs survive the Depression and return to prosperity. During the 1930s the ties with major league teams had become closer, and many brilliant young players tuned up for big league stardom by spending a year or two in the AA. The American Association was the sole minor league to survive the Depression decade with its membership unchanged. But by the end of the 1939 season, combat again had broken out in Europe, and in the 1940s the AA would face the severe problems of the Second World War.

1940–1949

Another War . . .
Another Heyday

The American Association was the only minor league that did not suspend operations, suffer a reduction in size, or see the disbanding of at least one franchise during the Depression decade. All eight AA cities maintained their clubs throughout the 1930s, and by the beginning of the new decade the rock-solid American Association looked forward to renewed prosperity. But by the opening of the 1940 season, Hitler's *blitzkrieg* was rolling unchecked across Europe. The only abbreviated season in AA history occurred during World War I, and the possibility of American participation in another global conflict would pose a threat to the league perhaps more serious than that of the Great Depression.

During the opening year of the decade, Bill Meyer guided Kansas City to first place for the second year in a row. The Blues' flashy-fielding shortstop, Phil Rizzuto (.347, 10 HR, 73 RBI, 35 SB), won the stolen base crown and was selected as the Minor League Player of the Year. Second baseman Gerry Priddy (.306, 16 HR, 112 RBI) swung a big bat for the second consecutive year, and so did first sacker John Sturm (.312) and outfielder Ralph Boyle (.316). Slugging outfielder Vince DiMaggio had been promoted to the National League, but he was adequately replaced by big league veteran Frenchy Bordagaray (.358 with 31 steals and 83 RBIs).

An AA All-Star team in Nicollet Park in 1940. The official 1940 All-Star Game, however, was played in Kansas City, with the Blues falling to the Stars before a record crowd of 18,449.

— Courtesy Minnesota Historical Society

The pitching staff featured righthanders Johnny Lindell (18–7), Don Hendrickson (16–7), and Charles Stanceau (15–8). On July 17, Kansas City again hosted the All-Star Game, again lost to the Stars (5–3) — and again set an attendance record with a crowd of 18,449.

For the second consecutive year, Kansas City lost the playoffs, as Louisville again finished fourth — and again was guided to the Governors' Cup by manager Bill Burwell. The Colonels were led by outfielder Chet Morgan (.317), first baseman Paul Campbell (.284 with a league-leading 17 triples), and righthander Charley Wagner (9–1 with a 1.84 ERA after being sent down by the Red Sox).

Johnny Lindell and Indianapolis lefty Robert Logan (18–14) tied for the league lead in wins, which was the first time the American Association victory leader had not been a 20-game winner (except for the war-shortened 1918 season, when Dickie Kerr went 17–7 for Milwaukee). Columbus southpaw Ernie White was the ERA and percentage titlist (13–4, 2.25), while Minneapolis out-

The 1940 Millers. Veteran Ab Wright (middle row, second from right) won the Triple Crown, and other hitting stars led Minneapolis to a league-leading .307 team average.

— Courtesy Minnesota Historical Society

fielder Roberto Estalella (.341, 32 HR, 121 RBI, 147 R, 132 W) led the league in runs and walks. First baseman Phil Weintraub (.347, 27 HR, 109 RBI), catcher Otto Denning (.329), outfielder Harvey Walker (.318, 25 HR), switch-hitting infielder Lin Storti (.313, 20 HR), and shortstop Eugene Geary (.308) helped Minneapolis record a .307 team batting average.

The greatest star of Minneapolis and the American Association in 1940 was Miller outfielder Ab Wright. A 6′1½, 190-pound righthander, Wright began his pro career in 1928 as a 22-year-old pitcher. Although he was 24–17 in his first three seasons, he hit so well that he was placed in the outfield, and in 1931 he won the batting title of the Western Association (.376, 30 HR, 104 RBI). At the end of the season he played 27 games for Minneapolis (.357). In 1932 Wright appeared in four leagues, including four games with the Millers, and the next year he made one appearance with Minneapolis before going down to Little Rock (.352). He spent the entire 1934 season with the Millers (.353, 29 HR, 131 RBI), then went up to the Cleveland Indians. Back in the minors after one year, he returned to Minneapolis in 1939 and led the league in

RBIs (.337, 21 HR, 134 RBI). He had a solid season for the Millers in 1941 (.284, 26 HR, 103 RBI), and the next year was the home run titlist (.291, 23 HR, 110 RBI). He fell off in 1943 (.280 in 101 games) and split 1944 between the Millers (.267 in 32 games) and the Boston Braves, then played two more years and retired with 323 home runs and a .326 average in 1,981 minor league games. But Ab Wright's most spectacular season was 1940, when he won the American Association Triple Crown (.369, 39 HR, 159 RBI).

In 1941 Burt Shotton, who had led Columbus to second place the previous year, sparked the Red Birds to a comfortable first-place finish. Columbus then dumped Kansas City, four games to two, to win the playoff opener, defeated Louisville in five games in the finals, then triumphed over Baltimore in the Junior World Series. The Red Birds led the league in hitting, featuring infielders Lou Klein (.367), Robert Repass (.317), Bert Haas (.315 with a league-leading 131 RBIs), and Ray Sanders (.308 and the league leader in runs and doubles). The pitching staff was superb: Murry Dickson (21–11) led the league in victories and strikeouts, and helped the team at the plate (.341 in 63 games); the ERA champ and percentage leader was Johnny Grodzicki (19–5, 2.58); and Harry Brecheen (16–6) and Preacher Roe (11–9) would become National League standouts. The only other 20-game winner of 1941 was Ray Starr (20–15) of Indianapolis, while the batting champ was the legendary minor league slugger Lou "The Mad Russian" Novikoff (.370), who played in 90 games after being sent to Milwaukee from the Chicago Cubs at the request of Bill Veeck.

Phil Wrigley, owner of the Chicago Cubs, long had subsidized the Milwaukee Brewers, but after he decided to withdraw his patronage the minor league club soon began to feel the pinch. During the 1941 season, with the Brewers off to a poor start, Milwaukee owner Harry Bendinger tried to sell his team to Wrigley. The gum magnate declined, but Bill Veeck, whose father had served the Wrigleys for 16 years as Cubs president and who had worked for the Cubs since boyhood, raised the money to buy the Brewers. Veeck also gave 25 percent of the club to Charlie Grimm, a 19-year big leaguer who had managed the Cubs to two pennants, so that he would join him in Milwaukee as his manager.

The last-place Brewers were 19–43, but Veeck livened up the league and built a team which would win three consecutive pennants. He borrowed $50,000 to refurbish splintery old (1888)

Borchert Field, and attracted crowds with a nonstop series of zany promotions and gag prizes. The breezy, outgoing Veeck sat with fans throughout his ballpark, second-guessing Grimm and shouting at the umpires. Grimm sometimes climbed into the stands to play a lefthanded banjo, he and Veeck consorted with fans in taverns all over the city, and the two men became hugely popular in Milwaukee.

Veeck was a fine judge of ballplayers. He built his club through shrewd purchases and trades, and kept his franchise solvent by developing players for profitable sale to the big leagues (he bought Eddie Stanky for $2,000, for example, then sold him a year later to the Cubs for $40,000). Veeck's first Milwaukee team had little speed, so he mixed sand into the basepaths to slow down the opposition. The club also had little power, and since he could not take advantage of the notoriously short right-field fence, he added a 60-foot high chicken wire fence to neutralize his opponents' left-handed sluggers. By the next season Veeck had acquired some power hitters, but when a visiting team possessed more left-handed power he had the chicken wire fence moved back and forth on a game-to-game basis with a hydraulic motor. Finally, he moved the fence from inning to inning to favor his team, and the next day the league legislated against such tactics. At a subsequent league meeting Veeck and his business manager contritely entered the conference room wearing football helmets and hockey masks to protect themselves from the ire of their colleagues.

On a trip to Columbus, which had a stable of fastballers and the weakest lights in the league, Veeck's players came onto the field wearing miners' caps, with the lights on to find their way. Brewers' coaches carried lanterns to the coaching boxes, and second baseman Packie Rogers used a light meter to monitor his position. On the same road trip, Indianapolis failed to turn on the lights in time for the Brewers to take batting practice, so the team hung the lanterns on the batting cage and entertained the fans — while infuriating Indians' owner-manager Donie Bush — by staging a pantomime batting practice. More constructive shenanigans included staging 9:00 A.M. "Rosie the Riveter" games for night-shift workers who were confined to a wartime seven-days-a-week schedule. All women wearing riveting masks or welding caps were admitted free, while ushers — clad in nightgowns and nightcaps — served breakfast. The idea attracted national publicity and was copied by big league clubs.

The 1941 Brewers finished last, but the next year Milwaukee charged to second place, being nosed out for the flag on the last day of the season. The Brewers then reeled off three consecutive first-place finishes, although Veeck missed the 1944 title run. He joined the Marine Corps late in 1943 and Grimm took over the club. But early in the 1944 season, Grimm returned to Chicago as manager of the Cubs, engaging Casey Stengel as his field replacement in Milwaukee. Veeck objected to Stengel from long distance, but Casey led the Brewers to their second straight pennant. Casey moved over to Kansas City for 1945 and finished seventh with the Blues, while the Brewers won their third consecutive flag. Bill Veeck returned for the last six weeks of the season, welcomed by an overflow crowd at Borchert Field. Veeck's leg, which had been broken during a college prank, then shattered by the recoil of an artillery piece, was amputated in 1946. Hoping to improve his marital situation, Veeck sold the Brewers after the 1945 season and purchased a dude ranch in Arizona. His marriage soon failed, however, and he returned to baseball as a colorful, controversial and exciting major league owner, displaying the same lively qualities he had brought to the American Association for half a decade.

World War II had affected the American Association and all of organized baseball as drastically as it had the life of Bill Veeck. There were 43 minor leagues in 1940, with a total paid attendance of almost 20 million. But by the next year attendance dropped to 16 million as the country became distracted by the threatening international situation. During the 1942 season, with the United States at war since the previous December, the number of minor leagues dropped to 31. President Roosevelt wrote to Baseball Commissioner Kenesaw Mountain Landis that he hoped professional baseball would continue to operate during the war as a boost to public morale. But wartime travel restrictions and a rapidly dwindling manpower pool caused most clubs, particularly in the lower minors, to cease operations; in 1943 and 1944 there were only 10 minor leagues (the number rose to 12 during the 1945 season, which opened shortly after the surrender of Germany). A shortage of materials reduced the quality of baseballs, and in the American Association, as well as all other leagues which continued to function, home run totals took a nosedive for the duration of the war.

The colorful Bill Veeck joined the Marines after the 1943 season, suffered severe leg injuries, and returned to his beloved Brewers late in the 1945 season.

— Courtesy Mariana York

In 1942 Kansas City returned to first place for the third time in four seasons. Victory leader Butch Wensloff (21–10), fellow righthander Tom Reis (13–5), and southpaw Herb Karpel (11–1) pitched the Blues to the pennant. Milwaukee led the AA in hitting behind batting champ Eddie Stanky (.342 with a league-leading 124 runs and 56 doubles), home run titlist Bill Norman (.301 with just 24 homers), first baseman Heinz Becker (.340), and fleet center fielder Hal Peck (.333). But Milwaukee and Kansas City were knocked off in the playoffs as Columbus went on to win the Governors' Cup and the Junior World Series for the second year in a row. Red Bird lefty Harry Brecheen (19–10), 156 K, 2.09 ERA) paced the league in strikeouts and ERA, then went up to the St. Louis Cardinals and a fine major league career.

The next year Milwaukee won the first of three straight pennants, again leading the league in hitting. Third baseman Grey Clarke (.346) took the batting championship, with strong support from RBI and home run titlist Ted Norbert (.293, 25 HR, 117 RBI), switch-hitters Heinz Becker (.326) and Herschel Martin (.307), outfielder Bill Norman (.275 with 18 homers), and slick-

The parking lot outside Louisville's Parkway Field in 1942 proved that large crowds sought diversion from World War II at AA ballparks.

— Courtesy Louisville Redbirds

Nelson Potter, warming up on opening day at Parkway Field, went 18–8 for Louisville in 1942.

— Courtesy Louisville Redbirds

The 1943 Mud Hens. Jack Kramer (front row, third from left) pitched the first no-hitter in the AA since 1935. Lin Storti (back row, far right) played 11 seasons for Milwaukee, Minneapolis, and Toledo.

— Courtesy Toledo Mud Hens

fielding shortstop Tony York (.287), who led the league in hits and at-bats.

But for the third year in a row Columbus won the Governors' Cup, dumping Milwaukee, four games to two, then sweeping second-place Indianapolis in three games, before going on to win a third consecutive Junior World Series, four games to one. Nick Cullop was named Minor League Manager of the Year by *The Sporting News*. As usual the Red Birds boasted a deep stable of pitchers, featuring strikeout leader Preacher Roe (15–7), fellow lefty George Dockins (16–8), and righthander Ted Wilks (16–8), while the offense was sparked by outfielders Chester Wieczorek (.328) and Gus Bergamo (.324), who led the league in walks and doubles, and catchers Tom Heath (.306) and Joe Garagiola (.293).

In 1944 Casey Stengel led the Brewers to another first-place finish, roaring to a 102–51 record and a .307 team batting average. Eight position players hit over .300, leadership was provided by Brewer veterans Heinz Becker (.346), Hal Peck (.345), Herschel Martin (.358), and Bill Norman (.296, 17 HR, 90 RBI), and a fine pitching staff was headed by 38-year-old righthander Earl Caldwell

The Milwaukee Brewers finished first in 1943. Grey Clarke (seated second from right) was the batting champ, Jittery Joe Berry (seated second from left) was the club's leading pitcher, Tony York (seated to the right of manager Charlie Grimm) led the AA in hits, and Ted Norbert (middle row, far right) was the home run and RBI leader. Bill Norman (middle row, second from left) was the 1942 home run champ.
— Courtesy Mariana York

(19–5 in his sixth and best season in the AA; he pitched another decade, winning 20 games in the Gulf Coast League when he was 47, copping his third straight ERA title the next year, and finally retiring after a 12–4 season in the Big State League when he was 49).

Third-place Louisville knocked off Milwaukee in the playoff opener, then swept St. Paul in four games in the finals. The Colonels boasted the ERA champ in Mel Deutsch (14–11, 2.47) and the strikeout, percentage, and co-victory leader in James Wilson (19–8). The Louisville offense was triggered by outfielder Steve Barath (.329), shortstop Frank Shofner (.317), utility man Mike Sabena (.317 in 61 games), second baseman Ben Steiner (.316), and first sacker Earle Browne (.312). Columbus failed to make the playoffs, but the Red Bird lineup included batting champ John Wyrostek (.358).

In 1945 Milwaukee recorded its third consecutive first-place finish, and Nick Cullop was named *The Sporting News* Minor

AA action in 1943.

— Courtesy Mariana York

League Manager of the Year for the second time in three years. The pitching staff was built around victory leader Owen Sheetz (19–8 with a 1.95 ERA and a league-leading 20 complete games in 25 starts), Wendell Davis (15–4), and veteran lefty Julio Acosta (15–10). Outfielder Lew Flick (.371) won the batting title, while third sacker Gene Nance (.316 with 106 RBIs) was the RBI champ. Louisville again finished third — and again won the playoffs — then defeated Newark in the Junior World Series. Outfielder-third baseman Ty LaForest spent one-third of the season with the Boston Braves, but in 91 games with Louisville (.353) he became the only Colonel to hit over .291.

World War II ended as the 1945 season closed, and organized baseball entered a banner period. Victorious after a long war, America was prosperous and in high spirits, and every form of public entertainment flourished. In 1946 the minor leagues mushroomed from 12 to 42, and American Association attendance jumped to a record 2,021,000. There were 52 leagues the next year with a total attendance of 40,505,210, and the American Association again set a record with cumulative crowds numbering 2,156,461, with an additional 154,384 at the postseason playoffs. In

Casey Stengel returned to the AA in 1944 to lead the Brewers to another pennant. He managed Kansas City the following season.

— Courtesy Mariana York

In 1944 Louisville third sacker Nick Polly (.290, 20 HR, 120 RBI) led the AA in RBIs and set a league record with 147 walks.

— Courtesy Louisville Redbirds

The Playoff Kings

The Columbus Red Birds won the first American Association postseason playoff and went on to emerge on top seven times in ten playoff appearances. In 1940 the Red Birds made it to the finals and came within one game of an eighth playoff triumph. The Columbus Senators lost the Little World Series in 1906 and 1907, but the Red Birds exhibited their accustomed postseason magic in the minor league classic, winning six times against their International League opponent. Only in 1937, with an injury-riddled roster, did the Red Birds bow, four games to three. In 94 AA playoff games, Columbus carved out a .617 winning percentage, and the Red Birds played at a .632 clip against the champions of the International League.

Year	Finish	Playoffs		Jr. World Series	
1933	First	4–2	Champs	Buffalo,	5–3
1934	Second	4–3	Champs	Toronto,	5–4
1937	First	8–4	Champs	Newark,	3–4
1940	Second	2–4			
1941	First	8–3	Champs	Montreal,	4–2
1942	Third	8–3	Champs	Syracuse,	4–1
1943	Third	8–3	Champs	Syracuse,	4–1
1948	Fourth	7–7			
1950	Third	8–5	Champs	Baltimore,	4–2
1954	Fourth	3–4			
		58–36	.617	29–17	.632

1948 the number of leagues rose to 58 with 40,949,028 in attendance. For the third year in a row, the AA broke the league attendance record, drawing 2,235,853, plus 133,099 in the playoffs. There were 59 minor leagues in 1949, with teams in 464 cities and an all-time attendance record of 41,872,762, although the American Association experienced a slight decrease.

When the 1946 season opened, therefore, AA ballparks filled with lively, enthusiastic crowds. Fans enjoyed the performance of Indianapolis shortstop Sibby Sisti, who won the batting title (.343) and became only the second AA player to be named *The Sporting News* Minor League Player of the Year. The home run champ was Toledo first sacker Jerry Witte (.312, 46 HR, 120 RBI), who had just completed three years in the service. Witte went up to the St.

Ace utilityman Joe Vitter was a key player for the 1944 St. Paul playoff finalists. He hit .273 and logged 140 games alternating between second, third, short, and the outfield. — Courtesy Joe Vitter

Louis Browns late in the season, but he could not hit big league pitching and returned to Toledo for the last third of 1947 (.279 with 13 homers and 46 RBIs in just 55 games). The next year he moved over to Louisville (.255, 29 HR, 98 RBI), then spent the last four years of his career in the Texas League, blasting 50 homers for Dallas in 1949. In 1946 the American Association authorized an official Most Valuable Player (later named the Mickey Mantle Award), and Witte was voted the first recipient.

Aside from Witte, just one other player — Minneapolis outfielder Babe Barna (.298, 28 HR, 112 RBI) — hit as many as 20 homers in 1946. The RBI leader, Minneapolis first sacker John McCarthy (.333 with 122 RBIs) managed just 16 roundtrippers. Despite a lack of power hitting throughout the league, pitching performances were generally unremarkable. St. Paul southpaw Tom Sunkel twirled a no-hitter but otherwise was unimpressive (6–6 with a 4.05 ERA). For the first time in league history three pitchers tied for the lead in wins — with the lowest victory total that had ever led the AA, even during war-shortened 1918. Toledo southpaw Fred Sanford (15–10 with 154 Ks in 230 IP) also paced the league in strikeouts and innings, but Milwaukee lefty Ewald Pyle

Crowds jammed AA ballparks after World War II.

— Courtesy Joe Vitter

(15–6) and St. Paul righthander Harry Taylor (15–7) had better winning percentages.

Indianapolis, St. Paul, and Minneapolis qualified for the playoffs, while Louisville finished first by four games. The Colonels led the league in double plays and built a solid offense around infielder Frank Shofner (.305) and outfielders John Welaj (.300) and Frank Genovese (.305), who completed a record-setting 268 games without an error, dating back to 1944. For the third year in a row, Louisville won the playoffs, downing St. Paul in the opener, four games to one, then executing a four-game sweep over Indianapolis in the finals. Unlike 1945, however, Louisville faltered in the Junior World Series, losing to Montreal, four games to two.

In 1947 Kansas City combined the managerial talents of Bill Meyer with a stable of Yankee farmhands to win first place by eight games. On June 26 righthander Carl DeRose (4–2 in eight games) pitched the first perfect game in AA history, stopping Louisville, 5–0. DeRose had missed three weeks with arm trouble and surgery was scheduled, but Meyer agreed to a final start before the operation. DeRose's arm was so painful that it brought tears, and after the game he could not even shake hands.

Other hurlers for the Blues included righthanders Bill Wight (16–9), Frank Hiller (15–5 and .311 at the plate) and percentage leader Fred Bradley (13–4 and .364), and southpaw Tommy Byrne (12–6). Ample offense was provided by left fielder Eddie Stewart (.358, 107 R, 102 RBI), catcher Gus Niarhos (.321), RBI champ Cliff Mapes (.308, 21 HR, 117 RBI), and outfielders Harry Craft (.315) and Hank Bauer (.313).

Saints righthander Phil Haugstad (15–6, 145 K) was the strikeout leader, but St. Paul finished in the second division. The batting champ was Milwaukee switch-hitter Heinz Becker (.363), the home run leader was Brewer outfielder Carden Gillenwater (.312 with 23 homers), while Alvin Dark (.323, 49 2B, 121 R) led all shortstops in putouts, assists and errors and all hitters in runs, doubles and at-bats. Milwaukee led the league in hitting and defeated first-place Kansas City in the opening round of playoffs. First baseman John McCarthy (.345, 22 HR, 102 RBI), MVP reliever Steve Gerkin (10–2 in a record 83 appearances), outfielder Babe Barna (.324 with 21 homers), and catcher Wes Westrum (.294 with 22 homers) led Minneapolis into the playoffs, but the Millers were knocked off by Louisville.

The Colonels had won three consecutive playoffs, and their 1947 effort was sparked by victory and ERA leader Clem Dreiseward (18–7, 2.15). But Louisville's playoff string at last was halted by Milwaukee in the finals, four games to three. The powerful Brewers then defeated Syracuse, also four games to three, to win the Junior World Series. Manager Nick Cullop, who had been voted *The Sporting News* Minor League Manager of the Year in 1943, when he won the AA playoffs and also downed Syracuse, became the first American Association field general to receive the award twice.

Milwaukee drew almost 300,000 fans during 1947, Indianapolis attracted over 316,000, Louisville nearly 340,000, and Kansas City brought in more than 379,000 fans. In 1948 Milwaukee improved to 365,000, St. Paul to 320,000, and first-place Indianapolis totaled an eye-popping 494,455. New manager Al Lopez led the Indians to their first pennant since 1928. First baseman Les Fleming (.323, 26 HR, 143 RBI) was named MVP after winning the RBI

Future Hall of Famer Duke Snider hit .316 for St. Paul in 1947 and won promotion to Brooklyn.

— Author's collection

In 1947 the league's color line was broken by St. Paul catcher Roy Campanella, who ripped AA pitching for a month, then moved up to a Hall of Fame career with Brooklyn.

— Author's collection

crown, righthander Bob Malloy led the league in victories (21–7), and right fielder Ted Beard (.301) demonstrated his arm spectacularly by throwing out the same runner three times at third in a single game to complete double plays. The talented Indians raced to the pennant (100–54) by an 11-game gap over second-place Milwaukee before being upset in the playoff opener by St. Paul.

During the early part of the season, St. Paul brought integration to the American Association in the form of hard-hitting catcher Roy Campanella. Jackie Robinson had broken the major league color line in 1947 with Brooklyn, and Dodgers President-GM Branch Rickey specifically planned to make Campanella the first black player in the AA while grooming him as Brooklyn's catcher of the future. Campanella opened the season with Brooklyn, but on the May 15 cutdown date he was optioned to St. Paul. The St. Paul press was unenthusiastic, and after Campy's historic debut on May 22, manager Walt Alston was accused of using him over the regular catchers "only because the Dodgers had sent Campanella to St. Paul to break the color line." It was reported with satisfaction that in his first game Campanella went hitless, fanned twice, and made a throwing error. But the future Hall of Famer quickly began to murder AA pitching (.325, 13 HR, 39 RBI in just 35 games), and by the time he was recalled to Brooklyn, St. Paul fans and press alike had begun singing his praises. The following year infielder Ray Dandridge (.363) and righthander Dave Barnhill (7–10) played for Minneapolis, and soon blacks were on rosters throughout the league. The most protracted opposition to integration was at Louisville, but the Colonels finally broke the color line in 1956.

The 1948 St. Paul club enjoyed the services of outfielders Robert Addis (.314) and Eric Tipton (.313, 28 HR, 126 RBI) throughout the season, while the other playoff finalists, Columbus, starred home run champ Mike Natisin (.305, 30 HR, 132 RBI) and catcher Joe Garagiola (.356 in 65 games). Alston's Saints defeated the Red Birds in a classic playoff series, four games to three, before losing to Montreal in the Junior World Series.

But Alston kept the Saints rolling in 1949, battling Indianapolis neck-and-neck throughout the season and sweeping a doubleheader on the last day of the season to win the pennant by half a game. The Saints showcased Phil Haugstad (22–7), reliever Clem Labine (12–6 in 64 appearances), outfielder Robert Addis (.346), and stolen base champ Henry Schenz (.345 with 30 steals). St. Paul was disappointed in the playoffs, losing the opener to Milwaukee, four games to three, while Indianapolis outlasted Minneapolis, also four games to three. For the third time in club history Minneapolis hit more than 200 homers (202), behind home run champ Charles Workman (.291, 41 HR, 122 RBI) and first baseman John Harshman (.270, 40 HR, 111 RBI, and a league-leading 121 runs and 122 walks), both lefthanders.

Indianapolis, still managed by Al Lopez, starred third baseman Froilan Fernandez (.312, 21 HR, 128 RBI), who won the RBI title and was named MVP. More offense was provided by first baseman Les Fleming (.340 in 95 games), while percentage leader James Walsh (15–4) and lefthanded reliever Royce Lint (14–3) offered strong pitching. The staff's best pitcher was righty Mel Queen, who led the league in victories, ERA, strikeouts, shutouts, innings pitched, and complete games (22–9, 24 CG, 178 K, 2.57 ERA), although his Triple Crown was marred by St. Paul ace Phil Haugstad, who tied for the lead in wins. The Indians beat Milwaukee in the playoff finals, four games to three, then downed Montreal to win the Junior World Series.

There were many outstanding performances during the 1949 season. On September 3 righthander Cot Deal, acquired by Columbus from Louisville early in the season, worked the entire 20 innings and banged out four hits to beat the Colonels, 4–3. Columbus first sacker Mike Natisin (.265 with 24 homers), the defending home run champion, went on a tear on May 30 and set a single-game record with 11 RBIs. On August 3, at Swayne Field, Toledo righthander Hal White gave up a single to the Minneapolis leadoff batter, then held the Millers hitless for nine innings. The next night, in the seven-inning lidbuster of a doubleheader, Toledo southpaw Walter Nothe pitched eight hitless innings as Minneapolis fell, 2–0, to a home run in the first extra inning. The Millers got a hit in the first frame of the next game, but the Toledo pitchers had established a new league mark with 17 consecutive no-hit innings (the old mark of 16⅔ innings had been set by Slim Harriss and Russ Van Atta in St. Paul in 1932).

The most spectacular individual feat of 1949 occurred on Tuesday night, May 24, during the second game of a doubleheader at Louisville. Colonels lefty Maurice McDermott, a 20-year-old fireballer (6–4 in 11 games) who would strike out 116 batters in just 77 innings before going up to the Red Sox, took the mound

Lefthanded Louisville fireballer Maurice McDermott (116 Ks in 77 innings) established an AA record with 20 strikeouts in one game in 1949.

— Courtesy Louisville Redbirds

against St. Paul. In the season opener, McDermott had struck out 17 Minneapolis hitters to come within one of the league record set by Dave Danforth in 1915 and matched by Archie McKain in 1934. McDermott struck out the side in the third, but after four innings he had recorded just six strikeouts. He fanned the side in the fifth and sixth, added two more in the seventh, then struck out the last six Saints he faced to establish a new single-game record of 20 Ks.

Also in 1949, on June 17, WFBM-TV of Indianapolis televised an Indians' game against St. Paul. Television was spreading around the country, and a number of AA cities experimented with televised baseball. But attendance across the AA in 1949 totaled 1,999,270, a drop of 236,000 from 1948, while the playoff crowds added up to 84,266 — barely half of the 1947 postseason attendance. Even though the American Association was one of only nine minor leagues to continue operations through World War II, in the fourth year of the postwar baseball boom there were indications that further difficulties lurked in the future. The spread of television was just one symbol of the prosperity that lay ahead in the 1950s, but ironically TV and other aspects of American prosperity would severely undermine the structure of minor league baseball.

1950–1959

End of Stability

During the 1950s the unmatched stability that had become the hallmark of the American Association was assaulted by forces that severely undermined all of minor league baseball. When AA cities began to experiment with televised games, there was scant realization that television would devastate minor league attendance. Not only would the televising of the Major League Game of the Week on Saturdays keep minor league fans at home on what had been vitally important attendance days; minor league play seemed alarmingly insignificant now that big leaguers actually could be *seen* in action — not just heard over the radio. More importantly, Americans rapidly became accustomed to staying at home in air-conditioned comfort on hot summer nights (no longer could the ballpark be advertised as a place to cool off) to watch their favorite network TV programs. When families did venture out during the 1950s for an evening of baseball, increasingly it was to a Little League park. As Little League ball mushroomed during the 1950s, families spent several evenings per week involved in practices, with little time or inclination left to attend minor league games. Another significant disruption of minor league baseball involved the movement of major league franchises to the most attractive minor league mar-

Louisville fans jammed Parkway Field on opening day in 1950. As the decade proceeded, such crowds became a rarity.

— Courtesy Louisville Redbirds

kets; indeed, the first transfer in each major league was to an American Association city.

The influence of at least some of these factors became obvious in 1950, when attendance in the AA plummeted by nearly half a million, a 25 percent drop to 1,504,845. Seventh-place Toledo attracted just 88,393, and crowd totals in the playoffs nosedived to 67,465. Attendance across the minor leagues fell off by seven million, and declined another seven million in 1951. National Association attendance dropped every year in the 1950s. In 1950 there were 58 minor leagues with a total attendance of 34,534,488 (down from 41,872,762 the previous year); by 1959 there were only 21 minor leagues with an attendance of just 12,171,848.

AA attendance in 1951 declined to 1,334,056, with 56,306 in the playoffs, and the next year the total sagged to 1,226,386, as Toledo attracted merely 41,497. Toledo's club shifted to Charleston, but in 1953 Toledo reorganized, won the pennant, and brought in 343,614 fans, which helped boost league attendance to 1,506,386. Attendance dropped to 1,225,863 in 1954, but for the next three years ranged between 1.5 and 1.6 million. The poorest playoff attendance was 21,697 in 1957, while the decade low across the

Ray Dandridge, a 36-year-old veteran of the Negro and Mexican leagues, was voted MVP as a hard-hitting infielder for the Minneapolis Millers in 1950.

— Author's collection

league was 1,194,364 in 1958. The next year, crowd totals moved up to 1,477,091, but there were 10 teams in 1959 for the first time in league history.

On the field the AA continued to showcase future stars and productive veterans. In 1950, for example, talented lefthander Harvey Haddix posted a pitcher's Triple Crown (18–6, 17 CG, 160 K, 2.70 ERA), leading the league in wins, strikeouts and ERA, as well as complete games, while sparking Columbus into the playoffs. First-place Minneapolis starred 36-year-old third sacker Ray Dandridge (.311), who was voted MVP and whose 16-year career in the Negro leagues would place him in the Hall of Fame.

Other major league standouts of the future included: Whitey Ford (6–3 before going 9–1 for the Yankees), Lew Burdette (7–7), Bob Cerv (.304), Bill Virdon (.341 in 14 games) and Billy Martin (.280 in 29 games) of Kansas City; Solly Hemus (.297) and Luis Arroyo (4–4) of Columbus; Johnny Logan (.296) of Milwaukee; Jimmy Piersall (.255) of Louisville; Hoyt Wilhelm (15–11) of Minneapolis; Clem Labine (11–7) of St. Paul; and Bob Friend (2–4) of Indianapolis. Johnny Mize, a noted big league slugger since 1936, worked himself back into shape (.298 in 26 games) with Kansas

During the first weeks of 1950, lefthander Whitey Ford tuned up for a Hall of Fame career with the Yankees by hurling for the Kansas City Blues.

— Author's collection

City before rejoining the Yankees. Righthander Kirby Higbe, whose long National League career stretched back to 1937, went down to Minneapolis (5–8 with a seven-inning no-hitter) from the New York Giants.

Righthander Marlin Stuart did not have a distinguished big league career (23–17 over six seasons), but he was an AA star with Toledo in 1950. The 31-year-old Mud Hen completed 10 of 12 starts (9–3 with a 2.23 ERA) before being called up to Detroit. On Tuesday, June 27, he took the mound at Swayne Field against Indianapolis. He retired 27 men in a row and outdueled the Indians, 1–0. There had been 46 seasons of AA ball before Carl DeRose pitched the first perfect game in league history, but three years later Marlin Stuart twirled a second perfecto.

Wilhelm, MVP Dandridge, righthander Millard Howell (14–2, a no-hitter, and .308 in 51 games), and first baseman-outfielder Bert Haas (.318, 24 HR, 106 RBI) led Minneapolis to first place. Home run and RBI champ Lou Limmer (.277, 29 HR, 111 RBI) and stolen base leader Jack Cassini (.276 with 36 steals) helped put St. Paul in the playoffs. Indianapolis reached second place behind manager Al Lopez, outfielder Dom Deessandro (.350 in 101

In his final minor league tuneup before going on to stardom with the Braves, Eddie Mathews hit .333 with Milwaukee late in the 1951 season.

— Author's collection

games), and reliable lefty Royce Lint (12–6 in 46 games).

Columbus, enjoying fine pitching from Haddix and right-hander Dutch Krieger (17–5), beat Minneapolis in the playoff opener, while Indianapolis swept St. Paul in four games. The finals went to seven games, with Columbus outlasting the Indians, then going on to defeat Baltimore in the Junior World Series.

Ball Hawk vs. Nighthawk

On Thursday, June 29, 1950, a routine game was in progress between the Millers and the Brewers at Milwaukee. In the fourth inning Minneapolis outfielder Bama Rowell lofted an easy fly to right center. Brewer right fielder Bob Jaderlund camped under the ball.

Suddenly, two nighthawks swooped across the field, and one alertly pecked the white sphere. Center fielder Bob Addis lunged at the deflected ball, but it rolled safely and Rowell steamed into second with a fluke double. Rowell went on to score what proved to be the winning run in a 4–3 decision.

During the 1950s, three slugging outfielders finished their minor league apprenticeship in the AA: Roger Maris (.293 with Indianapolis in 1956); Willie Mays (.477 in 35 games with Minneapolis in 1951); and Mickey Mantle (.361 in 40 games with KC in 1951).

— Author's collection

Two budding superstars flashed raw talent in the AA during 1951. Opening day brought snow in Minneapolis, but a helicopter blew the field clear and the Millers' center fielder, 19-year-old Willie Mays, made his AA debut with a double and a home run. Mays never cooled off, totally dominating AA pitchers (.477 with eight homers, 38 runs and 30 RBIs in 35 games) and making spectacular outfield plays before being called up to start for the Giants. In Kansas City another 19-year-old center fielder, switch-hitting Mickey Mantle, came down from New York after a disappointing start with the Yankees. At first Mantle's slump continued in the AA; following a bunt single his initial at-bat, he made 21 outs in a row. Disconsolate, he called his father in Commerce, Oklahoma, ready to quit baseball. The senior Mantle drove to Kansas City and angrily told his son, "You can go back and work in the mines like me!" Mickey talked at length with his father, decided to keep trying, and the next night in Toledo hit for the cycle: a bunt single, double, triple, and *two* homers over the light towers. Mantle went on a tear (.361, 11 HR, 50 RBI in 40 games) and was recalled to New York to stay.

Harry "The Hat" Walker, a 10-year National League vet, at the age of 32 became player-manager at Columbus and feasted on minor league pitchers, winning the batting title with the highest average (.393) since 1925 (Ed Murphy of Columbus — .397). But Columbus ended 1951 in the cellar.

Charlie Grimm returned to Milwaukee to guide the Brewers to another pennant. Grimm's deep pitching staff was led by ERA and percentage leader Ernie Johnson (15–4, 2.62), righthander Murray Wall (15–5), relief ace Virgil Jester (13–6 in 47 games), and righty Bert Thiel (14–9), who tossed a seven-inning no-hitter against Toledo. The Brewers led the league in fielding and hitting (.286). First baseman George Crowe (.339, 24 HR, 119 RBI) was the RBI champ, catcher Al Unser (.293 with 17 homers) was voted MVP, and other heavy hitters were shortstop Buzz Clarkson (.343), second sackers Bill Reed (.311) and Gene Mauch (.303 in 37 games), and outfielders Ben Thorpe (.299) and Cot Deal, a former pitcher who now was a switch-hitting outfielder (.262 with 18 homers). An impressive young slugger named Eddie Mathews played a few games late in the year — and unloaded a grand slam homer in his first at-bat. This talented club clinched first place by a nine-game margin, beat Kansas City and St. Paul to win the playoffs, then defeated Montreal in the Junior World Series.

Under Grimm, who was named *The Sporting News* Minor League Manager of the Year for 1951, the 1952 Brewers exploded to an even better start. On May 31, however, Grimm moved up to take over the managerial reins of the Boston Braves — just as he had left the Brewers for the Cubs during the 1944 season — but he would soon return to Milwaukee in an exciting capacity. After a week under Red Smith, Bucky Walters assumed the Brewer helm for the remainder of 1952. For the second year in a row the Brewers posted the best batting average (.292) and fielding percentage in the league, and again there was a deep mound corps, led by ERA and strikeout champ Don Liddle (17–4, 2.70, 159 K), Murray Wall (16–10), and NBA standout Gene Conley (11–4). At different times of the season the offense was triggered by outfielders Luis Marquez (.345) and Billy Bruton (.325), and infielders John Dittmer (.356 in 57 games), Gene Mauch (.324), Buzz Clarkson (.318 in 74 games), Bill Reed (.313 in 50 games), and Johnny Logan

(.301 in 42 games). The Brewer juggernaut was the last AA club to win 100 games (101–53), claiming the pennant over second-place Kansas City by a 12-game margin, then sweeping St. Paul in the playoff opener before dropping the finals to the Blues, four games to three.

St. Paul's playoff club was led by third baseman Robert Wilson (.334, 13 HR, 117 RBI), second sacker Jack Cassini (.308), and outfielders Sandy Amoros (.337), Dick Whitman (.333), Gino Cimoli (.319) and Bill Sharman (.294), the AA's other NBA star. Fourth-place Minneapolis again paced the league in homers (193) and made the playoffs behind outfielders Clint Hartung (.334 with 27 homers) and Bill Howerton (.307 with 24 homers and 61 RBIs in just 67 games), catcher Ray Kaat (.304 with 15 homers), shortstop Daryl Spencer (.294 with 27 homers), and 38-year-old third baseman Ray Dandridge (.291 with 10 homers). Infielder Davey Williams (.287 in 80 games) blasted four consecutive home runs during a two-game span on June 26–27.

The club that would win the playoffs was Kansas City, stocked with gifted Yankee farmhands such as Bill "Moose" Skowron, who played in the outfield in 1952, leading the league in homers and RBIs (.341, 31 HR, 134 RBI) and being named Minor League Player of the Year by *The Sporting News*. Skowron would be moved to first base the next year, but the Blues' 1952 first sacker was MVP John Bollweg (.325 with 23 homers). Righthander Ed Erautt led the AA in victories and winning percentage (21–5), and other key performers were infielder-outfielder Vic Power (.331 with 16 homers), second baseman Kal Segrist (.308 with 25 homers), and outfielder Bill Renna (.295, 28 HR, 90 RBI in 110 games).

At the other end of the AA, Toledo struggled with a last-place team that would finish 54½ games off the pace (46–107) and bring up the bottom in hitting (.241) and home runs (a meager 58). Attendance was miserable, and on June 23, in an action unprecedented in more than half a century of AA operation, the Toledo franchise folded and was transferred to Charleston, West Virginia. Such movements were common in other minor leagues, but since the American Association opened in 1902, only the shift of Toledo to Cleveland in 1914 and 1915 had disrupted the most notable stability in minor league history.

Once interrupted, the traditional AA constancy soon suffered even greater blows. The National League had maintained franchises in the same eight cities since 1900, the American League since 1903. But for years the movement of struggling franchises to more promising cities had been rumored. The transfer of the St. Louis Browns to Los Angeles was stopped by the entry of the United States into World War II. Bill Veeck, colorful and controversial owner of Milwaukee during the 1940s, now was the colorful and controversial owner of the Browns. Veeck petitioned the American League to move the Browns to Milwaukee, but he was voted down by other AL owners. Recognizing a good idea, Lou Perini, wealthy owner of the Boston Braves, requested permission to move the Braves to Milwaukee. The Braves had lost over $1 million the past three seasons, and in 1952 attendance totaled merely 281,000. Milwaukee already had constructed a 36,000-seat ballpark, the first stadium financed with public money, and Perini owned the Brewers, which would further facilitate the proposed move. On March 18, 1953, National League owners unanimously voted to approve the franchise transfer. Charlie Grimm returned to Milwaukee with the Braves and piloted the club to second place. Milwaukee fans responded with an NL record attendance of 1,826,397, and such an astounding success quickly spurred other franchise movement.

In 1953 the American Association had to respond quickly to the loss of a key city. Charleston remained in the league and again finished in the cellar, but the novelty of Triple-A baseball pulled in over 178,000 fans. The eighth AA franchise was placed by the Braves in Toledo, which finished in first place and incredibly brought a league-leading 343,614 customers into Swayne Field. The Braves' AA franchise therefore finished in first place for three consecutive seasons. Basketball star Gene Conley was the best pitcher of 1953 (23–9, 211 K, 2.90 ERA), leading the league in wins, strikeouts, ERA, innings pitched and complete games (24 CG in 32 starts). The offense was headed by switch-hitter Sam Jethroe (.309, 28 HR, 109 RBI) and returnees Luis Marquez (.292 with 37 steals) and Bill Reed (.290).

Elsewhere around the league Minneapolis won its seventh consecutive home run crown (170 HR) and another batting title (.281) behind home run king George Wilson (.315, with 34 homers), catcher Ray Katt (.326 with 28 homers), and third sacker Rance Pless (.322 with 25 homers). Indianapolis was boosted into the playoffs by defending batting champ Dave Pope (.352 in 1952,

At 6′8, Gene Conley was an NBA standout as well as a talented righthanded pitcher. He won the AA Triple Crown in 1953 and went on to enjoy an 11-year big league career.

— Author's collection

and .287 with 24 homers in 1953), first baseman Joe Macko (.234 with 20 homers) and RBI leader Wally Post (.289, 33 HR, 120 RBI). Post should have added a share of the home run crown to this RBI title. With the bases loaded in the second inning of a June 24 game against Charleston, Post lofted a drive over the Victory Field fence for an apparent grand-slam homer. But Dave Pope on first base waited to see if the ball would clear the fence, and Post ran past him. Post was declared out and what would have been homer number 16 was nullified. He was awarded a single and three RBIs, but at season's end he fell short of the home run title by one.

Kansas City had put together another powerhouse built around hitters who soon would become familiar to major league fans: batting champ Vic Power (.349), first sacker Bill Skowron (.318), shortstop Alex Grammas (.307), and outfielders Bob Cerv (.317 with 22 homers) and Elston Howard (.286). The pitching staff was held together by righthanded reliever Mel Wright (13–2 in 47 games). The Blues finished a strong second, beat Indianapolis in the playoff opener, then downed first-place Toledo, four games to three, to win their second consecutive playoff title.

How far can you throw it?

Although managers often flinch at the risk of injury to rifle-armed outfielders, long-distance baseball tosses always have been popular with minor league crowds. In 1953 Don Grate, an outfielder with Chattanooga of the Southern League, set a record with a herculean toss of 443 feet, 3½ inches. The following season slugger Rocky Colavito moved to Indianapolis and demonstrated his powerful right arm by standing on home plate and hurling a baseball over Victory Field's faraway center field. Colavito gave similar exhibitions until manager Kerby Farrell put an end to this potentially damaging exercise. But in 1956 Colavito spent a few weeks with San Diego of the Pacific Coast League, and he challenged Grate's record prior to a July 1 game at Lane Field. Rocky fired the ball over the center-field fence, but his longest measurement was 435 feet, 10 inches.

Grate played with Minneapolis in 1956, and on the Millers' annual Appreciation Night he attempted to break his own record before a crowd of 10,620. Center field in new Metropolitan Stadium was 405 feet from home plate, but a gate in the wire fence was opened to give Grate a running start. He took six steps before each throw, and he finally unleashed a ball that went almost to the box seats, setting a new record of 445 feet, 1 inch. Less than a year later, however, Glen Gorbous of the Omaha Cardinals broke the record with a throw of 445 feet, 10 inches.

The following year catcher Hal Smith of Columbus won the batting crown (.350), while Toledo first baseman George Crowe (.334, 34 HR, 128 RBI) was the home run and RBI leader. Minneapolis first baseman Gail Harris (.309, 34 HR, 113 RBI) tied Crowe for the home run championship, while righthanders Ike Delock (17–10) and George Susce (14–6) headed a deep pitching staff that earned second-place Louisville a playoff title.

Despite these and other accomplishments, however, 1954 was dominated by Indianapolis, which fielded one of the finest teams in American Association history. Manager Kerby Farrell controlled a nucleus of young but solid players: catcher Hank Foiles (.332), third baseman Bill Farrell (.307), first sacker Joe Altobelli (.287), second baseman Harry Malmberg (.286), left fielder Hal Simpson (.282), center fielder Gale Wade (.273 with a league-leading 24 steals), and fireballing righthander "Sad Sam" Jones (15–8 with 178

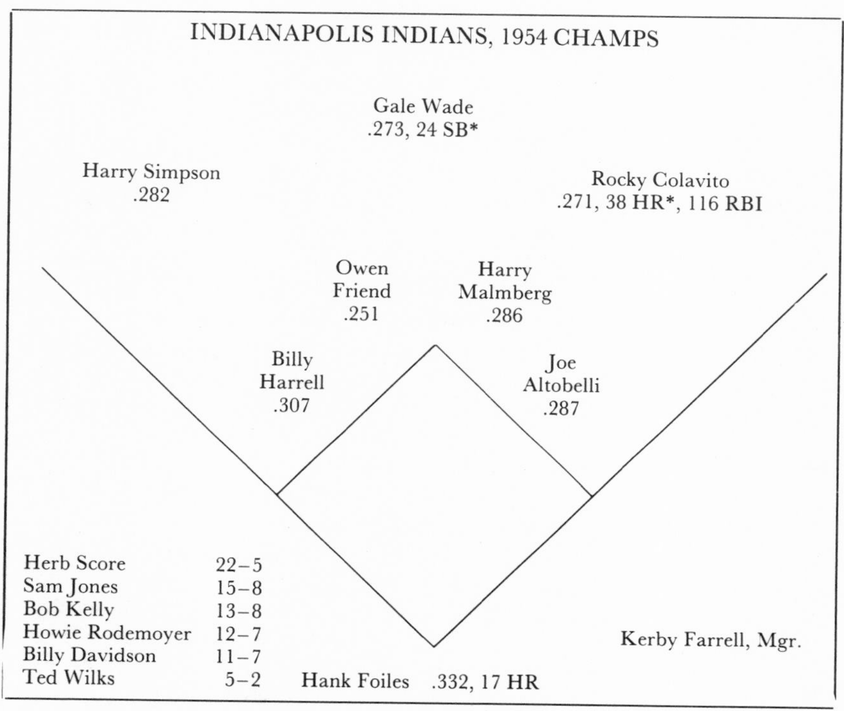

strikeouts and 129 walks in 199 innings). Stars of this roster, however, were 20-year-old roommates: home run champ and Indianapolis' Most Popular Player Rocky Colavito (.271, 38 HR, 116 RBI) and Rookie of the Year and MVP Herb Score (22–5, 330 Ks and 144 Ws in 251 LP, 2.62 ERA). Colavito was the league's most powerful slugger, while Score won the pitcher's Triple Crown and led the AA in almost every pitching category. Score and Sam Jones were one-two in strikeouts and walks, rendering opposing batters loathe to dig in against the Tribe aces.

The Indians dominated the league throughout the season, eventually outdistancing second-place Louisville by 10½ games. On August 9 the Indians took on the AA All-Stars at Victory Field, delighting a crowd of 10,948 fans by coming from behind to win, 3–2. The Indians specialized in come-from-behind victories, recording 28 one-run triumphs. When the playoffs opened, Herb Score was confined to a hospital bed with pneumonia, but the Indians de-

The Gold Dust Twins

Rocky Colavito and Herb Score, standouts on the Indianapolis pennant-winners of 1954, roomed together at an apartment near 34th and Fall Creek. They trundled around town in an old car they called "The Green Hornet," and during that memorable season the 20-year-old stars became known as "The Gold Dust Twins."

A native of the Bronx, Colavito was a 6′3 righthander with a rifle arm and a home run swing. He began his professional career at the age of 17 in 1951 at Daytona Beach, leading the Florida State League in home runs and putouts by an outfielder (.275, 23 HR, 111 RBI, 303 PO in a 140-game season). Two years later, while playing for Reading, Colavito led the Eastern League in homers and RBIs (.271, 38 HR, 116 RBI). The amiable Colavito would put on a show for pre-game crowds, standing on home plate and hurling a baseball over the center-field fence — until his alarmed manager, Kerby Farrell, halted these impromptu exhibitions. Voted by fans as the Tribe's Most Popular Player, Colavito wore an Indian uniform again in 1955 (.268, 30 HR, 104 RBI) and led all outfielders with 23 assists. He was moved to the Cleveland roster at the end of the year, playing for six major league clubs through the 1968 season. He blasted over 40 home runs three times, hit three homers in a game twice, and on June 10, 1959, he walloped four roundtrippers in consecutive at-bats. In 1965 he did not make a single error in 162 games, he established an American League record for consecutive errorless games (234) from 1964 to 1966, and for five years in a row he played more games than any other AL outfielder.

Like Colavito, Herb Score was born in 1933, in Rosedale, New York. A high school sensation at Lake Worth, Florida, the 6′2 southpaw fired six no-hitters and was given a $60,000 bonus to sign with Cleveland. Score had an overpowering fastball, but he was plagued by wildness. In 1953, while just 19, he was sent up to Indianapolis. He allowed just 37 hits in 62 innings and whiffed 61. But he walked 62 batters, his ERA was 5.23, and his won-lost record was just 2–5, and it was decided that he needed more seasoning. Back on the Indianapolis roster in 1954, he was so wild in spring training that he was almost sent down again.

Retained at the last minute as the club's fifth starter, Score became the sensation of the league, dominating opposing batters with his sizzling speed and a slow curve, along with enough of his old wildness to keep any sane hitter from digging in against him.

(continued)

He led the league in walks with 140, but he also established a new American Association strikeout record and produced one of the finest seasons in the history of the circuit. Score was the league leader in victories, winning percentage, strikeouts, ERA, complete games, and he fanned 17 Millers in a July 12 start against Minneapolis. In addition to the pitcher's Triple Crown, he was named Rookie of the Year and MVP. Score was 22–5 with a 2.62 ERA and 21 complete games in 32 starts; he allowed merely 140 hits in 251 innings while striking out 330 (the old record was 264, set in 1906 by Charles Berger of Columbus).

Score led the American League in strikeouts the next two seasons (245 Ks in 227 IP in 1955, and 263 Ks in 249 IP and a 20–9 record in 1956; this author saw him pitch in his rookie year with Cleveland, and he was simply overpowering). Tragically, however, he was struck in the eye by a screaming line drive early in the 1957 season. When he tried to come back from this injury, he developed arm troubles, and in five years he was out of the big leagues. Back in Indianapolis in 1962, he was 10–7 but his ERA was 4.82. He tried again the next year, but he walked 64 in 67 innings, struck out just 46, and was 0–6 with a 7.66 ERA.

feated Minneapolis, four games to two.

The playoff finals brought archrival Louisville to Victory Field, and all three games in Indianapolis went into extra innings. In the first contest first baseman Joe Altobelli squeezed in the winning run for the Indians with two out in the 12th. The next night, Score was a surprise starter. He twirled a one-hitter through 10 innings and struck out 14, including three straight batters in the ninth — after he loaded the bases with walks! But in the 11th a relief pitcher yielded two runs and lost the game. Two 10th-inning home runs by Louisville gave the Colonels an edge in the series. Louisville now had seized the momentum, and the Colonels returned home to nail down the playoff championship with 7–1 and 3–1 victories. The Colonels then downed Syracuse, four games to two, in the Junior World Series.

In 1954 the St. Louis Browns followed the Braves' example and moved their failing franchise, bringing big league baseball back to Baltimore. Like the Braves and the Browns, the Philadelphia Athletics had found it increasingly difficult to share the same city with another big league club. A group headed by Arnold Johnson purchased the Philadelphia Athletics and arranged to move the team to Kansas City for the 1955 season.

Again the American Association had to deal with the loss of a major market to a big league club. But also in 1955 another AA charter city lost its franchise. Although the 1954 Red Birds made the playoffs, Columbus ranked last in attendance for the second year in a row, and for the previous two years Columbus had been next-to-last to struggling Toledo. The parent St. Louis Cardinals decided to move their American Association franchise to Omaha, while Columbus civic leaders purchased the stadium from the Cardinals and bought an International League franchise. Meanwhile, Denver civic leaders had made a formal application for membership to the American Association in November 1954, and a few days later the Kansas City franchise was purchased for $78,000. Denver and Omaha had been the two strongest franchises in the Class A Western League, but similar wholesale disruptions now were occurring throughout minor league baseball.

Denver fans were delighted at the opportunity to watch New York Yankee farmhands play Class AAA baseball. The Bears were managed by Ralph Houk, and the roster included home run and RBI leader Marv Throneberry (.275, 36 HR, 117 RBI), Don Larsen (9–1 before being called up to New York), second baseman Bobby Richardson (.296), outfielder Whitey Herzog (.289, 21 HR, 98 RBI), catcher Darrell Johnson (.306), and, as player-coach, longtime American League infield star, Johnny Pesky (.343 in 66 games). The Bears finished third in the standings but first in attendance with a whopping 426,248. Omaha placed second behind a fine pitching staff which included ERA leader Willard Schmidt (12–5) and fellow righthanders Stu Miller (17–14) and Jim Pearce (12–5). Omaha, with a total of 316,012 admissions, finished second only to Denver in attendance, and the two new cities were the key to a league-wide attendance jump from 1.2 million in 1954 to 1.6 million in 1955.

In hopes of attracting big league baseball, Minneapolis and St. Paul each arranged to construct a new stadium. The Millers, in their last year at Nicollet Park, made the best use yet of the cozy field which had helped Minneapolis lead the league in homers 28 times in the 35 seasons from 1921 through 1955. The 1955 Millers established an all-time league record with 241 roundtrippers. The Millers had soared past 200 homers four times, a feat no other AA team could accomplish even once. The most productive Millers

Nicollet Park during an AA game on April 30, 1954. The double-decked right-field fence loomed just 279 feet down the line, and the right-center power alley was only 328 feet away.

— Courtesy Minnesota Historical Society

were MVP and batting champ Rance Pless (.337, 26 HR, 107 RBI), sensational outfielder Monte Irvin (.352 before being called up after 75 games), infielder Billy Gardner (.310 with 17 homers in 73 games), outfielders George Wilson (.307, 31 HR, 99 RBI) and Robert Lennon (.280, 31 HR, 104 RBI), and slugging catcher Carl Sawatski (.268 with 27 homers). Manager Bill Rigney also had victory leader Al Worthington (19–10), and he guided this talented club to first place. The Millers roared through the playoffs, pulling off a four-game sweep against both Denver and Omaha. In their first Junior World Series since 1932, the Millers battled Rochester, with workhorse righthander Al Worthington winning three of the first six games. In the seventh contest, Worthington came on as a reliever to nail down the victory and a triumphant postseason.

The forces that depressed minor league baseball during the 1950s and 1960s now undermined pro ball in Toledo. The Mud Hens had managed just two AA pennants, in 1927 and 1953, and after the 1955 season the franchise was moved to Wichita. By 1956, following more than half a century of almost inviolate franchise stability, the AA had lost four charter cities within four years. When

Cleveland pulled out of Indianapolis after the 1955 season, the toll almost became five, but nearly 6,700 local citizens became shareholders and kept the Indians in the AA. Louisville also nearly folded before the season, and the AA for a time considered admitting Miami, Florida, to the league.

The All-Star Game, which had been resumed in 1954 for more than a decade, was played in Denver in 1956 to a record crowd of 19,769. The first-place Bears downed the Stars, 10–8, to the delight of Denver fans. Again Denver led the AA in attendance with a total of 368,305 admissions, while Minneapolis attracted 318,326 fans to their new stadium.

Outfielders Willie Kirkland (.293, 37 HR, 120 RBI) and Don Grate (.316) sparked Minneapolis to the fourth-place playoff spot, while Omaha moved into third place behind batting champ Charles Peete (.350). Denver led the league in hitting (.298) and in homers (169); the rarefied air of Mile-High Stadium allowed the Bears to assume home run domination of the AA from Minneapolis. Although the Yankees made a number of callups that hurt the Bears at critical times, manager Ralph Houk again worked with a great deal of talent. For the second year in a row MVP first baseman Marv Throneberry was the home run and RBI king (.315, 42 HR, 145 RBI). Shortstop Tony Kubek (.331), second baseman Bobby Richardson (.328), Throneberry, and outfielder Bob Martyn (.314) were the top four hitters in the league after the batting champ, while other productive bats were swung by James Fridley (.291, 24 HR, 105 RBI), third sacker Woody Held (.276, 35 HR, 125 RBI), and catcher Darrell Johnson (.319), who went down with a broken hand after playing 107 games. Ralph Terry (13–4) and reliever John Kucab (12–4 in 43 appearances) were the best pitchers.

Denver led the league until injuries and callups took a deadly toll. Indianapolis, with the best team ERA and second-best team hitting, surged into first place. ERA champ Hank Aguirre (10–6, 2.50), fellow lefty Bud Daley (11–1) and righthander Stan Pitula (15–4) led a strong pitching staff. An offense capable of annihilating Louisville 24–0 was sparked by outfielders Dave Pope (.302 with 25 homers) and Roger Maris (.293 with 17 homers), catcher Russ Nixon (.319), third baseman Rudy Regalado (.322) and second sacker Larry Raines (.309). The Indians took first place by five games over Denver, outlasted Minneapolis in the playoff

Nineteen-year-old Orlando Cepeda enjoyed a stellar season with Minneapolis in 1957 (.309, 25 HR, 108 RBI), then went up to big league stardom in San Francisco.

— Author's collection

opener, four games to three, swept the Bears four straight in the finals, then executed another four-game sweep over Rochester in the Junior World Series.

In 1957, for the first time in four years, the AA franchise roster remained unchanged from the previous season. For the third year in a row, Denver led the league in attendance (305,625) and hitting (.291), as well as home runs (175) for the second consecutive season. Manager Ralph Houk enjoyed the services of batting champion Norm Siebern (.349, 24 HR, 118 RBI), catcher John Blanchard (.310 with 18 homers), veteran infielder Curt Roberts (.304 with a league-leading 23 steals), and third sacker Rance Pless (.299), who hit four grand-slam homers within a month after coming to Denver from Omaha. Flamethrower Ryne Duren (13–2 in 18 games with only 88 hits and 116 strikeouts in 114 innings) tossed a seven-inning no-hitter in his first game with the Bears on June 23. For the third consecutive year, slugging first sacker Marv Throneberry was the home run and RBI champ (.250, 40 HR, 124 RBI).

Minneapolis fielded another playoff team behind one of the Giants' most promising prospects, first baseman Orlando Cepeda (.309, 25 HR, 108 RBI), as well as righthander Max Surkont (15–

5) and fireballing lefty Pete Burnside (10–5). In the season opener, Millers righthander Stu Miller, who was called up by the Giants within a few weeks, beat Indianapolis 1–0 on a weather-shortened, six-inning no-hitter. Strikeout leader Stan Williams (19–7 with 223 Ks in 246 IP), first sacker Norm Larker (.323), and outfielder Don Demeter (.309 with 28 homers) propelled St. Paul into postseason play.

Heavy-hitting Denver was edged for first place by Wichita, which had the best pitching staff in the league. Righthander Carlton Willey (21–6) led the AA in victories, innings and winning percentage, and was voted Most Valuable Player. Joey Jay (17–10 with 18 CG in 32 GS) posted the most complete games, fellow righthander Red Murff was steady as a starter and reliever (11–9), and southpaw Juan Pizarro was unbeatable during his month with the Aeros (4–0 in five starts).

But fourth-place St. Paul upset Wichita in the playoff opener, while Denver rolled over the Millers in four straight games. The Bears beat St. Paul to win the playoffs, then took Buffalo apart in the Junior World Series by scores of 16–5, 9–1, and 13–9. The Bears then traveled to Buffalo, lost 2–1, then clinched the Junior World Series with an 8–1 victory. Denver had outscored their International League opponent 47–17.

In 1958 the league makeup remained unchanged for the third year in a row, although Louisville almost folded. Following a last-place finish in 1956, the Colonels became a community-owned club with no big league affiliation. The team plunged even deeper into the cellar in 1957 (49–105), then headed for a third straight last-place season in 1958, despite a working agreement with the Orioles. In May the club announced it could not meet its payroll or continue operations without assistance. AA President Ed Doherty called an emergency meeting of league directors, at which the Orioles' farm director pledged cooperation. A number of Louisville citizens pledged $1,000 apiece and the Colonels were given Fairgrounds Stadium rent-free. The AA did not want to lose another charter city, and directors certainly did not want to operate as a seven-team league for the rest of the season. Louisville officials estimated that it would take $44,000 to finish the year and felt that $20,000 could be raised locally. The league agreed to deposit an emergency fund of $24,000 in a Louisville bank, and another crisis had been averted.

The All-Star Game returned to Denver and again drew well (15,420). The Bears led the league in attendance for the fourth consecutive season, although the total (228,262) was just over half of the 1955 admissions figures. Denver once more paced the AA in hitting and homers behind batting champ Gordon Windhorn (.328), George Wilson (.299), Curtis Roberts (.298), John Blanchard (.291 with 19 homers), veteran outfielder Zeke Bella (.339 in 96 games), and pitcher-pinch hitter John Gabler (19–7 and .276 in 47 games). Denver held first place through midseason, but injuries and Yankee callups took a familiar toll, and the Bears dropped to fourth place.

Indianapolis dropped still further, into the second division, but provided the home run champ in 19-year-old outfielder Johnny Callison (.283, 29 HR, 93 RBI), while catcher John Romano was close behind (.291, 25 HR, 89 RBI). Longtime National League catching standout, 43-year-old Walker Cooper, managed the Indians and made the final appearances of his playing career (.211 in 38 games).

Wichita's second-place club featured southpaw Dick Littlefield (13–4), righthanded reliever Red Murff (11–5 in 51 games), outfielder Al Spangler (.292), and RBI titlist Earl Hersh (.237, 17 HR, 98 RBI) — for the first time in AA history the crown was won with fewer than 100 RBIs. Omaha shortstop Lee Tate (.292) set a record with 55 consecutive errorless games, and Louisville outfielder Willie Tasby (.322 with 22 homers) was named AA Rookie of the Year. Wichita ace Carlton Willey, who soon was promoted to the Braves, on May 22 fired the first nine-inning no-hitter in the AA since 1950.

Charleston took first place by 7½ games behind MVP second baseman Wayne Terwilliger (.269, 24 SB, 103 R), who led the league in steals and runs, and ERA champ Jerry Davie (17–5, 2.45), whose league-leading six shutouts included a no-hitter against Louisville. But Charleston fell to Denver in the playoff opener, four games to three, while Minneapolis downed Wichita. Minneapolis finished last in hitting (.248), although the pitching staff led the AA in ERA, and player-manager Gene Mauch (.243 in 65 games) guided his team to a four-game sweep of Charleston in the finals. The Millers then swept Montreal in the Junior World Series, a feat which garnered Mauch the first of two consecutive Manager of the Year awards.

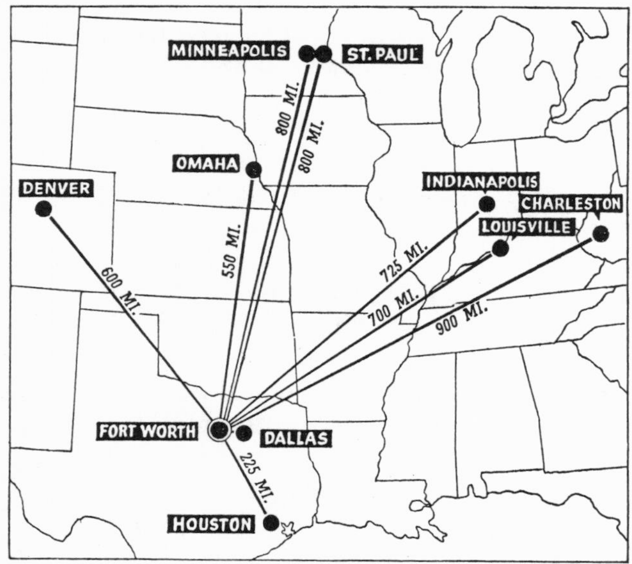

In 1959 the AA expanded to 10 teams, an unwieldy arrangement that lasted just one season.

— Author's collection

The most turbulent decade in AA history ended fittingly in 1959 with the greatest franchise adjustments that had yet occurred in a single year. Wichita dropped out of the circuit, but three Class AA Texas League cities — Dallas, Fort Worth, and Houston — moved up to the American Association. For the first (and only) time in its existence the AA was composed of 10 teams, and the schedule had to be expanded to 162 games. Charleston combined with the four remaining charter cities — Indianapolis, Louisville, Minneapolis, and St. Paul — to form an Eastern Division, while the Western Division was made up of the three Texas cities plus Denver and Omaha. There were no original AA cities in the West, several franchises had no traditional rivalries to offer fans, and travel distances were enormous — all factors which would work against the unwieldy arrangement.

The Western Division was weak. Denver was resentful of frequent callups by the Yankees, while New York was trying to maintain two Triple-A clubs. The Yankees and Bears severed ties after the 1958 season, and Denver President Bob Howsam decided to operate as an independent. Defending batting champ Gordon Windhorn was still aboard (.312), and Denver tied for the team batting lead (.274). But there was little pitching, the Bears had their first losing season in the AA, and finished third in attendance (161,127) — the first time since 1947 that Denver had failed to lead its league in admissions. None of the Texas clubs could rise above .500, and Houston became the last AA team to lose 100 games (58–104), although Dallas provided both the batting champ, in outfielder Luis Marquez (.345), and the ERA titlist, righthander Marion Fricano (12–4, 2.02). Omaha, sparked by stolen base leader Ellis Burton (.292 with just 18 steals) and righthander Frank Barnes (15–12), took the division title with the sole winning record in the West.

Indianapolis bolted to the early lead in the East behind the hitting of home run and RBI champ Ron Jackson (.286, 30 HR, 99 RBI), catcher Camilio Carreon (.311 with 91 RBIs), and outfielders Joe Hicks (.314) and Johnny Callison (.299). But the Indians sagged as Minneapolis and Louisville battled for first place during the latter half of the season, although all three clubs ended the year with better records than Western Division champ Omaha. Charleston placed last in the East, despite the efforts of strikeout leader Bob Bruce (11–13 with 177 Ks) and righthanded reliever George Spencer (11–7), who established a league record with 85 appearances.

Louisville finally produced the best mark in the league, bolstered by offensive production from switch-hitter Ken Wise (.302) and outfielder Al Spangler (.297) and the pitching of co-victory leaders Georges Maranda (18–6) and Don Nottebart (18–11). Lefty Juan Pizarro was sensational in five starts (4–1, with a 1.07 ERA and just 22 hits and 50 Ks in 42 innings), firing a 1–0 no-hitter over Charleston on June 16, then holding the Senators hitless for another 7⅔ innings in his next start before being called up by Milwaukee.

Minneapolis, with key contributions from outfielder Chuck Tanner (.319) and righthander Earl Wilson (10–2 and a .356 batting average) finished with the second-best record in the league. Gene Mauch, who would repeat as Manager of the Year, led the Millers past Omaha in the playoff opener. Fort Worth, second in the West but only a .500 club (81–81), shocked first-place Louisville with a four-game sweep, then battled to the seventh game of the finals before falling to Minneapolis.

The Millers then entered the Junior World Series against the Havana Sugar Kings. The first three games were to be played in

Ed Doherty, shown here making a presentation to 1949 batting champ Taft Wright (.368), served as AA president from 1954 through 1960.

— Courtesy Louisville Redbirds

Minneapolis, but a severe cold front prompted the Junior World Series Commission to move the classic to Cuba after two games. Five more games were played in Havana as Fidel Castro, a curve-balling pitcher who had attracted professional scouts when he was a young man, attended each contest with a large contingent of heavily-armed troops. Cuba was in upheaval; gunfire could be heard at times during play, much to the consternation of the Millers. But more than 100,000 Cubans crowded into the five games in Havana, making 1959 the attendance champion of all Junior World Series. After four games the Millers had won just one contest, but fought back to tie the series with victories in the fifth and sixth games. Minneapolis led, 2–0, in the eighth inning, but the Sugar Kings evened the score, then won with a run in the bottom of the ninth. A young second baseman who had claimed the batting championship of the Carolina League, Carl Yastrzemski, was declared eligible for the Junior World Series, and he hit .277 with a home run.

American Association officials were not pleased with the 10-team arrangement of 1959. Of the 10 clubs only Indianapolis (249,384) and Louisville (222,854) exceeded 161,000 in attendance, and 45,000 had attended the league playoffs — an average of only 2,600 per game. During the 1950s, 37 minor leagues had disbanded, and the surviving circuits struggled to remain in operation. Since 1953 the American Association, which for more than half a century was the most stable circuit in minor league baseball, had lost four charter cities and had scrambled to maintain league membership. For years Minneapolis and St. Paul had angled to obtain a big league franchise, but the loss of two more key cities would bring further chaos to the AA structure. League franchises were undermined by years of sagging attendance and revenues, while Minneapolis fans could muster no greater feeling of rivalry against Houston than Denver spectators could whip up against Charleston. The forces that had caused minor league baseball such damage during the 1950s seemed unrelenting, and as a new decade brought the likelihood of continued problems, there was a real possibility that the once rock-ribbed American Association might become another defunct minor league.

1960–1969

Death and Resurrection of the AA

The American Association entered the 1960s reeling from the disruptive blows of the previous decade. But problems intensified for the AA and for all of minor league baseball. There were 22 minor leagues in 1960 and 1961, but total attendance declined from 10,974,084 in 1960 (down almost 1,200,000 from 1959) to 10,100,986 in 1961. The next year there were only 20 minor leagues and attendance again slipped. In 1963 the number of leagues dropped to 18 with only 9,963,174 admissions, the lowest figures since World War II. Sadly, one of the leagues which folded in 1963 was the American Association. But the loss of one of the most important and historic leagues in baseball would not be permanent. By the end of the decade the AA would be resurrected, to enter upon a period which would prove highly eventful in the comeback of minor league baseball.

In 1960 the AA returned to eight teams when Dallas and Fort Worth combined into a twin cities franchise and Omaha left the league. The division format then was eliminated, and the schedule returned to 154 games per club. The pennant race was tight, with five teams battling for the lead and only Charleston, Indianapolis,

Future Hall of Fame outfielder Billy Williams played five games for Fort Worth in 1959 (.476), then performed so well for Houston in 1960 (.323 with 23 homers) that he went up to the Cubs to stay.

— Author's collection

and Dallas-Fort Worth posting losing seasons.

Denver's Bears, now affiliated with the Detroit Tigers, clawed their way to first place, once more hosted the All-Star Game (14,374), and again led the league in hitting (.286) and home runs (162). Bears first baseman Bo Osborne pounded his way to a Triple Crown (.342, 34 HR, 119 RBI), although third sacker Steve Boros matched his RBI total (.317, 30 HR, 119 RBI, and a league-leading 128 runs). Other heavy hitters included second baseman Jake Wood (.305) and infielder-outfielder Ozzie Virgil (.381 in 59 games).

Carl Yastrzemski now shifted to the Minneapolis outfield, posted a season (.339 with a league-leading 198 hits and a 30-game hitting streak) that vaulted him to a Hall of Fame career with the Red Sox. Millers outfielder Dave Mann (.293 with 50 steals) led the AA in thefts; in all he would record nine minor league stolen base titles during his career. Outfielders Billy Williams (.323 with 26 homers) and Dave Pope (.277), along with slugging first baseman Joe Macko (.239, 27 HR, 122 RBI) and player-manager Enos Slaughter (.289 in 40 games), led Houston to a third-place playoff

Enos Slaughter completed his big league career at the age of 43 in 1959, then spent the next season in the AA as player-manager at Houston. In 1937, on the eve of major league stardom, he was the AA batting champ (.387) with Columbus.

— Author's collection

berth. The 44-year-old Slaughter had starred for the 1937 Columbus Red Birds, and as manager of Raleigh in the Carolina League in 1961, he pinch hit effectively in 42 games (.341) to end his career as a player.

St. Paul made the playoffs behind first baseman Gail Harris (.315 with 22 homers), infielder John George (.306), outfielder Carl Warwick (.292 with 19 homers), and veteran righthander Art Fowler (13–10). The star of the Saints was righty Jim Golden (20–9, 2.32 ERA), who led the league in victories, ERA, complete games, shutouts (5), and innings pitched, and who became the last 20-game winner the AA has produced in three decades.

St. Paul fell to Louisville in the playoff opener, while first-place Denver struggled past Houston, four games to three. Louisville's playoff club was led by outfielder Mack Jones (.309), infielder Lee Tate (.284), southpaw Bob Hendley (16–9), and righthander Don Nottebart (13–5). The Colonels defeated Denver in the finals, then downed Toronto in the Junior World Series. But while the playoffs had been closely contested, attendance totaled less than 37,000. Denver was the season attendance leader

(209,783) but was the only team to draw more than 162,000 as total admissions fell to just one million.

After the season ended it was announced that the Washington Senators would move to Minneapolis-St. Paul, where Minneapolis' Metropolitan Stadium would host American League games. Indianapolis, which had staggered through a losing season as an independent, affiliated with Cincinnati for 1961, and sixth-place Charleston dropped out of the AA. The Los Angeles Dodgers moved their St. Paul affiliation into Omaha, but for the first time in league history there were only six teams in the American Association. A 150-game schedule was set up, with Indianapolis and Louisville the only charter cities remaining in the AA.

Future change in AA makeup was assured when Houston was awarded a National League franchise. For the past couple of years the baseball world had watched the development of the well-publicized Continental League, a proposed third major league apparently conceived to force the American and National leagues to expand beyond 16 franchises. The legendary Branch Rickey was at the forefront of the effort, and franchises supposedly would be placed in New York, Houston, Minneapolis-St. Paul, Denver, Dallas-Fort Worth, Atlanta, Buffalo, and Toronto. Several American Association cities would have been involved, but the Continental League never materialized. Efforts to launch the Continental League were halted in August 1960, when New York and Houston were promised expansion franchises in the NL, to begin play in 1962.

Houston, therefore, commenced its third and last year in the AA in 1961, and the Buffs headed for a playoff berth opposite first-place Indianapolis. The Indians would post the highest attendance with 179,423, while Denver dropped to 142,746. The playoffs attracted only 31,573, and the six-team league totaled only 788,704 admissions.

Cot Deal, familiar to AA fans as a pitcher and outfielder, managed Indianapolis to first place. The Indians boasted MVP Cliff Cook (.311, 32 HR, 120 RBI), who was the AA home run and RBI champ, stolen base titlist Chico Ruiz (.272 with 44 thefts), promising southpaw Claude Osteen (15–11), and victory leader Don Rudolph (18–9). Batting champ Don Wert (.328) and outfielder Jim McDaniel (.282, 30 HR, 114 RBI) led Denver to third place.

Despite a losing record (73–77), Houston edged Dallas-Fort

During a 1962 game between Oklahoma City and Louisville at All Sports Stadium, Colonels manager Jack Tighe prayerfully beseeches the plate umpire in a pose that was reproduced in newspapers all over the country.

— Author's collection

Worth for fourth place. The Buffs featured third baseman Jim McKnight (.283, 24 HR, 102 RBI), first sacker Marion Zipfel (.312 with 21 homers), outfielders Henry Mitchell (.292), Sam Drake (.307 in 83 games) and Jim McAnany (.318 in 80 games), and righthander Al Lary (15–9). On the eve of the playoffs, Hurricane Carla severely damaged Buff Stadium, and Houston was unable to play any home games during the postseason. But the Buffs ignored this disadvantage and upset Indianapolis in the opening round, four games to two, before losing to Louisville in the finals.

For the second year in a row, manager Ben Geraghty guided Louisville to second place and a playoff title. Mack Jones (.326) and Lee Tate (.291) returned to the Colonels, and starter-reliever Freddy Olivo won the ERA title (7–4 with a 2.66 ERA in 42

All Sports Stadium opened in 1962, when the Oklahoma City 89ers entered the AA.
— Photo by the author

games). Outfielder Howie Bedell led the league most of the season in batting, and he went on a 43-game hitting streak to tie Eddie Marshall's 1935 record. His bid to establish a new league mark was stifled by Dallas-Fort Worth, which held him hitless in five trips. When Bedell went out of action with a chipped left shoulder on August 24, Denver's Don Wert began to move up in the batting race. On September 7, with Bedell on the sideline, Wert went 4-for-7 in a closing-day doubleheader to win the batting title, .328 to .327.

After the season, Houston finally began its tenure in the National League, and the American Association shrunk to five teams. But Oklahoma City, which had left the Texas League in 1957, had built beautiful new All-Sports Stadium in hopes of returning to professional baseball. The Oklahoma City 89ers would provide a sixth team as the Triple-A affiliate of Houston, and the beleaguered AA managed to open play in 1962.

For the second year in a row, Indianapolis fielded a first-place team, and for the third year in a row Louisville won the playoffs. Hall of Fame shortstop Luke Appling managed the Indians to another pennant by a 10-game margin over second-place Omaha. The Tribe led the league in fielding and staff ERA, and finished second in hitting. Indianapolis provided the 1962 batting champ in first baseman Tom McCraw (.328), RBI king in Jim Koranda (.298, 19 HR, 103 RBI), and stolen base leader in Al Weis (.296 with 31 steals). Righthander Al Worthington (15–4) and lefty Franklin Kreutzer (15–10) led the pitching staff, while former ace Herb Score (10–7) and veteran major league outfielder Harry "Suitcase" Simpson (.279 with 19 homers) also were on hand.

Freddy Olivo again starred for Louisville, leading the league in strikeouts (13–11 with 151 Ks in 22 starts and 18 relief appearances), while fellow righthander Conrad Grob was the ERA champ (14–10, 2.86). Olivo and Grob also were the shutout leaders, spinning five scoreless games apiece. Colonels southpaw Danny Lemaster (10–4, 2.40 ERA, and 125 Ks in 124 IP before a Braves callup tied a record (set by Mud Hen Monte Pearson in 1933) by striking out seven batters in a row (during an April 23 game against Omaha, in which he whiffed a total of 14 Cardinals). Omaha lefty Nick Wilhite also struck out seven in a row (against Denver on May 29, fanning 13 Bears in all), while leading the AA in victories, starts, complete games, and innings pitched (18–14, 32 GS, 18 CG, 243 IP). Righthanded reliever Jack Smith (17–7 and a 2.06 ERA in 71 games) was voted Most Valuable Player.

Denver posted the best team average in the AA (.282). The most consistent Bears hitters were infielder-outfielder Frank Costro (.321), outfielders Jess Queen (.316 with 20 homers) and muscular Gates Brown (.300), and catcher Bill Freehan (.283). Gordy Seyfried (14–7) and starter-reliever Bob Dustal (12–8 in 57 games) were the best pitchers.

The opening series of the 1962 playoffs was reduced to a best-three-of-five format. Denver beat Omaha, three games to one, and fourth-place Louisville upset the pennant-winning Indians with a three-game sweep. Louisville then defeated Denver in the finals, four games to two, before losing to Atlanta in the seventh game of the Junior World Series.

Playoff attendance hit an all-time low with a meager total of 17,105, an average of just over 1,000 per game. Louisville, playoff winners for the third straight year, drew only 70,550 during the season, and last-place Dallas-Fort Worth recorded only 80,034 admissions. Denver attendance dropped to 165,614, while Omaha led the league with only 184,683. Total attendance was the worst yet, just 759,358.

Although the two remaining charter cities had dominated play in the 1960s, attendance continued to decline. Fan interest was dulled by the lack of traditional rivalries and by the frequent call-ups of key players to the parent clubs. But minor league teams were increasingly dependent upon their big league affiliates. In 1962, for example, Indianapolis hammered out an agreement with Cincinnati that the Reds would cover any salary commitment that exceeded $800 per month per player. Similar arrangements prevailed between other clubs, but the big leaguers soon would face greater demands from the minors. Despite five decades of model stability, the American Association, like other minor leagues, had been forced to scramble for franchise cities — a problem that became critical after the 1962 season.

Louisville, despite three consecutive playoff triumphs, finished last in attendance in 1962, and the Milwaukee Braves decided to pull out, transferring their Triple-A affiliation to Little Rock. The Los Angeles Dodgers had working agreements with two Triple-A clubs, Omaha and Spokane of the Pacific Coast League. The Dodgers elected to drop Omaha for 1963, reducing the AA to five teams. The Omaha club was willing to operate as an independent if big league teams would commit surplus players. Omaha insisted upon commitments for at least 20 athletes, but only about a dozen players were promised.

For two days National Association President George Trautman (former president of the American Association) met with officials of all three Triple-A leagues. Finally, on Thursday, November 29, Trautman announced that after 61 years of operation the American Association would be dissolved. The two remaining Triple-A leagues would expand to 10 teams: the International League took in Indianapolis and Little Rock, while the PCL temporarily dropped Vancouver and added Denver, Oklahoma City, and Dallas-Fort Worth.

"This is ridiculous," said DFW General Manager George Schepps. "The amount of money we spend for travel will cost more dollars than there will be in paid attendance." The major leagues, quite properly concerned about the problems assailing the top level of their farm system, agreed to absorb additional travel expenses, which the International League estimated at $7,000 per club. In 1964, however, the big leagues withdrew travel assistance, and the International League determined to cut back to eight teams. Indianapolis and Little Rock joined the Pacific Coast League, which expanded to two six-team divisions.

During the years that the American Association did not operate, the major leagues took important steps to reorganize the minors. As early as 1962, big league owners began to formulate a Player Development Plan which would pump substantial financial assistance into each farm system and which would restructure organized baseball. When the AA joined the National Association, the league was rated a Class A organization — the highest designation of the time. In 1908 the AA, PCL, and Eastern (International) League were promoted to the newly created Class AA designation, and these three circuits again were "promoted" in 1946 when a Class AAA rating was created. There also were Class D, C, B, A and AA leagues, and for a few years the PCL enjoyed a special "Open Classification" status. In 1963, however, the D, C, and B leagues were abolished, although "rookie" leagues were created. From 1963 through 1968 the International League and the PCL were the only Class AAA circuits in operation. Big league clubs each assumed major fiscal responsibility for five minor league teams, including one in Class AAA and one in Class AA.

After the 1968 season each major league expanded from 10 to 12 teams, creating a need for 24 Class AAA (and Class AA) clubs. The PCL still had 12 teams, and there were eight in the International League. As big league expansion became a reality in 1968, rumors abounded that the American Association would be reorganized to accommodate the necessary Class AAA expansion. A subcommittee of the major league planning committee recommended the revival of the American Association so that there would be three Class AAA leagues. A number of Class AAA owners and general managers were enthusiastic about such a revival, primarily because of the enormous travel distances and expenses of the current arrangements.

Yankee pitching great Allie Reynolds was asked to serve as president of the new American Association, and Carl Erskine, who had hurled superbly for Brooklyn and for St. Paul of the AA, at times lent assistance. Reynolds was a native of Bethany, a small town outside of Oklahoma City, and after he left baseball he became an Oklahoma City businessman. As AA president he accepted only minimal pay, ran the league's business from his own office, and utilized the services of his two secretaries without charge to the AA.

Indianapolis, Denver, Oklahoma City, and Tulsa agreed to leave the PCL to help resurrect the American Association, although these clubs shared in the territorial rights' compensation paid to the PCL for establishing big league teams in Seattle and San Diego. Tucson and Eugene joined the PCL, leaving that circuit with 10 franchises, while Omaha and Des Moines (the state capital franchise would be called "Iowa") enlisted in the AA. The new American Association would start up with six clubs, but it was planned to expand to eight teams the next year. The AA would play a 140-game schedule to a championship. There would be no playoffs, the Junior World Series would not be resumed, and the AA would not conduct an All-Star Game.

When the American Association returned to baseball, a significant change in roster composition had occurred. The Free-Agent Player Draft, first employed in June 1965, was conducted annually in January and June. At each session, clubs in organized baseball would select players, thereby acquiring the exclusive rights to each athlete. With National and American league franchises alternating, the major league teams would draft in reverse order of their standings the previous season. Major league teams would select just one player during each phase of each session, while Class AAA clubs would be permitted two selections apiece, Class AA teams four each, and each Class A team as many as it wanted. But since almost every minor league franchise has a major league affiliation, in effect all selections are made by parent organizations.

Climaxing a trend that had begun in the 1920s, minor league emphasis now was strictly focused upon developing players for the parent clubs. Although marginal players often bounced back and forth for years between the big leagues and Class AAA, career minor leaguers became virtually extinct. No longer would players spend 10 or 12 seasons with the same club or at least in the same league. Players would remain in the AA no longer than a few seasons, which meant that lifetime marks compiled by hitters and pitchers in earlier decades would never be threatened. Individual season records from the past were just as safe, because any player who posted spectacular numbers would be called up to the big leagues by midseason. Players tended to be younger and less experienced in Class AAA, rendering the quality of play less polished.

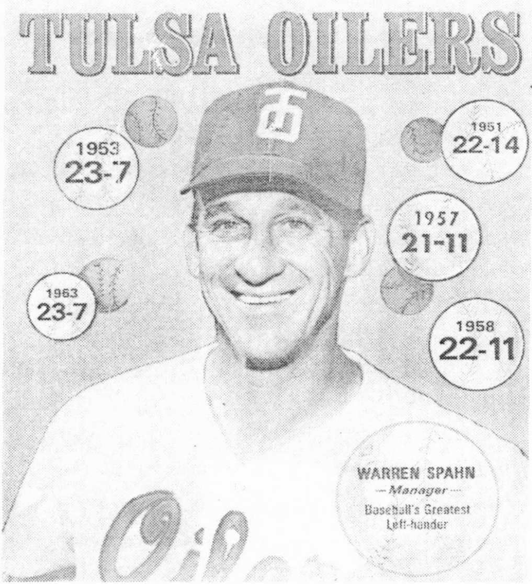

When Tulsa joined the reorganized AA in 1969, the Oilers were managed by famed southpaw Warren Spahn.

— Courtesy Wayne McCombs

Young talent was much in evidence around the new American Association in 1969. Future big league star Ted Simmons of Tulsa was the best catcher in the circuit (.317 with 16 homers). Tulsa left-hander Jerry Reuss, on the eve of a 20-year major league career, led the AA in victories, strikeouts, and innings pitched (13–11 with 151 Ks in 186 IP). A standout Kansas City Royals' outfielder of the 1970s and 1980s, Hal McRae, started the season with Indianapolis, but was limited by injuries to just 17 games. Bernie Carbo, an Indianapolis outfielder who was destined for 12 seasons in the major leagues, won the batting title (.359 with 21 homers) before being called up for his debut with Cincinnati. Lefthanded slugger John Mayberry tuned up for a 15-year big league career by playing first base for the Oklahoma City 89ers (.303 with 21 homers).

Tulsa reliever Sal Campisi (13–2 with a 1.99 ERA in 40 games) led the league in winning percentage and tied teammate Jerry Reuss for the most victories. Tulsa's manager was Hall of Fame lefty Warren Spahn, while Cot Deal, who had spent years in the AA as a player and manager, was field general at Oklahoma City. Oklahoma City outfielder Dan Walton was the home run and RBI champ (.332, 25 HR, 119 RBI). Denver resumed its accustomed role as the top hitting team in the AA behind outfielder Jim Holt (.336) and infielder Minnie Mendoza (.333).

Manager of the Year Jack McKeon led Omaha to the 1969 pennant. Outfielder George Spriggs won the first of two consecutive stolen base crowns (.311 with 46 thefts), while second baseman Luis Alcaraz (.301 with 13 homers) and shortstop Richard Severson (.263) were the top fielders at their positions. The pennant-winning pitching staff was built around righthanders Don O'Riley (12–5), Chris Zachary (11–6), Gerald Cram (10–4) and Alan Fitzmorris (10–6), and southpaw Paul Splittorff (12–10).

Omaha edged Denver for the highest attendance, 177,619 to 175,229. Admissions for the season totaled 882,547, or 100,000 more than in 1961 or 1962, the only other two years in which the AA has operated with six teams. Indianapolis was the only charter city that maintained a tie to the original American Association, but Denver and Omaha dated back to the 1950s, and two more cities were scheduled to be added in 1970.

The decade had begun with minor league baseball in general and the American Association in particular suffering obvious decline, and within three years the AA was forced to disband. But the minor leagues were propped up by the major leagues during the decade, and a reorganized AA would enter the 1970s with far greater optimism than it had at the beginning of the 1960s.

1970–1979

Comeback Decade

The American Association made a strong comeback during the 1970s. Attendance rose dramatically in 1970 and 1971 and remained solid throughout the decade. Two teams were added in 1970, the league makeup stayed unchanged for seven years, and there were only two franchise shifts during the 1970s. The AA permanently adopted the Eastern and Western division format in 1970, with the division winners pitted against each other in a post-season playoff. Indianapolis, the only charter city remaining in the league, finished first three times during the 1970s, while Denver recorded back-to-back championship finishes and three playoff titles. Denver established itself as a key franchise, leading the league in attendance the last five years of the decade.

According to plan, two franchises were added to the six-team AA in 1970. Wichita had played three seasons in the AA during the 1950s. Evansville, located in the southwestern corner of Indiana, near Illinois and Kentucky, would be the smallest city in the AA, but the "Triplets" would appeal to fans from the three-state area. Iowa and Evansville would team with Indianapolis and Omaha to form the Eastern Division, while Denver, Oklahoma City, Tulsa, and Wichita would make up the West, an arrangement that would endure unchanged through the 1976 season. During these years

The Evansville Triplets entered the AA in 1970.
— Courtesy Carl M. Wallace

travel distances would total fewer than 10,000 miles per club per season, far more favorable and less expensive than either the International League or PCL could offer.

When the AA was reorganized in 1969, there was no playoff, All-Star Game, or Junior World Series. In 1970 a 140-game schedule would be played, with a best four-of-seven series between division winners to end early in September, so that promising players could be brought up after major league rosters were expanded from 25 to 40 men. The Junior World Series, which had not been played since the AA disbanded in 1962, would be resumed after an interruption of nine years.

The All-Star Game drew just 4,286 fans, while the playoffs totaled 9,144 admissions — an average of fewer than 2,000 per game. Overall attendance for the eight-team AA added up to a satisfactory 1,353,187. A major factor in the increased fan interest was the amazing balance of the eight clubs. Only three teams had losing records, but every team remained in contention until late in the season. Just six games separated first-place Omaha (73–65, .529) from last-place Evansville (67–71, .486) in the East. The race in the West was even tighter. Denver (70–69, .504) edged Tulsa (70–

Lefthanded slugger Chris Chambliss began his pro career with Wichita in 1970 (.342).

— Author's collection

70, .500) by half a game, while Wichita had the worst record in the league (67–73, .479) but finished only three and a half games from the division lead. Indeed, Wichita sustained enough local interest to win the attendance title (256,824) by more than 81,000 admissions over Denver (175,746).

Wichita kept the crowds coming with the best offense in the league (.283), including batting champ Chris Chambliss (.342) and switch-hitter Richie Scheinblum, who led the league in RBIs, runs, hits, and total bases (.337, 24 HR, 79 R, 84 RBI). Outfielder Ted Ford (.326 in 106 games), catcher Ken Suarez (.301 in 84 games), and All-Star third baseman John Lowenstein (.295 with 18 homers) added to the hitting parade. Evansville first sacker Cotton Nash was the home run champ (.253, 33 HR, 83 RBI), while first baseman Gonzalo Marquez (.341) and outfielder Bill McNulty (.295 with 22 homers) batted well for Iowa.

Iowa southpaw Vida Blue was the best pitcher of the year (12–3, with 165 Ks and just 88 hits in 133 innings, as well as a 2.17 ERA). The sensational 21-year-old was called up before he could qualify for the ERA title, but he won the strikeout crown and posted the highest winning percentage in the league. Indianapolis

The Longest Game

On Thursday, May 28, 1970, Oklahoma City hosted Indianapolis in a game that went into extra innings. The score stood 5–5 after 17 innings when the curfew halted play. The game was resumed the next night prior to the regularly scheduled contest. The Indians scored a run in the top of the 20th, but the 89ers tied the game again in their half of the inning. In the 23rd Indianapolis tallied four times, then held the 89ers to one run to win the 10–7 marathon.

Playing time in the American Association's longest game was six hours and 37 minutes. A total of 13 pitchers took a turn on the mound. Ross Grimsley, the last of seven Indian hurlers, worked the last six innings to record the victory. It was Grimsley's only relief appearance of the season, as he went on to win the ERA crown.

With the 23-inning contest finally decided, the Indians and 89ers played the regularly scheduled game — and again went into extra innings. For the second night in a row, play was interrupted by the curfew. On May 30 the Indians won, 5–4, on a home run in the 12th, after five hours and 15 minutes. The Indians then won the regular May 30 game, 4–2, in a regulation nine innings.

righthander Ross Grimsley won the ERA championship but fell short of Blue's strikeout total (11–8, 2.73, and 162 Ks in 188 IP). Big righthander Ken Forsch pitched five games for Oklahoma City (4–0, 1.58 ERA) on his final minor league stop en route to 15 seasons in the big leagues.

Denver won the Western Division behind victory leader Francisco Carlos (13–9), switch-hitter Joe Patterson (.306), David Nelson (.359 in 53 games), and Richard Billings (.305). A key member of the club was 48-year-old pitcher-coach Art Fowler (9–5 with a 1.59 ERA and 15 saves in 45 appearances), who held the mound staff together, served as interim manager, and started a brawl in Denver by tearing after an offending hitter with a bat! Omaha starred MVP outfielder George Spriggs (.301 with 29 steals), who repeated as stolen base champ. Manager Jack McKeon led Omaha to the pennant for the second year in a row, posting the best record in the league, then defeating Denver in the playoffs, four games to one.

Denver bounded back in 1971 to win another Western Division crown. The Bears once more recorded the highest batting average (.276), and switch-hitting outfielder Richie Scheinblum had another standout season, receiving the MVP award after leading the league in hitting, RBIs, doubles, triples and total bases (.388, 25 HR, 108 RBI). The most consistent pitcher was righthanded reliever Garland "Shifty" Shifflett (12–7 with a league-leading 18 saves in 66 appearances).

Nine-inning no-hitters were pitched by Tulsa lefty Fred Norman (6–1 and a 2.14 ERA in nine games) and Wichita righthander Rich Hand (8–2 and a 1.89 ERA in 11 games). The most spectacular pitcher in the league was imposing righthander (6′8, 240 pounds) J. R. Richard. The 21-year-old fireballer won the strikeout and ERA crowns (12–7, 2.45, 202 Ks in 173 IP) before moving up from Oklahoma City to the Houston Astros. But Richard also was wild, leading the league in walks and beaning Evansville outfielder Al Yates (.342 in 35 games) on August 8. Sadly, Yates was out for the year, because if he had been able to play another seven days his contract would have awarded him an additional $5,000.

Iowa slugger Bill McNulty won the home run crown (.247 with 27 homers), while Oklahoma City outfielder Keith Lampard was the only man in the league besides batting champ Richie Scheinblum to hit over .300 (.337). First baseman John Mayberry spent half of the season with the 89ers pounding AA pitching (.324 with 12 homers in 64 games), and George Hendrick (.333 with 21 homers and 63 RBIs in 63 games) and Steve Hovley (.337 in 69 games) put in productive half-seasons with Iowa.

Indianapolis won the Eastern Division with the best record in the league. Southpaw Ross Grimsley (6–0 in six starts) helped the Tribe to a good beginning before returning to Cincinnati, while righthanded reliever Pedro Borbon (12–6 in 56 appearances) was dependable throughout the year. Outfielder-infielder Willie Smith (.351 in 77 games) was the best offensive performer.

The Indians took on the Bears in a playoff scheduled to conclude in Denver's Mile High Stadium, and the two teams battled evenly throughout the series. Because the Broncos were to play an NFL exhibition game on Sunday, AA playoff games six and seven had to be rescheduled as a day-night doubleheader on Saturday. Denver swept the doubleheader to win the playoff, as Indians' manager Vern Rapp was ejected from both games. During the final contest groundskeepers began readying the stadium for football, and as the crowd filed out, Broncos' fans were lining up to buy tickets. Because of the conversion of Mile High Stadium, the entire Junior World Series had to be played in Rochester. The Red Wings won, four games to three, and Denver baseball fans were angry that the Broncos' monopoly of the home field had cost the Bears at least one victory and the series.

But Denver's attendance was excellent (313,912), and Oklahoma City's was even better (329,513) as league attendance jumped to a decade-high 1,680,443. During the season Allie Reynolds, who had lent his prestige in the baseball world to the reorganization of the AA, resigned as league president. Joe Ryan, personable general manager at Wichita, was elected to serve as president, with only Oklahoma City — which did not want to lose league headquarters — casting a dissenting vote. Ryan moved AA offices to Wichita, and ran the league from Lawrence-Dumont Stadium even after the city lost its AA franchise in 1984. Ryan's father had been a major league catcher and the president of three minor leagues. Ryan had been a baseball executive all of his life, and he would give the American Association creative leadership for the next decade and a half. "Let's get our act in the 21st century," he often said in league meetings.

The close division races of 1970 and 1971 would be duplicated in 1972. Wichita dominated the West with the best record of the year, while Evansville ran away with the Eastern title. Wichita first baseman Pat Bourque (.279 with 20 homers) was voted Most Valuable Player, outfielder Cleo James was the stolen base champ (.281 with 39 steals), and the pitching staff was paced by ERA leader George Decker (12–7, 2.26 ERA), lefty Larry Gura (11–4), and righthanders Bill Bonham (10–4) and big Rick Reuschel, who went up to the Cubs after a fast start (9–2, 1.33 ERA).

Evansville righthander Lloyd Gladden led the AA in victories (15–9), fellow righty Jim Slaton posted the best winning percentage (11–2), and southpaw reliever Ray Newman (6–2 with a 2.05 ERA in 46 games) recorded 13 saves. First baseman Robert Hansen was the home run champ (.241 with 25 homers), and the offense was further fueled by outfielders Bob Coluccio (.300) and Robert Mitchell (.381 and 20 homers in 77 games), and third baseman Bill McNulty (.258 with 24 homers). The championship playoff had been altered to a best three-of-five series, but Evansville abruptly executed a three-game sweep over Wichita.

The Junior World Series had been suspended for 1972 so that

the Kodak World Baseball Classic could be conducted in Hawaii. The Eastman Kodak Company of Rochester, along with the Caribbean winter leagues and the three Class AAA circuits, sponsored the event. The Kodak Classic was a single elimination tournament made up of the host team (the Hawaii Islanders of the PCL), of an all-star squad of Latin American players from the winter leagues, and of the postseason playoff winners from the PCL (Albuquerque), the International League (Tidewater), and the AA (Evansville). Only 1,877 fans turned up for the first game, pitting the Islanders against the All-Stars. But the Islanders (along with Evansville) were eliminated early, and local interest disappeared — just 992 spectators were on hand to watch the All-Stars beat Albuquerque in the championship game. There was talk of playing another Classic between all-stars from Japan and the Caribbean and the Class AAA leagues, but the idea did not materialize, and it was decided to resume the Junior World Series in 1973.

A number of impressive pitching performances were made in the AA in 1972. Future big league righthanders Steve Busby of Omaha and Jim Bibby of Tulsa proved their potential as power pitchers: Busby won the strikeout crown (12–14 with 221 Ks in 217 IP), while Bibby had an even higher strikeout ratio (13–9 with 208 Ks in 195 IP). The highest ratio was recorded by J. R. Richard, who returned to the 89ers for 19 overpowering starts (11–8 with 169 Ks in 128 IP). From May 29 through June 21, Omaha lefthander Mike Jackson (11–8, 2.41 ERA) established a league record by pitching 42 consecutive scoreless innings. Nine-inning nohitters were spun by Jim Slaton of Evansville and Omaha righthander Tom Murphy (4–6 but a 2.41 ERA in 12 starts). On the next-to-last day of the season, Oklahoma City reliever Oscar Zamora (6–9 in 47 appearances) was given a start during a doubleheader with Denver. Zamora responded with a seven-inning perfect game, dominating the Bears so completely that only four balls were hit out of the infield.

Strong pitching continued in 1973. Omaha righthander Mark Littell led the league in ERA, victories, and complete games (16–6, 2.51, 15 CG in 22 starts). The strikeout king was Lowell Palmer of the 89ers (12–11 with 203 Ks in 196 IP). Palmer fired four shutouts, and so did Indianapolis righthander Tom Carroll (15–9), Iowa righty Stan Perzanowski (14–8), and Evansville southpaw Gary Ryerson (11–3). Veteran lefty Juan Pizarro was sent down to

Outfielder George Foster played with Indianapolis in 1973 before becoming a key member of Cincinnati's Big Red Machine.

— Author's collection

Wichita for nine games, with his usual domination of AA batters (6–1 and 68 Ks in 69 IP), while a future Cardinals' star, Tulsa righthander Bob Forsch (12–12), pitched a no-hitter over Denver.

Denver produced the MVP in DH Cliff Johnson, who led the league in homers and RBIs (.302, 30 HR, 117 RBI). Future Cincinnati Red and New York Yankee star Ken Griffey won the stolen base crown (.327 with 43 steals), despite plying just 107 games for Indianapolis (and 25 games for the Reds — .384!). Other AA players who soon would be big league stars included 20-year-old Omaha third baseman George Brett (.284), 21-year-old Iowa shortstop Bucky Dent (.295), and Indianapolis outfielder George Foster (.262 with 15 homers).

Nineteen-year-old first baseman Keith Hernandez came up from the Texas League to play for Tulsa during the stretch drive (.333 with five homers and 25 RBIs in 31 games). Tulsa also featured outfielder Jim Dwyer, who barely qualified for the batting title (.387 in 87 games) before going up to St. Louis. After a tight race, Tulsa (68–67) edged out Wichita (67–68) for the Western Division crown. Iowa, led by Stan Perzanowski, southpaw Ken Frailing (11–3), and fireballer Goose Gossage (5–4 with 59 Ks in

Fireballing righthander Goose Gossage played with Iowa in 1973.
— Author's collection

66 IP), stormed to the Eastern Division title with a nine-game margin and the best record of 1973.

The championship series had been returned to the familiar best four-of-seven format, and Iowa and Tulsa battled the full seven games. Tulsa, managed by Jack Krol, won the deciding game, but lost to Pawtucket, four games to one, in the Junior World Series. The Series had been resumed in 1973, following the Kodak World Baseball Classic of 1972, but after Pawtucket's victory the Junior World Series was permanently discontinued. The International League representatives had won the last five series, dating back to 1961, and, operating as the Eastern League, also had won the first four in 1904, 1906, 1907, and 1917. But the AA had taken five consecutive series from 1954 through 1958, and in 49 Little or Junior World Series the American Association held the edge, 26 to 23.

League attendance in 1973 had slipped below 1.2 million. Denver, Wichita, and Oklahoma City had registered the strongest attendance of the 1970s, but all three clubs suffered losing seasons in 1973 and fell off badly at the gate. These three key franchises again had losing years in 1974, with the same results at the box office. American Association attendance in 1974 sagged to 1,010,778, lowest of the decade, and it would remain barely above one million for two more seasons.

Keith Hernandez returned to Tulsa for much of 1974, winning the batting title (.351) before going back up to the Cardinals. ERA leader Ray Bare (12–4, 2.34), outfielder Danny Godby (.344 in 100 games), Bob Forsch (8–5 in 15 games), and defending batting champ Jim Dwyer (.336 in 36 games) were other key members of a club led by manager Ken Boyer to the Western Division championship. At a critical point in the season, J. R. Richard was sent down for a tuneup, and he responded with three shutouts in four starts (4–0 with only 15 hits in 33 innings). He did not allow a single earned run, losing his fourth shutout only because of a two-run error.

Vern Rapp piloted Indianapolis to another title in the East. The Indians led the league in fielding and staff ERA. First baseman Dave Revering, third sacker Ray Knight, and outfielder Tom Spencer (.291) were the top fielders at their respective positions. The pitching staff included righthanders Tom Carroll (8–4 with a no-hitter before his callup to the Reds), Joaquin Andujar (8–8), Rawly Eastwick (8–7), and Pat Zachry (10–7). Ken Griffey returned from the Reds to spark the offense for six weeks (.333 in 43 games), catcher Marc Hill (.278) was voted AA Rookie of the Year, and outfielder Joel Youngblood, who hit .317 in 1973, swung a solid bat all year (.285). Indianapolis again was disappointed in the playoff, losing to Tulsa, three games to four.

Righthander Jim Kern of the 89ers had a magnificent year, leading the league in victories and strikeouts (17–7 with 220 Ks in just 189 innings) and becoming the last AA pitcher to fan more than 200 batters in a single season. Two Iowa hurlers, righthander Joe Henderson (13–8) and veteran lefty Jim Stinson (3–3) twirled no-hitters. Iowa slugger Lamar Johnson (.301, 20 HR, 96 RBI) won the RBI title, 89er second baseman Duane Kuiper (.310 with 28 steals) was the theft leader, and Wichita first baseman Pete LaCock (.327, 23 HR, 91 RBI) was named Most Valuable Player.

In 1975 Denver vaulted from last place in the West in 1973 and 1974 to the top record in the league. The Bears finished first again in 1976, and won playoff titles in 1976 and 1977. Success on the field revitalized fan interest, and in 1975 Denver enjoyed the first of five straight attendance championships.

The 1975 Bears led the league in hitting (.290) and home runs (107), as well as attendance. Returning RBI leader Lamar Johnson won the batting championship (.336, 20 HR, 101 RBIs), while DH Sam Ewing (.318), outfielders Jim Lytle (.311 in 80 games) and Jerry Hairston (.367 in 40 games), and second baseman Chuck Estrada (.300) played key roles in an exciting offense. The pitching staff starred righthander Steve Dunning, who led the league in victories, strikeouts, innings pitched, and complete games (15–9, 16 CG, 196 IP, 139 K), southpaw reliever Rich Hinton (9–2 in 30 appearances), and righty Pete Vuckovich (11–4). The All-Star Game was held in Denver, and the Stars beat the Chicago White Sox, 7–4, before the largest crowd of the decade (11,615).

Returnees from the previous year distinguished themselves in 1975. Tulsa third baseman Hector Cruz won the home run and RBI titles (.306 with 29 homers and 116 RBIs in just 115 games). Indianapolis righthander Pat Zachry posted the same record as 1974 (10–7, 2.44 ERA) but won the ERA crown. Again hitting well were Keith Hernandez of Tulsa (.330), Tommy Smith of Oklahoma City (.302), and Mike Easler, who played for Iowa and Tulsa (.313). Righthander Mark Littell, who was the victory and ERA champ in 1973 with Tulsa, enjoyed a fine 1975 with Omaha (13–6).

Manager Fred Hatfield guided Evansville to the 1975 championship. Outfielder Robert Molinaro (.287 with 13 homers) and reliever Steve Grilli (11–4 with 12 saves) were the steadiest performers, with late-season help from colorful young righthander Mark Fidrych (4–1). Evansville won the Eastern Division, then beat Denver in the playoffs, four games to two.

When the AA was reorganized in 1969, two experimental tactics were tried: the automatic intentional walk and the "designated pinch hitter" for pitchers. The intentional walk soon was eliminated, but the DH was utilized for years. In 1975, however, the Cincinnati Reds decreed that none of their farm clubs could use the DH, which meant that Indianapolis would be the only team in the AA without the DH. The Indians fell 5½ games short of repeating as Eastern Division champs, and felt certain that use of a DH would more than have made up the gap. After the season, Indianapolis officials insisted that the league remedy their unique disadvantage. The American Association agreed to terminate the DH,

Colorful righthander Mark "The Bird" Fidrych came up late in 1975 to help Evansville win the pennant (4–1, 1.58 ERA). But after a brilliant rookie season with Detroit, arm troubles set in. Comeback efforts included stints with Evansville in 1980 and 1981, but Fidrych soon had to retire.

— Courtesy Carl M. Wallace

and in 1976 and 1977 AA pitchers hit for themselves (the DH returned to stay in 1978).

Vern Rapp, who had managed Indianapolis since the AA was reorganized in 1969, moved to Denver for 1976. Rapp, whose permanent home was in Denver, piloted the Bears to the league's best record for the second year in a row, then won the playoff title over Omaha. Denver again led the league in hitting behind MVP first baseman Roger Freed, who won the home run and RBI crowns (.309, 42 HR, 102 RBI), outfielders Warren Cromartie (.337) and Anthony Scott (.311), third sacker Pat Scanlon (.308 with 18 homers), and shortstop Rodney Scott (.307 with 35 steals). Outfielder Gary Roenicke spent the first half of the season with Denver (.290 with 12 homers in 77 games) before winning promotion to Montreal, but the Expos brought up future star Andre Dawson (.350 with 20 homers in 74 games) as a more than adequate replacement. The Bears' pitching staff was led by Joe Keener (14–4), Larry Landreth (13–9), Dave Gronlund (10–3), and reliever Bill Atkinson (6–3 with 15 saves). Vern Rapp was named *The Sporting News*

Minor League Manager of the Year, and he was hired to manage the St. Louis Cardinals.

Omaha, winners of the Eastern Division, had the league's stingiest pitching staff, led by reliever Gerald Cram (11–3 in 51 games). Another reliever, Indianapolis righthander Joe Henderson (7–3 with a 2.31 ERA in 54 games), worked 109 innings — exactly enough to qualify him as the ERA champ. Two AA vets, Mike Easler of Tulsa (.352 with 26 homers) and Sam Ewing of Iowa (.351), finished one-two in the batting race. Other impressive offensive performances were turned in by switch-hitting Garry Templeton of Tulsa (.321), and 89ers Dane Iorg (.326), Lonnie Smith (.308), and Richard Bosetti, who won the stolen base title (.306 with 42 thefts).

After the season, the first franchise transfer since the AA renewed operations in 1969 occurred when Tulsa moved to New Orleans. Owner A. Ray Smith would no longer tolerate Tulsa's decrepit old wooden ballpark, and when the city refused to build a new stadium he decided to move his franchise. League President Joe Ryan had been invited to place a team in the splendid Louisiana Superdome in New Orleans. A. Ray Smith, eager to explore the city's potential as the home of a future big league club, moved his team to New Orleans, which had not hosted professional baseball since 1959. But stadium rental proved excessive, and even though the last-place Pelicans drew almost 218,000 fans, Smith determined that he must again relocate his franchise.

The 1977 championship race was a duplicate of 1976. Denver and Omaha repeated as division titlists, then the Bears won the playoff series, again by a margin of four games to two. Denver trailed, one game to two, when the series moved to Omaha, but beat the Royals three straight in their own park. For the third year in a row, Denver led the league in hitting, and first baseman Moose Ortenzio (acquired after the 1976 season from Omaha) was named MVP when he pounded his way to the home run and RBI crowns (.311, 40 HR, 126 RBI). Gary Roenicke was sent back to Denver, where he played third or the outfield, as needed (.321). Outfielder Bomba Rivera (.302, 17 HR, 95 RBI), switch-hitter Jerry White (.313), and shortstop Stan Papi (.296) were other strong batters. The Bears' league-leading attendance rose to 288,167.

Omaha again recorded the best staff ERA (3.69 — Denver was last at 5.03). Reliever Gerald Cram was back for another good season (10–5 in 49 games), Gary Lance led the league in victories, starts and innings (16–7), Greg Shanahan missed the ERA title by a fraction of a percentage point (John Kucek of Iowa won, 2.538 to 2.541), and Lance and Shanahan tied for most shutouts (four). Omaha reliever Roger Nelson (5–3 and 16 saves in 58 games) was edged for the save title by Oscar Zamora of Wichita (7–2 and 17 saves in 59 games). Oklahoma City righthander James Wright (14–6) was named Pitcher of the Year.

Jim Dwyer, who was the batting champ in 1973 while playing with Tulsa, claimed another title with Wichita (.332 with 18 homers). Outfielder Clint Hurdle was Omaha's best hitter (.328 with 16 homers), and teammate Willie Wilson (.281 with 74 thefts) won the stolen base crown with the greatest total in league history. Doug Baird's record of 72 steals had stood since 1921, but Wilson's new mark would be exceeded in 1979, then again in 1980 and, most spectacularly, in 1984.

On July 21 the All-Star Game was held in New Orleans. The Texas Rangers beat the Stars, 9–1, in the Superdome before only 5,277 fans. Except for 1975, when a crowd of 11,615 gathered in Denver, attendance since the resumption of the All-Star Game in 1970 had ranged from 6,737 to merely 4,286. Furthermore, most officials had come to feel that All-Star Games caused a needless interruption in the schedule, particularly since stars who might soon be called up to the big leagues could squeeze in two or three more official games. It was decided not to play an AA All-Star Game in 1978, and the midseason exhibition has not been staged since.

The Superdome had booked a major event which would occur during a three-game weekend series between Evansville and the Pelicans, and stadium officials requested that the baseball teams play elsewhere. Businessmen in Springfield, Illinois, promoted a weekend of professional baseball at a local high school field, and the Pelican-Triplets series was a roaring success. A. Ray Smith, intrigued by the challenge of making Triple-A ball work in a city of 90,000, moved his club to Springfield.

An even bigger franchise move almost occurred at the same time. In November 1977 Charles O. Finley announced the sale of the Oakland A's to millionaire Denver oilman Marvin Davis, who intended to move the club to Denver. It was planned to shift the Bears' American Association franchise to Davenport, Iowa, and an indemnity fee for moving into AA territory would be split between the eight clubs and the league office. The fee probably would have been $300,000, giving at least $30,000 to each AA team — the difference between profit or loss to some clubs. But these negotiations hit a snag when Oakland refused to release Finley from a 20-year stadium lease. The AA could not even make out a schedule, and matters remained in limbo, when Finley decided to keep the A's in Oakland.

There also was talk of moving a big league team into New Orleans, which brought up another possibility of a territorial indemnity. Further talk involved enlarging the AA to 10 teams, since the American League had added two expansion franchises, necessitating two more Triple-A clubs. American Association owners wrangled over these matters. Throughout the 1970s a progressive faction had wanted to move into Canada and/or enlarge the league, but a conservative element pointed out that eight teams could be more readily scheduled than 10, and that the AA possessed the most limited — and least expensive — travel requirements of any Triple-A circuit.

Finally it was agreed to leave the AA unchanged, except for the transfer of Smith's franchise from New Orleans to Springfield, which further reduced travel. Springfield fit naturally into the Eastern Division, so Omaha shifted to the West. The designated hitter now returned as the league voted to allow the American League affiliates — Evansville, Iowa and Omaha — to use the DH. A. Ray Smith insisted that his club, a Cardinals' farm team, be allowed the DH, and Denver (Expos) and Indianapolis (Reds) followed suit. Only Oklahoma City (Phils) and Wichita (Cubs) would have to let pitchers hit for themselves, although the Reds decreed late in June that Indianapolis no longer could utilize the DH. As a courtesy, the other clubs would not use the DH against these teams.

Despite the handicap of not being able to use a DH during the latter part of the season, Indianapolis won a tight race in the East over Evansville. The Indians led the league in hitting (.286) and home runs (141). The heart of the offense was outfielder Champ Summers, who blasted his way to the home run and RBI crowns (.368, 34 HR, 124 RBI), and was voted Most Valuable Player. Summers and outfielder-first baseman Arturo DeFreites (.327, 32 HR, 101 RBI) gave Indianapolis the best one-two punch in the league. Righthanders Dan Dumoulin (12–6), Mike LaCoss (11–5), and David Moore (12–7) pitched well, while Larry Rothschild (4–0

Southpaw John Martin helped pitch Evansville to the 1979 pennant.
— Courtesy Carl M. Wallace

in eight games) and lefty Charlie Lebrandt (2–1 in four games) made brief contributions.

Evansville starter-reliever Sheldon Burnside (14–5) tied for the lead in victories and kept the Trips close on the heels of Indianapolis. Springfield first baseman Dane Iorg (.371 in 89 games) won the batting title from Summers, and Redbird outfielder James Lentine also hit impressively (.342). Another productive duo included stolen base champ Lonnie Smith (.315) and 89er teammate Kerry Dineen (.342).

No team in the West enjoyed a winning record, but Omaha (66–69) won the division behind righthander Bill Paschall (14–9), third baseman David Cripe (.300), and first sacker Randy Bass (.279 with 22 homers). Omaha surprised Indianapolis in the playoffs, winning the first two games on the road, then going on to down the Indians, four games to one. Indianapolis had finished first three times since 1971, but lost all three playoff series.

Evansville, on the other hand, reached the playoffs three times during the 1970s and won each season. The Trips finished with the best record of 1979, the only time during the 15-year Evansville tenure that the Trips posted a first place. Manager Jim Leyland

Kirk Gibson played outfield for Evansville's 1979 team, then went up to Detroit and big league stardom.

— Author's collection

controlled a stable of strong hitters: outfielders Dave Stegman (.302) and Dan Gonzales (.338 in 40 games); switch-hitter Richard Peters (.320); first sacker Joe Lis (.292); catcher Bruce Kim (.283); and infielder Tom Brookens (.306 in 77 games). The hard-hitting Trips won the East by five games over Springfield, then beat Oklahoma City in the playoffs, four games to two.

Lonnie Smith again starred for Oklahoma City (.330 with 34 steals), and Keith Moreland — soon switched to third base in the big leagues — was named All-Star catcher (.302, 20 HR, 109 RBI). John Vukovich was the AA's best-fielding third sacker (.291), and outfielder Orlando Gonzales (.313) and outfielder-first baseman John Poff (.293, 20 HR, 90 RBI) made major offensive contributions to the 89ers. Righthander Gary Beare proved almost unbeatable as a starter-reliever (12–1) while posting the league's best winning percentage (.923).

Indianapolis righthander Bruce Berenyi was the ERA champ and won the first of two consecutive strikeout titles (9–9, 2.82 ERA, 136 K). A relief pitcher, Iowa righty Dewey Robinson, rang up more victories than any other hurler in the league (13–7 in 49 relief appearances, along with nine saves).

Springfield outfielder Keith Smith won the batting crown (.350), and the stolen base champ was Omaha infielder German Barranca (.254 with 75 thefts). Denver led the league in hitting (.287) behind slugging first baseman Randy Bass (.333, 36 HR, 105 RBI) and outfielder Bobby Pate (.343 with 15 homers). The explosive Bears drew 335,684, Denver's greatest total since 1956.

On Fireworks Night, 38,490 fans flocked to Mile High Stadium, only to see the Bears trail the Omaha Royals, 14–7, in the bottom of the ninth. Suddenly, the league's best offense came to life, and with two out and two on the Bears had narrowed the margin to 14–13. Third baseman Jimmy Cox (.305 with 12 homers) blasted a three-run homer to win an incredible comeback, 16–14. The excited crowd then enjoyed a grand fireworks display, and even though the Bears finished with a losing record, attendance mounted.

Denver's magnificent fan support helped the league finish 1979 with an attendance of nearly 1.3 million. The "new" American Association had entered the 1970s with innovative, promotion-minded club executives who soundly reestablished the AA as a showcase for excellent baseball talent and stable franchises. Attendance remained solid throughout the 1970s, and the spectacular showing of Denver in 1979 would be a preview of attendance successes unparalleled in the history of minor league baseball.

1980–1989

Attendance Revolution

During the 1980s, significant changes occurred in minor league baseball, not the least of which was a steady increase in popularity. The American Association embodied and led these trends. Severe attendance problems had plagued all levels of minor league ball during the 1950s and 1960s. Ballparks were old and rundown, and often were located in disreputable sections of town. Tiny "crowds" were the norm, with a core of support only from a few diehard purists who found it increasingly difficult to adopt teams with constant roster turnover. Years of shrinking attendance discouraged the development of a younger generation of fans. Franchises could be acquired by daring entrepreneurs willing to assume existing debts. NFL football became the most popular professional sport, while television and youth-oriented movies and other sophisticated entertainments made baseball seem slow-moving and quaint. In minor league cities, the ballpark no longer was the place to go.

During the 1980s, however, a surprising upsurge of attendance occurred throughout the minors. At every level of the minor leagues expertly trained general managers aggressively staged a succession of attractive promotions. The public, perhaps a bit jaded by TV, VCRs, uncensored motion pictures, and the overexposure of televised football, began to exhibit a growing inclination to experience the "national pastime" firsthand. Cheap ticket prices, a result of many lean years when some GMs would desperately distribute free passes in an effort to build a following, made minor league baseball an incomparable entertainment bargain. A man who could *not* afford to take his family to an R-rated movie *could* treat the entire brood to a wholesome evening of baseball. As attendance swelled, ballparks were improved and new, streamlined stadiums were erected — frequently by cities eager to attract a major league franchise in the future. Although there was less roster continuity than ever, the presence of several experienced major leaguers on every AAA team offered a certain modified star quality to new fans.

The American Association led the way in the minor league attendance revolution of the 1980s. In 1980 Denver posted the AA's best record, winning the Eastern Division by a massive 21½-game margin before dropping the playoffs to Springfield. Denver's switch-hitting second baseman, Tim Raines, won the hitting and stolen base titles (.354 with 77 steals in just 108 games) and was named Rookie of the Year, while MVP Randy Bass was the home run and RBI champ (.333, 37 HR, 143 RBI). The Bears dominated the All-Star team with Raines, DH Bass, third sacker Tim Wallach (.281, 36 HR, 124 RBI), outfielders Art Gardner (.314) and Dan Briggs (.316), and victory leader Steve Ratzer (15–4). The Bears led the AA in almost every offensive category, and finished a close second to Springfield in team hitting and staff ERA.

Denver fans turned out in substantial numbers to watch this superb club. On Pepsi Night, Mile High Stadium boasted an attendance of 33,871; on Fireworks Night, Tim Raines beat the Royals, 2–1, with an inside-the-park homer as Denver set an all-time minor league attendance record for a single game. In 1950 the Dallas Eagles of the Texas League had staged spectacular opening-day promotions in the Cotton Bowl and attracted an eye-popping 53,578 fans; Jersey City once sold 61,164 tickets as a civic promotion, but that number far exceeded stadium capacity and the Dallas figure stood as the *attendance* record for three decades. But in Denver, on Fireworks Night of 1980, 58,980 fans filed into Mile High Stadium. Large crowds continued, and by season's end Denver had amassed a league-leading attendance of 565,214, an increase of 230,000 over 1979.

Denver's attendance was almost as good in 1981 (555,806), as

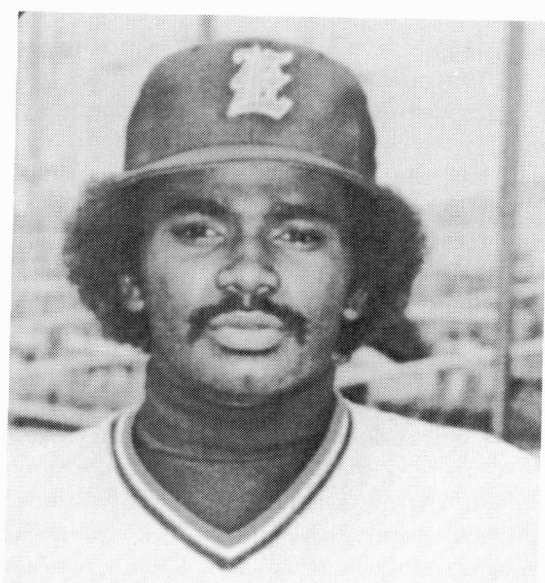

Darrell Brown roamed the Evansville outfield in 1979, 1980, and 1981.
— Courtesy Carl M. Wallace

the Bears outhit and outscored every club in the league. Omaha won the Western Division championship with the best record of the season. Royals' southpaws Atlee Hammaker (11–5) and Mike Jones (11–7), along with righthander Jeff Schattinger (8–4, 2.65 ERA in 59 relief appearances), were the leading pitchers on a staff that posted the league's lowest ERA, while switch-hitting third sacker Manny Castillo (.335 with 91 RBIs) paced the offense and was voted Most Valuable Player.

Manager Jim Leyland led Evansville to the Eastern Division title, but the 1981 playoff scheme called for the second-place team in each division to open the postseason with a series against the champions of the opposite division. Omaha downed Springfield in the opener, but Denver, which outhit and outscored every club in the league, defeated Evansville, then swept Omaha in four straight to win the pennant. The champion Bears featured RBI leader Dan Briggs (.314, 22 HR, 110 RBI), slugging first baseman Dave Hostetler (.318, 27 HR, 103 RBI), outfielder Terry Francona (.352), second sacker Mike Gates (.309), and victory and percentage leader Bryn Smith (15–5). Relief pitcher Dennis Lewellyn of the

Rick Leach was a regular for the Triplets in 1980, then shuttled back and forth between Evansville and Detroit the next two years.

— Courtesy Carl M. Wallace

Wichita Aeros (8–5 in 52 games) set a new league record with 25 saves.

After the 1981 season, A. Ray Smith was persuaded to move his Springfield Redbirds to Louisville, which had been without pro ball for nine years. Louisville banker Dan Ulmer headed a group that raised $4.5 million to convert Fairgrounds Stadium for baseball. Ulmer and his group wanted back into the American Association and they wanted a franchise with a strong major league affiliate, so they aimed their strategy specifically at Springfield, the league's smallest city. Contractually obligated to remain in Springfield, Smith spent considerable amounts to avoid legal action and move his club to a city which held the promise of supporting a big league club.

Smith provided delicious concessions and musical attractions, and the superb ballpark — renamed Cardinal Stadium — proved immensely popular with fans. An opening night crowd of 19,632 welcomed baseball back to Louisville. The Cardinals assembled a solid ball club, and fans continued to turn out in large numbers. Customarily attired in a checkered sportcoat, Smith wandered gregariously through the stands, and cheerful fans often would chant,

Iowa reliever Jon Perlman, wearing the traditional Cubs uniform in 1981. Perlman hurled for Des Moines in 1981, 1983, 1984 (11–6), and 1985, and he went up to pitch for the Cubs, Giants, and Indians.

— Courtesy Jon Perlman

"A. Ray! A. Ray!" On August 8 a midgame fireworks display celebrated a crowd which broke the all-time minor league attendance record of 670,563, set by the San Francisco Seals in 1946. By the end of the schedule, Louisville's amazing total had climbed to 868,418.

Despite their magnificent attendance record, the Redbirds failed to make the playoffs. Denver also did not reach the playoffs, although the Bears drew more than half a million for the third year in a row. Indeed, league attendance approached 2.5 million in 1982, up nearly a million over 1980. Overall attendance was boosted by the fact that seven of the eight AA clubs posted winning records, and even last-place Oklahoma City attracted nearly 181,000 fans.

The 1982 playoff scheme would pit the two division winners in a single championship series. Indianapolis won the East with the league's best record, but in the West Omaha and Wichita finished the schedule in a tie. Omaha shut out Wichita, 2–0, to claim the Western Division, but lost to Indianapolis, two games to four, in the pennant playoff. Wichita led the league in team average (.300) and home runs (165) behind batting champ Roy Johnson (.367), switch-hitter Chris Smith (.326), and MVP first baseman Ken Phelps (.333, 46 HR, 141 RBI), the home run and RBI titlist. Omaha's pitching staff was the stingiest in the league; lefthanded reliever Robert Tufts (10–6 with a 1.60 ERA in 59 appearances) was especially effective; and the offense was triggered by first baseman Ron Johnson (.336) and DH-outfielder Jesus Rivera (.318, 27 HR, 91 RBI). The Indianapolis pennant-winners starred stolen base champ Gary Redus (.333, 24 HR, 93 RBI, 54 SB), and third sacker Nick Esasky (.264 with 27 homers).

Louisville fans trooped into Cardinal Stadium to watch shortstop Kelly Paris (.328), DH Mike Calise (.272, 33 HR, 91 RBI), and victory leader Ralph Citarella (15–6). Elsewhere around the league there were stellar performances from Iowa's Pat Tabler (.342, 17 HR, 105 RBI), Mel Hall (.329, 32 HR, 125 RBI), Al Benton (.330), and Jay Howell (13–4 with a league-leading 2.36 ERA), from Denver outfielder-first baseman Pete O'Brien (.310, 25 HR, 102 RBI), and from Evansville slugger Mike Laga (.250, 34 HR, 90 RBI).

During the off-season, A. Ray Smith spent $750,000 on further stadium improvements, and boldly predicted that the Redbirds would become the first minor league club to reach one million in attendance. In addition to exciting promotions, splendid concessions and a superb stadium, Louisville fans enjoyed the best team of 1983. Managed by Jim Fregosi, the Redbirds roared to the Eastern Division title behind RBI leader Jim Adduci (.281, 25 HR, 101 RBI), stolen base leader Tom Lawless (.279 with 46 steals), and righthanded reliever Jeff Keener (11–5 and a league-leading 60 appearances). Crowds piled into Cardinal Stadium in unprecedented numbers, and by season's end Louisville had drawn 1,052,438. Spring weather had been colder than usual, summer temperatures were higher than normal, and the Louisville economy was depressed, but the Redbirds had brought in more than one million fans. Although the American Association had followed a 136-game schedule since 1973, Smith's Redbirds had outdrawn three big league teams (the major league schedule, of course, is 162 games long), and produced an average game attendance higher than that of five big league clubs. The American Association enjoyed another attendance gain to nearly 2.6 million as Denver recorded close to 483,000 admissions and Iowa, Indianapolis, and Oklahoma City

A. Ray Smith took his Redbirds to Louisville in 1982, and the next season more than one million fans jammed into Cardinal Stadium.

— Courtesy Louisville Redbirds

each exceeded 225,000. Smith and league president Joe Ryan began to dream of establishing the American Association as a third major league. Over the next few years there were visions of adding such cities as Brooklyn, Miami, Washington, Memphis and New Orleans to the strongest AA cities, so that rumored big league expansion could take the form of promoting the American Association to major league status.

Louisville beat Oklahoma City in the opening round of the 1983 playoffs, while Denver, champions of the Western Division, defeated Iowa. Iowa was led by home run champ Carmelo Martinez (.251, 31 HR, 94 RBI), second baseman Dan Rohn (.315), Rookie of the Year Joe Carter (.307 with 22 homers), and third sacker Fritz Connally (.288 with 22 homers); and Oklahoma City featured shortstop Curtis Wilkerson (.312). Dan Rohn set a league record for second basemen by playing 54 consecutive games without an error, while Indianapolis first sacker John Harris turned in a record-setting 78 errorless games in a row.

Denver again led the AA in hitting, and swept Louisville in four games in the championship playoff series. Denver's powerful club starred first baseman Chris Nyman (.319, 23 HR, 90 RBI), outfielder Dave Stegman (.334), victory and percentage leader Fernando Arroyo (14–4), and lefty Richard Barnes (11–6). The Bears entered the round-robin Triple-A World Series with PCL champ Portland and IL titlist Tidewater. Denver (1–3) won only the final game over Portland (2–2), giving Tidewater (3–1) the championship.

In 1984 the American Association voted to eliminate the divisional format, to expand the schedule from 136 to 154 games, and to stage a Shaughnessy playoff in postseason between the top four teams. Indianapolis, managed by Buck Rodgers, outdistanced the rest of the league, finishing 11 games ahead of second-place Iowa. Lefthanders Chris Welsh (13–4) and Joe Hesketh (12–3) posted the best two ERAs and winning percentages in the league, and DH-first baseman Ron Johnson (.303) was the team's offensive leader. Outfielder Mike Stenhouse, who won the 1983 batting title (.355) for Wichita, spent 27 games with the Indians in 1984, walloping three homers in a game against Evansville and hitting well enough (.333) to earn promotion to Montreal.

In the opening round of playoffs, however, the Indians were knocked off by Jim Fregosi's Louisville Colonels. The Colonels' speedy leadoff man, outfielder Vince Coleman, led the league in runs and at-bats, and set a new American Association record by stealing 101 bases (Coleman led the Appalachian League in steals his rookie year in pro ball, led the South Atlantic League with 145 thefts the next season, led the AA the following year, then went up to St. Louis and won the stolen base title his first five seasons in the National League). Louisville pulled 846,878 fans into Cardinal Stadium.

Iowa, led by home run champ Joe Hicks (.266, 37 HR, 90 RBI) and tall righthander Jon Perlman (11–6), drew over 275,000 fans, but fell to Denver in the playoffs. Third baseman Jose Castro (.316) and outfielder Daryl Boston (.312) spearheaded another hard-hitting Bear lineup, and Denver defeated Louisville for the AA pennant. Oklahoma City outfielder Tom Dunbar (.337) was the batting champ, but Wichita's Alan Knicely (.333, 33 HR, 126 RBI) won the home run and RBI titles, almost took a Triple Crown, and was voted Most Valuable Player.

Attendance in 1985 exceeded 2.7 million throughout the league. For the fourth consecutive year, Louisville posted the highest attendance in the minors (651,090), while Oklahoma City

(364,247), Denver (308,268), and new AA members Nashville (364,225) and Buffalo (362,762) each attracted well over 300,000 paid admissions. Five of the top 10 minor league teams in 1985 attendance were from the American Association, and the AA boasted six of the top 10 in 1984.

Larry Schmittou had purchased the Evansville franchise (100,326 in 1984) and moved it to Nashville, where the Sounds appealed to an entertainment-minded populace. Country-western stars frequently sang the national anthem at home plate, and several celebrities were enthusiastic owners. Buffalo, an old industrial city in transition to a white-collar economy, long had been a mainstay of the International League but had lost its franchise. Returning to organized baseball in the Class AA Eastern League, Buffalo played in old War Memorial Stadium, and experienced soaring popularity after Robert Redford filmed *The Natural* in the archaic facility. After the 1984 season, owner Robert Rich, Jr., sold the Eastern League franchise, then bought the Wichita Aeros (137,018 in 1984). Rich launched a well-financed, long-range strategy to bring major league baseball to Buffalo, and local fans responded in large numbers to a first-class Triple-A operation.

Early in the 1985 season, Buffalo traveled to Indianapolis and beat the Indians 15–9, pounding out 26 hits. The Indians added 19 hits for a combined total of 45 — a new American Association record. Over the season, however, offensive performances were modest. The batting champ was Nashville switch-hitter Scotti Madison (.341 in 86 games), but only two other season regulars hit above .300, outfielders Wally Johnson (.309) of Indianapolis and Paul O'Neill (.305) of Denver. The home run and RBI titles were won with comparatively low totals (.256, 29 HR, 89 RBI) by Dave Hostetler, who split the season between Indianapolis and Iowa.

After trying a Shaughnessy playoff in 1984, the AA decided to return to division play in 1985. Oklahoma City, led by the league's Most Valuable Player, third baseman Steve Buechele (.297), won the Western Division with the best record of the year. But Louisville, again managed expertly by Jim Fregosi, took the Eastern Division crown, then downed Oklahoma City, four games to one, to win the 1985 pennant. Louisville fireballer Todd Worrell (8–6 and 11 saves with 126 Ks in 128 innings) was the strikeout king, while Redbirds outfielder Curtis Ford (.255 with 45 steals) won the stolen base title. The Omaha staff produced two top righthanded hurlers, Pitcher of the Year Mark Huismann (5–5 with a 2.01 ERA and a league-leading 33 saves and 59 appearances) and ERA champ Steve Farr (10–4 with a 2.02 ERA in 17 games).

American Association attendance continued to rise in 1986 as Louisville led all minor league clubs (660,200) for the fifth year in a row. Nashville maintained its high attendance level (364,614) despite a losing team, and Buffalo stepped up its movement to build a new stadium and attain major league status, with impressive improvement at the box office (425,113 filed into "The Rockpile"). Denver, the league's perennial offensive leader, attracted over 300,000 fans, and the eventual pennant-winner, Indianapolis posted a robust "low" attendance mark with more than 220,000 fans.

For the second year in a row, Nashville fans were treated to the performance of the league's best hitter, outfielder Bruce Fields (.368), while Sounds righthander Jack Lazorko (8–6 with 119 Ks) was the strikeout leader. Buffalo lefty Pete Filson (14–3 with a 2.27 ERA) started 12 games, made 14 relief appearances, and led the AA in victories and ERA. Righthander Greg Maddux started the season in the Eastern League (4–3), performed brilliantly after a promotion to Iowa (10–1), then finished the season with the Cubs (2–4).

Denver won a close race in the West behind MVP infielder Barry Larkin (.329), home run champ Lloyd McClendon (.259, 24 HR, 88 RBI), and catcher Terry McGriff (.291). But Indianapolis, in its 100th year of professional baseball, topped the Eastern Division with the league's best record, then came from behind in the bottom of the ninth inning of the seventh playoff game to defeat Denver for the pennant. Indianapolis heroes included righthanders Rodger Cole (12–4) and Curt Brown (11–3), and second baseman Casey Candaele (.302).

As an economy move, in 1986 the major leagues reduced club rosters from 25 to 24, with important effects upon Triple A baseball. Big league clubs found that they needed a supply of veteran players who could be called up to fill roster needs caused by injury or poor performances. Experienced players, many in their thirties, filled Triple A rosters as insurance for big league affiliates. Triple A clubs began to resemble NFL taxi squads, and by the end of the 1980s bidding for experienced players pushed top salaries into the \$30,000–\$40,000 range. Such players began to appear on the same

In 1986 the Denver Zephyrs were champions of the Western Division and led the AA in hitting.

— Courtesy Denver Zephyrs

Triple A team for four, five or even six seasons, although two or three times a year they probably would go up to the big league club for a time. Good Triple A players might be traded from team to team within the same league, but were recognizable to regular fans. Greater recognizability came from periodically playing in the big leagues, which may offer one reason for growing fan interest in Triple A baseball. An increasing number of top prospects — such as Bo Jackson, Ken Griffey, Jr., Terry Steinbach, Mark Langston, Bret Saberhagen, Gary Gaetti, and Steve Sax — jumped from Double A to the majors. Of course, any Triple A player on a hot streak soon would find himself en route to "The Show," but American Association fans increasingly enjoyed quality baseball played by experienced, identifiable athletes.

For 1987 the league decided once more to eliminate division play and let the top four teams square off in a Shaughnessy playoff at season's end. There was an extremely tight race between defending champion Indianapolis, Louisville, and Denver. The Bears, leading the league in home runs with the highest total (192) since 1955 and in team hitting (.299) for the 19th time in the past 27 AA seasons, finished first by one game over Louisville. The potent Denver attack was spearheaded by infielder-outfielder Steve Stanicek (.352, 25 HR, 106 RBI, and the league leader in hits, doubles, and total bases), third baseman Steve Kiefer (.330, 31 HR and 95 RBI in just 90 games), switch-hitting second sacker Bill Bates (.316

Stars of the 1987 Nashville Sounds were infielders Chris Sabo (.292 — front row, fourth from right) and Jeff Treadway (.315 — second row, third from right), a 20-game winner with Cincinnati in 1985, who worked his way back from injuries with five games in Nashville.

— Courtesy Nashville Sounds

with 51 steals and a league-leading 117 runs), home run champ Brad Komminsk (.298, 32 HR, 95 RBI), and first baseman Joey Meyer (.311 with 29 HR and 92 RBI in only 79 games).

Louisville was led by MVP Lance Johnson (.333 with 42 steals), catcher Tom Pagnozzi (.313 with 14 HR and 71 RBI in just 84 games), and starter-reliever Paul Cherry (11–5 in 46 games). Oklahoma City, paced by outfielder David Meier (.320), also made the playoffs, but lost in the opening round to Denver. Indianapolis defeated Louisville, setting up a second consecutive championship series between the Indians and the Bears. Joe Sparks collected his second straight Manager of the Year award by guiding the Indians to another pennant, downing Denver four games to one. Sparks was able to work with a strong, versatile lineup: batting champ Dallas Williams (.357), first baseman Jack Daugherty (.312), second sacker Johnny Paredes (.312), shortstop Luis Rivera (.312), outfielders Tom Romano (.306), Alonzo Powell (.299) and Ron Shepherd (.291), reliever Tim Barrett (10–1 in 46 games), and ERA champ Pascual Perez (9–7, 3.79 ERA). Perez's ERA was the highest mark ever to take the American Association title.

League attendance again exceeded 2.7 million in 1987, ranging from over a quarter of a million in Indianapolis to more than half a million in Buffalo. This healthy distribution of attendance reflected the burst of popularity that had spread throughout minor league baseball. Eugene, Oregon, for example, had lost its Class AAA Pacific Coast League franchise after five seasons (1969–73) because of poor crowds, but in the 1980s, as a member of the short season Class A Northwest League, the Emeralds drew better total attendance with only half the schedule. During the 1970s, promotional genius Jim Paul transformed El Paso of the Texas League into one of the most successful franchises in minor league baseball, often attracting more than 300,000 fans per season, and the Class AA circuit pulled in more than one million admissions during each season of the 1980s. Attendance in the minor leagues in 1987 totaled more than 20 million. In the 1970s, when minor league attendance dropped steadily, the major leagues, which had owned about 90 percent of all minor league franchises, began unloading these clubs to public-minded local businessmen, who could utilize unsuccessful baseball investments as tax write-offs. Fewer than 15 percent of all minor league teams now are owned by the majors, and the value of "bush league" franchises has soared. A. Ray Smith sold his remarkably successful Louisville franchise to local investors in 1987 for $4.5 million.

In Buffalo, where the American Association franchise had been purchased in 1984 from Wichita for $1 million, Bisons' owner Bob Rich, Jr., took aim at reaching one million in attendance. In 1988 the Bisons moved into a splendid new $43 million stadium; Pilot Field seats 19,500, but it is built for a third deck, and the addition of the deck and bleachers could rapidly expand seating for a big league club to 45,000. Demand was so great for tickets in 1988 that Rich cut off season ticket sales at 9,000, so that walk-up fans could be accommodated. The promotions that had drawn half a million fans into The Rockpile were continued, and the Pittsburgh Pirates provided a solid roster, including All-Star shortstop Felix Fermin, victory leader Dave Johnson (15–12), and ERA champ Dorn Taylor (10–8, 2.14). Opening night brought temperatures in the twenties, but the first AA game in Pilot Field was a sellout. There were 22 sellouts during the 1988 season, and Buffalo became the second minor league team to achieve The Million (1,147,651), surpassing Louisville's 1983 record. Bob Rich, Jr., was selected by *The Sporting News* as minor league baseball's Executive of the Year.

The highlight of the season at Pilot Field was the first Triple-A Alliance All-Star Game. The Alliance was born after the 1987 season, when owners and executives of all three AAA leagues met

Four In One Game

On June 9, 1987, Iowa third baseman Wade Rowdon became the fourth slugger in American Association history to wallop four home runs in one game, and the only one of the four players to hit two of the four homers during one inning. Rowdon was the 1987 RBI champ, batting .337 with 18 four-baggers and 113 RBIs.

It had been 42 years since the feat had last been accomplished. Bill Hart was an infielder who had played three seasons during the war for Brooklyn, but he could not hit even against wartime pitching, and late in 1945 the Dodgers sent him down to St. Paul. He played shortstop for the Saints and went on a tear against AA pitchers, batting .368 with 18 homers and 46 RBIs in just 38 games. The biggest day of this spectacular streak came on September 4, when he blasted four home runs with poor-quality wartime baseballs. Home run champ Babe Barna hit just 25 homers all season, and Hart finished third in the home run race!

The first player to blast four homers during a single AA game was Kansas City first baseman Dale Alexander. Playing in the Blues' vast stadium, Big Alex (6′3, 215 pounds) hit .358 during the 1935 season, but collected only 16 home runs. One-fourth of this total came on June 14, when he sailed four roundtrippers out of cozy Nicollet Park in Minneapolis.

At Nicolett Park, during the morning game of the July 4 doubleheader in 1940, Minneapolis outfielder Ab Wright put on a slugging exhibition unmatched in any other contest played in nine decades of American Association baseball. Wright won the Triple Crown in 1940, batting .369 with 39 homers and 159 RBIs. On the morning of July 4 he cracked four home runs and a triple, establishing an all-time AA record with 19 total bases in a single game.

late in September at Hollywood, Florida. Harold Cooper, a longtime baseball executive from Columbus, had served as president of the International League since 1978, and for more than a decade Cooper and Joe Ryan, president of the American Association, had discussed the possibilities of interleague play. (Indeed, this idea went back far beyond Ryan and Cooper — in 1917 the AA and IL set up a schedule which would include 48 interleague games per club, but the United States entered World War I a week before the season opened, and the experimental format was abandoned . . . until 1988.)

Joe Ryan had suffered a stroke in 1987 and retired. (Since A.

Buffalo's splendid Pilot Field opened in 1988 and attracted a record minor league attendance totaling 1,147,651.

— Courtesy Buffalo Bisons

Ray Smith had sold Louisville and turned his energies to bringing big league ball to St. Petersburg, the loss of Ryan halted any hope of elevating the AA into a third major league.) Ken Grandquist, owner-president of the Iowa Cubs, was officially designated as president of the American Association, but league directors persuaded Harold Cooper to run the AA simultaneously with the IL. Cooper and his assistant, Randy Mobley, felt that the time was ripe for interleague play, an idea which also was being proposed for the major leagues. An informal meeting in Cooper's hotel room involved owners and GMs, and interleague play and an alliance were discussed late into the night. The next morning Cooper and Mobley breakfasted while the owners met officially. The two executives agreed that the new measures would not find approval — but later in the day they were surprised to learn that the Triple-A Alliance had been approved by directors of the American Association and the International League. The Pacific Coast League felt that the travel involved would be too difficult and expensive, but the AA and IL were geographically closer; indeed, Columbus and Toledo of the IL long had been members of the AA, while Buffalo had been a mainstay of the IL for decades. Harold Cooper would serve as

Harold Cooper became clubhouse boy for the Columbus Red Birds in 1936, later won promotion to general manager, and eventually served as president of the International League. Cooper was instrumental in the formation of the Triple-A Alliance in 1988 and served as first commissioner of the Alliance.

— Courtesy Harold M. Cooper

commissioner of the Alliance from offices in Grove City just outside Columbus, where Cooper had operated as president of the IL and, recently, of the AA.

Each Triple-A Alliance club would play 42 interleague games, six against each of the eight members of the other league — three at home and three away. Fans would be able to see Triple A players from 16 organizations instead of eight, a plan which was being counted on to boost attendance. A postseason Alliance Classic, a continuation of the Junior World Series, would be staged between the AA and IL champions (in 1983 Joe Ryan had organized the Triple-A World Series between the champions of the AA, IL and PCL, but the postseason tournament was staged only once). Umpiring crews would be used during the season in both leagues, which would reduce resentment in certain cities and by certain teams against specific officials. The most entertaining innovation, however, was the Triple-A All-Star Game.

The two 23-man rosters were made up of stars from all 26 Triple-A teams. The best players in the AA, IL and PCL were divided

The first Triple-A Alliance All-Star teams, which drew a capacity crowd at Buffalo's Pilot Field in 1988.

— Courtesy Buffalo Bisons

into American League and National League squads, and the game was scheduled for July 13, 1988, at Buffalo's showplace stadium. A capacity crowd thronged Pilot Field as ESPN telecast the first Triple-A All-Star Game to a national audience. Pam Postema, the only woman ever to umpire at the AAA level, called balls and strikes as the American League squad pushed across an unearned run in the top of the ninth to win, 2–1.

Indianapolis ran off the best record of the season, winning the Eastern Division by 16 games. Omaha, led by MVP first baseman Luis Delos Santos (.307 with a league-leading 87 RBIs), took the West by three games over Iowa, which paced the AA in hitting behind catcher Bill Bathe (.312), infielder-outfielder David Meier (.305), and outfielders Rolando Roomes (.301) and Doug Dascenzo (.295). Indianapolis, however, led the league in pitching behind righthanders Jeff Fischer (13–8, 2.69 ERA) and Bob Sebra (12–6, 2.94 ERA), while hitting was provided by second baseman Johnny Paredes (.295) and outfielder Billy Moore (.285, 17 HR, 80 RBI). Indianapolis beat Omaha, three games to one, to win the playoffs for the third consecutive year, then downed Rochester, four games to two, in the first Alliance Classic.

Veteran field general Joe Sparks was named Manager of the Year for the third season in a row. Nick Cullop (with Columbus in 1943 and Milwaukee in 1947), Kerby Farrell (with Indianapolis in 1954 and 1956), Gene Mauch (with Minneapolis in 1958 and

The pennant-winning 1988 Indianapolis club. The Indians have recorded four consecutive AA titles, 1986 through 1989.

— Courtesy Indianapolis Indians

Billy Moore led the AA in runs and doubles while playing for Indianapolis in 1988.

— Courtesy Indianapolis Indians

1959), Jack McKeon (with Omaha in 1969 and 1970), and Vern Rapp (with Indianapolis in 1972 and 1974) each won the award twice. But Joe Sparks had been named AA Manager of the Year twice (with Iowa in 1973 and Omaha in 1981) before winning the honor three consecutive years with Indianapolis, and his total of five is an impressive mark for any league.

An all-time minor league attendance record was set in 1988 as season admissions soared to 3,576,678, ranging from Buffalo's record-setting mark to Oklahoma City's 260,336. Louisville attracted 574,852, and Denver, Nashville, Indianapolis and Omaha each recorded well over 300,000 admissions. Total attendance in the AA increased by 766,288 over 1987. Everyone was pleased with the Alliance experiment, and during the winter meetings it was voted to continue the Alliance for three more years.

For 1989 the schedule was expanded from 142 to 146 games: members of the AA would play 102 league games, including 18 intradivisional and 12 interdivisional contests with each club, and there would be 44 interleague games. For the third time in four years, Indianapolis posted the best record in the AA, winning the Eastern Division by five games over Buffalo, which had a better record (80–62) than Western Division titlist Omaha (74–72). For the second year in a row, the AA set a new attendance record with admissions totals in excess of 3.6 million. Buffalo (1,116,441) became the only minor league club ever to record more than one million admissions in two seasons, and attendance at Louisville (603,788) exceeded half a million for an unprecedented eight years in a row.

Denver outfielder Greg Vaughn was the only man in the league to hit more than 19 homers (.276, 26 HR, 92 RBI); he led the AA in home runs and RBIs, and was voted Most Valuable Player. Louisville catcher Todd Zeile (.289) was named Rookie of the Year. Omaha repeated as Western Division champ behind returning first sacker Luis Delos Santos (.297), outfielder Nick Capra (.290), righthander Steve Fireovid (13–8), and lefty Stan Clarke (12–6). Indianapolis boasted the top two hitters in the league, second baseman Junior Noboa (.340) and shortstop Jeff Huson (.304 with 30 steals), and a six-year Indian veteran, switch-hitter Razor Shines, held down first base for half of the season (.305). The Indian pitching staff was the best in the AA: strikeout leader Mark Gardner (12–4, 2.37 ERA, and 175 Ks in 163 IP),

Pam Postema, who rose higher than any other female umpire, officiating at a Louisville game in 1989.

— Photo by the author

ERA champ Rich Thompson (9–6, 2.06), righthander Urbano Lugo (12–4, 2.94 ERA), and relievers Jay Baller (a league-leading 34 saves in 62 games with 2.02 ERA), Brett Gideon (7–2 with a 2.26 ERA in 47 games), and Jeff Dedmon (8–6 with a 2.71 ERA in 51 games).

In the first game of the playoffs, Indianapolis outlasted Omaha, 5–4, in 14 innings. Omaha won the next game, the Indians shut out the Royals in the third game, then Omaha evened the playoff at two apiece. Indianapolis took the deciding game, 5–0, to win an unprecedented fourth consecutive AA pennant, and field general Tom Runnels was voted Manager of the Year. In the second annual Triple-A Classic, Indianapolis brought the American Association its second victory by sweeping Richmond in four games.

The American Association opened the '90s with a Triple Crown pitching performance by Nashville southpaw Chris Hammond. The 23-year-old Hammond was brilliant in his second year at the Triple-A level, leading the 1990 AA in victories, winning percentage, strikeouts, ERA, and shutouts (15–1, .938, 149Ks in 149 IP, 2.17 ERA, 3 ShO). The league's best reliever was Louisville righthander Mike Perez, who recorded 31 saves in 57 appearances. Omaha lefty Gene Walters twirled a nine-inning no-hitter in the first game of a July 13 doubleheader.

The home run and RBI champ was Oklahoma City outfielder Juan Gonzalez (.258, 29 HR, 101 RBI), who was named Most Valuable Player, Rookie of the Year, All-Star MVP, and recipient of the "Star of Stars" Award. On May 9 Louisville left fielder Bernard Gilkey set an AA record by collecting three hits — two singles and a homer — during a 16-run third inning as the Redbirds pounded Nashville, 18–4; Louisville sent 21 men to the plate and collected 14 hits (but the previous night the Sounds had blasted out a 17–5 victory over the Redbirds).

Buffalo outfielder-first baseman Mark Ryal (.334) won the batting title with a 2-for-4 performance in a single-game playoff with Nashville for the Eastern Division crown. Ryal did not have enough at-bats to qualify, and it appeared that Omaha outfielder Gary Thurman (.331) would be the batting champ. But when the playoff game became necessary, Ryal had an opportunity to collect the four at-bats he needed. Ryal lined an RBI double in the first inning, recorded two more official at-bats, then came up again when the game went into extra innings and singled in the 10th to clinch the crown.

The playoff was forced when division leader Buffalo lost at Indianapolis on the last day of the season, while Nashville won at Louisville, which left the Bisons and Sounds deadlocked with identical 85–61 records. Buffalo had a head-to-head edge over Nashville during the regular season and was awarded the home field advantage. For the third year in a row the Bisons had attracted over one million fans, and despite only 19 hours' notice a crowd of more than 10,000 surged into Pilot Field on a Tuesday night to see the September 4 showdown. Ironically, the two franchises had played dead-even ball (63–63) since entering the American Association in 1985, and the opposing managers, Terry Collins of Buffalo and Pete Mackanin of Nashville, had once met in a single-game playoff in the Venezuelan winter league (Collins' team won in 14 innings). The two teams battled for five hours and 18 innings before Mackanin's Sounds finally prevailed, 4–3. Western Division winner Omaha, managed by Sal Rende, outlasted Nashville, three games to two, for the AA championship, then went on to win the Triple-A Alliance Classic over IL titlist Rochester, four games to two.

In 1991 Buffalo drew nearly 1.2 million at the gate, but was passed over by the National League for an expansion franchise. But righthander Rick Reed led the AA in victories, ERA and winning percentage (14–4, 2.15), offense was provided by Cecil Espy (.312) and Jeff Schulz (.300), and the Bisons won the Eastern Division with the best record in the league.

Denver — which *was* awarded an NL expansion franchise — won the Western Division behind batting champ Jim Olander (.325) and strikeout leader Calvin Eldred (13–9 with 168 Ks). Denver beat Buffalo, three games to two, to claim the AA championship, then won the Alliance Classic, four games to one, over Columbus.

During the 1991 season there was a bitter clash between minor league and big league owners, who intended to exert greater control over the minors while reducing expenditures to farm clubs. Although the minor leaguers finally agreed to a seven-year Professional Baseball Agreement, there was fierce opposition from AA owners. The Triple-A Alliance contract ran out after the 1991 season, and the increased travel expenses caused by the PBA rendered interleague play unprofitable.

Late in the 1989 season Harold Cooper announced his retirement from baseball, and owners of the AA and IL elected Randy Mobley to succeed Cooper as commissioner of the Alliance. In a surprise development, Cooper agreed to assume his old role as president of the American Association. Both leagues were run from president of the American Association. both leagues were run from Alliance headquarters in Grove City, Ohio, near Cooper's home. But Cooper decided to retire for good after the 1991 season, and AA and IL owners dissolved the Triple-A Alliance. Mobley accepted the presidency of the IL, while the AA elected a new president, Branch Rickey, III, who moved the league offices to Louisville.

Louisville was the site of the 1991 Triple-A All-Star Game. Almost 21,000 fans attended, and since all three Triple-A leagues participated in the All-Star Game, it was decided to continue the popular mid-summer classic. During 1991 AA season attendance increased to nearly 4.1 million, by far the highest total of any minor league. With attractive ballparks, capable and resourceful leadership, a product with increasing appeal as family entertainment, and a stability and prosperity reminiscent of the league's first half-century, the American Association marches toward the 21st century at the top of minor league baseball.

Nicknames

Countless bench jockeys and leather-lunged fans, as well as broadcasters and sportswriters in search of a touch of color, have produced a wealth of cleverly descriptive or insulting nicknames throughout the history of the American Association. Some of the AA players who attracted sobriquets on the baseball diamond include Nick "Tomato Face" Cullop, Al "Bozo" Cicotte, "Derby Day" Bill Clymer, Lou "The Mad Russian" Novikoff, Charles "Eagle Eye" Hemphill, "Toothpick" Sam Jones, Harry "The Hat" Walker, George "Twinkletoes" Selkirk, "Buzz" Arlett, "Dandy Dave" Danforth, John "Pepper" Clarke, Bob "The Rope" Boyd, "Showboat" Fisher, "Footsie" Marcum, "Buckshot" Wright, "Baby Doll" Jacobson, "Deerfoot" Milan, "Scout" Stovall, "Stoney" McGlynn, "Honey" Romano, "Unser Choe" Hauser, "Double" Dwyer, "Fuzzy" Hufft, "Bear Tracks" Greer, and "Howitzer Howie" Moss. Any number of ballplayers named Rhodes inescapably were called "Dusty," while "Doc" Gessler, a star football and baseball player for the Ohio Medical School Medics, was awarded a professional appellation because he had studied dentistry. "Bruno" Betzel probably was grateful for any nickname: his birth certificate read Christian Frederick Albert John Henry David Betzel.

Since 1902, hundreds of AA players have been labeled by the color of their hair. Among those who have received the most common nickname are "Red" Murff, "Red" Kress, "Red" McColl, "Red" Shannon, "Red" Kleinow — and, inevitably, "Red" Herring. "Rosy" Carlisle, "Rosy" Ryan, and "Pinkie" Pittenger were similarly branded, along with "Sandy" Vance, "Cotton Top" Turner, "Cotton" Nash, and "Cot" Deal. Appearance likewise dictated the nicknames of "Goldie" Rapp, "Specs" Hill, "Big Boy" Kraft, "Big Bill" Powell, "Piano Legs" Hickman, "Beauty" Bancroft, "Patcheye" Gill, "Splinter" Gerkin (he was 6′2 and weighed 162 pounds), "Slim" Harriss (6′6, 180 pounds), and husky Tommy Heath, "The Round Man." "Long Tom" Winsett and "Long Tom" Hughes each towered well over six feet, but "Pee Wee" Reese and "Little Phil" Geier had diminutive physiques, and "Midget" Reilly stood just 5′4. "Lefty" Gomez, "Lefty" Good, "Lefty" George, "Lefty" Davis, "Lefty" Dorkins, "Lefty" Heimach, and "Lefty" James were among scores of southpaws, mostly pitchers, who received the second most common appellation.

Brad "The Animal" Lesley was not the only player whose physique or style of play reminded onlookers of the animal world. Powerfully built "Moose" Skowron was an intimidating slugger, and similar qualities were exhibited to a lesser degree by "Moose" Ortenzio, "Moose" Werden, and "Moose" Grimshaw. "The Bull" Isaks may also have suggested these traits, but pitcher Lou "Bull" Durham saw his nickname on tobacco signboards in every ballpark in the league. The fowl family included "Ducky" Swann, "Chick" Brandom, "Chick" Fullis, and "Chick" Robertaille. Other species were represented in the nickname menagerie by strapping "Hippo" Vaughn, "Bunny" Brief, "Flea" Clifton, "Skeeter" Webb, Harry "The Cat" Brecheen, "Bird Dog" Hopper, "Sea Lion" Hall, "Ox" Eckhardt, and "Hoggy" Hogriever.

Regional origins provided sobriquets for Mississippian "Dixie" Davis, Georgian "Dixie" Walker, and North Carolinian "Reb" Russell. "Cowboy" Milstead and "Cactus" Johnson both hailed from Texas. Clyde "Pea Ridge" Day was a champion hog caller from Pea Ridge, Arkansas. Charles Dillon Stengel was a standout high school athlete in Kansas City, and as a professional baseball player from KC he became known as "Casey." Adding an international flavor were "Frenchy" Bordagaray, "Frenchy" Uhalt, Dave "Filipino" Altizer, "Jap" Barbeau, "Chink" Yingling,

"Big Finn" Fiene, "Dutch" Henry, "Dutch" Krieger, "Dutch" Zwilling, and "Heinie" Berger. A nautical touch was suggested by "Battleship" Gremminger, "Steamboat" Williams, "Steamboat" Ritter, and "Admiral" Jones, but "Sea Cap" Christensen was a St. Paul center fielder who frequently clowned by turning his Saints' cap sideways.

Personality traits named "Happy" Felsch, "Happy" McKain, "Pep" Clark, "Hi" West, "Gabby" Street, "Dummy" Kihm, and "Noisy" Flick. "Good Time" Lamar, "Bubbles" Hargrave, "Topsy" Hartsel, and Ted "Cork" Wilks could organize postgame celebrations. When young players, sometimes with a trace of the home farm still in evidence, arrived at the ballpark, they were called "Babe" Ganzel, "Babe" Barna, "Rube" Waddell, "Rube" Walberg, "Rube" Ellis, "Rube" Peters, "Country" Slaughter, "Schoolboy" Knight, and "Boy Wonder" Patterson. At the age of 20, Ted "The Kid" Williams won the American Association Triple Crown. Mature, confident pros earned such sobriquets as Art "The Great" Shires, "Ace" Winkles, and "Champ" Summers. A connection with officialdom was suggested by "Sheriff" Van Atta, "Sheriff" Gassaway, "Chief" York, "Chief" Eaves, and "Father" Marshall, but the highly competitive "Preacher" Roe was not noted for Christian charity while on the mound.

During a bench-clearing brawl, desirable teammates might include "Spike" Shannon, "Pug" Cavet, "Mutt" Williams, "Mutt" Riddle, "Rowdy" Bartell, "Rip" Schroeder, and "Dynamite" Dunn. Players who threw spitters or curves or who executed hook slides were assigned descriptive labels: "Spitball" Stricklett, "Hooks" Dauss, "Hooks" Iott, and "Hooks" Cotter. Hurlers Jake "Jerky" Northrup, "Jittery Joe" Berry, and "Shifty" Shifflet confused batters with herky-jerky deliveries. Chico Genovese was an award-winning center fielder, but his fielding percentage was increased by his refusal to attempt shoestring catches, and other players scornfully called him "One-Hop" Genovese.

Lefthanded hurler Irving Melrose Young was nine years younger than baseball's winningest pitcher, he was considerably smaller and threw from the opposite side, but he was frequently called "Cy the Second" and "Young Cy." In the early years of the century the popularity of fictional detective Nick Carter meant that a great many AA ballplayers named Carter were nicknamed "Nick." Harry Malmberg, "The Thin Man," received his sobriquet from a popular film sleuth. Pitcher Roy Parmalee sported a muscular physique and was called "Tarzan," and venerable reliever Art Fowler often was designated "King Arthur." Other famous nicknames included Vernon "George" Washington, "King" Cole, "Humpty Dumpty" Nixon, and Bob "Hurricane" Hazel. Students of nomenclature will find the American Association a rich source of nicknames.

The Ballparks

Baseball stadiums are the only athletic facilities called "parks." *The* national pastime is still that, a pastime, which intersperses moments of brilliant individual plays with time to relax and contemplate player shifts on the field, anticipated developments such as a tiring pitcher or a sacrifice bunt, and similar nuances of the game. The leisurely pace of baseball is in direct contrast to the fanatical violence of football and the frenetic pace of basketball. A major part of the seductive attraction of baseball is following the home team through a long season, becoming familiar with each player, enjoying the camaraderie of fellow fans — all at a friendly park which becomes a home away from home during six months of scheduled play.

When the American Association opened play in 1902, each of the charter cities enjoyed solid baseball traditions that had existed for decades. The playing facilities that had evolved featured covered wooden grandstands, unpainted bleachers, and plank fences encircling the outfield. These baseball parks were located near the downtown areas or at neighborhood sites serviced by trolley lines. Then as now, outfield fences were decorated with advertising, and at virtually every professional ballpark during the early 1900s the American Tobacco Company — manufacturers of Bull Durham

Louisville's Eclipse Park, like most professional stadiums early in the century, had a Bull Durham sign on an outfield fence. Manager Jack Hayden is showing the Colonels how to hit (Hayden was the 1908 AA batting champ).

— Courtesy Louisville Redbirds

Bosse Field, home of AA baseball from 1970 through 1984, was built in 1915.

— Photo by the author

Tobacco — erected a sign promising that any player who hit a ball against the sign would receive $25.

When Columbus' Recreation Park was built in 1887, construction included baseball's first concession stand, and the national anthem would first be played on a regular basis prior to Senators' games. In 1905 the Columbus Senators moved into baseball's first concrete-and-steel stadium. The double-decked grandstand at Neil Park seated 6,000, while wooden bleachers accommodated another 5,000 spectators. A second concrete, double-decked ballpark, Swayne Field in Toledo, opened to American Association play in 1909, the same year that Pittsburgh's Forbes Field became the first concrete structure in the big leagues.

A great deal of the charm of old ballparks was due to irregular and quaint features unique to each facility. For years a distinctive feature at Milwaukee's ramshackle, angular Athletic Park was a bar located behind home plate, which provided two rows of seats for patrons. Because not a single grandstand bench (there were no chair seats) offered a clear view of the entire playing field, the bar perches were regarded as the best seats in the house — until Prohibition shut down the home-plate watering hole. Owner Otto Borchert converted an outfield dressing room into a chicken coop for his prized White Rocks. A pet goat grazed the playing field during daylight hours, then was placed atop the grandstand roof for the night. But sportswriters complained that the resulting stench inside the pressbox was unbearable, and Milwaukee lost its team mascot. (In the late 1800s a center field stable in Columbus' Recreation Park housed the team *horse.*)

After Otto Borchert died of a heart attack in 1927, Athletic Park was renamed Borchert Field. On Thursday, June 15, 1944, the "Borchert Orchard" was the scene of a frightening storm. At 10:10 P.M., during the seventh inning of a 5–5 game with the Columbus Red Birds, a severe thundersquall suddenly struck Milwaukee with drenching rain and winds clocked at 56 miles an hour. The light standards whipped in the wind, then the field went dark as a 100-foot section of the grandstand roof near first base was ripped off. Part of the outfield fence was blown down, many autos parked on North 7th were damaged, and flying debris slammed into nearby houses. Although there was a panicky surge for the exits, someone turned on the grandstand lights and most members of the crowd of 5,100 remained calm. No players were hurt, but 30

Omaha's Johnny Rosenblatt Stadium is more than four decades old, but the home of the NCAA World Series has been beautifully expanded and renovated.

— Photo by the author

At Des Moines the PA announcer has his own little booth atop the grandstand roof.

— Photo by the author

fans were injured, some seriously, and police ambulances soon arrived to transport the worst cases to the hospital.

In 1951 a wind storm destroyed a large portion of the right-field fence at Lexington Park in St. Paul. Lexington Park was badly damaged by fire in 1906, and again in 1914. Fire claimed Louisville's ramshackle Eclipse Park after the 1922 season, but concrete Parkway Field opened the next year. Left field was close enough at Parkway to require a tall fence extension reminiscent of Fenway Park's "Green Monster." A "Red Monster" went up in right field in Wichita's Lawrence-Dumont Stadium in 1982. A second deck for advertising had been added above and four feet behind the original 10-foot outfield fence (line drives which hit the deck and bounced back onto the field were in play, but flies which dropped into the four-foot gap were ruled home runs). A local real estate firm then commissioned the Red Monster — a red sign attached to the scoreboard, 32 feet high and 33 feet wide.

Right field at Nicollet Park was so close that Minneapolis produced a succession of home run championships. Across the river in St. Paul, however, right field at Lexington Park was 365 feet down the line, and a 10-foot incline led to a 30-foot-high fence — which made homers to the right rare achievements. Even more impossible was right field in Kansas City's Meuhlebach Field, 450 feet from home plate with a 60-foot high wall. Lefthanded sluggers hit doubles — or long outs — at Meuhlebach. Toledo's Mud Hens were transferred to Cleveland for the 1914 and 1915 seasons, and AA hitters had to cope with a 375-foot, left-field foul line, a center field that was 420 feet from home plate — and an inviting right-field porch that loomed just 290 feet away, with a 40-foot-high wall.

Lighting systems began to be installed in minor league stadiums in 1930, and on June 9 six steel light standards around old Washington Park in Indianapolis illuminated the American Association's first night game. The last AA city to adopt the innovations was Minneapolis, in 1937. Night ball boosted attendance and saved franchises during the Depression, but no longer would it be possible to savor the delicious feeling of playing hooky that comes from attending a ballgame during a workday afternoon. Another innovation occurred during spring training of 1912, when cold weather forced the Indians to play a St. Patrick's Day exhibition game *inside* the State Fair Coliseum. Sixty-five years later the New Orleans

Right field at Louisville's Cardinal Stadium is just 312 feet down the line, necessitating the latest of a number of tall outfield extensions in AA ballparks.

— Photo by the author

Nostalgic Victory Field was built in Indianapolis in 1931, and was used as the celluloid home of the 1919 Black Sox in Eight Men Out.

— Photo by the author

War Memorial Stadium, built in Buffalo in 1936, was the film home of Robert Redford and the "New York Knights" in The Natural.

— Photo by the author

Pelicans hosted their AA opponents inside the Louisiana Super Dome.

Historical architecture is one of our most tangible links with the past. For Western history buffs, there is no keener pleasure than walking the streets of Tombstone or prowling around the abandoned structures of a deserted mining town or cavalry fort. An interstate highway has eliminated any trace of Milwaukee's Borchert Field; plaques are all that identify the rival stadiums of Minnesota's Twin Cities, Nicollet Park and Lexington Park; Toledo's Swayne Field has been razed and so has KC's Meuhlebach Field and a number of other grand old ballparks which once hosted American Association players and fans of decades past. But baseball buffs can travel to Evansville, where brick Bosse Field dates back to 1915, or to Indianapolis, where a night at Victory Field will link a nostalgic visitor with athletes and fans of six decades ago. Opened in 1931 as Perry Field, the Indians' classic ballpark is beautifully maintained, but so evocative of the past that it served quite convincingly as the celluloid home of the 1919 Black Sox in *Eight Men Out*. Also used effectively as a movie backdrop, for the Depression-era "New York Knights" of *The Natural,* was Buffalo's

War Memorial Stadium, which dates back to 1936 and which today stands vacant but presided over by a caretaker. Lawrence-Dumont Stadium in Wichita was opened in 1934, and baseball was first played in Columbus' Red Bird Stadium in 1932.

The Columbus facility offers a direct connection between baseball's past and present. Red Bird Stadium witnessed the feats of American Association ballplayers of the 1930s and 1940s, but in recent years it has undergone expansion and a multimillion-dollar renovation. Renamed for the Red Birds' clubhouse boy of 1935 who eventually organized the Triple-A Alliance, Cooper Stadium today boasts luxurious skyboxes and a dazzling concourse reminiscent of Buffalo's magnificent Pilot Field and other streamlined modern stadiums.

American Association Cities

Buffalo (Bisons)

Buffalo's first organized baseball club was the Niagaras, a quality amateur team which opened play in 1857 against other local nines and squads from neighboring communities. An independent team of professionals, the Buffalo Buffalos staggered through a 40-game schedule in 1877 (there were only 10 victories). The next year the Buffalo Bisons joined baseball's first minor league, the International Association, then moved up to the National League in 1879 and played major league ball for the next seven seasons.

In 1886 Buffalo began its long association with the International League, then called the Eastern League. There were several other name changes during the next 35 years, but the Bisons played continually — except for 1899 and 1900 — in the IL from 1886 through 1970. Buffalo also fielded a last-place team in the Players' League; the Buffalo catcher was Connie Mack, but the player-run circuit operated only in 1890. The Bisons won their first IL pennant in 1891, and manager George Stallings guided Buffalo to flags in 1904 and 1906. Other IL championships followed in 1915 and 1916, 1927, 1936, 1949 under Paul Richards, and 1959 under Kerby Farrell.

Buffalo tried the Western League in 1899 and 1900, and the Buf-Feds played in the upstart Federal League in 1914 and 1915. However, the city's primary baseball involvement for nearly a century was with the International League. In 1910 righthander Chet Carmichael pitched the first perfect game in IL history; the only other nine-inning perfect game in the International League also was twirled by a Buffalo hurler, Dick Marlowe, in 1952. In 1925 and 1926, left fielder Jimmy Walsh won back-to-back batting titles (.357 and .388) at the ages of 39 and 40, while first baseman Billy Kelly was the RBI leader (.318, 26 HR, 125 RBI, and .330, 44 HR — also tops in the league — and 151 RBI). On May 15, 1934, during a game with Albany, the Bisons hit five homers in one inning. From 1931 through 1941, Ollie Carnegie, who turned to pro ball at 31 after losing his job during the Depression, was a popular and hard-hitting outfielder. At 39, in 1938, he led the league in homers and RBIs (.330, 45 HR, 136 RBI), repeated in both categories the next year, and returned to Buffalo in 1945, hitting .301 in 39 games before retiring at 46. Another venerable and highly popular slugger, massive first baseman Luke Easter, won consecutive home run and RBI crowns when he was 41 and 42 in 1956 and 1957.

From 1889 through 1960, these and many other Bison heroes played at a diamond located on Michigan Avenue at East Ferry Street. The ballpark was called Olympic Park (1889–1907) and Buffalo Baseball Park (1908–1923), rebuilt as Bison Stadium (1924–1934), and renamed Offermann Stadium (1935–1960). Earlier the Bisons played at Riverside Park (1879–1883) and at the first Olympic Park (1884–1888). After Offermann Stadium was razed to be replaced by a school building, the Bisons moved into War Memorial Stadium. Built by the WPA in 1936–1937 as a football facility, "The Old Rockpile" had to be converted for use by professional baseball, and in 1983 it was used in the filming of Robert Redford's classic baseball movie, *The Natural.*

War Memorial Stadium was located in a deteriorating neighborhood which had become racist and threatening by the late 1960s. By 1970, attendance and the financial situation of the Bisons was so weak that the IL franchise was transferred to Winnipeg. Buffalo was without professional baseball for eight seasons, when a Class AA franchise was acquired in the Eastern League. The Bisons played in the Eastern League from 1979 through 1984, being purchased in 1983 by Rich Products Corporation, an immense frozen food company.

Robert E. Rich, Jr., president of Rich Products (and now of the Buffalo Bisons), approached baseball with resourcefulness and ambitions of a return to the major leagues. In his first year Rich almost tripled attendance at The Old Rockpile (77,077 in 1982 to 200,531 in 1983), and after an even more successful year in 1984

(223,443) he paid $1 million to purchase the Wichita franchise in the American Association.

In 1985 Buffalo fans welcomed the return of Triple-A ball with another surge of attendance (362,762). The Bisons' pitching staff finished dead last in ERA, but righthander Bill Long led the league in victories (13–6), while southpaw reliever Jerry Don Gleaton was the percentage leader (8–2 with a 2.44 ERA). The best hitters were infielders Steve Christmas (.298) and Joey DaSa (.287). On April 18 in Indianapolis, Buffalo exploded for a 15–9 victory in 10 innings. The Bisons hammered out 26 hits and the Indians added 19 more for a new AA record of 45 base hits in a single game.

The next season Buffalo's attendance improved again (425,113). For the second year in a row, first baseman Joey DaSa (.281, 17 HR, 83 RBI) was named to the All-Star team, and for the second year in a row a Buffalo pitcher led the AA in victories: left-hander Pete Filson (14–3), who also won the ERA title (2.27) while being voted the league's Pitcher of the Year. Outfielder Daryl Boston (.303 with 38 steals) had the team's top batting average, and the inviting right-field fence of War Memorial Stadium helped the Bisons lead the AA in home runs (129).

In 1987 slugging outfielder David Clark (.340 with 30 HR and 80 RBI in just 108 games) was the club's best hitter, and paid admissions reached nearly half a million. But Bob Rich wanted much more. Relentlessly pursuing a big league franchise, he assembled a long-range staff that eventually numbered 40, and by this time a splendid stadium was under construction a block from Buffalo's revitalized downtown area. Pilot Field would be ready by the 1988 opener, a 19,500-seat stadium which could be expanded to 40,000 within a matter of months. Built at a cost of $42 million, Pilot Field (Pilot Air Freight purchased the naming rights to the stadium) is comfortable and handsome, with a 50′x80′ state-of-the-art electronic scoreboard and two parking garages, which brought the package to $56.4 million. On a big night, 550 employees work at Pilot Field.

"We're going to put numbers on the board baseball just can't ignore," promised Rich. On opening day of 1988, Pilot Field welcomed the first of 22 sellout crowds as the Bisons downed Denver, 1–0. By June 15 the Bisons had roared past the half-million mark in attendance, and on July 13 the first annual Triple-A Alliance All-Star Game was conducted at Pilot Field. Buffalo became the second

Buffalo's Pilot Field, opened in 1988, is a streamlined, state-of-the-art downtown stadium.

— Photo by the author

minor league team ever to achieve The Million, establishing a new season attendance record (1,186,651). Righthander Dave Johnson (15–12) led the league in victories, while fellow righty Dorn Taylor (10–8, 2.14 ERA) won the ERA title.

The next year was even better as Buffalo posted the second-best record in the league. There was another strong pitching staff, led by Dorn Taylor (10–8, 2.58 ERA) and southpaws Bob Patterson (12–6) and Morris Madden (12–8). The offense was led by outfielders Albert Hall (.304 with 31 steals) and Steve Carter (.295), shortstop Jay Bell (.285), and All-Star DH Steve Henderson (.298). Again the Bisons set a new attendance mark, becoming the only minor league club to reach The Million (1,116,441) twice. Although Buffalo has high hopes of attracting big league baseball, the Bisons have helped the AA to achieve the highest attendance ever totaled by a minor league — over 3.6 million in 1988 and again in 1989.

"The dream that everyone in baseball shares is getting to the majors," explained Rich. "It's the thing that everyone shares, including the shortstop in Appleton, Wisconsin, and every city with a minor league team. Well, how does that shortstop get there? He does it by putting up the numbers. We decided to put up the numbers."

Year	Record	Pcg.	Finish
1985	66-76	.465	Seventh
1986	71-71	.500	Sixth
1987	66-74	.471	Fifth
1988	72-70	.507	Sixth
1989	80-62	.563	Second
1990	85-62	.578	Third
1991	81-62	.566	First (won Eastern Division, lost finals)

Charleston (Senators)

The state capital of West Virginia first fielded a professional team in the Class D Virginia Valley League in 1910. The next two years were spent in the Class D Mountain States League, and from 1913 through 1916 Charleston played in another Class D outfit, the Ohio State League. In 1931, when the Middle Atlantic League expanded to 12 teams — becoming the largest minor league up to that time — Charleston joined the Class C circuit. Charleston played in the Middle Atlantic until play was halted after the 1942 season, winning pennants in 1932 and 1942, and starring batting champ Barney McCoskey (.400) in 1936.

Following World War II, Charleston participated in the Class A Central League until the circuit, like so many other minor leagues, folded following the 1951 season. There was no pro ball in Charleston in 1951 — until the last-place Toledo Mud Hens collapsed in the face of hapless play and anemic attendance. On June 23, in the first (and only) mid-season franchise transfer in American Association history, the Toledo Mud Hens became the Charleston Senators.

The change of locale did not change the dismal performance (46–107) nor the pitiful attendance (just 41,407 for the entire season). Outfielders Babe Barna (.287 with 14 homers) and Lomax Davis (.319 in 77 games) were the only bright spots on the roster. Improvement was glacial, as the Senators finished in last place their first four years in the league, ranking last in team batting during their first five AA seasons and in fielding three of the first four years.

But in 1953, the Senators' first full AA season, attendance soared to 178,377 — more than double Charleston's population (although the metropolitan area totaled about 250,000). Crowds enjoyed the work of righthander Bill Powell (14–9), stolen base champ Don Nicholas (.263 with 41 steals), and outfielder Bob Boyd (.323 in 49 games), before he was promoted to the White Sox. In 1955 fans were entertained by legendary slugger Luke Easter, who played his only full season in the AA for Charleston (.283, 30 HR, 102 RBI). The massive (6′4½, 240 pounds), outgoing first baseman was 40, however, and he was sold to Buffalo for $7,500 — then led the International League in homers and RBIs for the next two years.

The Senators finally escaped the cellar in 1956, rising to sixth place behind infielders Harry Malmberg (.293) and Reno Bertoia (.289 with 12 homers), southpaw Hal Woodeschick (12–5), and fireballing righthander Jim Bunning (9–11 with 144 Ks in 163 IP). Charleston sagged into seventh place the next year. Indeed, in nine seasons in the AA, Charleston had eight losing teams, none of which rose above sixth place.

But the one winning Senators club exploded all the way to the pennant, taking first place in 1958 by a margin of seven and a half games. Righthander Jerry Davie led the league in ERA, winning percentage and shutouts (17–5 with a 2.45 ERA, six shutouts, and 18 CG in 26 starts). Don Lee also was a dependable starter (14–7, 2.95 ERA, and 18 CG in 30 starts), and George Spencer was excellent in relief (9–4 with a 2.01 ERA in 41 appearances). Brilliant in brief stints before being called up to the parent Detroit Tigers were righthanders Al Cicotte (5–1 in six starts) and Herb Moford (6–0 with a 0.95 ERA), who completed all three starts with two shutouts. Offensive leaders were first baseman Larry Osborne (.297, 19 HR, 97 RBI), shortstop Ron Samford (.301), stolen base champ Wayne Terwilliger (.269 with 24 steals), and outfielders Bill Taylor (.298 with 12 homers), Jim Delsing (.287 with 12 homers), and Stan Palys (.288).

Manager Bill Norman, who took over the Senators in July 1957, was promoted to the midseason managerial vacancy in Detroit. Bill Adair then stepped in at Charleston on June 10, 1958, and finished the successful pennant run. In the playoff opener Charleston faced fourth-place Denver and after five games led, three games to two. But the Bears had the best offense in the

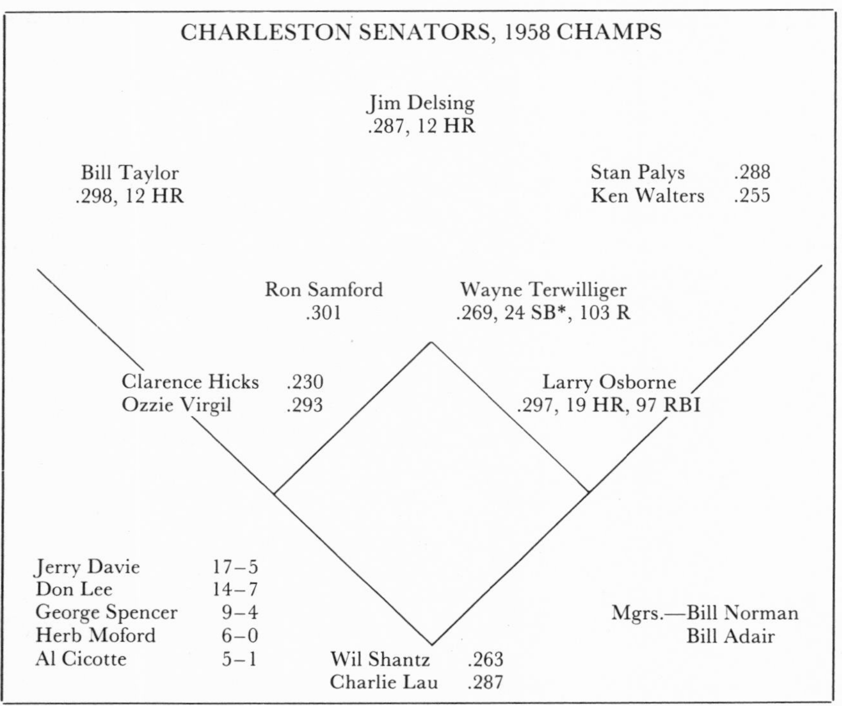

league, and the final two contests were in Denver. Charleston was beaten in both games and eliminated from the playoffs, but season attendance (162,914) was second only to Denver, and the Senators could proudly fly the American Association pennant.

In 1959 the AA expanded to 10 teams and split into two divisions. Bill Adair returned, and so did (for part of the season) Bill Taylor (.286 in 73 games), Clarence Hicks (.264 in 72 games), Stan Palys (.282 in 49 games), and Jerry Davie (4–8 in 14 games). Don Lee came back to become the most reliable starter (14–9), George Spencer returned to set a record for relief appearances (11–7 in 85 games), and righthander Bob Bruce (11–13 with four shutouts and 177 Ks in 222 IP) led the league in strikeouts. But the championship combination had been broken up, and the Senators dropped to the bottom of the Eastern Division.

The next season the AA returned to eight teams, and Charleston, now managed by former big league catcher Del Wilber, finished sixth. The team's best hitters were second baseman John

Schaive (.314) and first sacker Don Mincher (.306), who was called up to the Washington Senators and began a 13-year big league career. Season attendance dipped below 100,000 (95,976) for the only time in Charleston's AA tenure.

Charleston pulled out of baseball after the 1960 season but quickly returned to Class AAA baseball. The Miami Marlins of the International League had moved to San Juan for 1961, but the Puerto Rican city could not support the club, which finished the season in Charleston. Charleston was willing to keep the nickname — there certainly were no seas thriving with marlins near the city, but it was pointed out that the West Virginian mountains were crawling with men who carried Marlin rifles! In 1962 Charleston moved into the Class AA Eastern League for three seasons, winning the pennant in 1963. But the city's economy suffered severely during the 1960s, and as the population dropped from 86,000 to 71,000, Charleston gave up professional baseball. In 1971, however, Charleston re-entered the International League, playing for 13 seasons and finishing first in 1973 and 1978. In recent years the Charleston Wheelers have competed in the Class A Sally League.

Year	Record	Pcg.	Finish
1952	46-107	.301	Eighth
1953	60-94	.390	Eighth
1954	59-94	.386	Eighth
1955	50-104	.325	Eighth
1956	74-79	.484	Sixth
1957	67-87	.435	Seventh
1958	89-62	.589	First (lost playoff opener)
1959	77-84	.478	Seventh
1960	65-88	.425	Sixth

Cleveland

Cleveland coal magnate Charles W. Somers was a baseball enthusiast who became a key financial supporter of the early American League. Somers owned not only the Cleveland Naps of the AL but a number of minor league clubs, including the Toledo Mud Hens. Cleveland and Toledo are located on the south shore of Lake Erie, just a two-hour train ride apart, and for years Somers regularly shuttled players back and forth between the American League and the American Association (in the same way that today's marginal big leaguers bounce back and forth from Triple A to The Show three or four times per season).

When the Federal League challenged the American and National leagues in 1914, teams were placed in Chicago, Brooklyn, Pittsburgh, and St. Louis to offer direct competition to existing big league clubs. A similar "outlaw" circuit, the United States League, had attempted to operate in 1912. Although the USL collapsed in June, there had been a rival club in Cleveland, and Somers did not want such competition again. In Cleveland the only stadium suitable for major league play was League Park, built in 1891 at Lexington Avenue and East 66th Street. In 1910 Somers completed a major renovation of League Park, replacing the wooden grandstand with a concrete double-decked facility. Plank outfield fences also gave way to concrete construction, and in right field, where the foul line was only 290 feet from home plate, a tall screen made the fence 40 feet high all the way to center. Somers decided to provide daily baseball at his magnificent stadium, thereby monopolizing League Park and leaving a potential Federal League competitor with no place to play in Cleveland.

For 1914 Somers transferred his Toledo club to Cleveland. Local baseball fans could enjoy American League teams or American Association play on almost any given day. Of course, fans accustomed to big leaguers probably would not be attracted in large numbers to minor league ball, but at least the Federal League stayed out of Cleveland during the two years of its existence.

The 1914 American Association club was managed by 35-year-old outfielder Jimmy Sheckard, who had just finished a 17-year National League career; he hit under .200 with two NL teams in 1913 and could bat only .253 against AA pitching in 1914. The team's best average was recorded by first baseman-outfielder Jay Kirke, who hit well for Toledo in 1913 (.320), then split 1914 between Cleveland's AA team (.349 in 74 games) and the Naps (.273 in 87 games). Outfielder Dennis Wilie was a mainstay of the AA club (.316, 30 SB), and so was shortstop John Wesley "Schoolboy" Knight (.308), an eight-year American League veteran. Ray Bates was at third half of the season (.290), Earl Gardner was the second baseman (.287), and Bill Stumpf played second, third, and short as needed (.287 in 132 games); all were big league veterans.

The steadiest pitchers were John Scheneberg (16–10), Krum

Kahler (15–11), Buck Brenton (14–11), Lefty George (13–18), and Sad Sam Jones (10–4). Kahler pitched in a couple of games for the Naps, and Jones made the first appearance of a big league career that would last for 22 seasons. Lefty James split the season between the AA club (9–6 in 19 games) and the Naps (0–3 in 11 games), and so did Al Collamore (3–7 in 21 games for the Naps, and 5–4 in 9 AA games), rookie outfielder Elmer Smith (.333 in 13 AA games, and .311 in 23 AL games), and Jack Lelivelt (.295 in 92 games as a Naps first baseman, and .328 in 32 games as a minor league outfielder). The Naps had solid pitching and several good hitters, and finished a game above .500 (82–81) in fifth place.

The next year Schoolboy Knight was promoted to manager, and he continued to play shortstop in 1915 (.282). The second baseman again was Earl Gardner (.301), Al Nixon (.293) was an outfield fixture, and Lefty James (19–13) was the team's leading pitcher. Almost everyone else on the roster bounced back and forth between both Cleveland clubs. Jay Kirke again played well on both teams (.286 in 68 AA games, .310 in 87 AL games), but outfielder Dennis Wilie fared better in the AA (.311 in 93 games) than with the Naps (.252 in 45 games). Third baseman Joe Evans hit as well against big league pitching (.257 in 42 games) as he did against minor leaguers (.259 in 55 games), but outfielder James Eschen (.275 in 48 games) and Roy Wood (.288 in 89 games as an outfielder) performed better in the AA than in the AL (.239 in 15 games for Eschen, and .193 in 33 games for Wood as a first sacker). Most of the pitchers — such as Buck Brenton (11–11 in 28 AA games, 2–3 in 11 AL games) and Nick Carter (13–14 in 33 AA games, 1–2 in 12 AL games) — also saw duty with both Cleveland teams during the season.

Despite the presence of many current and former big leaguers on the roster, Cleveland's AA team sagged to seventh place in 1915. But the Federal League disbanded in December 1914, and Somers decided there was no further need to play minor league ball in Cleveland. After an absence of two years, the Mud Hens returned to Toledo.

Year	Record	Pcg.	Finish
1914	82-81	.503	Fifth
1915	67-82	.450	Seventh

Columbus (Senators, Red Birds)

Professional baseball in Columbus dates back to 1876, when a club of pros called the Buckeyes took on all comers. The next year the Columbus Buckeyes became charter members of the first minor league, the International Association of Baseball. When the old American Association added two teams during its second season of play, the 1888 Buckeyes brought major league ball to Columbus. (Buckeye pitcher Eddie "Dummy" Herndon, a deaf-mute, could not hear umpires' calls, and the arbiters developed a set of hand signals which proved so popular with fans that they solidified as the ball-strike and out-safe signals that are in use today.) Columbus pulled out of the American Association after two seasons, joined the Ohio State League in 1887, then became the Columbus Senators of the Tri-State League the next year.

In 1889 Columbus rejoined the American Association, dropping out after the 1891 season when the AA and the National League merged as a 12-team circuit. The Columbus Reds joined the Western League for its inaugural season of 1892, while the Columbus Statesmen entered the Inter-State League in 1895. Through 1901, reassuming the Senators' nickname, Columbus alternated between the Western and the Inter-State leagues.

When the new American Association opened play in 1902, the Columbus Senators held one of eight charter franchises. The Senators were second-division teams in 1902 and 1903, while "Derby Day" Bill Clymer was leading Louisville to consecutive second-place finishes. Clymer was hired as player-manager of the Senators in 1904, and promptly he guided the club into second place. It was just the beginning: Clymer was building a dynasty which would reel off three straight AA pennants.

The title clubs seemingly were inspired to championship play by moving into baseball's first concrete-and-steel stadium. The original Columbus Buckeyes played at a diamond laid out on a grassy lot located between the old Union Depot and North High Street. In 1883 wooden Recreation Park opened at a site bounded by Meadow Lane (later Monroe Street), Parsons Avenue, and Mound Street (roughly where Interstates 70 and 71 intersect today). The outfield fences were so deep that no ball ever was hit out of the park, and a small structure in far center field housed the club *horse.* A second Recreation Park went up in 1887 at a location closer to the heart of town between Kossuth, Jaeger (later Fifth), East Schiller (later East Whittier), and Ebner streets. The new Recreation Park boasted baseball's first concession stand, and outfield distances again were vast — 400 feet down the foul lines.

After the Western League disbanded in 1892, the ballpark site was sold to land developers, and the grandstand and fences were dismantled and peddled for lumber. When Columbus returned to professional baseball in 1895, games were played on a crude field at Spruce and High streets. By the next season Central Athletic Park had been erected at Jenkins and Moler avenues. The wooden stadium featured a center-field clubhouse with a shower (visiting teams, of course, had no facilities and had to return to the hotel for bathing). In 1900 the Senators leased from Robert Neil a location nearer to town, and 2,000-seat Neil Park quickly went up on Cleveland Avenue just west of Columbus Barracks and south of the Franklin Brewery.

After the second-place finish of 1904, business manager Bobby Quinn reported a profit of $10,000 and suggested that wooden Neil Park be substantially renovated. The owners purchased the site from Robert Neil for $41,000, then spent $23,000 on baseball's first concrete-and-steel stadium (Pittsburgh's Forbes Field would become the first concrete structure in the big leagues in 1909). The concrete grandstand at new Neil Park was double-decked and seated 6,000, and lumber from the old grandstand went into bleachers which could accommodate another 5,000 fans.

The financial gamble paid off immediately as the Senators reeled off three consecutive championships. Although Columbus, with a population of 125,000, was the smallest city in the American Association, the Senators led the league in attendance for the next eight years. In 1905 Columbus boasted the highest attendance of any minor league club, and posted larger numbers than five major league franchises. On September 1, 1907, a record overflow crowd of 20,531 fans jammed into the Senators' state-of-the-art stadium, and season attendance soared to 316,980.

Bill Clymer's dynastic teams of 1905, 1906, and 1907 featured superb pitching and defense. The Senators led the American Association in fielding in 1905 and 1906, and missed by a single percentage point in 1907. Gus Dorner led the American Association in victories in 1905 (29–8), Charles Berger (25–14 in 1905) was the league leader in 1906 (28–13), and southpaw George Upp paced the AA in 1907 (27–10). Senator mainstays during each of the pennant seasons were shortstop Rudy Hulswitt, second baseman Zeke Wrigley, and first sacker Dummy Kihm. Outfielders Ollie Pickering (.326 in 1905, .317 in 1906), Bill Hinchman (.314 in 1906), Bunk Congalton (.314 in 1905), and Doc Gessler (.325 in 1907) made outstanding contributions in one or another of the title years. Several of the Senators had big league experience, while Pickering, Berger, Dorner, Upp, Hulswitt, Hinchman, Gessler, outfielders Lefty Davis, Frank Jude and Midget Reilly, third baseman Jap Barbeau, and lefthander Patsy Flaherty (23–9 in 1906) went up to the majors after success in Columbus. When Clymer finally left Columbus at the end of 1909, he was succeeded as manager by Bill Friel (1911–12), third baseman on the 1906 and 1908 teams, then Bill Hinchman (1913–14) and Rudy Hulswitt (1915–16), from the championship teams.

In 1914 player-manager Hinchman was Columbus' first AA batting champ (.366), and led the league in hits (227) and runs scored (139). It was more than a decade before Eddie Murphy (.397 in 1925) brought another hitting title to Columbus. But the next year, in 1926, Columbus set all-time AA records for most losses (39–125) and runs allowed (1,299). Indeed, the Senators were mired in last place for three years in a row (1925, 1926, and 1927), and a pennant drouth lasted more than a quarter of a century.

But in 1931 the St. Louis Cardinals acquired control of Columbus as a key member of their vast and successful farm system. The team nickname was changed to Red Birds, and it was decided to construct a new stadium on West Mound Street. The brick outfield fence was far from home plate; left field was 457 feet away; and only Joe DiMaggio (in a 1946 exhibition) and Ralph Kiner (1947) ever hit home runs over the fence (eventually a chain-link fence reduced the incredible distances). On June 3, 1932, over 15,000 spectators — including the commissioner of baseball, Judge Kenesaw Mountain Landis, AA President Thomas J. Hickey, and Cardinal general manager Branch Rickey — viewed the inaugural game at Red Bird Stadium. The park was equipped with lights, and two weeks later a crowd of more than 21,000 viewed Columbus' first night game.

By 1933 the Red Birds were stocked with talented Cardinal farm hands. Paul Dean, who had paced the AA in strikeouts in 1932, won a rare pitcher's Triple Crown in 1933 (22–7, 222 Ks, 3.15 ERA). Bill Lee (21–9) and Lefty Heise (17–5) also turned in excellent performances in 1933, and Jim Lindsey (7–2) was almost invincible before an early-season promotion to the Cards. The offense was equally formidable: outfielders Nick Cullop (.313, 28 HR, 143 RBI), and John Rothrock (.347); second basemen Burgess Whitehead (.346) and Charles Wilson (.356); third sackers Bernard Borgmann (.340) and Gordon Slade (.353); and catchers Bill DeLancey (.285, 21 HR, 97 RBI) and Miguel Gonzalez (.324). The Red Birds roared to the pennant (101–51) with a 15½-game margin, then won the American Association's first postseason playoff series before defeating Buffalo of the International League for the Junior World Series crown.

Many of the championship players went to St. Louis and the famous Gas House Gang of 1934. But manager Ray Blades somehow molded another winner. Nick Cullop returned (.303, 27 HR, 130 RBI), while rookie center fielder Terry Moore was a sensation (.328), and second baseman Charles Wilson (.325) and shortstop William Myers (.313) added offensive punch from the infield. A late-season surge vaulted the Red Birds into second place and established momentum for the postseason. Blades engineered another playoff triumph, then downed Toronto in the ninth game of the Junior World Series.

In 1936 Burt Shotton replaced Ray Blades as manager, and a year later guided Columbus to another banner season. The 1937 Red Birds were led by batting champ Enos "Country" Slaughter (.382, with a league-leading 245 hits and 147 runs, along with 26 homers and 122 RBIs — in 1936 the young outfielder had hit .325 with 118 RBIs and a league-leading 20 triples). Outfielders Johnny Rizzo (.358, 21 HR, 123 RBI, and a 36-game hitting streak), and Lynn King (.302 and the first of two consecutive stolen base titles) helped establish a team batting average of .303, and so did pitchers Max Macon (.357) and Max Lanier (.308). Southpaws Macon (21–12) and Lanier (10–4) led the AA in victories and winning percentage respectively, while Bill McGee (17–7) was the ERA champ. At midseason the Red Birds hosted the fourth All-Star

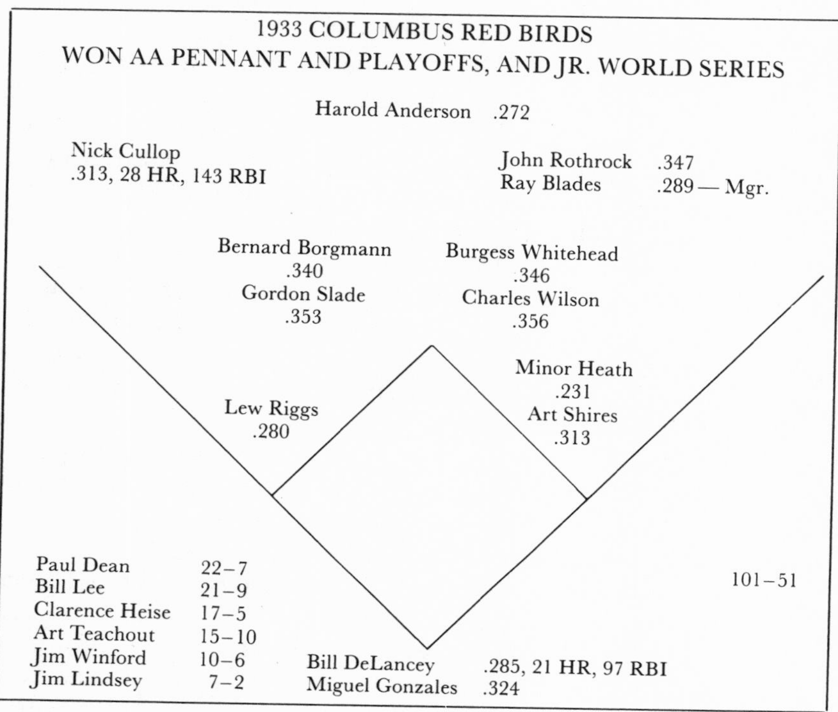

Game and downed the best of the rest of the league, 7–4, before a record crowd of 12,269. The Red Birds won the pennant on the last day of the season, then stormed into the playoffs to gain another postseason triumph.

In the Junior World Series, Shotton's team won the first three games at Newark, and needed to win just one of four games at Red Bird Stadium. But second baseman and team captain Jimmy Jordan (.285) broke a leg in a collision at second, and both catchers suffered injuries which allowed Bear baserunners to steal at will. Newark, one of the best teams in minor league history, won all four games at Columbus, creating the only disappointment in another stellar season for the Red Birds.

Three years later, Shotton produced another playoff club. Stars of the 1940 Red Birds were ERA champ Ernest White (13–4, 2.25), Murry Dickson (17–8), southpaw Harry "The Cat" Brecheen (16–9), catcher Walker Cooper (.302), and outfielders Coaker Triplett (.339), Harry "The Hat" Walker (.313), and Morris Jones (.322). The next season Shotton's club won first place by an eight-game margin. Murry Dickson (21–11) led the AA in victories and strikeouts and frequently was used as a pinch hitter (.341 in 63 games). Johnny Grodzicki (19–5 with a 2.58 ERA) was the ERA champ and percentage leader, and Harry Brecheen (16–6) and Preacher Roe (11–9) added more strength. The Red Birds paced the league in team hitting behind infielders Lou Klein (.367), Robert Repass (.317), Bert Haas (.315), and Ray Sanders (.308). Columbus won the playoff and the 1941 Junior World Series.

The Red Birds finished third in 1942 and 1943, but with customary postseason proficiency reeled off their second and third playoff and Junior World Series triumphs in a row (Columbus made the AA playoffs 10 times, winning seven times and missing another victory by just one game; the Senators had lost the Little World Series in 1906 and 1907, and the 1937 champs also dropped the classic, but the Red Birds beat the International League titlists in 1933, 1934, 1941, 1942, 1943, and 1950.)

Eddie Dyer managed the 1942 Red Birds. Although the team batting average (.254) was next-to-last in the AA, Harry Brecheen (19–10, 2.09 ERA) won the ERA and strikeout titles, and led a championship pitching staff. Former Columbus slugging star Nick Cullop assumed the managerial reins in 1943 and was named Minor League Manager of the Year by *The Sporting News*. Strikeout champ Preacher Roe (15–7) headed another strong mound corps, and an improved offense was sparked by catcher Tommy Heath (.302) and outfielders Chester Wieczorek (.328) and Gus Bergamo (.324).

Preacher Roe brought a fifth consecutive strikeout crown to Columbus in 1943. In five decades of American Association play, Columbus pitchers ran up 13 strikeout titles. Charles Berger won back-to-back titles in 1905 (25–14 with 200 Ks) and 1906 (28–13 with 264 Ks). In 1917 Grover Lowdermilk recorded the first pitcher's Triple Crown in AA history (25–14, 250 K, 1.70 ERA). Dave Danforth took back-to-back strikeout championships in 1920 and 1921 (25–16, 204 K, 2.66 ERA); he was a Triple Crown winner in 1921, but like Lowdermilk in 1917 his victory total was matched by another pitcher. Paul Dean won consecutive strikeout titles in 1932 and 1933, a Triple Crown season. Max Lanier was the strikeout king in 1939, followed by Frank Melton in 1940, Murry Dickson in

Catcher Joe Garagiola helped to bat Columbus to the 1948 playoffs.

— Author's collection

1941, Harry Brecheen in 1942, Preacher Roe in 1943, and, seven years later, Harvey Haddix for the 1950 championship club.

Such pitching exploits were abetted by the vast outfield expanses of Columbus ballparks, a factor which discouraged slugging feats by Senator and Red Bird hitters. In 1931 first baseman Cliff Crawford (.374, 28 HR, 154 RBI) won the home run and RBI titles. These two titles were copped in 1936 by outfielder "Long Tom" Winsett (.354, 50 HR, 154 RBI), who became the last of just three players to blast 50 or more homers — including three in one game — during an American Association season, despite being sold to Brooklyn after 141 games. Lefthanded first baseman Mike Natisin (.305, 30 HR, 132 RBI) won the 1948 homerun crown with more modest numbers.

Natisin's heroics, along with those of catcher Joe Garagiola (.356 in 65 games) and southpaw Harvey Haddix (11–9 and a .337 average, including 13 pinch-hitting appearances) helped to put the 1948 Red Birds into the playoffs. Despite the absence of Natisin, the fourth-place Red Birds made it to the last game of the playoff finals before going down. In 1950 the fireballing Haddix produced a Triple Crown (18–6, 160 K, 2.70 ERA) and led the Red Birds to another playoff title and Junior World Series triumph.

In 1951 veteran hitting star Harry "The Hat" Walker managed the Red Birds. The team sagged to last place, but Walker won the batting crown with a phenomenal performance (.393), then was summoned back to duty on the Cardinals' roster. Attendance plummeted as the Red Birds were mired in seventh place in 1952 (78,132) and 1953 (84,995). Batting champ Hal Smith (.350) led the 1954 Red Birds to fourth place, but the club uncharacteristically lost the first round of playoffs. Attendance improved (110,696) but remained the poorest in the league, and the Cardinals decided to move their American Association franchise to Omaha.

After 53 seasons, Columbus was out of the AA. But eleven local baseball enthusiasts put up $10,000 each to re-establish pro ball in the city. The Ottawa franchise of the International League was purchased for $50,000, while the stadium was bought from the Cardinals for $450,000. Nick Cullop was brought in as field manager, and Harold Cooper (who became clubhouse boy for the Red Birds in 1935 and worked in various capacities for the team until he entered the military in 1942) agreed to serve as general manager, a position he held until 1968. Eventually Cooper became president of the International League, and in 1988 the "Czar" took charge of the new Triple-A Alliance. Following a multimillion-dollar renovation, in 1984 the magnificent Columbus facility was renamed Cooper Stadium.

The Columbus Jets played in the IL for 16 years. In 1956 second sacker Curt Roberts blasted four homers in a seven-inning game against Havana, and the Jets recorded IL pennants in 1961 and 1965. But after the 1970 season, spiraling costs and declining attendance forced Columbus to surrender its franchise. Six years later, Harold Cooper was instrumental in returning IL baseball to his hometown. Franklin County purchased and refurbished the stadium, and George Sisler, Jr., was installed as general manager. Sisler, who announced his retirement following the 1989 season, has placed Columbus' proud baseball heritage on solid footing for the future.

Year	Record	Pcg.	Finish
1902	66-74	.471	Fifth
1903	56-84	.400	Sixth
1904	88-61	.591	Second

Red Bird Stadium opened in Columbus in 1932, but in recent years it has undergone expansion and a multimillion-dollar renovation. Today it is known as Cooper Stadium, renamed for the Red Birds' clubhouse boy of 1935 who eventually organized the Triple-A Alliance.

— Courtesy Columbus Clippers

1905	102-53	.658	First
1906	95-58	.622	First (lost Little World Series)
1907	90-64	.584	First (lost Little World Series)
1908	86-68	.558	Third
1909	80-87	.479	Seventh
1910	88-77	.533	Third
1911	87-78	.527	Third
1912	98-68	.590	Third
1913	93-74	.557	Fourth
1914	86-77	.528	Fourth
1915	54-91	.372	Eighth
1916	71-90	.441	Seventh
1917	84-69	.549	Fourth
1918	41-34	.547	Second
1919	70-84	.455	Sixth
1920	66-99	.400	Seventh
1921	67-96	.411	Eighth
1922	63-102	.382	Eighth
1923	79-89	.470	Fourth
1924	75-92	.448	Seventh
1925	61-106	.365	Eighth

1926	39-125	.238	Eighth
1927	60-108	.357	Eighth
1928	68-100	.405	Seventh
1929	75-91	.452	Sixth
1930	67-86	.438	Sixth
1931	84-82	.506	Fourth
1932	88-77	.533	Second (won playoff and Jr. World Series)
1933	101-51	.664	First (won playoff and Jr. World Series)
1934	85-68	.556	Second
1935	84-70	.545	Fourth
1936	76-78	.494	Sixth
1937	90-64	.584	First (won opener and finals, lost Jr. World Series)
1938	64-89	.418	Seventh
1939	62-92	.403	Seventh
1940	90-60	.600	Second (lost opener)
1941	95-58	.621	First (won opener, finals, and Jr. World Series)
1942	82-72	.532	Third
1943	63-90	.412	Eighth
1944	86-67	.562	Fifth
1945	63-90	.412	Eighth
1946	64-90	.416	Eighth
1947	76-78	.494	Fifth
1948	81-73	.526	Fourth (won opener, lost finals)
1949	70-83	.458	Seventh
1950	84-69	.549	Third (won opener, finals, and Jr. World Series)
1951	53-101	.344	Eighth
1952	68-85	.444	Seventh
1953	64-90	.416	Seventh
1954	77-76	.503	Fourth (lost opener)

Dallas (Rangers)

The Dallas "Hams" won the first Texas League championship in 1888, and the Dallas Giants, Submarines, Steers, Rebels, and Eagles played Texas League ball for seven decades. But when hard-driving oilman Dick Burnett bought the franchise in 1948, acquiring a major league team became the primary goal of Dallas baseball interests. In 1959 Dallas moved up to the American Association, along with Fort Worth and Houston.

The three Texas cities, along with Denver and Omaha, made up the Western Division of the expanded AA. The Dallas Rangers played at 10,500-seat Burnett Field in south Dallas. A treat for Ranger fans was Miss Inez (Inez Peddlie), the lovely organist who was a fixture at Dallas games for 15 years, playing every request with artistry, and convincing generations of fans that no seventh-inning stretch could ever be the same without her melodies.

In 1959 the Rangers had a losing record, despite the efforts of batting champ Luis Marquez (.345 with 18 homers), ERA titlist Marion Fricano (12–4 and a 2.02 ERA in 11 starts and 30 relief appearances), and lefthander Jack Spring (15–13). Attendance was 130,334 better than that of five other clubs in the league.

After the season, owners J. W. Bateson and Amon Carter, Jr., combined Dallas and Fort Worth into one club, hoping to achieve major league status with the proposed Continental League. But the third "major" league did not materialize, and the Dallas-Fort Worth Rangers played from 1960 through 1962 in the American Association. Steps had been taken to construct a major league facility, but Turnpike Stadium would not open until 1965. Rangers home games were alternated between Burnett Field and Fort Worth's LaGrave Field.

Outfielder Luis Marquez tailed off badly in 1960 (.264 with three homers), but fireballing lefthander Dick Tomanek won the strikeout crown (7–11 with 172 Ks in 181 IP). Outfielder Gale Wade (.270), second sacker Lou Klimchock (.270 in 72 games), and shortstop Dick Smith (.291 in 65 games) performed well, but overall the Rangers finished last in team hitting (.248), fielding, and staff ERA — and in the standings.

Catcher-manager Jim Fanning (.111 in 124 games in 1960) was replaced in 1961 by former National League catching standout Walker Cooper. But there was little improvement, and the Rangers came in fifth in a six-team league. The best players were first baseman Tommy Burgess (.288 with 14 homers), outfielders Chuck Tanner (.300 in 48 games) and Mike Harrington (.304 with 16 homers), catcher Bob Rodgers (.286), infielder Ray Jablonski (.341 in 44 games), righthanded starter Hugh Pepper (15–11), starter-reliever Dean Chance (9–12 in 63 games), and relievers Ron Blackburn (13–11 in 58 appearances) and Jack Hannah (5–4 in 52 appearances).

Pitcher Dick Littlefield was promoted to manager in 1962, but the Rangers plunged into the cellar and on July 19 Ray Murray took over the reins. Murray, an ex-major league catcher, was one of the stars of Dallas' 1955 Texas League champs, but he could do little to reverse the slide. The Rangers finished next-to-last in team hitting, fielding, and staff ERA. But the club did lead the league in homers (118), behind home run champ Leo Burke (.278, 27 HR, 85 RBI), first sacker Ray Jablonski (.281, 25 HR, 81 RBI), and third baseman-outfielder Wayne Graham (.311 with 17 homers). Outfielders Chuck Tanner (.315) and Mike Harrington (.296) also hit well, and righthanders Bob Baillargeon (11–11) and Ed Thomas (13–13) were the steadiest pitchers. Attendance bottomed out at 80,000, and the entire league totaled only 759,358.

The AA folded after the season, and Dallas-Fort Worth shifted to the Pacific Coast League for 1963. Fort Worth businessman Tommy Mercer bought the DFW franchise, intending to keep Dallas in the PCL and return the Fort Worth Cats to the Texas League, all the while angling for big league status. By 1965 Turnpike Stadium — seating just 10,000 in its initial phase — was completed in Arlington, and Dallas-Fort Worth re-entered the Texas League. The franchise drew well, despite several losing seasons. Late in 1971 the sale of the Washington Senators to Dallas-Fort Worth was announced, and in 1972 the Texas Rangers at last brought major league baseball to the Dallas area.

Year	Record	Pcg.	Finish
1959	75-87	.463	Ninth
1960	64-90	.416	Sixth
1961	72-77	.483	Fifth
1962	59-90	.396	Sixth

Denver (Bears, Zephyrs)

"If it was up to me," said Bears' fan Bob Gustafson, "I'd do everything possible to keep major league baseball out of Denver. I think it's perfect just the way it is now."

For three decades the Denver Bears have been one of the most important clubs in the American Association, consistently fielding winning teams and running up attendance figures that have sparked keen interest in major league circles. But the Bears have been so successful for so long in the AA that many hardcore fans seemingly would like to see Denver remain one of the showcase franchises in minor league baseball.

Baseball was played in Denver at least as early as 1862, and throughout the late nineteenth century there was enthusiastic support for numerous amateur, semipro, and professional clubs. Denver fielded a team from season to season in various versions of the Western League, and was a charter member when the circuit joined the National Association in 1902. The popular Theodore Roosevelt was president of the United States, and Denver's nine were called the "Teddy Bears," "Grizzlies" or "Cubs," eventually settling on the Denver Bears.

Denver won three consecutive Western League pennants (1910–12) but thereafter a succession of poor teams caused the Bears to suspend operations following the 1917 season. Home of the Bears had been Broadway Park, but when Denver re-entered the Class A Western League in 1922, Merchants Park was constructed two miles to the south. Nicknamed "The Brickyard" because of its hard playing surface, wooden Merchants Park seated 7,000 and featured deep outfield fences that encircled a vast graveyard for home run hitters.

During the Depression, poor attendance plagued the Bears, and other Western League clubs found the expense of travel to Denver oppressive. Denver gave up professional baseball after the 1932 season but rejoined the Class A Western League in 1947, when the circuit was reorganized after World War II. Ramshackle Merchants Park was replaced during the 1948 season by Bears Stadium, a beautiful half-bowl facility located at 20th and Federal Boulevard with a seating capacity of 18,523 — largest in the league. In 1949 Denver set a Class A attendance record of 463,069, and by the mid-1950s there was little doubt that the city was ready for a higher classification of baseball. When Kansas City moved into the American League, the Yankees needed an attractive new Class AAA affiliate, and Denver joined the American Association in 1955.

Stocked with Yankee talent, the Bears bounded into the playoffs during Denver's first four years in the league. Lefthanded first baseman Marv Throneberry was the team hero and the league's most productive slugger, leading the AA in both home runs and RBIs in 1955 (.275, 36 HR, 117 RBI), 1956 (.315, 42 HR, 145 RBI) and 1957 (.250, 40 HR, 111 RBI). In 1957 Norm Siebern (.349, 24

HR, 118 RBI) won the batting title, and manager Ralph Houk led Denver to its first AA playoff championship. The Bears failed to make the playoffs in 1959, then enjoyed playoff seasons the next three years. From 1955 until the AA folded in 1962, the Bears reached the playoffs seven of their first eight years in the league.

Norm Siebern was only the first of eight Denver batting champs: Gordon Windhorn (.328 in 1958), Larry Osborne (.342, 34 HR, 119 RBI for a Triple Crown in 1960), Don Wert (.328 in 1961), Richie Scheinblum (.388 and a league-leading 108 RBIs in 1971), Lamar Johnson (.336 in 1975), Tim Raines (.354 in 1980), and Lavell Freeman (.318 in 1988). After Marv Throneberry and Larry Osborne led the league in homers and RBIs in the same season, five other Bears pulled off the same slugging feat: Cliff Johnson in 1973 (.302, 33 HR, 117 RBI), Roger Freed in 1976 (.309, 42 HR, 102 RBI), Frank Ortenzio in 1977 (.311, 40 HR, 126 RBI), Randy Bass in 1980 (.333, 37 HR, 110 RBI), and Greg Vaughn in 1989 (.276, 26 HR, 92 RBI).

Steve Boros (.317, 30 HR, 119 RBI) marred Larry Osborne's 1960 Triple Crown by tying him for the RBI lead, and German Rivera (.300, 21 HR, 87 RBI) was the RBI co-champ in 1987. The Most Valuable Player award was voted to Marv Throneberry (in 1956), Steve Boros (1960), Richie Scheinblum (1971), Cliff Johnson (1973), Roger Freed (1976), Frank Ortenzio (1977), Randy Bass (1980), and Greg Vaughn (1989).

These and many other fine hitters have been aided by the carrying power of Denver's thin air, which also dulls the break of curve balls. Denver led the league in team hitting during its first six AA seasons. The Bears have played in the American Association 29 years and have recorded the highest batting average 19 times. Denver scored the most runs in the AA every season from 1956 through 1962, winning this category a total of 17 times. Twelve times the Bears led the league in home runs. The best total came in 1987 (192), which was the same year the Bears blasted out their highest average (.299).

These hard-hitting clubs have reached the AA playoffs 18 times, winning in 1957, 1971, 1976, 1977, 1981, and 1983. After the AA was split into divisions, Denver won the West in 1970, 1971, 1975, 1976, 1977, 1980, 1983, and 1987. The Bears ran up the best record in the league in 1960, 1975, 1976, 1977, 1980, and 1987. There were two appearances in the Junior World Series: a loss in seven games to Rochester in 1971, and a victory over Buffalo, four games to one, in 1957.

Such sustained success, and a constantly exciting offense, stimulated outstanding attendance. By 1955 the AA was plagued with declining attendance, but Denver hit the league with the stunning total of 426,248 admissions. The Bears led the AA in attendance their first four years in the circuit, again in 1960 and 1969, then seven straight seasons, 1975 through 1981. Attendance mounted steadily in the 1970s, then reached a peak of 565,214 in 1980. The 1981 total was almost as high at 555,806, but 537,914 the next year was second to Louisville. The Bears have been unable to post the highest attendance since 1981, despite totals which have ranged from 301,787 to 442,870. The most startling triumph occurred on Fireworks Night, July 3, 1984, when 65,660 fans crowded into Mile High Stadium for a game with Omaha. A heavily promoted opening day crowd of 53,378 was attracted to the Cotton Bowl in 1950 by the Dallas Eagles of the Texas League, but in 1984 the Eagles' minor league attendance record for a single game was claimed by the Denver Bears.

When Denver entered the AA in 1955, the club was owned by wealthy sportsman Bob Howsam, who bought the Kansas City franchise for $78,000. In 1959 Howsam began to invest heavily in the Denver Broncos of the fledgling American Football League, and soon his Rocky Mountain Empire Sports controlled the Broncos as well as the Bears and Bears Stadium. Bears Stadium began to undergo a series of expansions that would produce a seating capacity exceeding 75,000. Because of financial reverses, Howsam was forced to put Rocky Mountain Sports up for sale, and the major shareholder became Gerald Phipps, who owned the construction company in charge of Bears Stadium expansion. Rechristened Mile High Stadium (baseball diehards steadfastly continued to call it Bears Stadium), the facility could be converted from a baseball park to a football stadium within hours — but baseball "crowds" would be swallowed in the double-decked vastness that was filled for football games.

When the American Association disbanded after the 1962 season, Denver affiliated with the Milwaukee Braves and joined the Pacific Coast League. Six years in the PCL produced four losing seasons and no playoff appearances, and when the American Association was revived in 1969 Denver happily shifted back to the AA.

The Bears led the AA in hitting and attendance in 1969, despite a last-place finish, then won Western Division crowns the next two years, as well as the 1971 playoffs. Bear fans were deeply frustrated by the 1971 Junior World Series, which the Bears lost to Rochester, four games to three. Because of a conflicting Broncos' game, all seven contests were played in Rochester, and the home field advantage presumably would have accounted for one more Bears' victory and a Series triumph.

Despite back-to-back cellar finishes in 1973 and 1974, the Bears subsequently reeled off three straight Western Division titles and two consecutive playoff championships. The 1975 Bears were led by batting champ Lamar Johnson and Pitcher of the Year Steve Dunning (15–9). MVP Roger Freed sparked the 1976 team and MVP Frank "Moose" Ortenzio led the 1977 Bears, and both clubs posted the best record in the AA.

In 1980 the Bears again finished first behind batting champ Tim Raines, MVP Randy Bass, and Pitcher of the Year Steve Ratzer (15–4). The next year Denver won the playoffs, led by popular manager Felipe Alou, Pitcher of the Year Bryn Smith (15–5), Steve Ratzer (7–3 with 13 saves), and outfielder Terry Francona (.353 in 93 games). There were four playoff appearances from 1983 through 1987, with a playoff title in 1983 and a first-place team in 1987.

Chief architect of much of the Bears' enormous success was Jim Burris, who became general manager in 1966, and who previously had served as president of the Texas League and, concurrently, president of the AA (1960–62). The level of the Bears' attendance and the simultaneous prosperity of the Broncos continues to spur the possibility of major league baseball. Indeed, as early as 1960, Bob Howsam intended to bring big league baseball to Denver in the form of a Continental League franchise, but the proposed circuit failed to materialize. Late in 1977, Denver oil millionaire Marvin Davis negotiated with Charles O. Finley to buy the Oakland A's and move the American League club to Denver. The deal seemed so certain that the American Association planned to relocate the Denver franchise in Davenport, Iowa — and to split an anticipated $300,000 territorial infringement fee among the AA clubs. But late in January 1978 the deal began to collapse, primarily because Oakland would not release Finley from a 20-year stadium lease. During the next year, Davis continued to try to arrange a

The 1984 Denver Bears at Mile High Stadium, where the July 3 Fireworks Night attracted 65,660 fans — the largest single-game crowd in minor league history.
— Courtesy Denver Zephyrs

Finley, and he also looked into the possibilities of purchasing the Baltimore Orioles or the Chicago White Sox. In 1991 Denver was awarded a National League expansion franchise.

Several years ago a group of fanatical Bears' supporters formed the Throneberry Section. Located in Section 117 behind the visiting third-base dugout, these enthusiastic fans are experts at taunting the opposition. One specialty of the Throneberry Section is revealed when a disappointed strikeout victim trudges back to the dugout — and is met with chants informing him of his new batting average. One member of the Throneberry Section is Philadelphia native Jeff Aiken, who flatly states, "The best baseball I've seen is in the minor leagues." And fellow member Bob Gustafson when he said, "If it was up to me, I'd do everything possible to keep major league baseball out of Denver," reflected the conviction of every diehard minor league fan.

Year	Record	Pcg.	Finish
1955	83-71	.539	Third (lost opener)
1956	86-67	.562	Second (won opener, lost finals)

1957	90-64	.584	Second (won opener, finals, and Jr. World Series)
1958	78-71	.523	Fourth (won opener, lost finals)
1959	76-86	.469	Sixth
1960	88-66	.571	First (won opener, lost finals)
1961	73-73	.507	Third (lost opener)
1962	79-71	.527	Third (won opener, lost finals)
1969	58-82	.414	Sixth
1970	70-69	.504	Fourth (won Western Division, lost finals)
1971	73-67	.521	Second (won Western Division and finals, lost Jr. World Series)
1972	61-79	.436	Seventh
1973	61-75	.449	Eighth
1974	62-74	.455	Seventh
1975	81-55	.596	First (won Western Division, lost finals)
1976	86-50	.632	First (won Western Division and finals)
1977	71-65	.522	Third (won Western Division and finals)
1978	64-71	.474	Sixth
1979	62-73	.459	Seventh
1980	92-44	.676	First (won Western Division, lost finals)
1981	76-60	.559	Second (won Western Division and finals)
1982	68-67	.504	Seventh
1983	73-61	.545	Second (won Western Division and finals)
1984	79-75	.513	Third (won opener, lost finals)
1985	77-65	.542	Second
1986	76-66	.535	Second (won Western Division, lost finals)
1987	79-61	.564	First (won opener, lost finals)
1988	72-69	.511	Fifth
1989	69-77	.473	Sixth
1990	68-78	.466	Sixth
1991	79-65	.549	Second (won Western Division, finals and Alliance Classic)

Iowa CUBS

Des Moines (Iowa Oaks, Iowa Cubs)

Baseball was brought to Iowa after the Civil War by returning soldiers. In 1867 the first state baseball tournament was staged in Burlington, with a first-place prize of $200 and a $75 rosewood bat. The state capital, Des Moines, made its professional debut in 1887 in the Western League, and the next year the team won 26 consecutive games and claimed the pennant after winning a playoff from Kansas City.

During the twentieth century, Des Moines continued its association with the Class A Western League. League Park was located between Grand Avenue and Keosaqua Way at Fourth Street. In

1914 fiery evangelist Billy Sunday — an Iowa native and a former pro baseball player — conducted a revival at League Park and attracted 10,000 converts.

Early Des Moines professional teams were called Prohibitionists, Water Cures, Midgets, Undertakers (from the manager's off-season occupation), Politicians, and Underwriters. From 1925 through 1937 the team was known as the Demons, and the 1930 Demons became the first club to play under a permanent lighting system. At the 1929 minor league winter meeting, owner Lee Keyser announced his plan for financial survival during the Depression: installation of lights at League Park so that night games could be played regularly. But officials of the Independence Producers of the Class C Western Association decided to beat Des Moines to the gimmick. The Demons opened on the road, and Independence rigged temporary lights and played their opener against Muskogee at night — then took down the lights. Four days later, on May 2, the Demons scored 11 runs in the first inning and coasted to a 13–6 win over Wichita before an overflow crowd of nearly 11,000.

Night baseball saved numerous minor league franchises, but Des Moines was forced to halt operations after the 1937 season. A decade later, during the postwar baseball boom, the Des Moines Bruins re-entered the Western League, participating until the Class A circuit folded at the end of 1958. The Bruins then joined the Class B Three-I League until *it* disbanded following the 1961 season.

When the American Association reorganized in 1969, Dallas baseball executive Ray Johnston located a franchise in Des Moines. "Des Moines has a marginal population for triple-A baseball," said Johnston, and in order to broaden the appeal to surrounding communities he requested that the franchise be referred to as Iowa. Since the initial affiliation was with Oakland, the club would be called the Iowa Oaks. Players sent down from the big leagues often grumbled about "Death Moans" — all the more reason to stress *Iowa*. Home of the Oaks was Sec Taylor Stadium, named after the popular sports editor of the Des Moines *Register*. Although the ballpark is the smallest in the AA (the current seating capacity is 7,600), the location on the west bank of the Des Moines River offers an enchanting view of the state capitol behind the center-field fence.

Iowa's first year in the AA was uneventful. The Oaks tied for

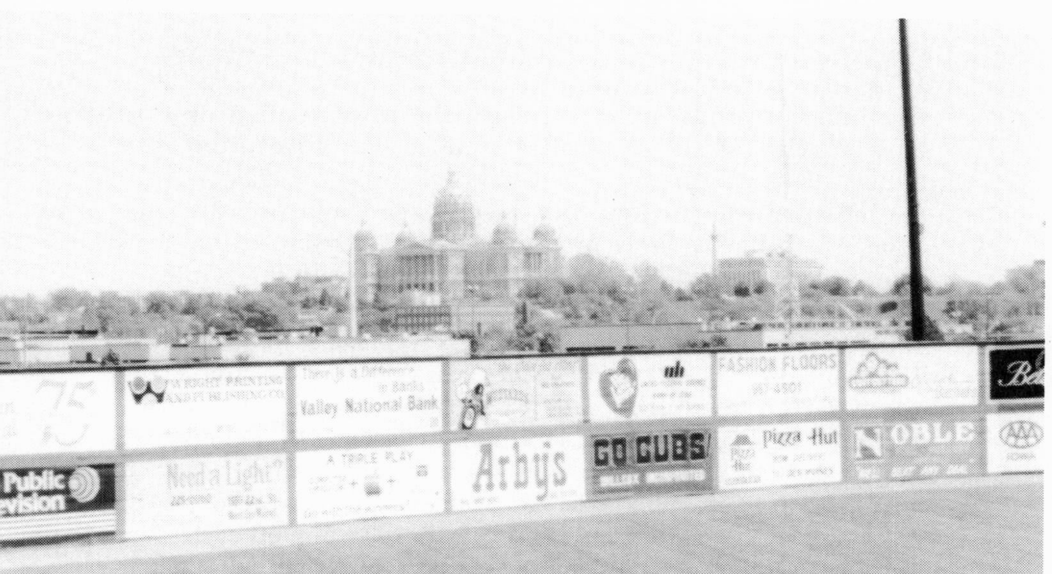

At Des Moines AA fans can view Iowa's handsome state capitol beyond the outfield fence.

— Photo by the author

fourth place in a six-team league, 23 games behind the pennant-winners. Jim Driscoll was named All-Star shortstop after leading the AA in walks (.286 with 82 Ws). Attendance was 130,000, and would remain at that level for three seasons.

In 1970 the Oaks finished a close second in the Eastern Division of the expanded AA. The offense was led by first baseman Gonzalo Marquez (.341), who missed the batting title by one point. Outfielder-third baseman Bill McNulty (.295 with 22 homers) and catcher Gene Tenace (.282 with 16 homers in 93 games) helped the Oaks lead the league in home runs.

But the most spectacular Oak of 1970 or any other year was 20-year-old southpaw Vida Blue. In just 17 games his sizzling fastball won him the strikeout title and the league's best winning percentage (12–3 with 165 Ks and only 88 hits in 133 IP). He pitched four shutouts and had the league's best ERA (2.17) — but lacked enough innings to qualify for the crown! Called up to Oakland, he pitched a no-hitter on September 21, then won 24 games for the A's the next year.

In 1971 Bill McNulty was the home run champ (.247 with 27 homers in just 107 games) as the Oaks again hit the most roundtrippers in the AA (160). Lefty Dave Hamilton (12–4) was the 1971 percentage leader, while the next year switch-hitting catcher Gene Dusan (.311) performed well. But attendance dropped to only 89,000, and the Oakland A's pulled out of Des Moines, although the team would continue to be known as the Oaks.

Des Moines affiliated with the Chicago White Sox, an association which immediately produced a championship team. Bucky Dent was on third (.295), except for 40 games with the White Sox. Southpaw Ken Frailing (11–3) and righthander Stan Perzanowski (14–8) were the top pitchers. Other key players were outfielder Ted Uhlaender (.278 in 51 games) and second baseman Hugh Yancy (.292), as well as catcher Richard Varney (.251 with 18 homers) and outfielder Ken Hottman (.224 with 19 homers), who helped the Oaks lead the league in home runs (127) for the third time in four years. The Oaks finished with the best record in the league and the Eastern Division crown. The playoff series with Tulsa went to seven games before the Oaks finally fell, but pilot Joe Sparks was named AA Manager of the Year.

It was to be the only division title and playoff appearance in Des Moines' first 21 years of AA participation, but there would be a number of highlights to come. In 1974 no-hitters were hurled by Joe Henderson (13–8) on July 31 against Wichita, and by Homer Stinson (3–3) on August 24 against Indianapolis. It was the first time that two no-hitters had been produced by an AA pitching staff in the same season since 1920. Also in 1974 the Oaks led the league in hitting (.293), behind RBI champ Lamar Johnson (.301, 20 HR, 96 RBI), third baseman Bill Stein (.328), and outfielder Joe Talley (.326).

Sam Ewing missed the batting title by one point in 1976 (.351), while outfielder Mike Squires was one of the league's top hitters in 1977 (.323) and 1978 (.312). Righthander Jack Kucek won back-to-back ERA titles in 1977 (2.54) and 1978 (2.46), and for good measure he threw in a no-hitter against the 89ers on May 26, 1978. Righthander Dewey Robinson was voted Pitcher of the Year after leading the AA in victories — as a reliever (13–7 in 49 relief appearances)!

In 1981 Iowa switched affiliations, from the Chicago White Sox to the Chicago Cubs. The club retained the Oaks nickname for a year, but when the Cubs began to send their uniforms to Des Moines, the team became the Iowa Cubs. Ray Johnston sold the club in 1982 for $600,000 to Ken Grandquist and 15 other local investors. Promotions were increased, seating was upgraded and expanded, lighting was significantly improved, and a vast new locker room was constructed. The Cub Club was built overlooking left field, offering excellent restaurant facilities with a view of the game. Cub Club members could even dine outside on the restaurant veranda, with old gloves available to catch stray baseballs.

The Pitcher of the Year in 1982 was ERA and percentage leader Jay Howell (13–4, 2.36), and teammates Pat Tabler (.342), Al Benton (.330), and Mel Hall (.329) stimulated record crowd interest. Attendance had never risen above 136,000 (1979), but in 1982 paid admissions jumped to 203,000, then 256,000 in 1983, and 275,00 the next year. Paid admissions have remained around a quarter of a million annually, but in 1988 the hard-hitting Cubs drew a club record 279,000.

The 1983 Cubs led the league in stolen bases (179), and starred home run champ Carmelo Martinez (.251, 31 HR, 94 RBI), outfielder Joe Carter (.307 with 22 homers), and second baseman Dan Rohn (.315), who set a record with 54 consecutive errorless games. First baseman Joe Hicks (.266, 37 HR, 90 RBI) was the home run king in 1984, while righthanders Reggie Patterson (14–7) and Jon Perlman (11–6) were two of the league's best pitchers. The next season Dave Hostetler led the AA in homers and RBIs (.256, 29 HR, 89 RBI), and the Cubs were the stolen base leaders in 1985 (179 steals, the same total as 1983) and 1986 (205 steals).

In 1986 Cubs righthander Greg Maddux was the percentage leader (10–1), infielder Steve Hammond hit for the second highest average (.330), and switch-hitter Rondin Johnson paced the league in triples (.289 with 14 3Bs). The following year, third baseman Wade Rowdon was the RBI champ (.337, 18 HR, 113 RBI), and on June 4, 1987, he became the fourth hitter in American Association history to blast four home runs in one game. In 1988 the Cubs led the AA in batting (.274) by featuring six of the league's top ten hitters: catcher Bill Bathe (.312), infielder-outfielder David Meier (.305 with 20 homers), first baseman Phil Stephenson (.293 with 22 homers), and outfielders Rolando Roomes (.301 with 16 homers), Doug Dascenzo (.295), and Dwight Smith (.293).

Des Moines has played in the American Association for 21 years, winning just one division title and making only one playoff appearance. But the Oaks and Cubs have provided baseball fans with many exciting performances, and the team has developed a devoted following which has made Des Moines a rock-solid AA franchise.

Year	Record	Pcg.	Finish
1969	62-78	.443	Fourth
1970	70-68	.507	Second
1971	71-69	.507	Third
1972	62-78	.443	Fifth
1973	83-53	.610	First (won Eastern Division, lost finals)
1974	74-62	.544	Third
1975	56-79	.415	Seventh
1976	68-68	.500	Fourth
1977	61-75	.449	Seventh
1978	66-70	.485	Fifth
1979	69-87	.507	Fourth
1980	59-77	.434	Seventh
1981	53-82	.393	Eighth
1982	73-62	.541	Second
1983	71-65	.522	Third
1984	80-74	.519	Second
1985	66-75	.468	Sixth
1986	74-68	.521	Third
1987	64-74	.464	Sixth
1988	78-64	.549	Third
1989	62-82	.431	Seventh
1990	72-74	.493	Fifth
1991	78-66	.542	Third

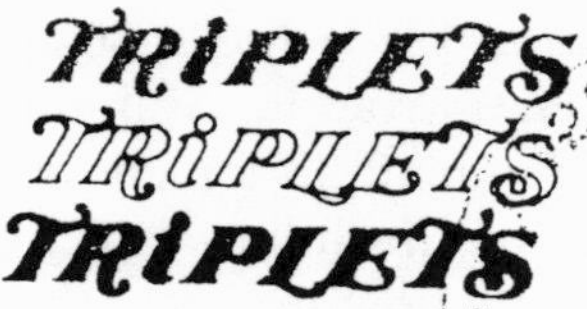

Evansville (Triplets)

"Evansville is blazing the trail out of minor league difficulties and showing the way to the baseball world. There is nothing else approaching it in the minor league world."

This proclamation was made in 1915 by Louis Heilbrenner, president of the Class B Central League. Heilbrenner was referring to Bosse Field, regarded as the first municipally-owned stadium in the history of organized baseball. Bosse Field was built at a cost of $100,000 by the Evansville school board and named for Mayor Benjamin Bosse, who had helped design and implement construction of the park.

Intended as an all-sports facility (indeed, after the opening baseball game of 1915 was played before a capacity crowd, that night 1,500 fans watched a wrestling match under improvised lighting) the 8,000-seat stadium was located just north of the downtown area in Garvin Park. The covered grandstand and outfield fences were built of brick, and even today Bosse Field is an evocatively handsome ballpark. The outfield was extremely deep until an interior wire fence was built in 1951, and there never has been a ball hit over the 477-foot center-field fence. President Heilbrenner's prediction eventually would prove true, as professional franchises at both the major and minor league levels regularly expect their stadiums to be provided by municipal, county, and state funding.

Evansville played in the Central League from 1903 until the circuit folded during the 1911 season. The next year Evansville was in the Class D Kitty League, then returned to the revamped Central League from 1913 through 1917. But the city spent its longest tenure in the historic Three-I League, appearing as the Evansville Evas in the circuit's inaugural season of 1902. The Evas played in wooden Louisiana Street Park, and catcher Frank "Germany" Roth walloped 36 homers, an amazing total for the dead-ball era (only first baseman Perry Werden, who hit 45 for Minneapolis in 1895, had ever recorded more home runs). Evansville returned to Three-I ball in 1919 and played for 13 seasons. In 1932 the city had to give up professional baseball because of Depression conditions, then came back into the circuit from 1938 through 1942, when the Three-I League suspended operations for the duration of World War II. Evansville and the Three-I League bounced back after the war, but minor league baseball experienced severe difficulties during the 1950s, and weak attendance caused the city to surrender its franchise after the 1957 season.

Through the years Bosse Field had hosted many fine players. In 1941 20-year-old Warren Spahn led the Three-I League in victories, winning percentage, and ERA (19–6, 1.83). Another 20-year-old future Hall of Famer, first baseman Hank Greenberg, led the 1931 Three-I League in doubles, games played, putouts, and assists (.318, 41 2Bs in 126 games). Outfielder Chuck Klein, who was voted into the Hall of Fame in 1980, made his professional debut with Evansville in 1927 (.327), while noted curveballer Tommy Bridges led the Three-I League in strikeouts before being called up to Detroit in 1930.

After Evansville dropped out of the Three-I League, eight

years passed before professional baseball returned to Bosse Field. The Esox played in the Class AA Southern League from 1966 through 1968. Again weak attendance cost Evansville its franchise, but local baseball enthusiasts were determined to resume professional play. When the reorganized American Association expanded from six to eight teams in 1970, a community-backed franchise brought Triple-A ball to Bosse Field, which was leased for one dollar per year.

For a decade and a half, Evansville would be one of the smallest cities in Class AAA, but the city's location in southwestern Indiana gave the team a potential following in Illinois and Kentucky. From the beginning, the team would attempt to attract fans from three states, as indicated by the new nickname: the Evansville Triplets (a $500 saving certificate to name the team attracted 3,218 entries).

During their first year in the American Association, the 1970 Trips finished dead last in team hitting, despite the efforts of outfielder Jim Nettles (.317) and first baseman Cotton Nash, whose 33 homers earned him the only AA home run title to be enjoyed by a Trips slugger (Nash's total gave him the greatest number of homers *ever* recorded at Bosse Field). The best team explosion came at Denver on June 29, when the Trips scored 13 runs in the third inning to beat the Bears, 16–6. Bert Blyleven dominated American Association hitters in eight games (4–2 with 63 strikeouts in 54 innings) and soon won promotion to Minnesota. On May 15 he pitched a 10-inning, 1–0 four-hitter over Iowa, walking just two and whiffing 17 Oaks batters. But the Trips finished at the bottom of the Eastern Division, and the Minnesota Twins pulled out of their Evansville affiliation.

The new parent club, the Milwaukee Brewers, immediately scored a coup with Evansville fans by bringing in Del Crandall as manager. In 1949 Crandall, then a 19-year-old catcher for the Evansville Braves, went on a tear early in the season (.351 with eight homers and 36 RBIs in 38 games), and the Boston Braves sent a plane to whisk him to the big leagues. Crandall eventually enjoyed an extremely successful managerial stint with Albuquerque, but the 1971 Trips again were last in team hitting and Evansville brought up the bottom of the standings. At midseason, team president Grayle Howlett had to borrow $7,000 from the league treasury to meet the July 15 payroll. The Triplets could not obtain a corporate credit line because local bankers did not consider Triple-A baseball a sound investment, and American Association President Allie Reynolds and Brewer officials traveled to Evansville to meet with Howlett. But in this crisis Carl Wallace, a restaurateur and amateur baseball supporter, launched a "Save the Triplets" movement. Twenty-four civic-minded businessmen purchased the club and placed the Trips on solid footing.

In 1972 Del Crandall exercised his managerial magic and won the Eastern Division, then swept Wichita in three games to seize the American Association pennant. Exhibiting unaccustomed power, the Trips led the AA in home runs: All-Star first baseman Robert Hansen was the league leader with 25; third sacker Bill McNulty hit 20; catcher Darrell Porter chipped in 13 in 88 games before being called up to Milwaukee; outfielder Robert Coluccio contributed the team's highest average (.300); and outfielder Bobby Mitchell recorded a spectacular half of a season (.381 with 20 HRs and 65 RBIs in 77 games). Righthander Lloyd Gladden led the AA in victories (15–9), and another righty, Jim Slaton (11–2), twirled a no-hitter against Wichita.

Crandall was promoted to the manager's position in Milwaukee, and most of the best players also moved up for 1973. Two mediocre seasons followed, but in 1974 a long and pleasant affiliation with the Detroit Tigers began, and one year later manager Fred Hatfield led the Trips to another pennant. The offense was sparked by All-Star outfielder Bob Molinaro (.287) and catcher Gene Lamont (.308). Late in the season, however, the Triplets were eight and a half games off the pace in the Eastern Division when the "Kiddie Korps" — four talented young pitchers — were called up from Class AA and propelled Evansville to the championship. Southpaw reliever Eddie Glynn posted a 2.48 ERA in seven appearances; Mark Lemongello went 7–4; Frank MacCormack was a perfect 3–0 in three starts, with a 1.42 ERA; and Mark Fidrych was 4–1 in six starts with four complete games, a shutout, and a 1.58 ERA. Fidyrich captivated the fans at Bosse Field. A lovable flake, off the field he dressed in cutoff jeans and a pajama top; on the mound "The Bird" talked to the ball and shook hands with teammates who made good plays.

"I used to throw any ball that someone got a hit off me back to the ump, so it could rub up against the other balls," reasoned The Bird. "Then, maybe the next time, it would come out as a pop fly."

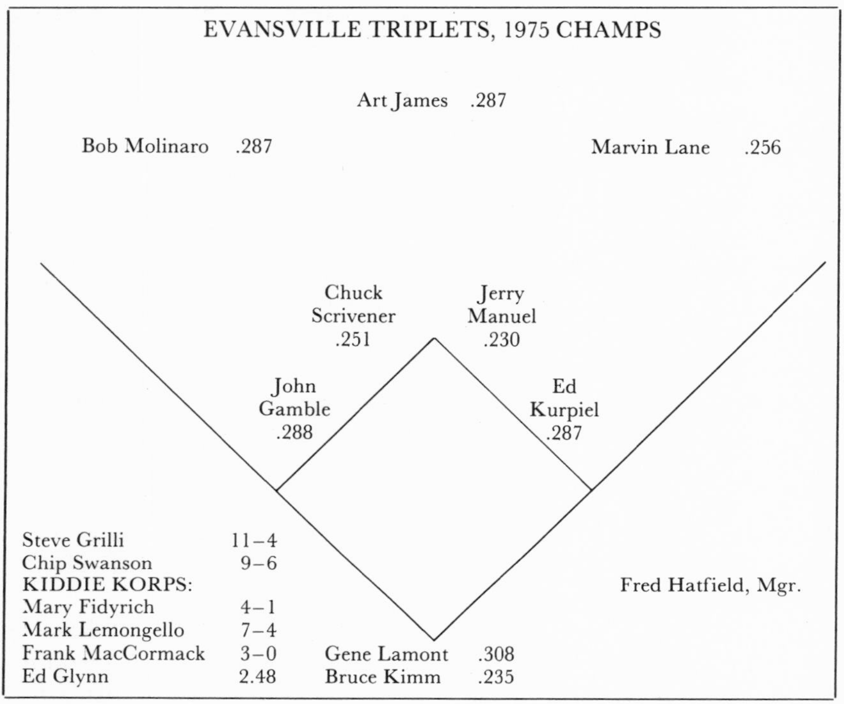

After winning the Eastern Division title, the Trips defeated the Denver Bears four games to two (the pennant was dramatically clinched in the 12th inning of the sixth game at Bosse Field, when light-hitting Jerry Manuel stroked a solo homer to win, 4–3). The Trips then downed Tidewater, the champions of the International League, to cop the Junior World Series and the winners' share of $363 per man (Tidewater players collected $242 apiece).

The winning combination of 1975 was broken up, and the 1976 Trips finished last in the American Association. The next year several of the championship players were held back, including second baseman Jerry Manuel (.272) and outfielder Bob Molinaro (.303, 17 HR, 91 RBI) and Art James (.288). Catcher Lance Parrish was the best newcomer (.279, 25 HR, 90 RBI), and the sixth-place Trips uncharacteristically led the league in homers.

In 1978 Less Moss was named AA Manager of the Year after posting the second-best record of the season. Although the Trips missed the Eastern Division title by half a game, Evansville posted the league's lowest team ERA, righthander Kip Young (11–3) led in winning percentage, and southpaw Sheldon Burnside (14–5) paced the AA in victories. The following season, Jim Leyland was awarded Manager of the Year honors by producing the identical record (78–58) and converting it into another pennant for Evansville. All-Star catcher Bruce Kimm (.283) was a mainstay of the club, along with switch-hitter Richard Peters (.320), center fielder Dave Stegman (.302), and first baseman Joe Lis (.292). Making strong contributions in part of a season were outfielder-first baseman Tim Corcoran (.338 in 87 games), infielder Tom Brookens (.306 in 77 games), and outfielder Dan Gonzales (.338 in 40 games). This hard-hitting roster led the American Association in homers, while the pitching staff rang up the league's second-lowest ERA — southpaw reliever John Martin was especially effective (7–1 with a 1.37 ERA). The Trips boasted the AA's best record and beat Oklahoma City, four games to two (right fielder Kirk Gibson ripped Oklahoma City at a sizzling 14 for 28 pace in the playoffs), to record Evansville's third pennant in eight years.

The 1980 Trips suffered a losing season, along with Mark Fidrych (6–7). The Bird had left Evansville for Detroit and enjoyed a spectacular rookie season in 1976. But a knee operation and a sore arm followed his magnificent debut, and Fidyrich returned to the Trips in 1980 to restore his effectiveness. His performance was mediocre, but in his final appearance 5,781 cheering fans watched him hurl seven shutout innings against Indianapolis. There was a late-season trial with Detroit, then Fidyrich was back in Evansville for 1981. He went 6–3, but his ERA was 5.75 and he finally retired in 1983. The Trips' best pitcher in 1981 was Larry Pashnick, who led the league in ERA (2.89) and who twirled a nine-inning, 1–0 no-hitter over Iowa on August 19. Tim Corcoran was back to lead the offense (.298), Rick Leach enjoyed a torrid start (.409) before being promoted to Detroit, and manager Jim Leyland again won the Eastern Division (the Trips' record was third-best in the league, and Omaha and Denver of the West battled it out for the pennant).

In 1982 the Trips finished last in team hitting and sixth in the league, despite the efforts of Howard Johnson (.317 with 23 homers in 98 games — then he went up to Detroit and hit .316 in 54 games). The following year the Trips dropped to last place, even though righthanded reliever Craig Eaton (7–6 with a 2.64 ERA in 53 games) won the ERA title, and catcher-outfielder-first baseman

Jim Leyland managed Evansville to Eastern Division titles in 1979 and 1981, and to the playoff championship in 1979.

— Courtesy Carl M. Wallace

Bill Nahorodny (.337) and outfielder-infielder Barbero Garbey (.321) turned in strong offensive showings. In 1984 switch-hitter Nelson Simmons (.307) and first baseman-outfielder John Harris (.303) led the offense, but the Trips could rise no higher than sixth place. Attendance was only 100,326, and it had never been greater than 147,807 (during the first pennant-winning season of 1972). With a population of only 130,000 and a charming but antiquated ballpark, it seemed unrealistic to expect Evansville to provide competitive Triple-A attendance: In 1984 every team recorded better home attendance than the Trips, five clubs easily exceeded 200,000, and Louisville recorded 846,878 — and the following year five clubs surpassed 300,000. Bowing to the inevitable, the Trips' board of directors sold the franchise during the 1984 season to Larry Schmittou, who had been attempting for at least a year to bring the team to Nashville. On the final night of the season, the Chicken helped entertain the last AA crowd at Bosse Field.

Bosse Field became the home of the University of Evansville Aces in 1985, and two years later the old stadium served as a host facility for the United States-Japan exhibition series. The Aces boast an excellent college baseball program, but local fans still harbor hopes that one day a professional franchise will return to Evansville.

Year	Record	Pcg.	Finish
1970	67-71	.486	Seventh
1971	60-78	.435	Eighth
1972	83-57	.593	Second (won Eastern Division and finals)
1973	66-70	.485	Fifth
1974	68-67	.504	Fourth
1975	77-59	.566	Second (won Eastern Division and finals)
1976	55-81	.404	Eighth
1977	65-68	.489	Sixth
1978	78-58	.574	Second
1979	78-58	.574	First (won Eastern Division and finals)
1980	61-74	.452	Sixth
1981	73-63	.537	Third (won Eastern Division, lost opener)
1982	68-65	.511	Sixth
1983	61-75	.449	Eighth
1984	72-82	.468	Sixth

Fort Worth (Panthers, Cats)

In 1888 Fort Worth became a charter member of the Texas League, competing for seven decades in the historic circuit and establishing one of the greatest dynasties in baseball history — six consecutive pennants from 1920 through 1925. Following a first-place finish in 1958, Fort Worth, along with Dallas and Houston, withdrew from the Class AA Texas League to move up to the American Association.

Because Fort Worth was a cowtown and gunfighters' haven late in the nineteenth century, a Dallas newspaper critically commented that the rowdy Main Street was "the noonday lair of the panther." Fort Worth proudly began to call itself Panther City, and the professional baseball team would always be known as the "Panthers," or "Cats" for short. Home of the American Association Cats was 13,000-seat LaGrave Field, rebuilt after a 1949 fire.

Addition of the three Texas cities in 1959 expanded the AA to 10 teams for the only time in league history. A Western Division was created by combining the Texas cities with Denver and Omaha. Fort Worth was managed by Lou Klein to second place in

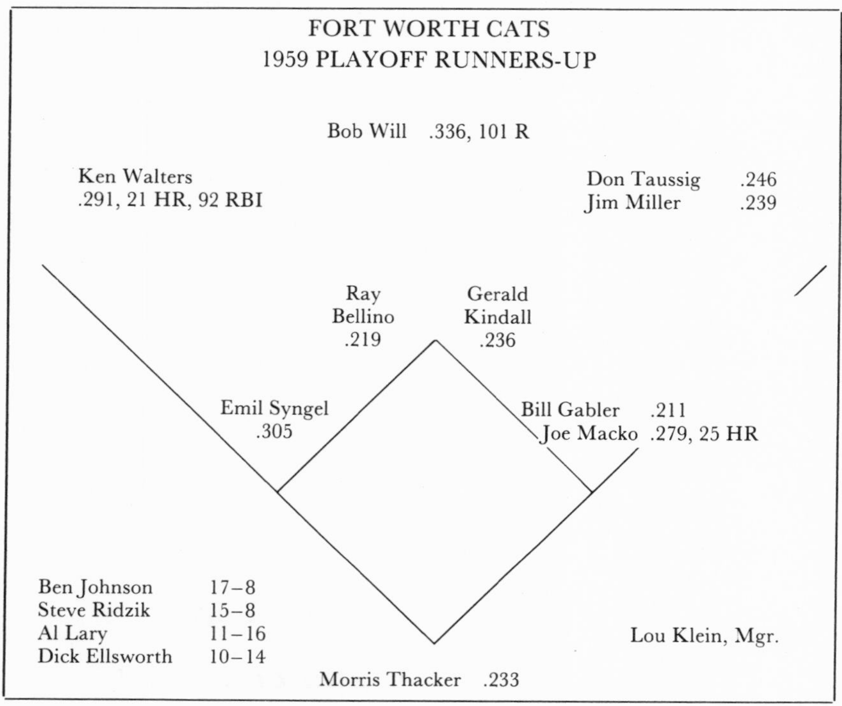

the West, good enough for a playoff berth despite a break-even 81–81 record.

The club did not hit well (.255), but outfielders Bob Will (.336) and Ken Walters (.291, 21 HR, 92 RBI), third baseman-outfielder Emil Syngel (.305), and first baseman Joe Macko (.279) offset other regulars who hit .211, .219, .233, and .236. But the pitching staff, led by righthanders Ben Johnson (17–8) and Steve Ridzik (15–8), recorded the league's second-lowest ERA (3.21).

In the opening round of playoffs the light-hitting Cats astounded the AA with a four-game sweep of first-place Louisville. The Cats took second-place Minneapolis to the seventh game of the finals before yielding the series, three games to four. Season attendance was 97,315.

There was general discontent with the 10-team format of 1959, and when Omaha dropped out of the league, Dallas and Fort Worth combined to form a single franchise and return the AA to eight clubs. Located just 35 miles apart, Dallas and Fort Worth for decades had maintained a bitter — and profitable — rivalry in the Texas League. But J. W. Bateson of Dallas and Amon Carter of Fort Worth, owners of the DFW Rangers, had hopes of placing their franchise in the Continental League, a proposed third major league scheduled to open play in 1960. In the fall of 1959 a Bi-County Sports Committee authorized $9.5 million in revenue bonds for construction of a major league, and Turnpike Stadium (later renamed Arlington Stadium) opened in 1965.

The Continental League did not materialize, and the Dallas-Fort Worth Rangers played in the AA for three years, alternating home stands between LaGrave Field and Burnett Field in Dallas. The Rangers finished dead last in 1960, rose to next-to-last the following year, then dropped back into the cellar in 1962. Southpaw Dick Tomanek (7–11 with 172 Ks in 181 IP) was the 1960 strikeout king, righthander Hugh Pepper (15–11) had a good season in 1961, and second baseman Leo Burke (.278, 27 HR, 85 RBI) won the 1962 home run crown. Attendance declined with the fortunes of the team: 113,849 in 1960, 105,933 in 1961, and just 80,034 in 1962.

After the 1962 season the AA disbanded, and Dallas-Fort Worth moved into the Pacific Coast League. One year later Fort Worth businessman Tommy Mercer bought the DFW franchise, left Dallas in the PCL, and returned the Fort Worth Cats to the Texas League. The Cats finished last in 1964, however, and Dallas and Fort Worth reunited at Turnpike Stadium to play for six more years in the Texas League. Attendance was excellent, Turnpike Stadium was expanded, and in 1972 the Texas Rangers entered the American League.

Year	Record	Pcg.	Finish
1959	81-81	.500	Fifth (won opener, lost finals)
1960	64-90	.416	Sixth
1961	72-77	.483	Fifth
1962	59-90	.396	Sixth

Houston (Buffs)

Houston became a charter member of the Texas League in 1888, and for the next 70 years the Bayou City was a mainstay of the circuit. Buffalo Bayou gave the Houston team its famous nick-

AA baseball in Houston was played in historic Buff Stadium, which was severely damaged by Hurricane Carla just before the 1961 playoffs.

— Author's collection

name, and in 1928 the 14,000-seat Buffalo Stadium opened at present-day Cullen Boulevard. For decades the Buffs were a key farm club of the St. Louis Cardinals and in 1952 there was talk of bringing the Cards to Houston. Other efforts to bring big league baseball to Houston occurred in 1954, when the Athletics were ready to leave Philadelphia, and in 1958, when the Indians considered pulling out of Cleveland.

The Houston Sports Association was formed in 1957 to acquire a major league baseball team for Houston. Judge Roy Hofheinz, multimillionaire R. E. Smith, and promoter George Kirksey were three primary members of the HSA, which began steps to finance a major league stadium in 1958. Hofheinz, who would become president of the big league club, had conceived the idea for a domed stadium after visiting the Roman Colosseum, and plans evolved to bring the revolutionary concept to reality.

An early step in moving Houston into the big leagues was upgrading the Buffs from the Class AA Texas League into Class AAA. Similar plans were afoot in the Dallas area, and in 1959 Houston, Dallas, and Fort Worth acquired franchises in the American Association. The Buffs made an inauspicious debut, plunging to the cellar of the 10-team league and becoming the last club in AA history to lose 100 games (58–104). Houston ranked last in team hitting (.243) and next-to-last in staff ERA. Veteran catcher Ray Noble (.294 with 15 homers) and outfielder Jim Fridley (.282 with 26 homers) were the only regulars who hit well, although outfielder Rod Kanehl tied for the stolen base title (.238 with 18 steals).

Houston fortunes quickly improved as the Buffs made the playoffs the next two years. In 1960 Enos "Country" Slaughter replaced Rube Walker as manager. The 44-year-old outfielder had just completed 19 years in the big leagues, and he appeared in 40 games as a pinch hitter and outfielder (.289) while instilling his hustling style of play in the Buffs. The Chicago Cubs stocked their Triple-A affiliate with such talent as future Hall of Famer Billy Williams (.323 with 26 homers) and Ron Santo (.268 in 71 games), who would star for 15 years in the big leagues. Outfielders Lon Johnson (.289) and Dave Pope (.277), catchers Dick Bertell (.289) and Ray Noble (.274), and infielders Jim McKnight (.291 in 67 games) and Joe Macko (.239, 27 HR, 91 RBI) led a solid offense. Righthander Al Lary (12–8) and reliever E. V. Donnelly (11–6 in 53 games) provided good pitching, and righty Moe Drabowsky was spectacular in five starts (5–0 with four complete games, two shutouts, and a brilliant 0.90 ERA) before an inevitable callup to the Cubs.

Houston, tied for third place, squared off against first-place Denver in the opening round of playoffs. After five games the Buffs led Denver, three games to two, with the final two contests scheduled for Houston. But Denver's league-leading offense exploded to win decisively, 9–1 and 15–6.

Slaughter became player-manager of Raleigh in the Carolina League for 1961. The parent Cubs featured a revolving system of managers in Chicago, while in Houston Grady Hatton, Freddy Martin, Lou Klein, and then Harry Craft handled the managerial reins. The Buffs again featured several strong batters, including returning third sacker Jim McKnight (.283, 24 HR, 101 RBI), first basemen Pidge Browne (.350 in 62 games) and Marion Zipfel (.312 with 21 homers in 101 games), infielder George Freese (.314 in 58 games), and outfielders Henry Mitchell (.292, 14 HR, 75 RBI), Jim McAnany (.318 in 80 games) and Sam Drake (.307 in 83 games). The most dependable pitchers were righthanded returnees

Al Lary (15–9) and E. V. Donnelly (4–4 in 48 games), and George Schultz (6–1 in 24 appearances).

Houston had a losing record but qualified for the playoffs by finishing fourth in a six-team league. Just before the playoff opener in Houston, Hurricane Carla destroyed the grandstand at Buff Stadium. Houston would have to play every postseason game on foreign soil, and traveled to Indianapolis to take on the first-place Indians at Victory Field. The Indians owned a 12–3 advantage over the Buffs at Victory Field, but Houston scored a stunning upset, winning four out of five games. The Buffs then fell to Louisville, four games to two, but the HSA was delighted with Harry Craft's late-season leadership.

Craft was hired to manage the Colt .45s in 1962. The .45s played in makeshift Colt Stadium as the world's first domed stadium went up nearby. In 1965 "The Eighth Wonder of the World" opened; it was an enclosed, air-conditioned facility that could seat 66,000. "The day the doors on this park open," stated legendary baseball executive Branch Rickey, "every other park in the world will be antiquated." The Astrodome has insured Houston's place in baseball history.

Year	Record	Pcg.	Finish
1959	58-104	.358	Tenth
1960	83-71	.539	Third (lost opener)
1961	73-77	.487	Fourth (won opener, lost finals)

Indianapolis (Indians)

Baseball was played in Indianapolis by 1867, if not earlier. On July 19, 1867, the Indianapolis Actives beat Lafayette, 54–31, and in the second game of the afternoon the Western Club of Indianapolis was trounced by the famous Washington Nationals, 106–21. By 1876 the Indianapolis Blues brought professional baseball to the city, playing on a diamond at the fairgrounds racetrack before moving to a wooden ballpark on South Street between Alabama and Delaware streets. The Indianapolis Blues played in the International League in 1877, then joined the National League the next year. There was not another professional club in Indianapolis until

1883, when a new park was built at Seventh Street and Tennessee Avenue (although a ban on Sunday baseball forced the team to shift to Bruce Grounds, located outside the city limits, for Sunday games). The Indianapolis Hoosiers played in the old American Association in 1884, shifted to the Western League for 1885, then returned to the National League from 1887 through 1889. Indianapolis re-entered the Western League in 1892 and moved into a vast park on East Ohio Street — the nearest fence was 469 feet from home plate. The team enjoyed Western League pennants in 1895, 1897, and 1899, then moved into yet another new ballpark on Washington Street.

When the American Association was organized late in 1901, Indianapolis switched to the new league — and the Indians would become the only club to participate in every AA season to date. Throughout the final weeks of the inaugural season, Indianapolis and Louisville were neck and neck, but the Indians won the first AA pennant on the final day of the 1902 season by taking *three* games from St. Paul: a postponed rainout and the scheduled doubleheader. The veteran Indian squad was led by longtime favorite George Hogriever (.290 with 37 SBs — the right fielder had hit .402 for the 1895 Western League champs), first baseman George Kihm (.296), shortstop Pete O'Brien (.295), and outfielder Art Coulter (.290). But all championship teams of the dead-ball era featured fine pitching, and the Indians boasted a magnificent staff: righthanders Tom Williams (24–12) and Jack Sutthoff (24–13), and southpaws Win Kellum (25–10) and Frank Killen (16–6).

The team returned intact the next year, and Kellum again went 25–10, while Kihm improved to .320. But the other veterans began to show their age: performances went down throughout the lineup, and the Indians sagged to fourth place. W. H. Watkins, longtime president and field manager (he had first managed the Indians in 1884), resigned to take over the Minneapolis Millers, and the Indians dropped into the second division for the next four years.

But W. H. Watkins was lured back to lead the Tribe in 1906. Soon he stepped down as field manager to devote all of his energies to the front office, and by 1908 he had built another championship club, again edging Louisville for the pennant. Future National League star Rube Marquard led the league in victories, innings and strikeouts (28–19, 367 IP, 250 Ks), and pitched a no-hitter and four shutouts in six consecutive games. Player-manager Charlie Carr hit over .300 for the third year in a row (.301), and outfielder John Hayden became the first Indian to win the AA batting title (.316). In September, Marquard was sold to the New York Giants for an eye-popping $11,000, while Hayden (Cubs), shortstop Donie Bush (Tigers), and righthander "Bull" Durham (Giants) also were peddled to big league clubs.

Another downward spiral ensued. W. H. Watkins resigned for good, and there were consecutive last-place finishes in 1912 and 1913. Compounding the club's difficulties was the presence of the Indianapolis Hoosiers, a Federal League team which won that circuit's first pennant in 1913. Indian management responded by hiring manager Jack Hendricks away from Denver of the Western League.

A former major league outfielder, Hendricks was a skilled field general and a fiery motivator who led the Tribe to third place in 1914 and 1915, second place in 1916, and to the pennant and a Little World Series championship in 1917. Outfielder Tommy Griffith led the offense in 1914 (.340), outfielder Joe Kelly was the stolen base champ the next year (.300 with 61 thefts), and fellow outfielder Duke Reilly was close behind (.288 with 47 SBs), and in 1916 Reilly (.292 with 37 SBs) and infielder Herman Bronkie (.290 with 45 SBs) paced the attack. In 1917 Reilly (.246) and Bronkie (.265) had off-years at the plate, and the Indians finished next-to-last in team hitting (.251). But the Tribe led the league in fielding and pulled off a triple play against Milwaukee to clinch the title on the last day of the season, then went on to down the Toronto Maple Leafs for another Little World Series triumph.

In 1918 Hendricks was hired to manage the St. Louis Cardinals, and future Hall of Famer Nap Lajoie became the Indianapolis player-manager (at the age of 42 he hit .282 in his final season as a player; the previous year, as player-manager of Toronto, he hit .380 to lead the International League in average, hits, and doubles). Jack Hendricks returned to Indianapolis in 1919, but even though he could not produce another pennant, he returned to the big leagues in 1924 after having managed the Tribe for nine seasons.

Southpaw Teller Cavet pitched for the club from 1918 through 1923, enjoying his best years in 1919 (with a league-leading 28–16 in 60 games) and 1921 (23–16). Mordecai "Three-Finger" Brown was part of the mound corps in 1919, and another former big leaguer, Bill Burwell, suffered a finger mutilation during World War I action, but found his curve to be *more* effective, and hurled for the Tribe from 1923 through 1934. He was the league leader in innings pitched in 1923, victories and ERA in 1925, and losses in 1929 (15–20). The righthander enjoyed back-to-back 20-win seasons in 1925 (24–9) and 1926 (21–14), overall he was 175–143 with the Tribe, and he returned to Indianapolis as manager in 1945 and 1946. Infielder Doug Baird, who had played for five National League teams, brought consecutive stolen base titles to Indianapolis as manager in 1921 and 1922. Righthander Carmen "Specs" Hill, who appeared in the National League at intervals from 1915 through 1930, pitched for the Indians from 1922 through 1926, winning 15 games or more in each season, with an especially effective showing in 1926 (21–7). Southpaw Jesse Petty was on the mound staff from 1920 through 1924; after leading the AA in victories and ERA (29–8, 2.83) in 1924, he was sold to Brooklyn. Reb Russell, once a fine major league pitcher, was acquired as a 37-year-old outfielder in 1926 (.322); he won the batting title in 1927 (.385 with 96 RBIs) and hit well again the next year (.311) before finally fading at the age of 40 in 1929 (.261). Catcher Johnny "Mutt" Riddle toiled 12 years for the Tribe (1928–37 and 1946–47).

Player-manager Bruno Betzel guided the Indians to a pennant in 1928. There was a solid pitching staff, led by Steve Swetonic (20–8), southpaw Emil Yde (19–12), Gorham Leverett (19–12), and Bill Burwell (13–10). But the strength of the club was an explosive offense. The team tied for first in batting (.302); third baseman Fred Haney (.334 with 43 steals and 6 triples) was the stolen base champ; outfielder Wid Matthews (.323) tied Haney for the league lead in triples; and fine performances also were turned in by outfielders Adam Comorsky (.357), Herman Layne (.347) and Reb Russell (.311), catcher Roy Spencer (.296), and second baseman M. T. Connolly (.291). The Tribe went on to wallop Rochester in the Little World Series, winning five games, tying one, and losing not a single contest to the International League champs.

The Great Depression began the next year, and Indian baseball fortunes also took a nosedive. In 1930 the club finished in last place, although light standards were installed at Washington Park

Grandstand and pressbox at Victory Field.

— Photo by the author

and the Tribe's first night game was played June 9, a 1–0 loss to St. Paul. But owner Norman Perry announced that a new, $350,000 stadium would be built on 16th Street, and the 14,500-seat facility opened before the end of the 1931 season.

Infielder Frank Sigafoos, who hit .326 in 1931 and .313 the following year, was the batting champ of 1933 (.370 with 126 RBIs). Lefthanded slugger Vernon Washington missed a hitting title by one percentage point (.367 with 120 RBIs) the next year, but Johnny Cooney, who had become an Indian outfield star after his big league pitching career ended, won the batting championship in 1935 (.371). Reliable hurlers during this period were future major leaguers Jim Turner (1933 through 1936) and Vance Page (1934 through 1938), and Robert "Lefty" Logan (1931 through 1946), who set the American Association record for longevity with a single club.

Turner (18–13, with a .282 batting average in 51 games), Page (15–13), and Logan (16–9) were the best pitchers when the Indians went to the playoff finals in 1936. The explosive batting order included the legendary Ox Eckhardt (.353, including a 6-for-6 game on July 4), first baseman Dick Siebert (.330), catcher

Johnny Riddle (.325), and outfielders Fred Berger (.323 with 106 RBIs) and Hubert Bates (.324). Two years later the Tribe again reached the playoffs behind Vance Page (15–5), third baseman Buck Fausett (.339), infielder Steve Mesner (.331), and outfielder Glenn Chapman (.308 with 103 RBIs). Although most of the key players moved up, outfielders Milton Galatzer (.325) and Myron McCormick (.318), and catcher Bill Baker (.338) led the team to the 1939 playoff finals.

In 1942 Owen J. "Donie" Bush became part owner. A native of Indianapolis, Bush played shortstop on the Indians' 1908 pennant-winners, played in the American League until 1923, then managed the Tribe from 1924 through 1926. In 1943 Bush resumed the managerial post, and he guided his club to the playoff finals. Southpaw Jim Trexler led the league in wins and ERA (19–7, 2.14), while the best hitters were outfielder-third baseman Gil English (.322), catcher Stew Hofferth (.301), and outfielders Jess Pike (.318) and Joe Moore (.305).

During World War II, the name of the stadium was changed to Victory Park, and after the 1944 season — after the Indians hit a meager total of *two* home runs in Victory Park all year — the fences were moved in. Former pitcher Bill Burwell became manager in 1945 and promptly led the Indians to back-to-back playoff berths. ERA leader Jim Wallace (17–4, 1.83), a southpaw, and right-hander Ed Wright (13–5) were a lethal one-two mound combination in 1945, and Emerson Roser (7–3, 1.73) kept the ERA title in Indianapolis in 1946. Outfielder Stan Wentzel (.321 with 30 steals and 106 RBIs) was the Rookie of the Year and MVP of 1945, and he had another good season in 1946 (.299). Other productive hitters in both 1945 and 1946 were Gil English (.286 with 97 RBIs, and .304) and first baseman Vince Shupe (.315 and .297). Outfielder Art Parks (.312) was an offensive leader in 1945, while key producers in 1946 were outfielder Joe Bestudik (.279, 15 HR, 109 RBI), second sacker Al Roberge (.310) — and shortstop Sibby Sisti, who won the batting title (.343) and was named Minor League Player of the Year by *The Sporting News*.

In 1948 Al Lopez, who had just ended a 19-year major league catching career, was hired as manager of the Tribe, and he promptly engineered the only 100-victory season in Indianapolis baseball history (100–54). After this first-place finish, Lopez had to settle for second place in 1949 and 1950 (during his long big league managerial tenure, he was dubbed "Bridesmaid" because of *nine* second-place finishes). The 1948 pennant-winners — the first for Indianapolis since 1928 — were knocked off in the first round of playoffs. But the 1949 Indians, who missed first place by just one game, won the playoffs, and the 1950 team grudgingly yielded the playoff finals to Columbus, four games to three.

Righthander Bob Malloy (21–7) led the league in victories and innings in 1945. Malloy sagged badly the next year (4–9, 6.77 ERA), but another righthander, Mel Queen, won the pitcher's Triple Crown in 1946 (22–9, 178 K, 2.57 ERA). Jimmy Walsh was hard to beat in 1946 (15–4), while southpaw Royce Lint was effective in both 1946 (14–3) and 1950 (12–6). Right fielder Ted Beard led the AA in walks in 1948 (.301 with 128 Ws) and 1949 (.277 with 132 Ws), while Jack Cassini was the 1948 stolen base champ (.305 with 33 steals) and a .300 hitter again the next year. MVP first sacker Les Fleming won the 1948 RBI title (.323, 26 HR, 143 RBI — plus a .340 average the next season), and third baseman-outfielder Froilan Fernandez kept the crown in Indianapolis in 1949 (.312, 21 HR, 128 RBI). Shortstop Pete Castiglione (.308) and outfielder Culley Rikard (.285 with 107 RBIs) were key offensive performers in 1948, and outfielder-pinch hitter Dom Dallesandro was impressive in 1949 (.342 in 44 games) and 1950 (.350 in 101 games). A different highlight of this period occurred on June 17, 1949, when the first telecast of a Tribe contest went out over WFBM-TV.

Lopez left to manage the Cleveland Indians after the 1950 season, ending a highly successful three-year reign in Indianapolis. Outfielder Dave Pope won a batting title in 1952 (.352), and he hit well (.287, 24 HR, 88 RBI) for the club that reached the playoffs in 1953. Infielder Al Smith also was impressive in 1952 (.288 with 20 homers) and 1953 (.332 with 18 homers and 75 RBIs in just 86 games), while outfielder Wally Post was the 1953 RBI champ and missed the home run title by the margin of a baserunning mistake (.289, 33 HR, 120 RBI — Wally was called out and awarded a single when he ran past Pope, who was on first when Wally hit a ball over the fence).

The Tribe enjoyed a magnificent season in 1954. Managed by Kerby Farrell, the Indians defeated the AA All-Stars, 3–2, at Victory Field, won the pennant by a 10½-game margin, then took the playoff opener before losing the finals to Louisville. Stars of the team included such future big leaguers as home run champ Rocky Colavito (.271, 38 HR, 116 RBI), lanky righthander "Toothpick" Sam Jones (15–8), catcher Hank Foiles (.332), left fielder Harry "Suitcase" Simpson (.282), third sacker Billy Harrell (.307), and first baseman Joe Altobelli (.287). The most outstanding performance came from the explosive left arm of 20-year-old Herb Score, who was named MVP and Rookie of the Year after leading the league in almost every pitching category (22–5, 21 CG in 32 GS, 2.62 ERA, 251 IP, 330 K, 140 W). Score established the all-time American Association strikeout record, led the league in walks (Jones was number two in both categories — no one dug in at the plate against Score or Toothpick Sam), struck out 17 in one game, and won the pitcher's Triple Crown.

Fifteen players from the 1954 championship club were promoted, sold or traded, and despite the presence of Colavito (.268, 30 HR, 104 RBI, and the fans' Most Popular Player for the second consecutive year), the Tribe sagged to seventh place. Despite good attendance, Cleveland had lost money for years on its Indianapolis club, and after the 1955 season announced its intention to pull out of the city. But within weeks 6,672 shareholders, buying stock at $10 per share, put up almost $205,000, and on January 1, 1956, the Tribe became a community-owned franchise. The affiliation with Cleveland was retained, along with field manager Kerby Farrell, while "Mr. Baseball" in Indianapolis, Owen J. Bush, assumed the role of president-general manager (in 1967, after the city purchased Victory Field, the handsome old ballpark was renamed Bush Stadium).

The 1956 Indians delighted their 6,672 owners by storming to the American Association pennant, winning the playoffs with a four-game sweep of Denver in the finals, then sweeping Rochester in the first four games of the Junior World Series. Russ Nixon (.315) was the Tribe's catcher until he was called up by Cleveland after playing 105 games. Righthander Stan Pitula (15–4) led the club in victories, but lefty Hank Aguirre (10–6) was promoted to Cleveland in July — and replaced by a razor-sharp Bud Daley (11–1, 2.31 ERA). Outfielder Carroll Hardy, who had spent the previous fall as a halfback with the San Francisco 49ers, was red-hot (.385) until he was summoned by his draft board after 21 games. But Cleveland obtained Dave Pope as a replacement, and the veteran returned to Indianapolis by leading the club in homers (.302,

25 HR, 76 RBI in 100 games). Billy Harrell (.279), Rudy Regalado (.322 after a .316 in 1955), and Joe Altobelli (.245, 19 HR, 81 RBI) were other familiar faces, while infielders Larry Raines (.309) and Bobby Young (.330) added hot bats to a productive lineup. The most notable newcomer was right fielder Roger Maris (.293, 17 HR, 75 RBI), who exploded for a pair of homers and seven RBIs in the second game of the Junior World Series.

After the season, Cleveland broke off their lengthy affiliation with Indianapolis, but young Max Schumacher joined the club as ticket manager, eventually rising to general manager and president and earning widespread respect as a baseball executive. The next few seasons were disappointing, but in 1957 fans enjoyed the performances of towering (6′7) first baseman Ron Jackson (.310, 21 HR, 102 RBI) and outfielder Neil Chrisley (.343). Ted Beard, long a popular member of the Tribe, was promoted to the White Sox after playing 96 games, but the 36-year-old outfielder had logged enough at-bats to win the 1957 batting crown (.347). Noted big league catcher Walker Cooper was the Tribe's player-manager in 1958 and 1959, and in his first season 19-year-old outfielder Johnny Callison (.283, 29 HR, 93 RBI) and catcher John Romano (.291, 25 HR, 89 RBI) finished one-two in the league's home run derby. In 1959 slugger Ron Jackson returned to man first base and win the home run and RBI crowns (.286, 30 HR, 99 RBI), lefty Gary Peters (13–11) hurled a no-hitter at Bush Stadium, and catcher Camilio Carreon (.311, 10 HR, 91 RBI) was named Rookie of the Year.

In 1961 and 1962 the Indians posted the best record in the AA, although each year the Tribe fell in the opening round of playoffs. The best pitchers of 1961 were victory leader Don Rudolph (18–9) and fellow southpaw Claude Osteen (15–11), while the offense was sparked by left fielder Joe Gaines (.315), shortstop and Rookie of the Year Chico Ruiz (.272 with a league-leading 44 steals — the Tribe led the league in stolen bases for the fifth year in a row), and the "Bombsie Twins," catcher Don Pavletich (.295 with 22 homers) and third baseman Cliff Cook (.311, 32 HR, 119 RBI), who led the league in home runs, RBIs and runs, and who was named Most Valuable Player. In 1962 Hall of Fame shortstop Luke Appling managed the Tribe to its second consecutive pennant by a 10-game margin. First baseman Tom McCraw won the batting title (.328), shortstop Al Weis kept the stolen base crown in Indianapolis (.296

with 31 steals), third sacker Ramon Conde wielded a dangerous bat (.353 with 76 RBIs in 89 games), and Al Worthington (15–4) and southpaw Franklin Kreutzer (15–10) led the team in victories.

The American Association ceased to exist before the next season. The Tribe and the Arkansas Travelers were added to the International League for 1963, and Indianapolis finished in first place for the third year in a row. The Indians moved to the Pacific Coast League in 1964, but there were no championships recorded during the five seasons spent by Indianapolis in the PCL.

The 1969 the American Association was reorganized, and the Tribe produced the batting champ and MVP in outfielder Bernie Carbo (.359 with 21 homers in 111 games). The next season righthander Milt Wilcox (12–10 with five shutouts) was voted Pitcher of the Year and southpaw Ross Grimsley (11–8, 2.73 ERA) won the ERA title. Grimsley rocketed to a 6–0 start in 1971 before being promoted to Cincinnati, but he had sparked the Tribe to a lead it would not relinquish. First baseman-outfielder Willie Smith came down from the Reds at midseason to lead the offense (.351 in 77 games), Milt Wilcox also returned for the last half of the year (8–5), and Pedro Borbon provided outstanding righthanded relief (12–6 in 56 appearances). The Indians posted the league's best record and won the Eastern Division by a whopping 13½-game margin, but lost to the Western Division champs, the Denver Bears, in the seventh game of the playoff series.

Outfielder Gene Locklear won the 1972 batting title (.325), first baseman Roe Skidmore (.290 with 89 RBIs) was RBI champ, and reliever Steve Blateric fashioned a 1.58 ERA in 63 appearances. In 1973 Indianapolis fans enjoyed the exploits of future big league standouts George Foster, stolen base champ and Rookie of the Year Ken Griffey (.327 with 43 steals in 107 games), and third sacker Dan Driessen (.409 with 46 RBIs in 47 games before a callup by the Reds). Vern Rapp, who had guided the Tribe to the best record of 1971, repeated the feat in 1974. Like the 1971 Tribe, the 1974 Indians lost to the Western Division champs in the seventh game of the playoffs. Righthander Tom Carroll (8–4) pitched a no-hitter, Ken Griffey was outstanding (.333) in 43 games, and second baseman Junior Kennedy (.284) went 6-for-6 in a 28-hit explosion at Denver when the Tribe trounced the Bears, 15–7.

In 1975 Pat Zachry was 10–7 for the second year in a row, and he won the ERA title (2.43). The 1978 Tribe rang up the league's best record and brought to Indianapolis the third Eastern Division title since 1971, although once again the Tribe would lose in the playoffs. Outfielder John "Champ" Summers (.368, 34 HR, 124 RBI) won the home run and RBI titles, and was named MVP and the Minor League Player of the Year. First baseman Art DeFreites (.327, 32 HR, 101 RBI) gave the Indians a powerful one-two punch in the batting order, while center fielder Lynn Jones (.328) and third sacker Harry Spilman (.295) also helped the Tribe lead the league in team hitting (.286) and homers (141 — an all-time Indianapolis high).

Norm Beplay, who became a part-time public address announcer for the Indians at old Washington Park in 1929 and who had been the regular PA man since 1942, retired at the end of the 1979 season. In 1982, despite a steady stream of callups by Cincinnati during the season, the Tribe stubbornly battled toward a championship, as typified by a seven-inning doubleheader opener against the 89ers on July 14. Oklahoma City scored seven runs in the top of the seventh to take a 13–7 lead. But as a home crowd of 12,612 screamed in delight, the Indians fought back with seven runs of their own to win, 14–13. Stolen base champ Gary Redus had a magnificent year (.333, 24 HR, 93 RBI, 54 SB). Important contributions were made by catcher Steve Christmas (.306), second baseman Tom Lawless (.308 with 35 steals in 86 games), outfielder Dallas Williams (.300), third sacker Nick Esasky (.264 with 27 homers in 105 games), southpaw reliever Dave Tomlin (9–2 in 60 appearances), and colorful righthander Brad "The Animal" Lesley (6–4 in 40 appearances).

After a disappointing 1983 season, during which the Cincinnati Reds refused to permit the Tribe to use a DH, Indianapolis severed a 16-year relationship and became the Triple-A affiliate of Montreal. The new association was an immediate success, as manager Buck Rodgers led the Indians to the league's best record and was named Minor League Manager of the Year by *The Sporting News*. The Tribe roared to a first-place finish with a whopping 11-game margin, although there was a disappointing end to the season when the Indians fell in the opening round of playoffs. Indianapolis was sparked by a pitching staff which featured southpaws Chris Welsh (13–4 with a league-leading 3.01 ERA), Joe Hesketh (12–3, 3.05 ERA), and Dave Schuler (8–0 in 42 relief appearances). The brightest offensive stars during the season were second baseman

Mike Gates (.297), third sacker Brad Mills (.315 in 66 games), infielder Wally Johnson (.283 with 27 steals in 97 games), center fielder Roy Johnson (.270 with 22 steals in 107 games), left fielder Mike Fuentes (.251, 22 HR, 80 RBI), and Razor Shines (.282, 18 HR, 80 RBI) and Ron Johnson (.303), who divided duties at first and DH. The next year Wally Johnson (.309 with 35 steals) returned, along with Razor Shines for part of the season (.308 in 65 games), while first baseman Andres Gallaraga was named Rookie of the Year (.269, 25 HR, 87 RBI). But Buck Rodgers departed for Montreal and the injury-plagued Expos put 46 men in Indianapolis during the season, which sentenced the Tribe to last place.

True to form, however, the Indians rebounded in 1986, compiling a remarkable first-to-last-to-first sequence of finishes over three years. Indianapolis, celebrating its centennial season of professional baseball, won the Eastern Division title by nine games, then downed Denver, four games to three, for the playoff championship. In the seventh game of the playoff the Tribe, which came from behind to win 34 times during 1986, trailed 4–2 in the bottom of the ninth, before rallying to score the winning run before a frenzied home crowd. Righthanders Rodger Cole (12–4), Curt Brown (11–3 as a reliever), and Bob Sebra (9–2 before a callup to Montreal) led the mound corps, while All-Star second baseman Casey Candaele (.302) and outfielders Dallas Williams (.289), Derrell Baker (.284), and Billy Moore (.256, 23 HR, 82 RBI) formed the heart of the offense.

Joe Sparks, Manager of the Year in 1986, earned the honor for the second year in a row by leading the Tribe to third place, then defeating Louisville and first-place Denver in the playoffs to repeat as pennant-winners. Batting champ Dallas Williams (.357), in his fifth year as an Indian, posted the highest average in Class AAA. Other productive members of a talented roster included shortstop Luis Rivera (.312), second sacker Johnny Paredes (.312 with 30 steals), switch-hitting first baseman Jack Daugherty (.312), four-year Tribe veteran Razor Shines (.279), outfielders Tom Romano (.306), Alonzo Powell (.200, 19 HR, 74 RBI), and Ron Shepherd (.291), righthanded reliever Tim Barrett (10–1 in 46 games), and ERA leader Pascual Perez (9–7), in a comeback season following injuries and drug problems.

The Tribe was better than ever in 1988. For the third consecutive year, Sparks was voted Manager of the Year for guiding the

Indians to first place and the Eastern Division title, defeating Omaha for a third straight flag, then downing International League champion Rochester, four games to two, to win the first Triple-A Alliance title. Returning to lead the offense were second baseman Johnny Paredes (.295 with 43 steals), outfielder Billy Moore (.285 with a league-leading 88 runs and 34 doubles), and first sacker Jack Daugherty (.285). The pitching staff was formidable, leading the league in ERA (a sparkling 2.96), shutouts (17) and strikeouts (966), and featuring returnee Bob Sebra (12–6), righthanders Jeff Fischer (13–8, 2.69 ERA) and Brian Holman (8–1 with a 1.99 ERA in 42 games), Richard Sauveur (7–4, 2.43 in 43 games), and Mike Smith (5–1, 2.57 in 32 games).

In 1989 Indianapolis won an unprecedented fourth consecutive American Association pennant. The Tribe posted the best record in the league, defeated Western Division champ Omaha three games to two for the AA flag, then swept Richmond in four games to win a second straight Alliance playoff. New field general Tom Runnels was named Manager of the Year. His pitching staff featured strikeout king Mark Gardner (12–4, 2.37 ERA, 175 Ks in 163 IP), righthander Urbano Lugo (12–4, 2.94 ERA), ERA titlist Rich Thompson (9–6, 2.06), and relievers Jay Baller (2.02 ERA with a league-leading 34 saves in 62 games), Brett Gideon (7–2 with 2.26 ERA in 47 appearances), and Jeff Dedmon (8–6 with a 2.71 ERA in 51 games). Second baseman Junior Noboa won the batting title (.340), shortstop Jeff Huson was runner-up (.304 with 30 steals), outfielder Larry Walker (.270 with 36 steals) came back from a severe knee injury, and popular Razor Shines returned for a fifth season with the Tribe (.305).

Since 1982 Indianapolis has recorded five first-place finishes, four Eastern Division titles, five playoff championships, victories in the only two Alliance Classics staged to date, and has become the sole franchise to claim four consecutive American Association pennants. In more than a century of professional baseball, Indianapolis has enjoyed its most remarkable success during the past eight seasons.

Year	Record	Pcg.	Finish
1902	95-45	.681	First
1903	78-61	.561	Fourth
1904	69-85	.448	Sixth
1905	69-83	.454	Sixth
1906	56-98	.383	Eighth

1907	73-81	.473	Sixth
1908	92-61	.601	First
1909	83-85	.494	Fourth
1910	69-96	.418	Seventh
1911	78-88	.470	Seventh
1912	56-111	.335	Eighth
1913	68-99	.407	Eighth
1914	88-77	.533	Third
1915	81-70	.536	Third
1916	95-71	.572	Second
1917	90-63	.588	First (won Little World Series)
1918	41-34	.547	Third
1919	85-68	.556	Fourth
1920	83-83	.500	Fifth
1921	83-85	.494	Fourth
1922	87-80	.521	Fourth
1923	72-94	.434	Seventh
1924	92-73	.558	Second
1925	92-74	.554	Second
1926	94-71	.570	Second
1927	70-98	.417	Sixth
1928	99-68	.593	First (won Little World Series)
1929	79-89	.467	Fourth
1930	60-93	.393	Eighth
1931	86-80	.518	Third
1932	86-80	.518	Fifth
1933	82-72	.532	Third
1934	77-75	.507	Fifth
1935	85-67	.559	Second
1936	79-75	.513	Fourth (won opener, lost finals)
1937	67-85	.441	Sixth
1938	80-74	.519	Fourth (lost opener)
1939	82-72	.532	Third (won opener, lost finals)
1940	62-84	.425	Sixth
1941	65-88	.425	Sixth
1942	76-78	.494	Sixth
1943	85-67	.559	Second (won opener, lost finals)
1944	57-93	.380	Sixth
1945	90-63	.592	Second (lost opener)
1946	88-65	.575	Second (won opener, lost finals)
1947	74-79	.484	Sixth
1948	100-54	.649	First (lost opener)
1949	92-61	.604	Second (won opener, finals, and Jr. World Series)
1950	85-67	.559	Second (won opener, lost finals)
1951	68-84	.447	Seventh
1952	75-79	.487	Sixth
1953	82-72	.532	Fourth (lost opener)
1954	95-57	.625	First (won opener, lost finals)

1955	67-86	.438	Seventh
1956	92-62	.597	First (won opener, lost finals)
1957	74-80	.481	Sixth
1958	72-82	.468	Sixth
1959	86-76	.531	Third
1960	65-89	.422	Seventh
1961	86-64	.573	First (lost opener)
1962	89-58	.605	First (lost opener)
1969	74-66	.529	Third
1970	71-69	.507	Second
1971	84-55	.604	First (won Eastern Division, lost finals)
1972	61-79	.436	Seventh
1973	74-62	.544	Second
1974	78-57	.578	First (won Eastern Division, lost finals)
1975	71-64	.526	Fourth
1976	62-73	.459	Sixth
1977	72-64	.529	Second
1978	78-57	.578	First (won Eastern Division, lost finals)
1979	67-69	.493	Fifth
1980	58-77	.430	Eighth
1981	62-74	.456	Seventh
1982	75-61	.551	First (won Eastern Division and finals)
1983	64-72	.471	Seventh
1984	91-63	.591	First (lost opener)
1985	61-81	.430	Eighth
1986	80-62	.563	First (won Eastern Division and finals)
1987	74-64	.536	Third (won opener and finals)
1988	89-53	.627	First (won Eastern Division, finals, and Alliance Classic)
1989	87-59	.596	First (won Eastern Division, finals, and Alliance Classic)
1990	61-85	.418	Seventh
1991	75-68	.524	Fourth

Kansas City (Blues)

Like other charter cities of the American Association, Kansas City became the site of enthusiastic amateur baseball competition during the post-Civil War years. By the 1870s a diamond at Riverview Park near 14th and Oak streets was the home of the crack Kansas City Antelopes, but when the club traveled to Atchinson they were soundly thrashed by the Pomeroys. On the return contest at Riverview Park, a riot erupted and the umpire fled for his life. A replay was scheduled for the following Saturday, but to insure

Frontier gunfighter Wild Bill Hickok was utilized as an umpire to control the violence at an early Kansas City game in Riverview Park.

— Courtesy Kansas State Historical Society

order the services of Wild Bill Hickok were engaged as umpire. Hickok, a famous frontier gambler, scout, lawman and pistoleer, also was a baseball krank, and he gladly officiated at Riverview Park armed with a brace of sixguns. Understandably, there was no trouble as the Antelopes downed the Pomeroys, 48–28. Asked by Antelope partisans how they could repay him, Hickok requested an open carriage with a matched pair of white horses from Frank Short's livery stable, and the gunfighter-umpire proudly drove around Market Square waving at admiring citizens.

Late in May 1884, Altoona of the Union Association, a one-year major league, lost its 6–19 club to Kansas City. Playing at Athletic Park at Southwest Boulevard and Summit Street, Kansas City staggered to a 14–63 record, and the team finished the season — with a characteristic 2–15 mark — at Wilmington. After a taste of big league ball, Kansas City acquired a National League franchise in 1886, but the KC Cowboys finished next-to-last. The following season Kansas City joined the Western League, and by 1888, togged in blue stockings, the team had acquired a nickname that would prevail for two-thirds of a century in KC: the Blues (although Cowboys also would be used for years). Kansas City returned to the big leagues in 1889 by spending a losing season in the old American Association, then the Blues played for 10 years in the Western Association. After playing in the Western League in 1901, the Blues became charter members of the newly-formed American Association.

Kansas City began AA play in Exposition Park, but soon the club was treated to a new stadium, 11,000-seat Exposition Park at 20th and Prospect. Although the Blues would not win a pennant until war-shortened 1918, Kansas City fans responded enthusiastically to a succesion of fine performances. The first two AA home run champs wore Blues uniforms: outfielder Mike Smith in 1902 (.312 with 10 roundtrippers), and first baseman Mike Grady (.324 in 1902) the next year (.355 with 16 homers). The 1905 Blues (still called the cowboys in many quarters) finished last and lost 17 in a row, but on June 14 pulled off *two* triple plays — a feat unique in American Association history.

On August 10, 1906, righthander Ducky Swann (22–13) pitched the league's first no-hitter. Swann pitched well again the following season (21–19), while first baseman Jake Beckley won the batting title (.365). In 1908 two members of the pitching staff, righthanders Chick Brandom (17–13) and 18-year-old Smokey Joe Wood, twirled no-hitters within eight days, on May 14 (Brandom) and May 21. Brandom (20–15) and big league veteran Dusty Rhoades (21–15) were 20-game winners for the 1910 Blues, and Rhoades repeated the feat the following year (20–16). In 1912 Rhoades pulled off a third consecutive 20-win season (21–15), while righthander "Big Bill" Powell (27–12, 340 IP, 174 K) led the AA in innings and strikeouts. Bert Gallia led the league in victories (26–12) in 1914 and outfielder Bash Compton was the stolen base champ (.325 with 58 steals). In 1915 Compton tied for the home run lead (.343 with a dead-ball total of nine homers) and first baseman Jack Lelivelt paced the AA in batting, hits, doubles, and total bases (.346, 41 2B). For the next two seasons outfielder Beals Becker reigned as hitting and home run king (.343 and .323, with 15 homers both in 1916 and 1917). Jack Lelivelt (.306) and catcher Bubbles Hargrave (.317) also hit well for the 1916 Blues, and Mike Regan (22–17 with a league-leading 340 IP) and Roy Sanders (20–18) were 20-game winners, but the team finished in the second division.

The long pennant drought finally came to an end in 1918,

when the first-place Blues were awarded the championship as the season suddenly was terminated because of wartime conditions. Charles Adams (14–3) and outfielder Wilbur Good (.321) starred for the club. Good played eight seasons for the Blues, 1917 through 1924, when he was 39 (but he remained active as a player until 1931, retiring at the age of 46 after 27 seasons with a .334 lifetime average). While with Kansas City he led the league in hits three times and in runs once. From 1919 through 1923 Good batted .348, .334, .349, .352, and .350.

Late in the 1913 season the Blues acquired a 6′1, 185-pound first baseman from the St. Louis Browns. Bunny Brief (his real name was Antonio Bordetski) would spend eight more years with Kansas City, as well as five seasons with two other American Association clubs, and the righthanded slugger went on to establish numerous league hitting records. In 1914, his first full year in KC, Bunny performed impressively enough (.318, 51 2B, 16 3B, 12 HR, 38 SB, 123 RBI, and a 30-game hitting streak) to return to the American League. During the next three seasons he bounced from the Chicago White Sox to the Salt Lake City Bees to the Pittsburgh Pirates to the Louisville Colonels. Bunny returned to Kansas City in 1918, and the next year he ripped out the first of eight consecutive 100-plus RBI seasons (.324 with 101 RBIs).

Beginning in 1920 (.319, 23 HR, 120 RBI) Bunny won four RBI titles in a row and three consecutive home run crowns. He enjoyed his finest season at the age of 29 in 1921 (.361, 42 HR, 191, and a league-leading 51 doubles and 166 runs), but again dominated AA pitching in 1922 (.339, 40 HR, 151 RBI). The next season Bunny led the league in RBIs and runs scored (.359, 161 R, 29 HR, 164 RBI). His numbers slipped in 1923 (.338, 17 HR, 104 RBI), and he was dealt to Milwaukee, where he led the league in homers and RBIs in 1924 and in home runs again the next year.

Another slugger who became familiar to Kansas City fans during the 1920s was lefthanded first baseman Dud Branom. A Texan who stood 6′1 and weighed 190 pounds, Branom wore a Blues uniform from 1920 through 1926. During the first three years, he split each season between Kansas City and other teams. But he was the everyday first sacker in 1923 (.348), 1924 (.318 with a league-leading 22 triples), 1925 (.294), and 1926 (.351 with 116 RBIs). By the time Branom was promoted to the Philadelphia Athletics another Texan, Fred Nicholson, had become a regular in the outfield. Nicholson already had spent 13 years as a pro, including five seasons in the big leagues and four in the AA with St. Paul and Toledo. He spent six seasons, 1926–31, with the Blues, and hit over .300 four times: his best seasons were 1917 (.320 with 113 RBIs and 20 SBs) and 1929 (.324).

During these same six years, Tom Sheehan pitched for the Blues. The big righthander (6′3, 220 pounds) had led the AA in victories, ERA and games in 1922 and 1923, and in 1927 he paced the league in wins and innings for Kansas City (26–13 with 331 IP). Jimmy Zinn, another fine righthander, was a mainstay of the Blues' staff from 1922 through 1928, winning 138 games in seven seasons. An excellent hitter (.301 lifetime), Zinn batted over .300 in every season for the Blues except the last. Frequently used as a pinch hitter, first baseman and outfielder, his best seasons at the plate came in 1923 (.354) and 1926 (.366), when he went 6-for-6 while hurling the Blues to victory over Columbus. Zinn came to Kansas City from Pittsburgh for the latter part of 1922 (18–5), enjoyed a banner year for the 1923 champs, had another standout season in 1928 (23–13), and won the ERA title in 1927 (24–12, 3.08). Also in 1927, fabled minor league slugger Joe Hauser spent his only season in Kansas City. Hauser was a lefthanded power hitter. The vast expanses of right field in Meuhlebach Field cut down on his homer production but helped him lead the league in triples (.353, 49 2B, 22 3B, 20 HR, 134 RBI, 145 R, 25 SB).

Brewer owner George Meuhlebach, who had purchased the Blues from the estate of George Tebeau, built a 17,500-seat, $400,000 stadium at 22nd Street and Brooklyn Avenue. Meuhlebach Field, constructed on the site of a former frog pond and ash heap, was a bowl — fans entered the upper row of the concrete park at ground level, and box seat holders walked down toward the level of the playing field. Right-field dimensions were astounding: 450 feet from home plate with a 60-foot-high wall. Five seasons passed before Joe Hauser somehow powered the first two stratospheric home runs over the right-field fence.

Meuhlebach Field opened in 1923, and the Blues responded by bringing Kansas City its second AA pennant with 112 victories (St. Paul was right behind with 111 wins), then downing Baltimore in the Little World Series. Jimmy Zinn posted the best record (27–6) of his 25-year career, and the hard-hitting lineup led the league in batting by 20 points with a record .315 team average while lofting 109 homers, also the top mark in the circuit. Bunny Brief led the AA in runs and RBIs (.359, 29 HR, 164 RBI, 161 R), player-manager Wilbur Good (.350, 136 R) and Dud Branom (.348) enjoyed banner seasons, and so did catcher Bill Skiff (.335) and Buckshot Wright (.313), who was propelled into an 11-year big league career as a shortstop.

In 1929 Kansas City put together another superb championship club (111–56), and once again St. Paul finished second with an excellent team of its own (102–64). The mound corps boasted no overwhelming stars but permitted the fewest runs in the league, while the batting order bristled with lethal hitters: outfielders Denver Grigsby (.345), Fred Nicholson (.344), Robert Seeds (.342) and Ollie Tucker (.336); catchers Tom Angley (.389) and John Peters (.320); and infielders Joe Kuhel (.325) and Harry Riconda (.320). The Blues went two-for-two in the Little World Series, beating Rochester five games to four.

The next several seasons brought few highlights. Outfielder Eddie Pick was acquired from Milwaukee in 1930 and performed impressively for three seasons (.310 with a league-leading 107 walks, .318 and 125 runs, and .344 with 121 RBIs). On June 11, 1935, during a game at Minneapolis, big (6′3, 215 pound) first baseman Dale Alexander (.358) rifled four home runs out of Nicollet Park. "Big Alex" hit only 12 other homers during 1935, and the next season (.315) he collected merely five. But Alexander helped the 1936 Blues make the playoffs, although the club lost the opener to first-place Milwaukee.

By now the New York Yankees owned the Blues and their ballpark, which was rechristened Ruppert Stadium in 1937, after Yankees owner Jacob Ruppert. A 12-foot-high fence cut across the vast outfield: the distances now measured 350 feet down the lines and 400 in center. Yankee talent began to assert itself in 1938, when the Blues finished second, then won the playoffs and went on to defeat Newark, four games to three, in the Junior World Series. Under manager Bill Meyer the Blues featured pitching, defense, and baserunning, leading the AA in fielding and stolen bases while yielding the fewest runs. Outfielder Joe Gallagher paced the league in hits (.343, 200 H, 24 HR, 119 RBI), and key pitchers were righthanders George Washburn (12–4) and Sandy Vance, who split the season between the Yankees and KC (8–1).

Meyer led Kansas City to first place the next two seasons, al-

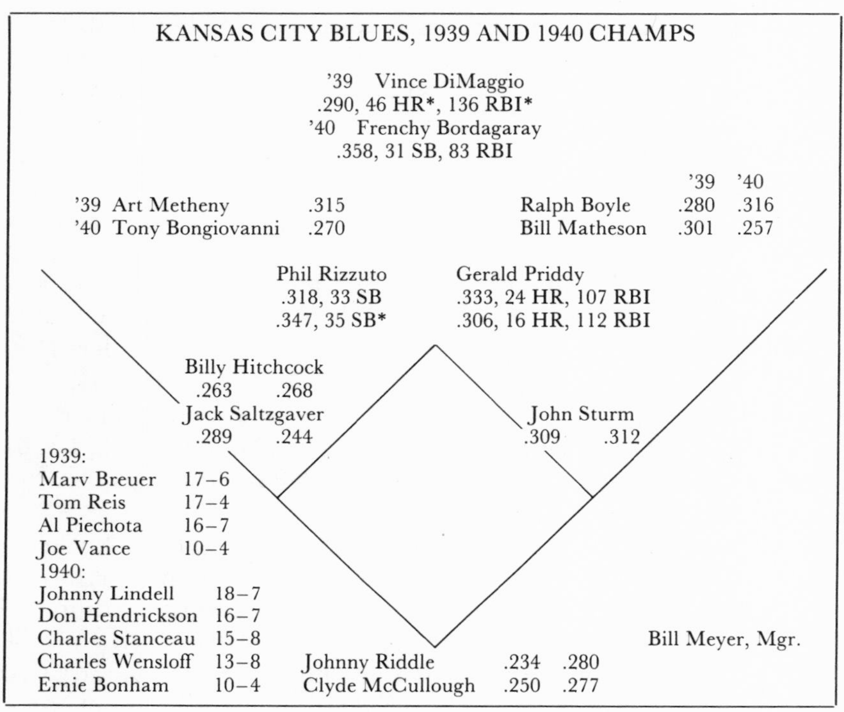

though neither pennant winner was able to capture the playoffs. The 1939 Blues established the all-time AA mark for victories in a 154-game season (107–47), and both clubs led the league in stolen bases and ERA. The Blues' brilliant young shortstop, Phil Rizzuto, starred in both championship seasons (.316 with 33 steals, and .347 with a league-leading 35 steals), and was named Minor League Player of the Year by *The Sporting News*. Other two-year standouts were second baseman Gerry Priddy (.333, 24 HR, 107 RBI, and .306, 16 HR, 112 RBI), first sacker and leadoff hitter Johnny Sturm (.309 and .312), slick-fielding Billy Hitchcock in the hot corner, and outfielder Ralph Boyle (.316 both seasons). Outfielder Vince DiMaggio was the 1939 home run and RBI leader (.290, 46 HR, 136 RBI) before being sold to Cincinnati. Frenchy Bordagaray was obtained from the Reds for 1940 and proved to be an excellent replacement both in the outfield and at bat (.358 with 31 steals and a league-leading 214 hits); a six-year big-leaguer, Bordagaray bet Blues infielder Jack Saltzgaver that he would bat at least .350, and the Yankees brought him back to the majors after his performance in KC. The pitching staffs featured Marv Breuer (17–6 with a 2.28 ERA), Tom Reis (17–4, 2.30), and John Babich (17–6), who ranked one-two-three in the 1939 ERA standings, and the 1940 victory leader, Johnny Lindell (18–7).

The Yankees brought up most of the key players for 1941, but somehow Meyer adroitly fielded another playoff team. Hitchcock (.296) moved over to short, walk leader Mike Chartak (.293, 100 W) shifted first to the outfield as needed, and outfielder Colonel Mills (.307) and second baseman Al Glossup (.301) provided solid hitting. The next year rookie manager Johnny Neun produced the Blues' third flag in four seasons, although the team was defeated in the opening round of playoffs. First baseman Ed Levy (.306) and outfielder Eric Tipton (.305) hit well, but the strength of the team was a pitching staff led by victory leader Butch Wensloff (21–10), veteran Tom Reis (13–5), and lefty Herb Karpel (11–1).

For the next four years, Kansas City suffered losing seasons. Casey Stengel, who had been signed by his hometown team after starring in high school athletics, was the manager in 1945 at Kansas City. (The Blues had farmed him out to lower classifications, but at the end of 1910 he was one-for-three as a pinch hitter, and early in his career he was dubbed "Casey" after KC.) Longtime Kansas City infielder Jack Saltzgaver managed the last-place Blues in 1944, Bill Meyer returned as manager in 1946, and in the latter year the ballpark was rechristened Blues' Stadium.

Meyer wasted little time in producing another pennant, claiming his fourth flag for KC in 1947. Characteristically, his team led the league in stolen bases, featured an excellent pitching staff—and lost the playoff opener. Righthander Carl DeRose (4–2 in eight games) twirled the first perfect game in AA history on June 26 against Minneapolis. The 24-year-old DeRose had been a fireballer before the war, and he was 12–6 with KC in 1946, but a series of injuries had almost ended his career when he somehow threw the perfecto. Fred Bradley pitched excellent ball (13–4) before falling to injuries, and Bill Wright (16–9), Frank Hiller (15–5), and Tommy Byrne (12–6) also were formidable hurlers. Rifle-armed center fielder Cliff Mapes (.308, 21 HR, 117 RBI) was the RBI champ. Other strong hitters were outfielders Eddie Stewart (.358), Harry Craft (.315) and Hank Bauer (.313), catcher Gus Niarhos (.321) and first baseman Steve Sonchak (.294).

Although Kansas City slipped into the second division for the next three seasons, infielder Al Rosen was the 1948 Rookie of the Year (.327, 25 HR, 110 RBI). Hank Bauer (.305, 23 HR, 100 RBI) and catcher Ralph Houk (.302) also posted good seasons in 1948, and the next year first baseman Joe Collins led the league in triples (.319, 18 3B, 20 HR). The 1951 Blues reached the playoffs behind Mickey Mantle (.361 in 40 games), strikeout king Robert Wiesler (10–9 with 162 Ks in 194 IP), and catcher Clint Courtney (.294).

The next two clubs finished second, then went on to win the playoffs. Infielder-outfielder Vic Power was a key member of both teams, leading the league in doubles and triples in 1952 (.331, 40 2B, 17 3B, 109 RBI) and winning the batting title the next year (.349, 39 2B, 93 RBI). Outfielder Bill Skowron was named 1952 Minor League Player of the Year by *The Sporting News* after leading the AA in homers and RBIs (.341, 31, 134 RBI), then was switched to first base the next year (.318, 15 HR, 89 RBI). Righthander Ed Erautt was the victory and percentage leader (21–5), while first baseman Don Bollweg (.325 with 23 homers) and second sacker Kal Segrist (.308, 25 HR, 92 RBI) were other stars of 1952. The next year former Blues' outfielder Harry Craft managed a team which featured, in addition to Power and Skowron, outfielders Bob Cerv (.317, 22 HR, 91 RBI) and Elston Howard (.286), shortstop Alex Grammas (.307), and righthanded relievers Melvin Wright (13–2) and Rex Jones (7–2).

In 1954 Craft's club sagged to seventh place, despite the efforts of walk leader Kal Segrist (.291 with 99 Ws) and catcher Gus Triandos (.296 with 18 homers). It was to be the final edition of the KC Blues in the American Association. In 1953 the Boston Braves had moved to Milwaukee with spectacular success, and the next year the St. Louis Browns went to Baltimore. Arnold Johnson purchased the Philadelphia Athletics and moved the A's to Kansas City for 1955. Blues' Stadium, now renamed Municipal Stadium, was rebuilt and expanded in time for opening day. Former president Harry Truman, who threw out the first ball, and longtime owner-manager of the Athletics Connie Mack were on hand to help welcome major league baseball back to Kansas City after an absence of 66 years.

Year	Record	Pcg.	Finish
1902	69-67	.507	Fourth
1903	69-66	.511	Fifth
1904	60-91	.387	Seventh
1905	45-102	.301	Eighth
1906	72-83	.464	Fifth

1907	78-76	.510	Fourth
1908	70-83	.456	Seventh
1909	71-93	.432	Eighth
1910	85-81	.512	Fifth
1911	94-70	.573	Second
1912	85-82	.509	Fourth
1913	69-98	.413	Sixth
1914	84-84	.500	Sixth
1915	71-79	.473	Fifth
1916	86-81	.515	Fifth
1917	66-86	.434	Seventh
1918	44-30	.595	First
1919	86-65	.570	Second
1920	60-106	.361	Eighth
1921	84-80	.512	Third
1922	92-76	.548	Third
1923	112-54	.675	First (won Little World Series)
1924	68-96	.415	Eighth
1925	80-87	.474	Fifth
1926	87-78	.527	Fifth
1927	99-69	.589	Third
1928	88-80	.524	Sixth
1929	111-56	.665	First (won Little World Series)
1930	75-79	.487	Fifth
1931	90-77	.539	Second
1932	81-86	.485	Sixth
1933	57-93	.360	Eighth
1934	65-88	.425	Eighth
1935	84-70	.545	Third
1936	84-69	.549	Third (lost opener)
1937	72-82	.468	Fifth
1938	84-67	.556	Second (won opener, finals, and Jr. World Series)
1939	107-47	.695	First (lost opener)
1940	95-57	.625	First (won opener, lost finals)
1941	85-69	.552	Third (lost opener)
1942	84-69	.549	First (lost opener)
1943	67-85	.441	Seventh
1944	41-110	.272	Eighth
1945	65-86	.430	Seventh
1946	67-82	.450	Seventh
1947	93-60	.608	First (lost opener)
1948	64-88	.421	Sixth
1949	71-80	.470	Fifth
1950	54-99	.353	Eighth
1951	81-70	.536	Third (lost opener)
1952	89-65	.578	Second (won opener and finals, lost Jr. World Series)
1953	88-66	.571	Second (won opener and finals, lost Jr. World Series)
1954	68-85	.444	Seventh

Louisville (Colonels)

Few cities can claim as rich a baseball heritage as Louisville. On April 19, 1865, the Louisville Club played the Nashville Cumberlands in an open field that is today 19th and Duncan. Although Louisville triumphed, 22–5, it was the city's first game and the spectators had to ask the official scorer who won. The scorer was Mrs. John Dickens, wife of the Nashville captain and shortstop and the first woman ever identified officially with the new sport. The Louisville catcher was Theodore F. Tracy, who courageously became the first backstop ever known to play "under the bat" — catchers had no protective equipment and always positioned themselves 30 or 40 feet behind the plate.

Members of the Louisville Club had to pay $2 per month in dues, and were fined 10 to 25 cents for swearing on the field — $3.30 was collected in 1865! By the next year the team played at a diamond bounded by Third, Fifth, Oak and Park streets, although the ballpark soon was moved to a site now occupied by St. James Court.

This park would be the home of Louisville's first professional team. Late in 1875 a series of meetings was held in Larry Gatto's Saloon on Green Street to organize the National League, and when play began in 1876 Louisville fielded one of the original eight NL teams. After it was learned that four Louisville players accepted $100 each to throw a crucial series with Hartford, the players were banned from professional baseball and Louisville dropped out of the National League.

But in 1882 the American Association was organized as a major league to challenge the National League, and Louisville provided one of six charter clubs. Eclipse Park was located at 28th and Elliott streets, and the team was called the Louisville "Eclipse," an awkward nickname which gave way to several sobriquets during succeeding seasons (after a disastrous storm killed 75 Louisville residents in 1890, the players were dubbed "Cyclones"). Throughout the 1880s the team's best hitter was Pete Browning, who won AA batting crowns in 1882 (.382) and 1885 (.367). In 1884 Browning broke his favorite bat — one he had made himself (shades of

Hillerich & Bradsby's
1st bat was turned
for Pete Browning.
Played for Louisville
Colonels 1882-1889.
Lifetime BA .341.

Pete Browning, Louisville batting champ of the 1880s, was responsible for the creation of the famed Louisville Slugger bats.

— Courtesy Louisville Redbirds

Roy Hobbs and "Wonder Boy") — and he went to the shop of wood-turner J. F. Hillerich at First Street near Market. Hillerich and Browning worked into the night to craft a bat that the slugger praised throughout the league. Within a short time the little wood-turning shop became Hillerich & Bradsby, the bat-making giant which turned out Louisville Sluggers.

The best pitcher of the 1880s was lefthander Toad Ramsey (37–27 in 1886 and 39–27 the next year). Once offered $100 to pitch a game, Toad suggested that instead he be paid $5 per strike-out. He whiffed 24, and earned $120! In 1888 Louisville players conducted baseball's first player strike when new owner M. H. Davidson decided to levy a fine for every fielding error. For two days the team boycotted games in Baltimore, causing Louisville to forfeit, but on the third day resistance crumbled. The players returned to the field, continued to make errors — and paid Davidson's fines!

During the calamitous Johnstown Flood of 1889, the team was on a train which was marooned by high waters, and the Colonels were missing and presumed lost for two days. The 1889 Colonels were hapless, losing 26 games in a row, changing managers seven times during the season, and finishing 27–111 (.195). But the next year the club rocketed from last to first, winning Louisville's only major league pennant. The American Association folded after the 1891 season, but Louisville was absorbed into the National League.

During the 1890s, future Hall of Famers Rube Waddell, Hughey Jennings, Fred Clarke, Jimmy Collins, Dan Brouthers, and the legendary Honus Wagner played for the Colonels, and Wagner became the first player to have his autograph inscribed on a Louisville Slugger bat. In his first game as Louisville's third baseman, Jimmy Collins became the first third sacker to leave his base, playing toward shortstop or into left field, as the situation dictated (and in an 1885 game at Eclipse Park, St. Louis first baseman Charles Comiskey became the first man at his position to play off the bag). Late in the 1899 season the grandstand at Eclipse Park burned, forcing all remaining games to be played on the road. The Louisville "Wanderers" won what proved to be Louisville's final major league game, 25–4 over Washington. After the season the National League reduced its size from twelve to eight teams, and Louisville was one of the clubs eliminated.

In 1901 Louisville formed its first minor league team, the Colonels of the Western Association. By June, however, the club folded and was sold to Grand Rapids, and the league shut down before the month ended. But when the minor league American Association was organized in 1902, a new team of Colonels became charter members (replacing Omaha, which was to be one of the eight original cities — until it was decided that Omaha was too far away from the other seven cities). Owner George "White Wings" Tabeau had hastily built a new Eclipse Park at 7th and Kentucky, which was not quite finished for the season opener. The grandstand was soaked with paint and roofed with tar paper; Eclipse Park was a fire trap, and would eventually succumb to flames, but it hosted American Association baseball for 21 seasons.

Outfielder Derby Day Bill Clymer (.296) managed the Colonels to second place in 1902. Louisville and Indianapolis battled for the flag throughout the year, with a race so close that each club had to play three remaining games on the final day of the season. First sacker Babe Ganzel (.370 with 135 runs scored in 138 games) led the league in hitting and runs. The Colonels paced the AA in team batting (.293), runs, total bases, and steals (235), and boasted a trio of iron-armed pitchers: victory and winning percentage leader

Ed Dunkle (30–10), Pat Flaherty (26–16 with a league-leading 363 innings), and a hurler named Coons (24–10). The next year the Louisville mound staff again featured the AA victory and percentage leader in Tom Walker (26–7) and the league workhorse in Wish Eagan (24–16 with 359 innings), but again Louisville came in second. Bill Clymer (.350 with 31 steals) rapped out the team's best batting average, but he was hired away by Columbus.

In 1904 Louisville again led the league in batting (.284) and, for the only time in AA history, home runs (a dead-ball era total of 36). Southpaw Bill Campbell (26–14) was one of the best pitchers in the league, but Louisville dropped to fourth in the standings. Although in 1906 Louisville again led the league in hitting (.276, with a league-leading 100 triples — and just 14 homers) and produced the batting and stolen base titlist in outfielder Billy Hallman (.342 with 54 steals), the Colonels suffered their first AA losing season. Southpaw Ambrose Puttman (21–20 with 174 Ks) was the 1907 strikeout leader. The next year fourth-place Louisville had three 20-game winners: Puttmann (26–12), fellow lefty John Halla (23–16), and future National League star Babe Adams (22–12). Also during 1908, outfielder Orville Woodruff played 62 consecutive games without an error, while on April 28 Jesse Stovall hurled the second no-hitter in American Association history.

Catcher Henry Peitz was promoted to player-manager in 1909, and immediately he led the Colonels to Louisville's first pennant in two decades. Although the Colonels batted an anemic .233, they paced the league in stolen bases for the second season in a row, turned the most double plays for the fifth time in a six-year period, and recorded the circuit's highest fielding percentage. A late-season surge allowed Louisville to overtake Milwaukee and Minneapolis during the final week of the schedule. Several members of the championship team were sold, however, and in 1910 the Colonels plunged to last place. The Colonels again occupied the cellar in 1911, followed by a seventh-place finish the next year.

Louisville returned to contention in 1913, 1914, and 1915. Righthander Grover Cleveland Lowdermilk won back-to-back strikeout crowns in 1913 (20–14 with 197 Ks) and 1914 (18–16 with 254 Ks). Jake Northrup, a righthander who would win — and lose — more games (222–189) than any other American Association pitcher, tied for the lead in victories in 1914 (26–10), and was almost as good the next year (25–15). In 1915 Texas southpaw

Dave Danforth (12–8 with 173 Ks in 189 IP) struck out 18 Kansas City Blues to establish a single game strikeout record. Archie McKain, pitching for the Colonels against St. Paul in 1934, matched the record, which would be broken by yet another Louisville fireballer in 1949.

Derby Day Bill Clymer, who had managed Columbus to three consecutive pennants since leaving Louisville in 1903, was hired to guide the Colonels in 1916. Clymer's Colonels led the league in fielding, but first baseman Jay Kirke (.303), acquired from Milwaukee after the start of the season, was the only regular who hit above .277. Joe McCarthy, who had played for Clymer at Buffalo in 1914, was brought in to play second base, but he typified the good-field-no-hit (.259) characteristics of the 1916 Colonels. The performance of Jake Northrup sagged (16–13), although John Middleton (21–9) and Cuban righthander Dolf Luque (13–8) tried to take up the mound slack. Seven different players were regularly interchanged in the outfield. But Clymer performed managerial magic and fielded lineups that won 101 games and Louisville's second AA pennant.

Northrup was dealt to Indianapolis, while Middleton and Kirke went up to the New York Giants, and the Colonels would not return to the throne room for five years. McCarthy became a fixture at second base, and he was named player-manager in 1919. Dolf Luque got off to an 11–2 start in 1918, then was sold to Cincinnati and resumed a 20-year National League career. Righthander Frank "Dixie" Davis led the league in victories in 1917 (25–11), went up to the Philadelphia Phillies the next year, returned to Louisville in 1919 to pace the AA in strikeouts and innings pitched (22–20, 372 IP, 165 Ks), then spent the next seven seasons with the St. Louis Browns. In 1919 outfielder Tim Hendryx, a six-year American League veteran, won the batting title as a Colonel (.368), then was purchased by the Boston Red Sox. The Colonel mound corps had not recorded a no-hitter since 1903, but in 1920 southpaws Ernie Koob (17–17) and Tommy Long (18–13) each hurled no-hitters.

The next season Koob was the most dependable pitcher (22–9) as McCarthy guided the Colonels to the pennant and to victory over Baltimore in the Little World Series. The Colonels led the league in fielding and double plays, and hammered the ball at a .309 rate. Outfielders Merito Acosta (.350 with 135 runs and 116 walks), Rube Ellis (.336 with 100 RBIs) and Roy Massey (.316 with 134 runs), third sacker Joe Schepner (.317 with 109 RBIs), second baseman Bruno Betzel (.313), and catcher Bill Meyer (.312) filled a dangerous batting order. Popular first baseman Jay Kirke, who had led the 1916 champs in hitting, was the league's most explosive batter (.386, 43 2B, 17 3B, 21 HR, 157 RBI), winning the batting title and establishing the all-time league record for hits (282).

Righthander Ben Tincup was 9–0 for the 1921 pennant winners, and he played 62 games as an outfielder, posting a .284 average in 102 games. A full-blooded Cherokee Indian, Tincup was a fine batter who often was used as a pinch hitter or in the field (.271 lifetime in 1,203 minor league games). He played three seasons for the Philadelphia Phillies and twirled a perfect game for Little Rock of the Southern Association in 1917. He went to Louisville in 1919 (11–8) and stayed for 13 seasons. Tincup won 180 games for the Colonels; his most productive years were 1922 (20–14) and 1924 (24–17), although he was 14–3 in 1930 at the age of 39. During the 1931 season, Tincup was dealt to Minneapolis (1–4, 8.68 ERA), and after spending the next year with Sacramento in the Pacific Coast League he retired. But in 1936 he began to play again in lower classification leagues, and he pitched his last game in the Northern League when he was 51.

In 1922 a swift, hard-hitting outfielder named Earle Combs was signed by the Colonels off the campus of Eastern Kentucky State Teachers College. During his rookie season Combs led the league in triples (.344 with 18 3Bs), and the next year he rapped out the most hits (.380 with 241 hits, 46 doubles, and 145 RBIs). He went to New York in 1924, played with the Yankees for 12 years (.325 lifetime), appeared in four World Series (.350), and was voted into the Hall of Fame in 1970. Jay Kirke had another superb season in 1922 (.355 with 123 RBIs and a league-leading 236 hits), but the most spectacular event of the year occurred after the end of the playing season.

On the night of November 20, 1922, a fire destroyed Eclipse Park in less than an hour. The next day the club president, Colonel William Knebelkamp, announced that a new steel and concrete stadium would be erected. Parkway Field, costing $100,000 and seating 14,500, opened on May 1, 1923, and would serve as home of the Colonels for 33 years. The outfield was vast, with dead center located 507 feet from the plate, although left field was near enough to cause construction of a tall, Fenway Park-style fence. The forbidding dimensions of right and center were reduced somewhat when the bullpens were moved to the outfield, with a five-foot-high fence in front.

In 1924 nine-year American League veteran Elmer Smith became the only Colonel ever to win a home run title (.334 with 28 homers). Other hard-hitting Colonels in 1924 were shortstop Red Shannon (.340), outfielder Ty Tyson (.331), and veteran infielders P. A. Ballenger (.322) and Bruno Betzel (.311), but after a tight pennant race Louisville finished third.

By 1925, however, McCarthy had built a juggernaut which would run away with two consecutive pennants. There was a mixture of proven veterans and talented newcomers. Returnees from the 1921 champs included second baseman Bruno Betzel (.312 in 1925 and .322 in 1926), catcher Bill Meyer (.287 and .306), P. A. Ballenger, moved over from short in 1921 to third by 1925 (.291), Ben Tincup (14–16 and 18–7), and outfielders Rube Ellis (.352 in 1926) and Merito Acosta (.310 in 1925). Veteran outfielder Ty Tyson (.352) and shortstop Red Shannon (.294) were steady hands in 1925. Hooks Cotter was installed at first base (.326 and .273) and John Anderson was added to the outfield (.314 and .310). In 1926 catcher Al DeVormer was acquired (.368), Pinkie Pittenger came in as shortstop (.312), and Earl Webb patrolled the outfield (.333).

Joe Guyon, a Chippewa Indian who was an All American footballer at Georgia Tech in 1918, began a Hall of Fame NFL career in 1920 and, preceding Bo Jackson, started in minor league baseball as a speedy outfielder the same year. He was purchased by the Colonels in 1925 and played spectacularly for both championship clubs (.363 with 152 runs and 106 RBIs, and .343 with 132 runs — he hit .358 in 1927, but in 1928 an injury ended his pro football and baseball careers, although he played sporadically in the lower minors in 1931, 1932, and 1936). The pitching load in both seasons was carried by five righthanders: Nick Cullop (22–8 and 20–8), Joe DeBerry (20–8 and 17–13), Ed Holley (20–7 in 1925), Joe Dawson (17–7 in 1926), and Ben Tincup.

Joe McCarthy led the 1925 Colonels to a 106–61 record, then moved up to a Hall of Fame managerial career with the Cubs, Yankees, and Red Sox. Longtime Colonels catcher Bill Meyer was selected to replace McCarthy, and he responded with a 105–62 mark. The 1925 colonels led the league in fielding and hit .299 as a team, while the 1926 club posted a .308 mark, best in the AA.

Several key players were sold from the pennant winners, but the club quickly began to rebuild. Ed Sicking, an experienced National League infielder, became a regular in 1928 (.368), and in the same year Texan Dud Branom became the Colonels' first baseman and led the AA in RBIs (.310 with 128 RBIs). His numbers improved the next year (.332 with 129 RBIs), and in five seasons Branom annually produced from 110 to 134 RBIs for Louisville. In 1929 Butch Simons (.340) became a Colonel, roaming the Louisville outfield for nine seasons. A career .329 hitter, Simons batted above .350 three times for Louisville.

Simons' best season was 1930 (.371 with a league-leading 248 hits and 49 doubles), when he led the Colonels to a pennant. Outfielder Herman Layne paced the league in triples and stolen bases (.330 with 19 triples and 40 steals), while other offensive stars were third sacker Babe Ganzel (.338), first baseman Dud Branom (.314 with 123 RBIs), catcher Ray Thompson (.336), and future Hall of Fame second baseman Billy Herman (.305). Joe DeBerry (19–10), Ben Tincup (14–3), strikeout leader Phil Weinert (16–11), and Roy Wilkinson (17–11) were the best pitchers.

The next year Billy Herman (.350), Herman Layne (.346), Babe Ganzel (.306), and Dud Branom (.300) returned to have good seasons. Herman, signed out of semipro ball for $250 a month in 1928, was sold to the Cubs in 1931 for $60,000, finished the season in Chicago (.327), and quickly established himself as a National League star. Herman Layne had a twin brother, Harry. The Layne twins broke into pro ball with Bristol of the Appalachian League in 1922 and retired together after the 1934 season. A career .316 hitter, Harry played just 26 games in the American Association, with Columbus in 1925 and 1926. Herman, who hit .327 lifetime, played in the AA from 1927 through 1933 (.325, .347, .307, .333, .346, .302 and .274), splitting seven seasons between Louisville and Indianapolis.

Despite good hitting in 1931, the Colonels sagged to seventh place and remained a second division club throughout most of the decade. Louisville fans had to content themselves with standout individual performances. Butch Simons led the offense throughout most of this dismal period, and he was in top form in 1935 (.352)

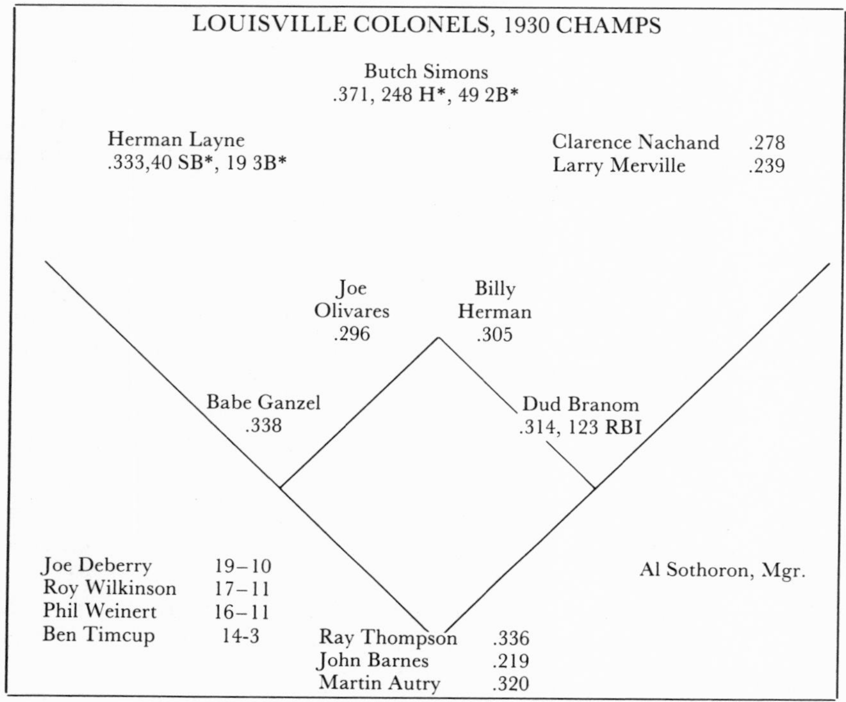

and 1936 (.353 with a league-leading 220 hits). Righthander Jack Tising, who joined the pitching staff in 1934, recorded strikeout titles in 1935 (230 Ks) and 1937 (174 Ks). In 1938 an 18-year-old rookie won the shortstop position (.277), and after another season in Louisville, Pee Wee Reese became a fixture with the Brooklyn Dodgers.

The Colonels produced a Cinderella story in 1939, posting another losing season but inching into fourth place and a playoff slot on the next-to-last day of the season. Louisville then decisively defeated Minneapolis and Indianapolis, each by four games to one, to win the playoffs. The Junior World Series with Rochester went down to extra innings in the seventh game at Red Wing Stadium, but in the 11th the Colonels scored four runs to win, 7–3. Pee Wee Reese (.279 with 18 triples and 35 steals) led the league in triples, stolen bases, and putouts by a shortstop. But no regular batted .300 (outfielder Chet Morgan hit .291), the Colonels totaled the fewest home runs as a team, and James Weaver (16–14) and Charles

Wagner (13–10) had the best records on the pitching staff.

In 1940 the Colonels again puffed into fourth place with a modest 75–75 record — and again won the playoffs, dumping Columbus and first-place Kansas City in the playoffs, before losing to Newark in the Junior World Series. Chet Morgan (.317 with just nine strikeouts in 150 games) was the only regular to hit .300, and James Weaver (13–9) again was a mainstay of the pitching staff. Charley Wagner started the season with the Red Sox, but Boston sent him down late in the year, and in 10 starts he was 9–1 with a 1.84 ERA. For the second year in a row, the Colonels won a third consecutive fielding title in 1941. Shortstop Johnny Pesky (.325) led the offense, while Ossie Judd (13–5), Tex Hughson (7–1), and George Dickman (7–5, 1.94 ERA) each split the season between Louisville and Boston. For the third year in a row, Bill Burwell guided the Colonels into the playoffs, although this time Louisville lost to first-place Columbus in the finals.

The Colonels failed to reach the playoffs the next two years, but in 1944 manager Harry Liebold began a new reign in the AA throne room. The 1944 ERA champ was righthander Mel Deutsch (14–11, 2.47), while righty James Wilson (19–8 with 147 Ks) was the victory and strikeout leader. Third baseman Nick Polly (.290, 20 HR, 120 RBI) won the RBI title and set the all-time league record for walks (147 — he was the first Colonel ever to lead the AA in bases on balls). Other offensive contributors were outfielders Steve Barath (.329) and Chico Genovese (.279 with 130 runs and 33 steals), shortstop Frank Shofner (.317), second baseman Ben Steiner (.316), and first sacker Earle Browne (.312). The third-place Colonels downed first-place Milwaukee in the playoff opener, then swept St. Paul in four games to win the Governors' Cup.

The next year, despite wartime personnel turnover, Shofner (.298), Barath (.291), Genovese (.279), and Browne (.273) returned to form the nucleus of another championship club. The best newcomer was outfielder-infielder Ty LaForest (.353 in 91 games), who also played 50 games with the Red Sox. Liebold again brought the Colonels in third, again defeated first-place Milwaukee in the opener, again beat St. Paul to claim the Governors' Cup, then bested Newark to win the Junior World Series.

The Colonels were even better in 1946, winning first place and the Governors' Cup, with a four-game sweep of Indianapolis, before dropping the Junior World Series to Montreal. Louisville hit merely .265 as a team and managed just 43 homers, the lowest total in the league. But the club led the league in double plays, and right-hander Al Widmar was the ERA champ (12–9, 2.43). There was offensive punch from outfielders John Welaj (.300 with a league-leading 37 steals), Frank Genovese (.305) and James Gleeson (.306), who came over from Columbus at midseason, and from veteran infielders Frank Shofner (.305) and Charles Koney (.286). During the championship years of 1944, 1945 and 1946, Chico Genovese established a record for AA outfielders by playing 268 consecutive games without an error. Genovese patrolled the vastness of Parkway Field, but he shunned shoestring catches, preferring to play the ball on the first hop; this conservative style led to few errors — and the nickname "One Hop" Genovese.

In 1947 the Colonels came within a game of winning a fourth straight playoff title. Liebold guided Louisville to second place, then won the opening series over Minneapolis, four games to three, before dropping the finals, three games to four, to Milwaukee. Southpaw Clem Dreiseward (18–7, 2.15) led the league in victories and ERA, while infielder-outfielder Billy Goodman, on the eve of a productive big league career, sparked the offense (.340). The next year Louisville descended to last place, and the Colonels would not return to the playoffs until 1951. In 1949 outfielder Tom Wright won the batting title (.368), but the next highest average by a full-season regular was almost 100 points lower (.271), turned in by 19-year-old outfielder Jimmy Piersall.

Early in 1949 Louisville fans were treated to the fireballing heroics of stringbean southpaw Maurice McDermott (6–4 in 11 games, with an eye-popping 116 strikeouts in just 77 innings). In the season opener, McDermott whiffed 17 Millers, coming within one of the single-game record of 18, set by Louisville's Dave Danforth in 1915 and equalled by Archie McKain of the Colonels in 1934. But on May 24, in the second game of a night doubleheader against St. Paul, McDermott mowed down 20 Saints to establish a new mark. Three weeks later, however, the Red Sox recalled McDermott.

The next year, victory leader James Atkins (18–9) and outfielder Taft Wright (.335, 15 HR, 115 RBI) sparked Louisville to a playoff berth, and there were consecutive playoff appearances in 1953, 1954, and 1955. Lefthander Frank Baumann (10–1 with a .368 batting average) was spectacular in just 13 games for the 1953

Colonels, while stars of the 1955 club included strikeout leader Jerry Casale (17–11 with 186 Ks) and third baseman Frank Malzone (.310). Outfielder Marty Keough led the league in triples in 1954 (.292, 90 RBI, 17 3B) and 1955 (.393 with 14 3B). The 1954 Colonels finished second under manager Mike Higgins, won the playoffs, then defeated Syracuse in the Junior World Series.

After the 1955 season, the long affiliation between Louisville and the Red Sox was terminated after Louisville fans became disenchanted over frequent callups of star players. For three years, 1956–58, Louisville was mired in last place, although Ted Abernathy (12–16 with 212 Ks) was the strikeout champ in 1956, and in 1958 outfielder Willie Tasby (.322, 22 HR, 95 RBI) was named Rookie of the Year. In 1956 both the team and the grandstand seating arrangements were integrated, and in 1957 the Colonels moved out of Parkway Field in favor of Fairgrounds Stadium. The stadium was provided rent-free when the community-owned club struggled through 1957 without a major league affiliation.

Beginning in 1959, Louisville enjoyed four highly successful seasons. The 1959 Colonels won the Eastern Division with the best record in the 10-team American Association, before being swept in the playoff opener. Switch-hitter Ken Wise (.302) and outfielder Al Spangler (.298) were the best batters, while righthanders Georges Maranda (18–6) and Don Nottebart (18–11) led the league in victories. Southpaw Juan Pizarro was brilliant at midseason in a five-game stopover which vaulted him to the Milwaukee Braves (4–1, 42 IP, 22 H, 50 K, 1.07 ERA, and three shutouts which included a 1–0 no-hitter over Charleston).

The 1960 Colonels finished second, beat St. Paul and Louisville to win the playoffs, then downed Toronto in the Junior World Series. Bill Adair was voted Manager of the Year as his club led the league in fielding, ERA, and complete games. Don Nottebart again led the pitching staff (13–5), along with southpaw Bob Hendley (16–9) and Ted Abernathy's excellent relief work during part of the season (2.29 ERA in 22 appearances, with just 30 hits in 51 innings).

The next year the Colonels again finished second and won the playoffs before suffering a sweep by Buffalo in the Junior World Series. Outfielder Howie Bedell tied Eddie Marshall's 1935 league record by hitting in 43 consecutive games. Bedell was leading the AA in hitting (.327) late in the year when a chipped bone in his shoulder sidelined him as Denver's Don Wert (.328) passed him on the final day of the season. The pitching staff again posted the league's best ERA, while starter-reliever Freddy Olivo (7–4 with a 2.66 ERA in 42 games, including eight starts) won the ERA title. The catcher was Bob Uecker (.309), who provided offensive punch while keeping the clubhouse loose with constant jokes and horseplay.

The following season Olivo (13–11, with 22 starts in 40 games, and 151 Ks) was the strikeout champ, and fellow right-hander Connie Grob (14–10 with a 2.86 ERA) took the ERA crown. The Colonels posted the lowest batting average in the AA and finished fourth in a six-team league, but swept first-place Indianapolis in three games, then beat Denver to win a third consecutive playoff title. The Colonels lost the Junior World Series to Atlanta in seven games, but this disappointment paled when the American Association disbanded after the season. Efforts to join the International League were fruitless, and Louisville suddenly found itself without professional baseball for the first time in the twentieth century.

Early in 1964, Charles O. Finley, the colorful but controversial owner of the Kansas City Athletics, signed a two-year contract for his team to play in Fairgrounds Stadium, but American League owners blocked his attempt to move the A's to Louisville. Finally, in 1968, Walter Dilbeck, an Evansville real estate man, bought Toronto's International League franchise and moved the club to Louisville. A year later Bill Gardner, a Louisville attorney and shopping center magnate and a nephew of longtime Red Sox owner Tom Yawkey, purchased the Colonels from Dilbeck. But the Kentucky State Fair Board decided to expand and redesign Fairgrounds Stadium primarily for football, and after the 1972 season the pennant-winning Colonels were evicted.

Nine years passed without pro ball in Louisville — until A. Ray Smith exploded on the local sports scene. Smith, a Texan who made a fortune in the construction business in Tulsa, bought the Tulsa club in 1961 and operated there until 1977, when stadium problems triggered a move to New Orleans. Smith's team, the Triple-A affiliate of the St. Louis Cardinals, stayed in the Louisiana Superdome merely one season before transferring operations to Springfield. But in 1981 Louisville banker Dan Ulmer headed a group dedicated to obtaining an American Association club, and

Ulmer persuasively sold Smith on Louisville. Smith was under contract to Springfield, and he had to pay half a million dollars in legal and moving expenses.

The Louisville Baseball Committee financed a $4.5 million remodeling of Fairgrounds Stadium (the state matched city and county pledges). When the facility had been converted to football a decade earlier, the seating capacity was nearly doubled to 40,000 as stands were built across right field. These stands now were dragged 50 feet back, but since the right-field corner was just 312 feet from home plate, a Fenway-type wall was built. Renamed Cardinal Stadium, the park featured superb concessions and a delightful scoreboard that periodically would race three electronic horses (Louisville being a racing town, considerable wagering would occur throughout the stands on the outcome of the electronic race).

The timing of Smith and Ulmer proved perfect. Louisville citizens were starved for baseball, and anxious for a pleasant, wholesome, affordable center for family entertainment. The 1982 Redbirds provided a winning club, fans turned out in droves from opening night, and Smith became so popular that when he wandered through the stands each evening in his checkered sport coat the crowd would chant, "A. Ray! A. Ray!" On August 8, Smith interrupted the game in the sixth inning for a fireworks display to celebrate a new minor league attendance record. During the postwar baseball bonanza of 1946 the San Francisco Seals established a record minor league attendance of 670,563 that had held up for 36 years. The Redbirds soared past the Seals' mark on August 8 and by the end of the season Louisville's record-setting total had risen to 868,418.

But A. Ray Smith and his Redbirds were just getting started. Smith spent at least $750,000 on a splendid concessions area, 8,000 plastic seats, and numerous other improvements to sparkling Cardinal Stadium. With confidence bolstered by the success of his first season in Louisville, Smith predicted that the Redbirds would draw a million fans in 1983. Although the spring was cold and wet and the summer unusually hot, and although unemployment was severe, the club was good enough to win the Eastern Division with the best record in the league. Outfielder Jim Adduci (.281, 25 HR, 101 RBI) was the RBI champ. Jim Fregosi was voted Manager of the Year, and the pitching staff showcased Todd Worrell and Danny Cox. The Redbirds may have fallen in the opening round of playoffs, but disappointment was more than offset by unprecedented triumphs at the ticket office. On August 25 a crowd of 31,258 broke the one million mark, and the eye-popping total finally reached 1,052,438. In 1983 three *major* league teams failed to draw a million, despite enjoying about 13 more home dates apiece, and Louisville's per game average attendance of 16,191 exceeded that of five big league clubs.

Jim Fregosi engineered a third consecutive winner in 1984, and for the third year in a row the Redbirds led all minor league clubs in attendance (846,878). All-Star shortstop Jose Gonzalez (.279), power-hitting DH Gary Rajsich (.286, 29 HR, 95 RBI), outfielders Gene Roof (.302) and Jim Adduci (.289) formed a solid core, while Vince Coleman, an outfielder with incredible speed, led the league in runs and set the all-time AA record for stolen bases (.257, 97 R, 101 SB). The Redbirds had to defeat Wichita in a single-game playoff just to secure fourth place and a postseason berth, but then rolled through first-place Indianapolis and Denver to take the pennant.

The next year Louisville again led the minors in attendance (651,090), while Fregosi somehow worked another miracle on the field. Fireballing righthander Todd Worrell, splitting his time between the bullpen and the starting rotation (17 starts, 16 relief appearances), led the league in strikeouts (8–6 with 126 Ks in 128 IP). The Redbird offense ranked dead last with an anemic .239 average, but Louisville managed to win the Eastern Division, then downed Oklahoma City in the playoffs to repeat as AA champs.

In 1986 Jim Fregosi left during the season to manage the Chicago White Sox, and the Redbirds sank to last in the Eastern Division, despite the efforts of RBI leader Jim Lindeman (.251, 20 HR, 96 RBI). But A. Ray Smith continued to pull fans into Cardinal Stadium (660,200), leading all minor league teams in attendance for the fifth consecutive year. After the season, however, super salesman Dan Ulmer persuaded Smith to sell the Redbirds to a group of Louisville investors (including John A. Hillerich III, president of Hillerich & Bradsby) for upwards of $4 million. Ulmer became chairman of the board, while Smith headed for Florida to try to bring major league baseball to St. Petersburg.

The 1987 Redbirds starred MVP and Rookie of the Year Lance Johnson (.333 with 42 steals). Third-year catcher Tom Pagnozzi (.313) hit three homers in one game, southpaw Paul Cherry (11–5) led the pitching staff, and Louisville finished second by just one game. The Redbirds lost the playoff opener, but again Louisville paced the AA in attendance (516,329).

Despite a last-place finish in 1988, Louisville once more enjoyed excellent attendance (574,852). Sixth-place Buffalo became the second minor league club to draw over one million (1,147,651), but the Pilots' new attendance record was greatly facilitated by the precedent-setting Redbirds of 1983. Louisville finished last in the East in 1989, but attendance increased at Redbirds games (603,788), while Buffalo again broke one million. Redbird catcher Todd Zeile (.289, 19 HR, 85 RBI) was named Rookie of the Year. "Big Leon" Durham attempted to play his way back to the big leagues (.287), and Cardinal outfielder Willie McGee came down to play out of an injury (.407). Righthanders Bob Tewksbury (13–5) and Howard Hilton (12–5) were two of the best pitchers in the league. In 1990 the Redbirds again performed before large, enthusiastic crowds attracted by a streamlined facility and an unusually bountiful baseball tradition.

Year	Record	Pcg.	Finish
1902	92-45	.671	Second
1903	87-54	.617	Second
1904	77-70	.524	Fifth
1905	76-76	.500	Fourth
1906	72-83	.464	Sixth
1907	77-77	.500	Fifth
1908	88-65	.575	Second
1909	93-75	.554	First
1910	60-103	.363	Eighth
1911	67-101	.398	Eighth
1912	66-101	.395	Seventh
1913	94-72	.520	Fourth
1914	95-73	.565	Second
1915	78-72	.520	Fourth
1916	101-66	.605	First
1917	88-66	.571	Second
1918	43-36	.544	Fourth
1919	86-67	.562	Third
1920	88-79	.527	Second
1921	98-70	.583	First (won Little World Series)
1922	77-91	.458	Sixth
1923	94-77	.550	Third

1924	90-75	.545	Third
1925	106-61	.635	First (lost Little World Series)
1926	105-62	.629	First (lost Little World Series)
1927	65-103	.387	Seventh
1928	62-106	.369	Eighth
1929	75-90	.452	Fifth
1930	93-60	.607	First (lost Little World Series)
1931	74-94	.440	Seventh
1932	67-101	.399	Eighth
1933	70-83	.458	Sixth
1934	78-74	.513	Fourth
1935	52-97	.349	Eighth
1936	63-91	.409	Seventh
1937	62-91	.405	Eighth
1938	53-100	.346	Eighth
1939	75-78	.490	Fourth (won opener, finals, and Jr. World Series)
1940	75-75	.500	Fourth (won opener and finals, lost Jr. World Series)
1941	87-66	.569	Second (won opener, lost finals)
1942	78-76	.506	Fifth
1943	70-81	.464	Fifth
1944	85-63	.574	Third (won opener and finals, lost Jr. World Series)
1945	84-70	.545	Third (won opener, finals, and Jr. World Series)
1946	92-61	.601	First (won opener and finals, lost Jr. World Series)
1947	85-68	.556	Second (won opener, lost finals)
1948	56-98	.364	Eighth
1949	70-83	.458	Sixth
1950	82-71	.536	Fifth
1951	80-73	.523	Fourth (lost opener)
1952	77-77	.500	Fifth
1953	84-70	.545	Third (lost opener)
1954	85-68	.556	Second (won opener, finals, and Jr. World Series)
1955	83-71	.539	Fourth (lost opener)
1956	59-93	.388	Eighth
1957	49-105	.318	Eighth
1958	56-95	.371	Eighth
1959	97-65	.599	First (lost opener)
1960	85-68	.556	Second (won opener, finals, and Jr. World Series)
1961	80-70	.533	Second (won opener and finals, lost Jr. World Series)
1962	71-75	.486	Fourth (won opener and finals, lost Jr. World Series)
1982	73-62	.541	Second
1983	78-57	.578	First (won Eastern Division, lost opener)
1984	79-76	.510	Fourth (won playoff, opener and finals)
1985	74-68	.521	Third (won Eastern Division and finals)
1986	64-78	.451	Seventh
1987	78-62	.557	Second (lost opener)
1988	63-79	.444	Eighth
1989	71-74	.490	Fifth
1990	74-72	.507	Fourth
1991	51-92	.357	Eighth

Milwaukee (Brewers)

As early as 1836 a primitive form of baseball was staged in Milwaukee, and in 1860 Rufus King, a future Civil War general, organized a club of paid players to represent the Cream City. A Milwaukee team was drubbed, 85–7, by the famous Cincinnati Red Stockings of 1869, but enthusiasm for baseball continued, and in 1878 the Cream Citys represented Milwaukee in the National League, playing at grounds bounded at West Michigan, West Clybourn, and North 10th and 11th streets. "If they could keep their expenses as low as their scores," remarked a local newspaper writer, "it would not require much money to run the club," and predictably Milwaukee stayed just one year in the early National League. In 1884 Milwaukee held a franchise in the Union Association, but the league folded after a single season. Milwaukee entered the Western League in 1885, played the following year in the Northwestern League, then joined the Western Association, soon becoming called the Brewers.

Athletic Park, future home of the American Association Brewers, was dedicated in 1888. Built on a city block at Eighth and Chambers, originally the park had only a grandstand back of home plate, bleachers down the base lines, and no outfield fences. Later the grandstand was extended along the third base line, then behind first, but there were no chairs — only long benches which could seat a crowd of 10,000 (overflows of as many as 17,000 spectators were accommodated by a roped-off outfield, which always resulted in numerous ground-rule doubles). When a plank fence was erected the foul lines were extremely short, but the distances to the power alleys were enormous, and the grandstand angles were so misplaced that not a single seat offered a full view of the playing field. Until the onset of Prohibition, there was a bar behind home plate, and the two tiers of seats were considered the best vantage point in Athletic Park. High school football also was played at Athletic Park, and in winter an ice skating rink was set up, with a skaters' dressing room located just beyond left field. After buying the club in 1919, Otto Borchert turned the skaters' room into a chicken coop for his White Rocks. For a time the Brewers boasted a goat as mascot. The goat grazed on the playing field when there were no games, but at night was placed on the grandstand roof. A foul stench seeped into the pressbox, however, and the writers protested that the goat had to go.

In 1901 Milwaukee became a charter member of the American League, but the Brewers dropped out after a last-place finish, then joined the newly organized American Association. Southpaw Nick Altrock (28–14) and stolen base champ Billy Hallman (.322 with 46 steals) starred for Milwaukee's first AA entry, but the Brewers had a losing season and would not record a pennant until 1913. In 1903 righthander Claude Elliott (24–10 with 226 Ks) became the league's first strikeout king (strikeouts were not tallied in 1902), and the next year righty Clifton Curtis (24–20 with 210 Ks in 355 IP) kept the title in Milwaukee. Curtis enjoyed another fine season in 1906 (22–14), and two years later he tossed a no-hitter against Indianapolis. Also launching long careers with Milwaukee in 1904 were infielder and future manager Harry Clark (1904–16, 1922–23) and pitcher-outfielder Tom Dougherty (1904–15). Shortstop Germany Schaefer (.356 with 56 steals) was another star of the 1904 second-place Brewers, but every performer in the league was overshadowed by outfielder George Stone (.405 with 254 hits), who banged out the highest batting average in AA history.

Dougherty was at the top of his form in 1905 (22–17) and 1909 (21–11). In the latter season a big (6′1, 200-pound) righthander with the stamina of a bull joined the Milwaukee pitching staff, with spectacular results. Ulysses Simpson Grant "Stoney" McGlynn played his first full season of pro ball with York of the Tri-State League in 1904, leading the circuit in victories and innings for the next three years (30–11, 28–16, 36–10). In 1906, after winning 36 games for York, he went over to Steubenville of the Penn-Ohio-Maryland League (5–1), then finished the season with the St. Louis Cardinals (2–2). In all McGlynn was 43–13 in 1906, working 511 innings in 64 games and fanning 300 batters. He pitched for St. Louis for two more years, then was purchased by Milwaukee in 1909. Stoney led the AA in wins, losses, games, innings and strikeouts (27–21, 64 games, 446 IP, 183 Ks), along with a record 14 shutouts. He was a workhorse again in 1910 (16–21 with a league-leading 392 IP in 63 games) and 1911 (22–15 in 55 games). Suspended for the 1912 season, McGlynn would pitch just 35 more games of pro ball.

The 1906 Brewers at Athletic Park.
— Courtesy Milwaukee Public Library

In 1913 veteran third baseman Harry Clark was appointed manager, and promptly he produced Milwaukee's first two pennants. The roster remained almost intact in 1913 and 1914 as the Brewers rolled to consecutive championships. Clark was a steady performer in both years (.286 and .301), along with Tom Dougherty (14–9 and 14–4), Irving "Young Cy" Young (15–10 and 20–16), and outfielder Newt Randall (.288 and .321). Standouts in 1913 were Cy Slapnicka (25–14), Ralph Cutting (21–9), and batting champ Larry Chappelle (.349), who was sold to the Chicago White Sox after 85 games and 350 at-bats. In 1914 Milwaukee native Oscar Felsch won a regular position in the outfield and took the home run title (.304 with 19 homers), while banner performances were turned in by Ed Hovlik (24–14), outfielder John Beall (.312), and second baseman Phil Lewis (.295).

Beall had another good year in 1915 (.334) and Chappelle returned from Chicago (.309), but many of the best players were sold or traded, and there would not be another pennant for more than two decades. During the 1916 season, however, Brewer fans were able to watch America's most famous athlete, Jim Thorpe, roam the vast outfield at Athletic Park and win the stolen base title (.274

with 48 steals). During the war-shortened 1918 season, Milwaukee first sacker Doc Johnston won the batting title (.374), the Brewers ran away with the stolen base championship (137 in 73 games — no other team had more than 85), and southpaw Dickie Kerr led the league in victories, innings, and strikeouts (17–7 with 99 Ks in 207 IP).

Otto Borchert bought the Brewers in 1919, and following his death by a heart attack in 1927 Athletic Park was renamed in his honor. In 1920 Dinty Gearin joined the club for a 12-year stay; the southpaw tossed a no-hitter in 1926, enjoyed his best year in 1925 (20–13), and had stints in the National League in 1923 and 1924. Ivy Griffin took over first base in 1922 and pounded opposing pitching for the next eight years (.303, .362, .305, .335, .335, .323, .325 and .328 — he was a lifetime .320 hitter in 2,300 minor league games).

In 1922 catcher Glenn Myatt interrupted a 16-year big league career long enough to win a hitting title (.370) for Milwaukee, and shortstop Lester Bell was the 1924 batting champ (.365 with 18 homers) before becoming a National League regular. Slugging outfielder-first baseman Bunny Brief played the final four years of his legendary career (.331 lifetime with 342 minor league homers) in Milwaukee: 1925 (.358, 37 HR, 175, winning the home run and RBI titles), 1926 (.352, 26 HR, 122 RBI, winning his second consecutive home run crown), 1927 (.308), and 1928 (.309). Brief retired at the age of 36 in Milwaukee, dying in his adopted city in 1963.

Outfielder Lance Richbourg starred for the Brewers in 1924 (.321), 1925 (.312), and 1926 (.346), when he led the league in hits (247), runs (151), triples (28), and stolen bases (48). Shortstop Jim Cooney was the stolen base champ in 1923 (.308 with 60 steals), and in 1927 the Brewers led the league in hitting (.313) behind shortstop Harry Riconda (.353), outfielders Frank Wilson (.337, including four doubles in one game) and Frank Luce (.324), second baseman Fred Lear (.330), first sacker Ivy Griffin (.323), and six-year (1923–24, 1926–29) third baseman Harry Strohm (.312), along with pitcher-outfielder Oswald Orwoll (.370 in 99 games, and 17–6 from the mound). Southpaw Rube Walberg won the strikeout crown in 1924 (18–14 with 175 Ks) and lefty Ernie Wingard posted the most victories of 1928 (24–10, and a .331 batting average in 80 games). Righthander Claude Jonnard won 97 games for the Brewers from 1926 through 1932, recorded strikeout titles in 1928 and 1931, and was a 20-game winner in 1927 (22–14) and 1928 (20–11).

In 1931 versatile, rangy (6′2, 175-pound) Tedd Gullic joined the Brewers, playing outfield, first and third through 1942, except for 1933, when he was with the St. Louis Browns. At Milwaukee he hit over .300 eight times, led the league in doubles in 1934 (.334 with 53 2B), 1935 (.323, 44 2B, 33 HR, 131 RBI), and 1940 (.323, 40 2B, 31 HR, 100 RBI). Other top performances came in 1932 (.354, 27 HR, 123 RBI) and 1937 (.321, 26 HR, 138 RBI). First baseman Art "The Great" Shires was the 1931 batting champ (.385), and in 1934 outfielders Earl Webb (.354) and John Kloza (.326, 26 HR, 148 RBI) won the hitting and RBI titles. In 1934 switch-hitting infielder Lin Storti (.330, 34 HR, 145 RBI) joined the Brewers for five productive seasons, and in 1935 shortstop Eddie Marshall established an all-time American Association record by hitting in 43 consecutive games — even though his overall season average was just .290.

Al Sothoron became manager in 1934 and two years later led the Brewers to a first-place finish, victory in the first Shaughnessy Playoff held in the American Association, and a triumph over Baltimore in the Junior World Series. The pitching staff was led by Joe Heving (19–12), Duane Hamlin (19–14), and southpaw strikeout champ Clyde Hatter (16–6, 190 Ks), who had won the ERA title the previous year. Outfielder Frenchy Uhalt (.322 with 36 steals) won the stolen base championship, despite playing in only 116 games. MVP Rudy York (.334, 21 3B, 37 HR, 148 RBI), Lin Storti (.307, 31 HR — including three in one game — 108 RBI), Tedd Gullic (.329), catcher George Detore (.330 with 22 HR and 78 RBI in just 89 games), and slugging outfielder Chester Laabs (.324, 42 HR, 136 RBI) were instrumental in Milwaukee's finest season in 22 years.

In 1937 Milwaukee led the league until June, despite losing several star players. The Brewers faltered to a fourth-place finish, then made it to the playoff finals behind the hitting of Tedd Gullic (.321 with 138 RBI), outfielder John Heath (.367), third baseman Ken Keltner (.310 with 27 homers), Lin Storti (.308, 25 HR, 125 RBI), and first baseman Minor Heath (.296, 25 HR, 113 RBI). The next season Al Sothoron again guided a rebuilt roster into the playoffs. Nine-year American League veteran Whitlow Wyatt was brilliant in winning the pitcher's Triple Crown (23–7, 208 Ks, 2.37 ERA), which vaulted him to seven succeeding seasons in the National League. The offense, led by Tedd Gullic (.313, 28 HR, 107 RBI), Minor Heath (.294 with 32 homers), and Lin Storti (.265 with 21 homers), paced the AA in home runs (163).

Al Sothoron, who had pitched for 11 seasons in the big leagues before becoming Milwaukee's field general, died at the age of 46 in 1939. Minor Heath (.259) took over the managerial reins, Tedd Gullic turned in another solid season (.301 with 26 homers), and Lin Storti (.281, 30 HR, 105 RBI) set a league record for third basemen by playing 49 consecutive games without an error. But the club suffered a losing season, then sagged to last place in 1940 and 1941. In 1940 Lou "The Mad Russian" Novikoff, who had played 11 games for Milwaukee in 1939, donned a Brewer uniform after playing 62 games for the Cubs. A legendary minor league hitter, Novikoff appeared in 90 games for the Brewers and won the batting title — his fourth in a row in four different leagues — with a 5-for-8 performance on the last day of the season (.370).

Novikoff's batting title was the first of three in a row by a Brewer, and five in a seven-year period (1941–47). Beginning in 1942, Milwaukee won the first of four consecutive team hitting championships, skipped a year, then won again in 1947. The offensive explosion led to regular playoff appearances, although for four years in a row, 1942–45, the Brewers lost in the opening round. A major factor in the Brewer resurgence was the leadership of Bill Veeck and longtime major league first baseman and manager Jolly Cholly Grimm.

At midseason of 1941, Brewers owner Harry Bendinger sold the club to 28-year-old Veeck. Veeck's father had served as president of the Chicago Cubs until his death, and Bill long had worked for the Cubs in numerous capacities. Cubs owner Phil Wrigley for years had maintained a highly generous working agreement with the Brewers, but the Chicago subsidy had been removed and Milwaukee was headed for the cellar when Veeck purchased the team with borrowed money. Veeck offered Grimm, a close friend, 25 percent of the club to serve as manager.

Veeck bounded into Milwaukee determined to rejuvenate the franchise by offering constant excitement and entertainment at Borchert Field. "Sport Shirt Bill" immediately borrowed $50,000 to refurbish his splintery ballpark, launched a nonstop succession of zany promotions, and scoured organized baseball to acquire players for the Brewers (he obtained Novikoff, Eddie Stanky, Grey Clarke and Heinz Becker, each of whom would win a batting crown for Milwaukee). Banjo-playing Jolly Cholly, like Veeck, was outgoing and popular, and he had managed the Cubs to National League pennants in 1932 and 1935 (in 1941, five years after retiring as an active player, the 43-year-old Grimm inserted himself as a pinch hitter and lined a triple to the right-center field fence).

In 1942, behind scrappy shortstop Stanky (.342, 124 R, 56 2B — all league-leading figures), first baseman Becker (.340), speedy outfielder Hal Peck (.333), home run champ Bill Norman (.301 with 24 homers), and old reliable Tedd Gullic (.287 — his last season before going to Portland of the PCL to finish his career), the Brewers were nosed out of the pennant on the last day of the season. Veeck, who had purchased Stanky for $2,500, sold him to the Cubs for $40,000.

Grimm led the 1943 Brewers to first place with an offense sparked by batting champ Grey Clarke (.346), home run and RBI leader Ted Norbert (.293, 25 HR, 117 RBI), Heinz Becker (.326), outfielder Herschel Martin (.307), and shortstop Tony York (.287). The most consistent pitchers were righthanders "Jittery Joe" Berry (18–10) and Wes Livengood (18–10), although Veeck astounded Grimm when southpaw Julio Acosta (3–1) burst out of a 15-foot cake at a Borchert Field ceremony for Jolly Cholly's 45th birthday (he had told reporters that he wanted "a left-handed pitcher" for his birthday).

After the season Veeck joined the Marines, turning the club over to Grimm, who engineered a 10–2 start. But he could not turn down a sudden offer again to manage the Cubs, and Casey Stengel answered an SOS to take over the Brewers. Although Veeck at first objected strenuously to the choice, Stengel expertly guided Milwaukee to the highest win total (102–51) of any American Association team of the 1940s. "I had the horses," modestly remarked Casey, who had become immensely popular with the fans and press. Indeed, 38-year-old Earl Caldwell led the league in victories (19–5), while first baseman Heinz Becker (.346) and outfielders George Binks (.374) and Hal Peck (.345) were among eight Brewers who hit over .300. The team compiled a .307 batting average, led the league in homers (135) for the second year in a row, and scored a record 28 runs against Toledo on May 23.

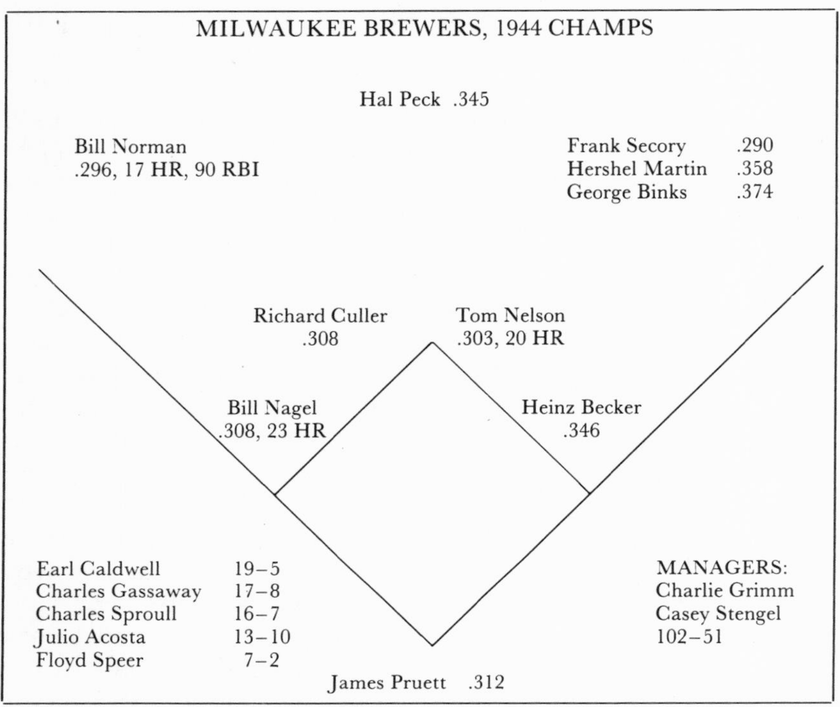

Veeck asked Stengel to return in 1945, but Casey moved over to Kansas City. Nick Cullop, who had just ended 25 years as a player, managed the Brewers to a third consecutive first-place finish. The offense again led the league in hitting (.292), provided the batting champ in outfielder Lew Flick (.374) and the RBI leader in third baseman Gene Nance (.316, 17 HR, 106 RBI). Owen Sheetz paced the league in victories (19–8, 1.95 ERA), while Wendell Davis (16–4) and southpaw Julio Acosta (15–10) were standouts on a solid pitching staff.

At the end of the season Veeck, who was on crutches because of a leg shattered in the service, sold the Brewers to Chicago lawyer Oscar Salinger. With his marriage in trouble, Veeck bought a guest ranch in Arizona, but soon returned to baseball as an innovative and exciting big league club owner. "Milwaukee was my proving grounds. It was the place where I tried out all my ideas, the good and the bad, without the terrible pressure to succeed that comes with a major league franchise. Milwaukee was all fun, even when I was running from loan company to loan company. It was all light, all laughter."

Milwaukee missed the playoffs in 1946, but Nick Cullop guided the team into postseason play the next three seasons. Indeed, from 1942 through 1952 the Brewers made the playoffs nine times, missing only in 1946 and 1950, and posted the league's best record five times, 1943–45 and 1951–52. The 1947 club finished third, then gathered momentum by defeating Louisville in seven games to win the Governors' Cup, then capped a splendid season by winning the Junior World Series, four games to three, over Syracuse. Milwaukee boasted its customary explosive offense, once more leading the league in hitting, providing the batting champ in switch-hitter Heinz Becker (.363), the home run titlist in outfielder Carden Gillenwater (.312 with 23 homers), and the Rookie of the Year in shortstop Al Dark (.303 with a league-leading 121 runs, 49 doubles, 290 putouts, and 454 assists). Cullop was named Manager of the Year by *The Sporting News,* an honor he had won in 1943 with Columbus.

Lefthander Glenn Elliott (14–5 in 1947) was the 1948 ERA champ (14–7 with a 3.76 ERA) and first baseman Heinz Becker had another good year (.319). Outfielders Froilan Fernandez (.318, 23 HR, 124 RBI) and Marvin Rickert (.302, 27 HR, 117 RBI) were other major contributors to a second-place finish in 1948. The next year Cullop managed the Brewers to third place, 16 games behind second-place Indianapolis and 16½ games behind champion St. Paul. In the playoff opener Milwaukee pulled a stunning upset, four games to three, over St. Paul, before losing the finals to Indianapolis. Second baseman Roy Hartsfield (.317) was voted Rookie of the Year, and power was provided by outfielder Howard Moss (.294, 29 HR, 117 RBI) and first baseman Nick Etten (.280, 20 HR, 108 RBI).

In 1950 the Brewers suffered a losing season, despite the efforts of batting champ Bob Addis (.323), second baseman Bill Reed (.313), shortstop Johnny Logan (.296), and outfielder Howard Moss (.285 with 26 homers). The next year Jolly Cholly Grimm, Milwaukee's favorite lefthanded banjo player, returned to manage the Brewers, and the club responded with a remarkable season. The Brewers finished first by nine games, won the Governors' Cup with playoff triumphs over Kansas City and St. Paul, then downed Montreal in the Junior World Series. Tall righthander Ernie Johnson led the league in ERA and winning percentage (15–4, 2.62), catcher Al Unser (.293 with 17 homers) was voted MVP, and first baseman George Crowe (.339, 24 HR, 119 RBI) won the RBI title and was named Rookie of the Year. Other fine performances were turned in by shortstop Buzz Clarkson (.343), righthander Murray Wall (15–5), and second baseman Bill Reed (.311).

The Brewers were even better in 1952, becoming the last American Association team to win 100 games (100–53) and sprinting to the pennant. Charlie Grimm was called up to manage the Boston Braves on May 31, but longtime coach Red Smith capably took over managerial duties in Milwaukee. For the second year in a row, the Brewers led the league in batting average, fielding percentage and fewest errors, and also ran up the largest total of stolen bases. Outfielders Luis Marquez (.345) and Billy Bruton (.325), and infielders John Dittmer (.356 in 57 games), Gene Mauch (.324), Buzz Clarkson (.318 in 74 games), Bill Reed (.313 in 50 games) and Johnny Logan (.301 in 42 games) gave his lineup depth and hitting punch. The pitching staff was equally strong: ERA and strikeout leader Don Liddle (17–4, 159 K, 2.70 ERA), fellow southpaw Dick Hoover (10–5), and righthanders Murray Wall (16–10), Gene Conley (11–4), Ed Blake (10–3), and W. H. Allen (8–3). This talented club outdistanced second-place Kansas City by 12 games, swept St. Paul in four games in the playoff opener, but lost to the Blues in the seventh game of the finals.

By this time construction was under way on long-delayed Milwaukee County Stadium (efforts had been made to construct the ballpark since the 1930s, and ground finally was broken in 1950 on the publicly-financed $5 million stadium). Bill Veeck, now owner of the St. Louis Browns, had petitioned the American League to move his club to Milwaukee, but he had been voted down. Wealthy Lou Perini, owner of the hapless Boston Braves (parent club of the Brewers) approached the National League with the same proposal, and his fellow owners unanimously approved the move on March 18, 1953. Perini had hoped to move his franchise to Toronto, but he controlled the Milwaukee territory and there was a brand-new 36,000-seat stadium. Charlie Grimm managed the Braves to second place, and a team that had drawn merely 281,000 fans in Boston established a National League record with a whopping 1,826,397 attendance. Borchert Field, home of American Association baseball for 51 years, was torn down in the spring of 1953, and today an interstate highway crosses the site. The franchise shift was the first major league move in half a century, and the eye-popping success story would trigger a succession of similar movements.

Year	Record	Pcg.	Finish
1902	65-75	.464	Sixth
1903	77-60	.562	Third
1904	89-63	.585	Third
1905	90-61	.598	Second
1906	86-70	.552	Second
1907	72-84	.460	Seventh
1908	71-83	.461	Sixth
1909	90-77	.539	Second
1910	76-91	.455	Sixth
1911	79-87	.476	Fifth
1912	79-85	.479	Fifth
1913	100-67	.599	First
1914	98-68	.590	First
1915	67-81	.453	Sixth
1916	54-110	.329	Eighth
1917	71-81	.467	Fifth
1918	38-35	.521	Fifth
1919	58-93	.384	Eighth
1920	78-88	.470	Sixth
1921	81-86	.485	Fifth
1922	85-83	.506	Fifth
1923	75-91	.452	Fifth
1924	83-83	.500	Fourth
1925	74-94	.440	Seventh
1926	93-71	.567	Third
1927	99-69	.589	Second
1928	90-78	.536	Third
1929	69-98	.413	Seventh
1930	63-91	.409	Seventh
1931	83-85	.494	Fifth
1932	88-78	.530	Third
1933	67-87	.435	Seventh
1934	82-70	.539	Third
1935	75-79	.487	Sixth
1936	90-64	.584	First (won opener, finals, and Jr. World Series)
1937	80-73	.523	Fourth (won opener, lost finals)
1938	81-70	.536	Third (lost opener)
1939	70-83	.458	Sixth
1940	58-90	.392	Eighth
1941	55-98	.359	Eighth
1942	81-69	.540	Second (lost opener)
1943	90-61	.596	First (lost opener)
1944	102-51	.667	First (lost opener)

1945	93-61	.604	First (lost opener)
1946	70-78	.473	Fifth
1947	79-75	.513	Third (won opener, finals, and Jr. World Series)
1948	89-65	.578	Second (lost opener)
1949	76-76	.500	Third (won opener, lost finals)
1950	68-85	.444	Sixth
1951	94-57	.623	First (won opener, finals, and Jr. World Series)
1952	101-53	.656	First (won opener, lost finals)

Minneapolis (Millers)

The Minneapolis Unions provided the Flour City its first organized baseball club in 1867. During the next several years, other amateur teams from Minneapolis included the Browns, Blue Stockings, and White Shirts. The first professional aggregation was the Minneapolis Millers, who played in the Northwestern League in 1884. Because the Millers' owner hired "real ball players" from outside the city, three of the best Minneapolis athletes crossed the Mississippi River to play for St. Paul's Northwestern League club. The first meeting between the two teams occurred on June 23, 1884, in St. Paul and was won by the locals, 4–0.

During the 1880s and 1890s, Minneapolis continued to field professional clubs in the Western League. In 1889 the Millers moved into Athletic Park, on the current site of Butler Square. Right field loomed so close that batters sometimes were thrown out at first on an apparent single to right, and in 1894 and 1895 first baseman Perry Werden walloped 42 and 45 homers, totals which remained unmatched in professional competition until Babe Ruth blasted 54 in 1920. But in May 1896, the Millers were given 30 days to abandon cozy Athletic Park, because the downtown location had been sold for commercial purposes. Late in May the Millers left on an extended road trip while a new ballpark was hastily erected at 31st Street and Nicollet Avenue. The ground was graded and plank fences, bleachers, and grandstands went up in just three weeks, and even though the new facility would not become known as Nicollet Park until 1897, it would be the home of professional baseball in Minneapolis for 60 years. In 1897 the Millers romped to a Western League pennant behind player-manager Walter Wilmot (.391) and righthander Bill Hutchison (38–13).

The Western League disbanded for a year after the 1900 season, and Minneapolis was without a professional team in 1901. But in 1902 the Millers became charter members of the new American Association. Wilmot continued to guide the club, but the Millers finished seventh in 1902 and 1903. Although Minneapolis began to enjoy winning records in 1904, there would be no pennant during the inaugural decade of the American Association. In 1907 first baseman Buck Freeman (.335, 38 2B, 18 HR) led the league in doubles and homers — the first of 21 home run titles won by Miller sluggers between 1907 and 1953. Right field at Nicollet Park was just 279 feet from home plate and the right-center power alley measured only 328 feet. In 1907 the Millers topped the AA in team homers — the first of a record 32 times Minneapolis would pound its way to the home run title. From 1921 through 1955 the Millers hit the most homers in 28 of 35 seasons, including seven straight from 1924 through 1930, six straight from 1932 through 1937, and seven straight from 1947 through 1953.

Mike Cantillon bought the Millers after the 1906 season for $27,500, and he determined to build a championship club by acquiring players with major league backgrounds. The Millers' third baseman-manager for 1909, for example, was future Hall of Famer Eddie Collins, at 36 a 14-year big league veteran. Collins (.273) guided the club into third place behind batting champ Tip O'Neill (.296 — the only AA hitting title under .300), stolen base leader Warren Gill (.242 with 41 steals), and hurlers Fred Olmstead (24–12 with nine shutouts) and "Young Cy" Young (23–18), who pitched shutouts in both halves of a doubleheader against Milwaukee on July 13. Collins moved on at the end of the season, and Mike Cantillon hired his brother Joe as manager. Joe had been a good minor league second baseman and umpire, a scout credited with discovering Walter Johnson, Rube Waddell and Amos Rusie, and he had managed the Washington Senators. With the front-office support of his brother, Joe would win the next three pennants, and add a fourth in 1915.

The infield remained intact throughout the championship seasons of 1910, 1911, and 1912: the first baseman was Warren Gill, who added another stolen base title in 1911; at second was Jimmy Williams, a hard-hitting (.315, .332 and .296) veteran of 11 big league seasons; the shortstop was six-year big league vet "Daredevil

Dave" Altizer, who won stolen base crowns in 1910 and 1912 (.300 with 65 SB, .335 with 30 SB in 1911, and .294 with 68 SB); and at third was Hobe Ferris, who had played nine seasons in the major leagues and whose best year with the Millers was 1911 (.303). Light-hitting but prankish Yip Owens caught in all three championship seasons, and outfielders Otis Clymer (.308 with 38 SB, .342 with 51 SB, and .307 with 61 SB) and Claude Rossman (.278, .356 and .322) were five-year major league vets who roamed the Nicollet gardens for all three pennant-winners.

Roy Patterson, a veteran of seven major league seasons, was the only starting pitcher who played for the three consecutive champs (21–12, 24–10, 21–9), and he led the AA in victories in 1911. Ten-year big league vet Long Tom Hughes led the league in wins in 1910 (31–12) and pitched his way back to the majors. In 1911 Mike Cantillon acquired the gifted, eccentric southpaw, Rube Waddell. The 35-year-old future Hall of Famer won both ends of a doubleheader against Louisville — a three-hitter and a one-hitter — in 1911, and he turned in the last two solid seasons of his career for the 1911 and 1912 AA champs (20–17 and 12–6).

The star of 1910 and 1911 was outfielder Gavvy Cravath, who led the league in batting average, hits, homers, doubles, and total bases both years (.326, 14 HR, 41 2B, and .363, 29 HR, 53 2B, 33 SB). Cravath had played two unsuccessful seasons in the American League, but after his standout performance for the Millers he went on to nine years in the National League.

Minneapolis outdistanced the other AA teams with 107 victories in 1910, 99 the next year, and 105 in 1912. The Millers led the league in hitting in each of these seasons, provided the stolen base champ and victory leader all three years, and established the all-time stolen base record with 292 thefts in 1912. A hallmark of the Minneapolis dynasty was the remarkable stability which kept eight key veterans on the roster. But by 1913 age was beginning to take its toll, and several players were purchased by big league clubs. Joe Cantillon threatened to win a fourth consecutive pennant in 1913, but the Millers faded to second place in the final week of the season, then sagged to seventh place in 1914.

The next year found Minneapolis in last place as late as July, but Cantillon rallied the Millers and stormed to another pennant. The club again led the league in hitting, as well as runs, doubles, total bases, and hits. This potent attack was triggered by outfielders Henri Rondeau (.333) and Roy Massey (.292), infielder-outfielder Jay Cashion (.327), catcher Patsy Gharrity (.308), shortstop J. Jennings (.307), and 38-year-old Dave Altizer (.302 with 118 runs), who played mostly in the outfield but led the AA in runs. Chink Yingling (19–13 with a 2.17 ERA) won the only ERA title ever recorded by a Miller pitcher, while Mutt Williams led the league in victories, games, complete games, and innings pitched (29–16, 64 G, 32 CG, 441 IP). Harry Harper, a wild southpaw with a blistering fastball (7–9, 154 IP, 99 H, 127 W, 148 K) pitched a no-hitter against St. Paul in March, but in July he issued a record-setting 20 walks in eight innings against the Saints. The Washington Senators, however, were sufficiently impressed to bring up Harper in exchange for righty "Bird Dog" Hopper, who was incredibly effective during the pennant drive in the last two months of the season (18–3).

There would not be another pennant until 1932, but in the interim Minneapolis fans enjoyed watching a number of fine individual performances, especially players who became fixtures at Nicollet Park. Dave Altizer wore a Miller uniform from 1910 through 1918, when he was 41. Daredevil Dave led the AA in runs scored four times, twice was stolen base champ, set the all-time league record for sacrifices, and was a .300 hitter five times, including 1917 (.322), 1914 (.331), and 1911 (.335). Happy-go-lucky catcher Yip Owens was with the club 10 seasons during the period 1910 through 1922. Roy Patterson, four times a 20-game winner from 1908 through 1914, returned to Minneapolis in 1917 for three more years; in 10 seasons the righthanded spitballer was 135–73 for the Millers. Outfielder-catcher Henri Rondeau was with the Millers in all or part of a record 12 seasons, 1913 through 1924, and he hit over .300 seven times. In 1922, 31-year-old Earl Smith, a six-year American League veteran, went to Minneapolis for nine seasons as a slugging outfielder. He hit over .300 every year but one and drove in more than 100 runs six times; his best seasons were 1924 (.353, 23 HR, 127 RBI, 139 R, 25 SB, and a league-leading 64 2B), 1925 (.313, 31 HR, 54 2B, 156 RBI, 132 R), and 1927 (.342, 25 HR, 49 2B, 135 RBI, 132 R).

In 1916 Chink Yingling led the AA in victories (24–13) and was almost matched by Charles Burk (21–16), and the next year Claude Thomas paced the league in games and innings pitched

(20–24 in 62 games and 374 IP). Former big league pitcher Reb Russell joined the Millers in 1919, attempting to resurrect his career as an outfielder. The next year the 31-year-old lefthander began to wield a dangerous bat (.339 in 85 games), and in 1921 he hit his way (.375, 33 HR, 132 RBI) into a contract with the Pittsburgh Pirates. From September 1921 through June 1922, the hard-hitting Millers went 238 consecutive games without being shut out. Reb Russell and fellow outfielder Dick Wade (.327, 32 HR, 126 RBI) helped the 1922 Millers become the first AA club to hit more than 100 homers, and in 1924 the team pounded out 354 doubles. The 1923 home run champ was outfielder Carl East (.375, 31 HR, 175 RBI), who was dealt to the Washington Senators in exchange for outfielder George Fisher. Early in 1924, however, East angrily left the Senators, and the club demanded the return of Fisher. Commissioner Kenesaw Mountain Landis ordered Fisher to report to Washington, but the Senators soon traded him to Milwaukee, whereupon the Millers protested and persuaded Landis to assign him to Minneapolis (he hit .309 in 1924).

Architect of the East-Fisher trade was Mike Kelley, who had been the Millers' owner-president-manager in part of the 1905 and 1906 seasons, and who again bought the franchise after the 1923 season. Kelley kept his club solvent by acquiring veteran sluggers who padded their statistics in the friendly confines of Nicollet Park, then arranging profitable sales to big league clubs. In 1928 Kelley acquired a superb center fielder, Spence Harris, who had played two years in the American League. Harris led the AA in home runs, doubles, runs, total bases and at-bats (.327, 32 HR, 127 RBI, 133 R), and after another stellar performance in 1929 (.340, 100 RBI, 139 R) he was sold by Kelley to Washington. But again he was a disappointment and soon was back in Minneapolis. In 10 seasons with the Millers his batting average ranged from .363 to .301, he led the league in runs three times, recorded 100 or more RBIs in six seasons, and was the league's best center fielder (he spent 28 years as a pro, and became the minor league career leader in runs, hits, doubles, and total bases). Another great outfielder, future Hall of Famer Zack Wheat, finished his career in a Miller uniform in 1928, hitting .309 at the age of 40. Shortstop Frank Emmet led the AA in homers and runs scored in 1927 (.330, 32 HR, 116 RBI, 154 R), and in 1929 he was the league's stolen base champ (.317 with 36 steals). Kelley acquired slugger Nick Cullop (420 minor league

Miller owners and managers, 1902–39. (1) Clarence Saulpaugh. (2) Walter Wilmot. (3) Mike Cantillon. (4) Joe Cantillon. (5) George Belden. (6) 1902 Millers. (7) Mike Kelley. (8) Donie Bush. (9) Dave Bancroft. (10) Tom Sheehan.

— Courtesy Minnesota Historical Society

homers) from Brooklyn in 1930; although wracked by family tragedies, the righthanded outfielder led the league in homers, RBIs and runs (.359, 54 HR, 152 RBI, 150 R), then was sold to Cincinnati.

During a five-year period the Miller mound corps produced three strikeout kings: Robert McGraw in 1925 (22–13), Pat Malone in 1927 (20–18 with 214 Ks), and John Brillheart in 1929 (20–16). Rube Benton joined the staff in 1926 and won 115 games for the Millers during the next eight years, enjoying his best season in 1929 (20–14). The 1929 season was memorable not only because Benton and Brillheart were 20-game winners. The Millers set another new team record for home runs (158), Wes Griffin (.351) played all nine positions in one game, and the perennial rivalry between Minneapolis and St. Paul exploded into an unusually violent brawl during a Fourth of July doubleheader at Nicollet Park.

After 17 seasons without a pennant, Minneapolis began another dynasty in 1932. Noted field general Donie Bush replaced Mike Kelley as manager and immediately produced a champion (100–68). Bush was hired by Cincinnati in 1933, but after finishing last he returned to Minneapolis to win consecutive championships. League champs in 1932, 1934 and 1935, the Millers came in second in 1933 and won the Western Division. In each of these seasons the Millers led the AA in homers, recorded the most hits in 1932 and 1933, posted the highest batting average in 1933 (.303) and 1934 (.308), and scored the most runs in 1932, 1933 and 1934, including an all-time AA record of 1,162 in 1932.

All four clubs were bolstered by hard-hitting Spence Harris, slugging first baseman Joe Hauser, southpaw Jesse Petty (18–8 in 1933, 19–7 in 1934 at the age of 39), third sacker Babe Ganzel (.311, 23 HR, 143 RBI in 1932, then .314, .301 and .294), and second baseman Andy Cohen (.311 in 1934). The explosive 1932 team boasted the batting champ in outfielder Art Ruble (.376, 29 HR, 141 RBI), the home run king in Joe Hauser (.303, 49 HR, 129 RBI), and the all-time American Association run leader in outfielder Joe Mowry (.348, 175 runs, and a league-leading 257 hits). Utility man Harry Rice hit so well (.345) that he appeared in 117 games, while catcher Paul Richards was spectacular in 78 games (.361, 16 HR, 69 RBI). Rosy Ryan pitched in 60 games and tied for the lead in victories (22–13), while 42-year-old Rube Benton enjoyed one of his best years with the Millers (18–7). The Millers outdistanced the rest of the AA by nine and a half games, but dropped the Junior World Series to Newark.

In 1932 Joe Hauser put on one of the most spectacular hitting displays in baseball history (.332, 153 R, 69 HR, 182 RBI), leading the league in runs and RBIs and, of course, in home runs for the second year in a row. A lefthander, he walloped 50 of his homers in Nicollet Park. Hauser had cracked 63 home runs for Baltimore in 1930, and his 1932 total set the all-time American Association record. He is the only player to hit 60 home runs twice, and only Joe Bauman, playing first base for Class C Roswell in 1954 (.400, 72 HR, 224 RBI) ever hit more in a season. Hauser led the 1932 Millers to the league's second-best record and the championship of the Western Division, but Minneapolis lost a postseason playoff with Columbus.

Hauser was headed for an even better year in 1934 when he

broke a kneecap in July (.348, 33 HR and 88 RBI in just 82 games). But switch-hitting slugger Buzz Arlett was acquired from Birmingham late in May, and he won the home run crown despite playing in just 116 games (.319, 41 HR, 132 RBI). Other offensive stars included run leader and first baseman Spence Harris, catcher Pinky Hargrave (.356), outfielder Ab Wright (.353, 29 HR, 131 RBI), and infielders Leo Norris (.310, 23 HR, 116 RBI) and Ernie Smith (.325). Righthander Wally Tauscher led the AA in victories (21–7); Tauscher pitched nine years for the Millers, 1933–41, running up a record of 133–78. The 1934 All-Star Game was played in Nicollet Park, and the powerful Millers beat the Stars, 13–6, as Joe Hauser recorded two home runs and six RBIs. Despite the loss of Hauser soon afterward, Donie Bush still brought the Millers into first place with another Western Division title, although Columbus again registered a playoff triumph.

In 1935 Hauser was hobbled by two crippled knees (.262, 23 HR, 101 RBI), Buzz Arlett lost part of a finger (.360, 25 HR, 101 RBI), Pinky Hargrave missed two months with broken fingers (.242), Wally Tauscher missed numerous starts with a sore shoulder (18–9), Babe Ganzel suffered eye and ankle injuries (.294), Spence Harris chipped a bone in his ankle (.337), and other players were battered. But newcomer Johnny Gill led the AA in homers, runs and RBIs (.361, 148 R, 43 HR, 154 RBI), and rifle-armed center fielder Fabian Gaffke, another Miller rookie, also helped at the plate (.302 with 19 homers). Donie Bush artfully juggled his injury-plagued roster, as the Millers again beat the All-Stars, 4–3, and somehow took first place by a six-game margin.

Gaffke had an even better season the next year (.342, 25 HR, 132 RBI), and newcomer Earl Browne also was impressive (.328, 35 HR, 126 RBI), but the Millers sagged to fifth place despite blasting 212 home runs. In 1937 the Millers rose to third place behind RBI champ Red Kress (.334, 27 HR, 157 RBI), home run titlist Roy Pfleger (.326, 29 HR, 121 RBI), and doubles and triples leader Carl Reynolds (.355, 49 2B, 17 3B, 17 HR, 110 RBI).

At the beginning of 1938 the starting right fielder was lanky, 19-year-old Ted Williams, whose temper tantrums supposedly drove an exasperated Donie Bush to inform owner Mike Kelley, "Either that kid goes or I go" ("We're going to miss you, Donie," came the legendary reply). Williams won a Triple Crown (.366, 43 HR, 142 RBI) and led the league in runs, walks and total bases, then departed for a Hall of Fame career with the Red Sox.

The 1939 Millers came in second behind a home run barrage led by Phil Weintraub (.331, 33 HR, 126 RBI), second sacker Lin Storti (.281, 30 HR, 105 RBI), and outfielders Ab Wright (.337, 21 HR, and a league-leading 134 RBI), James Wasdell (.323, 29 HR, 102 RBI in just 102 games), and Harvey Walker (.304 with 24 homers). Herb Hash led the league in victories (22–6), while Wilburn Butland (19–10) and veteran Wally Tauscher (13–6) also posted good seasons. In 1940 the Millers again led the league in homers (183) as well as team hitting (.307). The lineup bristled with heavy hitters such as Phil Weintraub (.347, 27 HR, 109 RBI), switch-hitter Lin Storti (.313 with 20 homers), outfielders Roberto Estalella (.341, 32 HR, 121 RBI, with a league-leading 147 runs and 132 walks), and Harvey Walker (.318 with 25 homers), and catcher Otto Denning (.329).

But the biggest gun on the roster was outfielder Ab Wright who, like Ted Williams two years earlier, won a Triple Crown (.369, 39 HR, 159 RBI). Although Wright was righthanded — and therefore unable to take full advantage of the short right-field fence in Minneapolis — he boomed four home runs and a triple at Nicollet Park on July 4, 1940, setting the all-time AA standard for total bases in a single game. Wright began his professional career in 1928 as a pitcher, but his hitting ability soon made him a regular outfielder. He played 27 games in Minneapolis in 1931 (.357), then appeared in four games the next year and one in 1933. A good season with the Millers in 1934 earned a promotion to the Cleveland Indians, but after a year he was back in the minors. Wright returned to Minneapolis in 1939, won the RBI title, then took the Triple Crown. In 1941 he repeated as home run champ (.284, 26 HR, 103 RBI), and early in 1944 the 38-year-old outfielder was purchased by the Boston Braves. After the war he played two more years of minor league ball before retiring with a .326 lifetime average in the minors.

In 1941 slugging first baseman Zeke Bonura entered the service after a fine start (.366 in 46 games), and newcomer Babe Barna was the stolen base champ (.336, 24 HR, 105 RBI, 29 SB). At the end of the season Barna was sold to the New York Giants, but he would return to Minneapolis in 1944. The strapping (6′2, 210-pound) outfielder, a lefthanded slugger, led the league in home runs and walks in 1944 (.298 with 24 homers) and 1945 (.309 with

25 homers), and in runs the next year (.298, 28 HR, 112 RBI, 122 R). He recorded his highest batting average as a Miller in 1947 (.324 with 21 homers), but after one more season (.288 with 23 homers) he was dealt to Nashville. At the Sulphur Dell he enjoyed another short right-field porch (.341, 42 HR, 138 RBI in 1949, .358 in 1951), then finished his career in the AA with Toledo and Charleston in 1952 (.287).

From 1943 through 1945, the Millers led the league in stolen bases and produced the stolen base champ: infielder Herman "Flea" Clifton in 1943 (.282 with 16 steals, the lowest total ever to win the AA title); outfielder Jim Cookson in 1944 (.305 with 47 steals); and second baseman Frank Danneker (.308 with 50 steals). In 1946 owner Mike Kelley arranged an April doubleheader with the archrival Saints and pulled in a crowd of 15,761; 5,000 fans stood on the field, and special ground rules produced 24 doubles in the doubleheader, which was swept by St. Paul. But at the end of the season Kelley, last of the independent owners, sold the Millers to the New York Giants. Kelley, who had managed for 30 years in the minors, remained in Minneapolis until he died in 1955.

In 1946 lefthanded first baseman John McCarthy was the RBI champ (.333 with 122 RBIs), and another good season in 1947 (.346 with 22 homers) gave the 10-year National Leaguer a final shot with the Giants. The 1947 MVP was righthanded reliever Steve "The Splinter" Gerkin, who made a record-setting 83 appearances (10–2). In 1948 future Hall of Famer Billy Herman played in 10 games (.452) while managing the Millers, and the next year the home run king was outfielder Charlie Workman (.291, 41 HR, 122 RBI), while first sacker Jack Harshman led the league in runs (.270, 40 HR, 110 RBI, 121 R). Minneapolis fielded its first black players in 1949, 35-year-old Ray Dandridge (.362), a future Hall of Famer who hit safely in 28 straight games, and pitcher Dave Barnhill (7–10).

After the 1935 Millers finished in first place, there had been a 14-year pennant drought. There were playoff appearances in 1936, 1939, 1940, 1941, 1946, 1947 and 1949, but in each of these seven seasons the Millers were eliminated in the opening round. In 1950 the Millers finally recorded another first-place title, although once again Minneapolis was stymied in the playoff opener. Ray Dandridge (.311 with a league-leading 195 hits) was voted Most Valuable Player, while outfielder-first baseman Bert Haas (.318, 24

HR, 80 RBI) finished second in the balloting. Outfielder John Jorgensen (.330) and outfielder-infielder Bill Milne (.312 in 54 games) were two lefthanded hitters who performed superbly in part of a season. The pitching staff demonstrated excellent depth behind Dave Barnhill (11–3), knuckleballer and future Hall of Famer Hoyt Wilhelm (15–11), southpaw Adrian Zabala (11–4), and Dixie Howell (14–2), who twirled a no-hitter against Columbus and who was often used as a pinch hitter because of his batting prowess (.308 with five homers).

The next year Dandridge (.324), Milne (.300), home run champ Tookie Gilbert (.273, 29 HR, 100 RBI), Howell (.337 with seven homers), catcher Ray Kaat (.308), and even Zabala (.375) hit well, but the pitching sagged and Minneapolis slipped into the second division. For a few weeks, though, Miller fans were entertained by the brilliant play of Willie Mays, who was promoted to the Giants after just 35 games (.477 with eight homers and 30 RBIs) and finished the season with Rookie of the Year honors in the National League. Minneapolis fans, accustomed to a home-owned franchise, were nettled when Mays and other star performers were pulled up to the major league club during the season. In addition to this unsettling change of procedure, plans were being formulated to build a new stadium in hopes of attracting a big league team.

But there would be a few more seasons in the friendly confines of Nicollet Park, and the Millers took full advantage. The 1953 season was more than a month old when George Wilson joined the roster, but the lefthanded outfielder pounded his way to the home run title (.315 with 34 homers). The lineup still boasted catcher Ray Kaat (.326, 28 HR, 98 RBI), as well as third baseman Rance Pless (.322, 25 HR, 88 RBI), and outfielder Charles Diering (.322). Wilson was back in 1954 (.302, 27 HR, 92 RBI) to lead the league in runs, and he was joined by lefthanded first baseman Gail Harris (.309, 34 HR, 113 RBI).

The 1955 Millers would be the last to play at Nicollet and the team blasted 241 home runs, breaking the 200 mark for the fourth time. Minneapolis was the only AA team to hit 200 homers in a season, and the 1955 total was their greatest number. Infielder Rance Pless won the batting crown, along with several other offensive titles, and was named MVP (.337, 26 HR, 107 RBI). Outfielder Monte Irvin put in a superb half season (.352), and a prize newcomer was catcher Carl Sawatski, a powerful lefthanded hitter (.268 with 27 homers). George Wilson (.307, 31 HR, 99 RBI) and Robert Lennon (.280, 31 HR, 104 RBI) were as reliable as ever, and righthander Al Worthington led the league in victories (19–10). Manager of the Year Bill Rigney guided Minneapolis to first place by an eight-game margin, then the Millers shattered the post-season jinx by sweeping both series, becoming the first AA team to win eight consecutive playoff games. In the Junior World Series — the Millers' first since a 1932 collapse against Newark — Al Worthington won three games, then came in as a reliever to finish off Rochester in a fittingly triumphant finale at Nicollet.

The next season opened at Bloomington Park (later renamed Metropolitan Stadium), a $4.5 million, 18,200-seat facility located in the suburb of Bloomington. For the inaugural game an overflow crowd jammed into the showplace stadium, and the 1956 Millers became the only minor league club in Minneapolis history to draw over 300,000 (318,326). With Bill Rigney promoted to the Giants, Eddie Stanky took over as the Millers' pilot. Slugging outfielders Willie Kirkland (.293, 37 HR, 120 RBI) and Don Grate (.316) led the team to a fourth-place finish but, reverting to form, the Millers went down in the opening round. In 1957 the rifle-armed Grate (.296) and powerful first baseman Orlando Cepeda (.309, 25 HR, 108 RBI) sparked the Millers to third place, but Minneapolis suffered a four-game sweep in the playoff opener.

Throughout 1957 there were strong hopes in Minneapolis that Horace Stoneham, who had announced that he was pulling the Giants out of New York at the end of the season, would bring National League baseball to Metropolitan Stadium. But Stoneham took his team to San Francisco, and he transferred his Minneapolis affiliate to Phoenix. But the San Francisco Seals, Class AAA farm club of the Boston Red Sox, moved to Minneapolis.

Although the movement to acquire a big league club continued, the Red Sox affiliation paid off immediately. Under player-manager Gene Mauch the new Millers made the playoffs in 1958 and 1959, won both playoff rounds each year, and triumphed in the 1958 Junior World Series. Mauch was voted Manager of the Year both seasons and was named to lead the Philadelphia Phils. The 1958 Millers finished last in hitting but second in fielding and first in staff ERA. The following season the team again led the league in ERA — the only time in AA history that Minneapolis pitchers allowed the fewest runs in the league — and in fielding as well. Pitching and defense were the keys to the Millers' success in 1958 and 1959; the only full-season regular to hit .300 was infielder Chuck Tanner in 1959 (.319 with a league-leading 41 doubles). In 1958 the Millers swept Denver in four games to win the playoff finals, then won four straight against Montreal to record their second Junior World Series victory. The next year the Millers outlasted Fort Worth in a seven-game playoff final series and went on to participate in perhaps the most remarkable of all Junior World Series against the Havana Sugar Kings. The Millers blew a two-run lead in the eighth inning of the seventh game to lose the series, but the last five games were played in Havana — with Fidel Castro and squads of gun-toting soldiers present — and over 100,000 Cubans attended, giving the 1959 series the all-time attendance record.

In 1960 Minneapolis recorded its 40th winning record in 59 years in the AA, although the Millers failed to reach the playoffs. Star of the final Millers club was young Carl Yastrzemski, who won the 1959 batting crown of the Carolina League, then capped his first year as a pro by playing against the Sugar Kings. Yaz was a starting outfielder for the 1960 Millers, leading the league in base hits and missing the batting title by just three percentage points (.330 with 193 hits). Outfielder Dave Mann (.293 with 50 steals) was the stolen base champ. The Millers finished AA participation with a 4,800–4,366 record and the best winning percentage ever accumulated in the league. The Millers won nine pennants, hosted a record five All-Star games, and became the only American Association club never to finish last.

Year	Record	Pcg.	Finish
1902	54-86	.385	Seventh
1903	50-91	.355	Seventh
1904	78-67	.538	Fourth
1905	90-64	.584	Third
1906	91-68	.544	Third
1907	80-74	.520	Third
1908	77-77	.500	Fifth
1909	88-79	.527	Third
1910	107-61	.637	First
1911	99-66	.600	First
1912	105-60	.636	First
1913	97-70	.581	Second
1914	75-93	.446	Seventh
1915	92-62	.597	First
1916	88-76	.537	Third

1917	68-86	.442	Sixth
1918	34-42	.447	Seventh
1919	72-82	.468	Fifth
1920	85-79	.518	Fourth
1921	92-73	.558	Second
1922	92-75	.551	Second
1923	74-92	.446	Sixth
1924	77-89	.464	Sixth
1925	86-80	.518	Fourth
1926	72-94	.434	Seventh
1927	88-80	.524	Fifth
1928	97-71	.577	Second
1929	89-78	.533	Third
1930	77-76	.503	Fourth
1931	80-88	.476	Sixth
1932	100-68	.595	First (lost Little World Series)
1933	86-67	.562	Second (lost playoff)
1934	85-64	.570	First (lost playoff)
1935	91-63	.591	First
1936	78-76	.506	Fifth
1937	87-67	.565	Third (lost opener)
1938	78-74	.513	Sixth
1939	99-55	.643	Second (lost opener)
1940	86-59	.593	Third (lost opener)
1941	83-70	.542	Fourth (lost opener)
1942	76-78	.494	Seventh
1943	67-84	.444	Sixth
1944	54-97	.358	Seventh
1945	72-81	.471	Fifth
1946	76-75	.503	Fourth (lost opener)
1947	77-77	.500	Fourth (lost opener)
1948	77-77	.500	Fifth
1949	74-78	.487	Fourth (lost opener)
1950	90-64	.584	First (lost opener)
1951	77-75	.507	Fifth
1952	79-75	.513	Fourth (lost opener)
1953	76-78	.494	Fifth
1954	78-73	.517	Third (lost opener)
1955	92-62	.597	First (won opener, finals, and Jr. World Series)
1956	78-74	.513	Fourth (lost opener)
1957	85-69	.552	Third (lost opener)
1958	82-71	.536	Third (won opener, finals, and Jr. World Series)
1959	95-67	.586	Second (won opener and finals, lost Jr. World Series)
1960	82-72	.532	Fifth

Nashville (Sounds)

For more than a century, baseball in Nashville centered around the Sulphur Dell. Originally known as Sulphur Spring Bottom, the low-lying area featured a sulphur spring and salt lick, and became a trading, watering and picnic spot in the earliest pioneer times. Baseball was introduced in 1862 by soldiers of the Union Army of occupation. There were spirited amateur games and enthusiastic crowds, which led to the support of various semipro and professional clubs.

In 1901 Nashville became a charter member of the Southern Association, participating until the Class AA circuit disbanded after the 1961 season. The Nashville Fishermen (later called Volunteers or Vols) won the first two pennants, as well as other flags in 1916, 1940, 1943, 1944, 1948, and 1949. There were playoff titles from 1939 through 1944, 1949, 1950 and 1953, and Dixie Series championships from 1940 through 1942 and in 1949. Much of the championship success was credited to Larry Gilbert, who managed the Vols from 1939 through 1948.

Nashville's stadium was first called Athletic Park, then Sulphur Springs Bottom. Grantland Rice, who won fame as a poetic sportswriter, became the first sports editor of Nashville's *Tennessean* in 1907, and renamed the ballpark Sulphur Dell. Rice pointed out that it was easier to write rhyming couplets with Dell than with Bottom, and the name became famous among baseball people. Located north of the state capitol, Sulphur Dell had a short right-field fence, even after the diamond was turned around in 1927; left-handed sluggers thrived in Nashville. Pitchers, however, called the park "Suffer Hell." In 1930 first baseman Jim Poole pounded out 50 home runs and 167 RBIs; in 1948 outfielder Larry Gilbert blasted 52 homers and 182 RBIs, an all-time record; and in 1954 outfielder Bob Lemon won a Triple Crown (.345, 64 HR, 161 RBI), and his 64 homers (42 of them over The Fence) established the all-time league mark. There were 16 batting champs, including Phil Weintraub in 1934 (.401), Les Fleming in 1941 (.414), and Hugh Hill in 1902 (.416), who hit for the highest average in league history.

When the South Atlantic League went up to Class AA in 1963, Nashville fielded a team, but attendance was poor. The Vols disbanded, Sulphur Dell was razed, and today the historic site is used for parking. But the city's baseball tradition was too strong to die, and in 1978 Nashville again joined the Sally, which had been renamed the Southern League in 1964. Energetic Larry Schmittou brought professional baseball back to Nashville at a time when the home of country-western music was reaching new heights as an entertainment haven.

Herschel Greer Stadium was built south of downtown at the foot of St. Cloud Hill in Fort Negley Park (Fort Negley atop the hill was a key point in Nashville's Civil War fortifications). The stadium, which now seats 18,000, has pulled more than five million fans through the turnstiles since 1978. Schmittou's new team, nicknamed the Sounds, played in the Southern League from 1978 through 1984 before stepping up to the American Association. Schmittou purchased the Evansville Triplets in 1984, then moved the franchise to Nashville.

In 1985 the Sounds finished second in the Eastern Division. Switch-hitter Scotti Madison, who played catcher, third base, first base and outfield, won the batting crown (.341 with 16 homers in 86 games), and another switch-hitter, outfielder Darrell Brown, also had a good year (.294 with 32 steals in 97 games). On July 7, righthander Bryan Kelly (8–8) twirled a 5–0 no-hitter over the 89ers. Attendance was a robust 364,225.

The next season brought another hitting title to Nashville. Outfielder Bruce Fields (.368) was the batting champ, but the club slumped to a losing record, although attendance again exceeded 364,000. German Rivera was selected as All-Star third baseman (.298 with 14 homers), and Scotti Madison (.257) and Bryan Kelly (5–5) were back with the Sounds, but not as effective. In 1987 Nashville sank into the AA cellar, but attendance, stimulated by constant promotions and the presence of C&W stars, was the best yet (378,715). The Sounds were last in team hitting, despite the efforts of third sacker Chris Sabo (.292) and Jeff Treadway (.315), who led all second basemen in fielding. The most effective pitchers were righthander Scott Terry (11–10 with a 3.97 ERA, second best in the league) and Jeff Montgomery (8–5).

The Sounds improved to a winning record in 1988, although there was a dizzying succession of managers — Jack Lind, Wayne

The Oak Ridge Boys posing for an album cover at Herschel Greer Stadium in 1989. Bass singer Richard Sterben, nearest the camera, has been a Sounds' stockholder since 1978.

— Photo by the author

Garland, Jim Hoff, George Scherger and Frank Lucchesi. Outfielder Van Snider was the home run champ (.290 with 23 homers), second baseman Lenny Harris won the stolen base title (.277 with 45 thefts), lefthander Norm Charlton was the strikeout king (11–10 with 161 Ks in 182 IP), and righthander Jeff Gray led the league in saves (8–5 with a 1.97 ERA and 19 saves in 42 games).

In 1989 Van Snider (.222 with 12 homers) and Jeff Gray (4–4 with a 3.66 ERA and seven saves in 45 games) tailed off, but Jack Armstrong tied for the victory lead (13–9) and outfielder Skeeter Barnes was the doubles leader (.303 with 30 2Bs). The Sounds again won more than they lost (74–72), and although Nashville finished 13 games off the pace, there were over 441,000 paid admissions at Herschel Greer Stadium.

When the Sounds reintroduced professional baseball to Nashville after an absence of 15 years, Larry Schmittou consciously identified his team with the city's entertainment scene. Country music stars such as Larry Gatlin, Jerry Reed, Conway Twitty, and Richard Sterban are Sounds stockholders. When the author visited Herschel Greer Stadium on May 10, 1989, the Oak Ridge Boys were photographing an album cover with the ballpark as a backdrop. Fans were able to talk with the singers and take photos, and during pregame ceremonies the Oak Ridge Boys stood at home plate to sing the national anthem (through the years "The Star Spangled Banner" has been delivered by the Oaks, Larry Gatlin, the Statler Brothers, Lee Greenwood, Loretta Lynn, Charlie McCoy, Boots Randolph, Charlie Pride, Lynn Anderson, Tiny Tim, and a host of other stars). After the game started, Oaks' bass singer Richard Sterban, who has been a Nashville club owner since 1978, donned a Sounds cap, took his seat in the pressbox, and enthusiastically related to the author his experiences with the Sounds. As attendance figures indicate, Nashville has warmly embraced Triple-A baseball, and in just seven years the Sounds have become one of the strongest and most glamorous franchises in American Association history.

Year	Record	Pcg.	Finish
1985	71-70	.504	Fifth
1986	68-84	.479	Sixth
1987	64-76	.457	Eighth
1988	73-69	.514	Fourth
1989	74-72	.507	Fourth
1990	86-61	.585	Second (won Eastern Division, lost finals)
1991	65-78	.455	Sixth

New Orleans (Pelicans)

During the late nineteenth century, the New Orleans Pelicans proved to be the bellwether franchise of the struggling Southern League and participated in its successor, the Southern Association, from 1901 through 1959. When the Class AA Southern League was organized in 1964, New Orleans did not field a team. And by the time the Louisiana Super Dome opened, there had been no professional baseball for years.

While traveling through New Orleans, American Association President Joe Ryan stopped off to tour the Super Dome. A casual conversation with stadium manager Jim Chandler led to an invitation to stay overnight, at the expense of the Dome, and meet with state officials the next day. Ryan made it clear to Dome executives that the American Association was not major league, but he received an earnest invitation to bring a team to New Orleans.

When Ryan relayed the invitation around the AA, Tulsa owner A. Ray Smith eagerly investigated. Oiler Park in Tulsa was a decaying wooden structure which Smith had to repaint annually at great expense, and which city officials refused to replace. Smith arranged to move his franchise, a Cardinals' affiliate that would be called the Pelicans, to "Oiler Park South" for the 1977 season.

Outfielder Benny Ayala led the club in batting (.298, 18 HR, 73 RBI), and catcher Tom Harmon (.292 in 94 games) also hit well, but the Pelicans finished last in team average (.248). Ayala and infielders Ken Oberkfell (.251) and Tony LaRussa (.250 in 50 games) would log considerable playing time in the big leagues. The busiest starters were righthanders Earl Bass (10–10) and Steve Dunning (8–13), while relievers Stan Butkus (5–3 in 59 games), Johnny Sutton (5–4 in 42 games), and Mike Beard (4–2 in 31 games) found plenty of action. Eddie Solomon (4–2 with a shutout in eight starts) won promotion to the National League, but overall the staff ERA (4.68) was next-to-last in the AA.

Although the Pelicans finished in the cellar, nearly 218,000 fans filed into the Super Dome. On Thursday, July 21, the All-Star Game was held in the Super Dome, although only 5,277 showed up to watch the Texas Rangers beat the Stars, 9–1. Season attendance was second only to Denver, but Smith and his fellow owners lost heavily because stadium rental was $6,000 per game, the Pelicans were given no share of parking or concession revenue, and transportation expenses to and from New Orleans were by far the greatest in the league. Smith decided that such conditions made it impossible to avoid financial losses, and he moved his club to Springfield after just one season. In the intervening years there has been talk of bringing in a Texas League or Southern League or big league franchise, but to date there has been no professional baseball in New Orleans since the AA Pelicans of 1977.

Year	Record	Pcg.	Finish
1977	57-79	.419	Eighth

Oklahoma City (89ers)

The Oklahoma City 89ers joined the American Association in 1962 and, in the city's first year of Triple-A ball, led the AA in attendance. The original 89ers founded Oklahoma City in 1889 and wasted no time in nailing together a grandstand of planks and beer kegs. During the late 1800s, local kranks enjoyed the play of Oklahoma City nines such as the Dudes, Pirates, Statehoods, and Browns. Oklahoma City helped organize the Southwestern League in 1904, won the pennant, then switched to the Class C Western Association in 1905. After four seasons, Oklahoma City moved up to the Texas League in 1909, but three years later the franchise was moved to Beaumont. In 1914 the Oklahoma City Indians rejoined the Western Association, then switched to the Class A Western League in 1918.

The Indians were readmitted to the Texas League in 1933, competing in the Class AA circuit through the 1957 season. Three consecutive weak teams and the problems confronting all minor league operations in the 1950s caused attendance to plunge to 51,000 in 1957 (down from more than 333,000 for a losing club in 1951). Oklahoma City withdrew from professional play after 1957, but would find a new baseball future in Class AAA. When Houston moved into the National League in 1962, the American Association shriveled to five teams. But the Oklahoma City 89ers, American Association affiliate of the Houston Colt 45s, moved into beautiful new All Sports Stadium, a 12,000-seat bowl in the west end of the city. Although the 89ers finished next-to-last, attendance was a league-leading 184,000.

When the AA disbanded following the season, the 89ers shifted into the Pacific Coast League, winning the championship in 1963 and again in 1965. But travel in the sprawling PCL was difficult and expensive, and when American League expansion triggered the reorganization of the American Association, Oklahoma City happily moved back into the AA. Allie Reynolds, former American League pitching great and a successful Oklahoma City businessman, consented to serve as president of the new AA, and ran the league from his Oklahoma City offices.

Despite a losing record in 1969, the 89ers featured home run and RBI king Dan Walton (.332, 25 HR, 119 RBI) and ERA champ Ron Cook (8–8, 3.11). On July 20, 1969, Oklahoma City and Denver established the all-time league futility record for runners left on base, as each club stranded 20 players. The next year, on May 28 and 29, the longest game in AA history was played at All Sports Stadium, with Indianapolis finally outlasting the 89ers after 23 innings and six hours and 37 minutes.

In 1971 a truly intimidating fastballer, 6′7 righthander J. R. Richard, won the ERA and strikeout crowns (12–7 with a 2.45 ERA and 202 Ks in only 173 innings), and led the 89ers to their only winning record in their first eight AA seasons. Oklahoma City led the league in attendance with 330,000, and there were 245,000 paid admissions in 1972. In 1973 Lowell Palmer brought another strikeout title to Oklahoma City (12–11 with 203 Ks in 196 IP), and the next year Jim Kern kept the crown in town (17–7 with 220 Ks in just 189 IP). It was the last time that an AA pitcher would fan more than 200 batters in a season, but other strikeout titles were recorded by 89ers Randy Lerch in 1976 (13–11 with 152 Ks) and Dan Warthen in 1978 (13–8 with 144 Ks).

Attendance had steadily declined because of a succession of losing teams, and in 1975 the last-place 89ers drew merely 46,752 fans. Bing Cox and Patty Hampton, who operated the Cox Advertising Agency, were hired to improve attendance. A series of offbeat promotions was staged to popularize "Goodtime Baseball," and admissions jumped to more than 122,000. Two years later, Patty and Bing bought a majority interest, despite advice that Oklahoma City sports centered around Sooners football. The promotions increased, the stadium was constantly improved, Patty was named AA Executive of the Year in 1979 and 1980, and Bing and Patty married in the latter year. The 89ers developed a solid core of supporters and attendance continued to grow. A Western Division title in 1979 helped, and when the 89ers won another division crown in 1985, paid admissions exceeded 364,000 — the fourth-highest total in minor league baseball.

Twenty-year-old Lonnie Smith arrived in Oklahoma City in 1976, and the fleet outfielder would star for the 89ers for four seasons, until he made the big leagues to stay. During his first year as an 89er, Smith led the league in runs (.308, 93 R, 26 SB), and performed almost as well in 1977 (.277, 91 R, 45 SB). He was the sto-

The Oklahoma City 89ers promote "Good Times Baseball."
— Courtesy Oklahoma City 89ers

len base champ in 1978 (.315, 103 R, 66 SB), then repeated as run leader (.330, 106 R, 34 SB) while sparking the club to the 1979 Western Division championship. Keith Moreland (.302, 34 2B, 20 HR, 109 RBI) and John Poff (.293, 34 2B, 20 HR, 90 RBI) tied for the lead in doubles, while Orlando Gonzales (.313), percentage leader Gary Beare (12–1), Fred Beene (10–5), and Martin Bystrom (9–5) were other key players. It was Oklahoma City's first AA division title and playoff appearance, but the 89ers fell in the finals to Eastern Division winners Evansville, two games to four.

Orlando Gonzales nearly won the 1980 batting crown (.3541 to .3543 for Tim Raines of Denver), but outfielder Bob Dernier led the league in stolen bases and runs (.302, 72 SB, 105 R). Len Matuszek also was impressive in 1981 (.315, 21 HR, 91 RBI), and the 89ers recorded their fifth stolen base title as a team (there had been other crowns in 1974, 1975, 1977, and 1978). In 1984 outfielder Tommy Dunbar won the hitting title (.337). It was the only AA batting crown won by an 89er to date; Oklahoma City has not yet recorded a team hitting or home run title, nor a no-hitter.

The 89ers won a second Western Division championship in 1985 behind MVP Steve Buechele (.297), triples leader Robert

Brower (.249 with 18 3B), and righthanders Jose Guzman (10–5), Bob Sebra (10–6), and Glen Cook (9–5). The pitching staff allowed the fewest runs in the league, and the team fielding percentage was the AA's highest. Once again the 89ers were frustrated in the playoffs, losing to Louisville, four games to one.

Robert Brower led the league in walks and runs the next year (.287, 130 R, 94 W, 53 SB), and Tommy Dunbar also enjoyed another good season in 1986 (.290, 10 HR, 91 RBI). In 1987 righthander Bill Taylor was the victory leader with the lowest total (12–9) ever to win this crown in the AA. Righthander Mike Jeffcoat pitched well in 1987 (11–8) and 1988 (9–5).

The 89ers finished last in 1989, but still totaled nearly a quarter of a million admissions. Bing and Patty Hampton Cox sold the 89ers to a New York group headed by art dealer Jeffrey Loria and Marvin Goldklang, a lawyer who is part-owner of the New York Yankees and three other minor league franchises. Former Yankees' outfielder Bobby Murcer was named new president of the 89ers, and he announced that the franchise would remain in Oklahoma City. The sale brought an estimated $4.5 million, a record price for a Triple-A club, and an accurate reflection of the esclating value of minor league baseball franchises in general and Oklahoma City in particular.

Year	Record	Pcg.	Finish
1962	66-81	.449	Fifth
1969	62-78	.443	Fourth
1970	68-71	.489	Sixth
1971	71-69	.507	Third
1972	57-83	.407	Eighth
1973	61-74	.455	Seventh
1974	62-73	.459	Sixth
1975	50-86	.368	Eighth
1976	72-63	.533	Fourth
1977	70-66	.515	Fourth
1978	62-74	.456	Seventh
1979	72-63	.533	Third (won Western Division, lost finals)
1980	70-65	.519	Third
1981	69-67	.507	Fourth
1982	43-91	.321	Eighth
1983	66-69	.489	Fourth (lost opener)
1984	70-84	.455	Seventh
1985	79-63	.556	First (won Western Division, lost finals)
1986	63-79	.444	Eighth

1987	69-71	.493	Seventh
1988	67-74	.475	Seventh
1989	59-86	.407	Eighth
1990	58-87	.400	Eighth
1991	52-92	.361	Seventh

Omaha (Cardinals, Dodgers, Royals)

Although Omaha did not play a game in the American Association until 1955, the Nebraska city had a part in forming the league. In 1879 pioneer baseball organizer Ted Sullivan formed the Northwest League, the first professional circuit not centered on the Eastern seaboard. Teams were located in Dubuque (Sullivan's home) and Davenport in Iowa, Rockford in Illinois, and Omaha. There was a 1,500-seat ballpark on Sherman Avenue (now North 16th Street), but a Fourth of July game with 1,000 kranks in attendance made up the largest crowd of the season. Within just three weeks the last-place Omaha "Mashers" (the players were notorious womanizers) folded. The next season Sullivan reorganized his circuit as the Western League, which later spawned both the American League and the American Association.

During the 1880s, Omaha's population tripled from 30,000 to 90,000, and the growing city was better able to support professional baseball. Omaha joined the Western League in 1885, again disbanded before the end of the season, then rejoined the circuit two years later and played through 1894, winning a pennant in 1889 behind future Hall of Famer Kid Nichols (36–12). In 1899 William A. Rourke, experienced as a player and manager, helped reorganize the Western League, and successfully operated the Omaha franchise for 20 years. When the American Association was formed in the fall of 1901, Omaha was intended to be one of the eight charter cities. But before the initial season began, it was decided that Omaha was too far removed from the other cities, and Louisville was hastily enlisted as a replacement.

Omaha remained a mainstay of the Western League, winning championships in 1904, 1907, 1916, and 1924. Three-Fingered Brown played for Omaha, and so did Babe Herman, Heinie Manush, Fred Haney, Hank Severeid, and Monty Stratton. Western League Park was located at 15th and Vinton streets, but the grandstand burned in August 1936. Depression conditions made it impossible to rebuild the park, and Omaha dropped out of pro ball for more than a decade.

During the postwar baseball boom, Omaha reentered the Western League as part of the vast St. Louis Cardinal farm system. The city built Rosenblatt Stadium at 13th and C streets for the Cardinal-owned club, but in 1950 the ballpark became the permanent home of the NCAA College World Series, a 10-day event around which the pros must arrange their schedule. The Omaha Cardinals won Western League pennants in 1950 and 1951, and in 1955 jumped from Class A to AAA to replace Columbus in the American Association.

Loaded with St. Louis farmhands and managed by Johnny Keane, the Omaha Cardinals marched to second place in 1955, then defeated Louisville in the playoff opener before falling to first-place Minneapolis in the finals. The Cards had strong pitching from ERA leader Willard Schmidt (12–5, 2.56), Stu Miller (17–14) and Jim Pearce (12–5), while offensive production came from outfielders Frank Carswell (.351 in 107 games), Charles Peete (.317 in 99 games), and Dan Schell (.326 with 18 homers), and second baseman Don Blasingame (.302).

The following season Keane led the Cards to third place and another playoff appearance. Charles Peete was the batting champ (.350), but first-place Denver eliminated the Cardinals in the opening round of playoffs. Although there was little hitting the next two years, righthander Frank Barnes won the 1957 ERA title (12–10, 2.41), hurling six shutouts and a no-hitter. In 1958 righty Bob Blaylock was the strikeout champ and Lee Tate (.292) set an AA record for shortstops by playing 56 consecutive errorless games.

The AA expanded to 10 teams in 1959, and Omaha won the Western Division behind Frank Barnes (15–12), southpaw Ray Sadecki (13–9), and stolen base leader Ellis Burton (.292 with just 18 steals). Again the Cardinals were defeated in the playoff opener. When the AA cut back to eight teams after the season, Omaha was squeezed out for a year but returned in 1961 as a Los Angeles Dodger affiliate. The following season Danny Ozark guided the Omaha Dodgers to second place, although the playoff hex continued, this time in the opener against Denver. Lefty Nick Wilhite led the AA in victories, starts, complete games, innings, and losses (18–14 with 19 CG in 32 starts, and 243 IP). But the AA, now diminished to six clubs, was disbanded, and Omaha again was left without professional ball.

For six years the best baseball in town was the NCAA World Series, but the American Association reorganized, and Omaha enlisted as the Triple-A affiliate of the expansion Kansas City Royals. The Omaha Royals dominated the league for two years, recording back-to-back first-place finishes and the club's first playoff title. Jack McKeon was the pilot of these teams and was named Manager of the Year both seasons. In 1969 the AA had only six teams and no playoff, and the Royals took the pennant by a six-game margin. Their fine pitching staff included Don O'Riley (12–5), Gerald Cram (10–4), Alan Fitzmorris (10–6), and southpaws Paul Splittorff (12–10) and Chris Zachary (11–6). Throughout the season good performances were rewarded with promotion to Kansas City, but McKeon skillfully juggled his changing lineup: outfielders Scott Northey (.327 in 69 games), Joe Keough (.314 in 52 games), Lee Green (.295 in 80 games), and Alfredo Rico (.296); third baseman Steve Boros (.272 in 102 games) and Paul Schaal (.374 in 65 games); catchers Francis Healy (.282 in 64 games) and Al Campanis (.244 in 78 games); and first basemen Dennis Paepke (.295 in 98 games) and Larry Osborne (.280 in 72 games). The double-play combination was the best in the league, leading the AA in fielding at their respective positions: second baseman Luis Alcaraz (.301) and shortstop Richard Severson (.263).

Outfielder George Spriggs was the stolen base champ in 1969 (.311 with 46 thefts), and he was with Omaha long enough in 1970 to win another stolen base crown (.301 with 29 steals in 105 games) and be voted Most Valuable Player. Catcher Francis Healy also was back for part of the year (.294 in 82 games), but there were few other returnees. First baseman Charles Harrison (.279 with 21 homers) and outfielders Charles Day (.311 in 85 games) and Hilario Valdespino (.300 in 54 games) were the best of the newcomers. The Royals won the Eastern Division with the best record in the league, then beat Denver in the playoff, four games to one.

Six seasons would pass before Omaha reappeared in the playoffs, but the 1972 Royals boasted AA Rookie of the Year James Wohlford (.291). The 1972 pitching staff included fireballing righthander Steve Busby (12–14 with 221 Ks in 217 IP), who won the strikeout crown and tied a league record by fanning eight batters in a row; righty Tom Murphy (4–6, 2.61 ERA), who tossed a no-hitter against Indianapolis; and southpaw Mike Jackson (11–8 with a 2.41 ERA and only 138 hits and 158 Ks in 172 IP), who set an all-time AA record with 42 consecutive shutout innings. In 1973, 20-year-old third baseman George Brett (.284) was named to the All-Star Team, and righthander Mark Littell led the league in victories and ERA (16–6, 2.51).

Beginning in 1976 the Royals won three straight division titles, and recorded another first-place finish and a playoff championship. The 1976 Eastern Division champs led the league in staff ERA and featured second baseman Steve Staggs (.283) and reliever Gerald Cram (11–3 in 51 games). The next year the Royals won the East with the best record in the league and, once more, the lowest staff ERA. Standout players included victory leader Gary Lance (16–7), stolen base champ Willie Wilson (.281 with 74 thefts), outfielder Clint Hurdle (.328), third sacker Dave Cripe (.282), and catcher Craig Perkins (.313). For the second year in a row, the Royals lost to Denver in the playoffs. In 1978 Omaha captured the Western Division crown with a losing record (66–69), but upset Indianapolis in the playoffs, four games to one. Bill Paschall tied for the 1978 victory lead (14–9), while John Sullivan managed both the 1977 and 1978 Royals.

There was another losing season in 1979, but infielder German Barranca (.254 with 75 steals) won the stolen base title. The 1981 Royals claimed the Western Division and the league's best record, as third sacker Manny Castillo (.335, 10 HR, 91 RBI) was named MVP. Veteran righthander Bill Paschall (9–7) and southpaws Mike Jones (11–7 with a no-hitter) and Atlee Hammaker (11–5) helped the mound corps lead the league in ERA, but hard-hitting Denver shelled the Royals for a four-game sweep in the playoffs. Manager of the Year Joe Sparks produced another Western Division crown in 1982 behind lefthanded reliever Robert Tufts (10–6 with a 1.60 ERA in 59 games), first baseman Ron Johnson (.336), and outfielder-DH Jesus Rivera (.318, 27 HR, 91 RBI).

Ron Johnson had another good year in 1983 (.317), and the next season Steve Farr was the ERA champ (10–4, 2.02) and reliever Mark Huismann (5–5 with a 2.01 ERA and a league-leading 33 saves in 59 games) was voted Pitcher of the Year. In 1986 outfielder Dwight Taylor (.259, 67 SB) was the stolen base leader, and the following year the crown was claimed by outfielder Gary Thurman (.293, 58 SB).

Upper left: 1988 Omaha Royals celebrate clinching the 1988 Western Division title. Upper right: Royals' owner Gus Cherry thanks fans for their support. Lower left: Bill Swaggerty pitches the 5–3 title-winning victory over Oklahoma City. Lower right: Infielder Dave Owen crosses the plate after slamming a two-run homer in the fourth inning against the 89ers.

— Courtesy Omaha Royals

The Royals were purchased for almost one million dollars from Kansas City in 1985 by Gus Cherry. The outgoing Cherry, a former minor league pitcher, enjoyed his first Western Division title in 1988. First baseman Luis Delos Santos (.307 with 87 RBIs) led the league in RBIs and was named MVP, while Luis Aquino (8–3) twirled a no-hitter in interleague play against Columbus. Although the Royals lost the playoffs to Indianapolis, Cherry's promotions with a winning team attracted a record attendance of 308,080.

Results were even better the next year, with another Western Division crown (but another playoff loss to Indianapolis), and paid admissions totaling 314,645. Luis Delos Santos again was a key player (.297), along with outfielder Nick Capra (.290, 31 SB), victory leader Steve Fireovid (13–8), and southpaw Stan Clarke (12–6). Since the AA was reorganized in 1969, Omaha has compiled the best record in the league five times, made nine playoff appearances, won three playoff championships and nine division titles — more than any other club during the same period.

Year	Record	Pcg.	Finish
1955	84-70	.545	Second (won opener, lost finals)
1956	82-71	.536	Third (lost opener)
1957	76-78	.494	Fifth
1958	80-74	.519	Fifth
1959	83-78	.516	Fourth (won Western Division, lost opener)
1961	62-87	.416	Eighth
1962	79-68	.537	First
1969	85-55	.607	First
1970	73-65	.529	First (won Eastern Division and finals, lost Jr. World Series)
1971	69-70	.496	Fifth
1972	71-69	.507	Fourth
1973	62-73	.459	Sixth
1974	54-82	.397	Eighth
1975	67-69	.493	Sixth
1976	78-58	.574	Second (won Eastern Division, lost finals)
1977	76-59	.563	First (won Eastern Division, lost finals)
1978	66-69	.489	Fourth (won Western Division and finals)
1979	65-71	.478	Sixth
1980	66-70	.485	Fifth
1981	79-57	.581	First (won Western Division and opener, lost finals)
1982	71-66	.518	Fourth (won Western Division, lost finals)
1983	64-72	.471	Sixth
1984	68-86	.442	Eighth
1985	73-69	.514	Fourth
1986	72-70	.507	Fourth
1987	64-76	.457	Seventh
1988	81-61	.570	Second (won Western Division, lost finals)
1989	74-72	.507	Third (won Western Division, lost finals)
1990	86-60	.589	First (won Western Division, finals, and Alliance Classic)
1991	73-71	.507	Fifth

Springfield (Redbirds)

"You get feelings in your bones."

A. Ray Smith so described to the author the primary reason he picked Springfield, Illinois, as the new home for his American Association franchise in 1978. After spending the 1977 season in New Orleans, Smith was convinced that it was impossible for a minor league baseball team to make money in the Super Dome. Smith happened to drive through Springfield, and he was strongly impressed with the Illinois city of 90,000.

When Super Dome officials, faced with a schedule conflict because of an extravaganza event, asked Smith to play a weekend series with Evansville somewhere else, Springfield businessmen arranged to host the games. Support was excellent, and Smith — with good feelings in his bones — began serious explorations to bring his club to Springfield. The city had played in the Class B Three-I League during 1903–14, 1925–32, 1935, 1938–42 and 1946–49, then shifted to the Class D Mississippi-Ohio Valley League for 1950. There had been no pro ball since 1950, and high school coaches, backed by a local newspaper, opposed Smith's move. But a Class AAA club is an enormous economic asset to a community, and the city spent hundreds of thousands of dollars to upgrade a high school ballpark to professional standards. Springfield is only 95 miles from St. Louis, and Smith's club was a Cardinal affiliate in Cardinal country.

The Springfield Redbirds were managed in 1978 by Jimy Williams to the third-best record in the AA. First baseman Dane Iorg (.371 in 89 games — he spent the rest of the year with the Cards) won the batting title. Other solid hitters were outfielders Jim Lentine (.342), Mike Potter (.266, 22 HR, 90 RBI) and John Scott (.281), catcher Terry Kennedy (.330 in 64 games), switch-hitter John Tamargo (.302 in 65 games), infielder Ken Oberkfell (.285 in 64 games), and second baseman Tommy Herr (.279 in 33 games). The leading pitchers were righthanders Bill Rothan (10–5), Greg Terlecky (8–5), and Silvio Martinez (5–2 in seven starts), who pitched a no-hitter before being called up to the Cards.

Hal Lanier managed the Redbirds the next two years. The

1979 club finished second in the East, and again the Redbirds provided the batting champ, outfielder Keith Smith (.350). Another outfielder, Leon Durham, came up from Class AA Arkansas and demonstrated the hitting ability that would make him a big league star (.310, 23 HR, 88 RBI). Returning for another year with the Redbirds were switch-hitting third baseman Manny Castillo (.323), second sacker Tommy Herr (.293), catcher Terry Kennedy (.293), outfielder Jim Lentine (.285), and righthander Greg Terlecky (9–5).

In 1980 Lanier guided the Redbirds to the Eastern Division title, then won the playoffs over Denver, four games to one. The Redbirds led the league in fielding and staff ERA, and southpaw Al Olmstead won the ERA title (10–5 and a 2.77 ERA with three shutouts in 17 games). Righthander Jim Otten was unbeatable in seven starts (6–0, 1.69 ERA). Keith Smith (.295 in 69 games), Tommy Herr (.312) and Leon Durham (.258) split the season between Springfield and St. Louis. First baseman Joey DeSa (.293), second sacker Neil Fiala (.296), and outfielder Gene Roof (.258) were the best fielders in the league at their positions, and outfielder Terry Landrum (.303) added a strong bat.

The next year Springfield suffered its only losing season in the AA, even though the Redbirds placed second in the East. Gene Roof (.348), Neil Fiala (.323), and Joey DeSa (.292) came back in good form, while catcher George Bjorkman (.254 with 28 homers) was home run champ. Dave LaPoint was the strikeout leader (13–9 with 129 Ks), and fellow righthander Benny Edelen was extremely effective while with the Redbirds (9–1 in 16 games).

Despite the losing record, attendance exceeded 120,000 — the best total in four seasons. In 1978 first-year attendance was more than 110,000 — all excellent totals for a city of 90,000. Smith, having proved to numerous doubters that a Class AAA club could be profitable in Springfield, now wanted to proceed with the challenge of acquiring a big league franchise. After the City of Springfield had invested heavily in renovating and expanding the Redbirds' stadium, Smith had signed a five-year contract to keep his club in town. He negotiated with a local group to sell the franchise, but enthusiastic investors from Louisville persuaded him to transfer the Redbirds. Springfield took Smith to court, but AA President Joe Ryan came in to help with negotiations. Smith finally agreed to pay almost half a million dollars in legal and settlement fees, and

Springfield obtained a franchise in the Class A Midwest League, a classification more suitable for the city's size.

Year	Record	Pcg.	Finish
1978	70-66	.515	Third
1979	73-63	.537	Second
1980	75-61	.551	Second (won Western Division and finals)
1981	66-70	.485	Fifth

St. Paul (Saints)

The first baseball game in Minnesota was played on August 15, 1857, in Nininger, which would become the state's most famous ghost town. Within two years there were twice-weekly games in St. Paul pitting bachelors against married men at a diamond "near Dr. Pattison's church." The summer after the Civil War, St. Paul's best club was the North Stars, and in 1866 there was a fierce intra-city rivalry between the Olympics (representing the Upper Town) and the Saxons (Lower Town). An even bitterer — and far longer-lasting — rivalry began in 1867 when the North Stars ventured across the Mississippi River and thumped a Minneapolis nine, 56–26. The return game resulted in another St. Paul victory, 47–29, and one of baseball's keenest rivalries would continue for nearly a century. Other St. Paul clubs were organized enthusiastically in 1867, including the Lake City Union team and the Rochester Gopher States team, as well as nines in several nearby towns, and that season the Minnesota State Association of Ball Players was organized in St. Paul. St. Paul made a successful bid of $600 for the right to host the first state baseball tournament in September, and the North Stars emerged the victors.

St. Paul and Minneapolis played in the League Alliance in 1877 and 1878, and in 1884 St. Paul joined a circuit called the Northwestern League. The Minneapolis Millers shunned local talent and hired outside players, but St. Paul snapped up these stars from the Flour City. When the Twin City rivals first met at St. Paul's West Seventh Street Grounds, 4,000 kranks witnessed a 4–0 St. Paul victory. Many visitors from Minneapolis bet large sums on the Millers, but watched in dismay as St. Paul did not allow a single runner past second base. The Northwestern League folded in September, but St. Paul joined the Union Association, a major league which operated for just one season. St. Paul played only eight games (2–6), all on the road; there would be no more big league ball involving the Twin Cities until 1961.

In ensuing years, St. Paul and Minneapolis clashed as members of the Western League, but after the 1899 season Charles Comiskey moved his Saints from St. Paul to Chicago, where the club would become the White Sox of the new American League. But in 1902 St. Paul, as well as Minneapolis, became charter members of the American Association. The Saints' AA home in 1903 was Lexington Park at Lexington and University, but the next year the club began to play at a downtown ballpark between 12th and 13th and Robert and Minnesota streets. In 1909 the team ventured back to Lexington for weekend games, and the next season Lexington Park became the permanent playing field of the Saints. Just outside the park and adjacent to the outfield fence from deep left to center was the Coliseum; home runs to left would land on the roof of the big building. A 10-foot incline led to the right-field fence, which was 30 feet high and an uninviting 365 feet from home plate.

St. Paul finished third in the inaugural AA campaign, showcasing outfielder Spike Shannon (.337) and second baseman Miller Huggins (.328). The playing manager was first sacker Mike Kelley (.277), a legendary minor league figure who was involved with the AA as a player, manager, and club owner-president until 1946. He engineered 2,293 victories in the AA (2,390 during his entire career), the highest total ever amassed by a manager for one league, and he managed St. Paul to six pennants over 18 seasons (1902–1905, 1908–1912, and 1915–1923). Miller Huggins shared a room with Kelley in St. Paul, and in conversations with the masterful Saints' manager, Huggins began to develop strategic concepts that he would later employ as the pennant-winning field general of the New York Yankees.

Kelley led the Saints to back-to-back championships in 1903 and 1904, managing artfully and holding down first base in both seasons (.309 and .298). Other two-year standouts were outfielder Jim Jackson (.307 with 42 SB, and .335 with 13 HR and 59 SB), who won the 1904 home run and stolen base titles, third sacker Ed Wheeler (.293 and .296), and hurlers George Ferguson (19–10 and 14–8) and Charles Chech (24–9 and 27–8), who posted the most victories of 1904. The Saints led the league in stolen bases both seasons, and in hitting and fielding in 1903. Stars of 1903 included batting champ Phil Geier (.362), outfielder Spike Shannon (.308, 41 SB, and a league-leading 132 runs), diminutive second baseman Miller Huggins (.308 with 48 SB), and Joe Stewart (16–10). Sold to National League clubs were Geier and Stewart (Boston), Shannon (St. Louis), and Huggins (Cincinnati). Returnees carried the Saints to another flag, but after the 1904 season Jackson (Cleveland) and Chech (Cincinnati) also were sold to the big leagues.

The sale of so many stars by owner George Lennon caused a losing season in 1905, despite the efforts of batting champ Charles Hemphill (.364). Kelley clashed with Lennon and moved across the river to Minneapolis for 1906, while the Saints finished next-to-last in 1906 and sank to the cellar the following two seasons.

In 1908 Charles "Sea Lion" Hall joined the Saints' pitching staff. A rawboned righthander (6′3, 187 pounds) whose real name was Carlos Clolo, Sea Lion was spectacular as a teenaged rookie with Seattle of the PCL in 1904 (28–19). He pitched with Cincinnati in 1906 and 1907 before being sent down to Columbus. After spending half of 1909 with last-place St. Paul he was sold to the Boston Red Sox, despite a miserable record (4–13). Hall was with the Red Sox through 1913, then returned to St. Paul in 1914 and 1915 (24–10), when he was sold to the St. Louis Cardinals. Except for six games with Detroit in 1918 after the AA had halted their season because of the war, he was back with St. Paul from 1918 through 1923, recording 20-win seasons in four straight years. Sea Lion Hall retired at the age of 40 in 1925, after spending part of the year with Minneapolis, and having played 10 seasons for St. Paul.

Of even longer tenure for the Saints was outfielder Joe Riggert, who moved to St. Paul in 1912 after a disappointing year with the Boston Red Sox (.212). Following a good season with the Saints in 1913 (.293 with a league-leading 12 homers and 23 triples) he was sold to Brooklyn, but he hit poorly (.203) and was back in St. Paul for 1915. He spent the next 10 years with the Saints, except for 1919, when he was with Boston in the National League for the last half of the season. During 12 years with St. Paul he led the AA three times in home runs and triples, once in doubles, stolen bases and runs, and was a star on four championship teams. Riggert played pro ball for 20 years, hit .301 in the minors, and became the all-time career leader with 228 triples.

For a decade and a half St. Paul fans had to content themselves with favorites like Joe Riggert and Sea Lion Hall. Shortstop-outfielder Art Butler was the 1912 batting champ (.329), and first baseman Leo Dressen won the first of three stolen base championships in 1917 (.291, 55 SB). Strikeout titles were claimed in 1911 by righthanded spitballer Martin O'Toole (15–11 with 199 Ks in 204 IP) and in 1915 by southpaw Robert Steele (20–16 with 183 Ks).

The most important development of 1915 was the acquisition of the Saints by John W. Norton, who brought Mike Kelley back to St. Paul after a two-year absence and who shrewdly began building a productive stable of players. Norton's Saints would win four AA pennants in six seasons. Each of these clubs led the league in stolen bases, and the 1920 and 1921 pitching staffs allowed the fewest runs.

In 1919 outfielder Elmer Miller led the AA in home runs and total bases (.314, 16 3B, 15 HR), first sacker Leo Dressen again was the stolen base titlist (.272, 46 SB), and hard-hitting catcher Bubbles Hargrave (.303) was the leader in putouts at his position. Key members of the mound corps were Richard Niehaus (23–13), Rusty Griner (21–14), Howard Merritt (19–9), and Sea Lion Hall (17–13). Delighted over the first pennant in 15 years, St. Paul fans presented the players with wristwatches and collected $1,400 for Kelley. The Saints then took a train to Los Angeles and played a best-five-of-nine series with the Vernon Tigers, champions of the Pacific Coast League. Vernon used an ineligible player and watered the diamond to slow down the speedy Saints, and St. Paul lost, five games to four. The series drew nationwide attention and the Saints were praised in the press, but the American Association discontinued postseason play with the PCL until 1924.

The next year the Saints waded through a 168-game schedule, dominating play with one of the most magnificent teams in AA history. Posting a record of 115–49 (.701), Kelley's club outdistanced second-place Louisville by 28½ games and set the all-time league mark for victories. The Saints led the league in team fielding and in almost every offensive category: hitting (.301, 21 points higher than the next team), runs (961 — Toledo was next with 819), hits, doubles, triples, home runs, and, for the second year in a row, stolen bases. Third baseman Joe Rapp was the batting champ (.335 with 49 steals) and first sacker Leo Dressen won his third stolen base title and led the league in runs (.294, 50 SB, 131 R). The rest of the batting order featured outfielders Elmer Miller (.333, 108 R, 104 RBI), Dave Duncan (.313), Bruno Haas (.307) and Joe Riggert (.286 with a league-leading 17 triples), catcher Bubbles Hargrave (.3347, 22 HR, 109 RBI), second baseman Martin Berghammer (.304), and shortstop Danny Boone (.297). The mound corps allowed the fewest runs in the league for the second consecutive year. Southpaw Fritz Coumbe (19–7) was a welcome addition from the big leagues, and the heart of the 1919 staff returned: Rusty Griner (16–13), Howard Merritt (21–10), Steamboat Williams (20–6), and 35-year-old Sea Lion Hall, who enjoyed his best year (27–8, 2.06 ERA) by leading the AA in victories and ERA, while pitching his second no-hitter in three years. This powerhouse club was overconfident going into the Little World Series, which was resumed in 1920 on a permanent basis. International League champion Baltimore had won its final 25 games and recorded the second of *seven* consecutive pennants. Jack Dunn's Orioles beat St. Paul, 5–1, but 10,000 fans overflowed Lexington Park to cheer the Saints.

Mike Kelley and John Norton were experts at developing talented young players or reviving the careers of fading big leaguers, then selling them from the Saints to a major league club for profits that kept the St. Paul franchise comfortably in the black. Back in 1911 Kelley peddled strikeout champ Marty O'Toole and his favorite catcher, William Kelly, to Pittsburgh for the princely sum of $22,500. Norton sold Bubbles Hargrave to Brooklyn for $20,000, Charlie Dressen went to Cincinnati for $35,000, catcher Leo Dixon was acquired for $3,500 and peddled to the St. Louis Cardinals a year later for $15,000 and four players, and pitcher Rube Benton was picked up for $1,000 and sold after two seasons for $20,000.

With the sale of several stars from the 1920 championship club the Saints dropped to sixth place in 1921, despite strong performances from Sea Lion Hall (20–14 and a .291 batting average in 56 games), Marty Berghammer (.315), Elmer Miller (.313 with 96 RBIs in just 102 games), and Bruno Haas (.324), who would play outstanding ball for the Saints for 11 seasons (1920 through 1930). Kelley and Norton quickly rebuilt, however, and the Saints bounded back into the throne room in 1922 (107–60 and a 15-game victory margin). The pitching staff featured three 20-game winners: victory and ERA leader Tom Sheehan (26–12, 3.01), 37-year-old Sea Lion Hall (22–8), and southpaw Rube Benton (22–11). Kelley's Saints, as usual, led the league in stolen bases, and the offense was sparked by veteran outfielders Bruno Haas (.331) and Joe Riggert (.316), big league retread Tim Hendryx (.341), and third baseman Charlie Dressen (.304). In the Little World Series, however, the Saints again fell to Baltimore, five games to two.

The next year Charlie Dressen (.304), catcher Mike Gonzalez (.303), outfielder Sea Cap Christensen (.296 with 102 RBIs), Joe Riggert (.289), and Marty Berghammer (.288) led an offense which once more posted the most steals but finished seventh in hitting. The Saints battled to the last day of the season before settling for second place, and the key to another successful year (111–57) was perhaps the best starting rotation in AA history: Tom Sheehan again led the league in victories and ERA, tying the record for most victories (31–9, 2.90) and working in the most games (54); Cliff Markle won the strikeout title (25–12 with 184 Ks, also in 54 games); Sea Lion Hall, now 38, had the team's highest batting average (24–13, .309); and Howard Merritt recorded another 20-win season (20–11 in 51 games).

In 1924 St. Paul again led the league in stolen bases and, for the second year in a row, recorded the best fielding percentage and permitted the fewest runs. Tom Sheehan and Sea Lion Hall were sold after the 1923 season, but Cliff Markle (19–9) and Howard Merritt (19–17) returned and were aided by righthander Tony Faeth (15–4). Third baseman Charlie Dressen led the league in RBIs (.347, 18 HR, 151 RBI), while first sacker Johnny Neun (.353) and outfielders Sea Cap Christensen (.314), Joe Riggert (.294), and Bruno Haas (.293) provided solid offensive punch. Mike Kelley had returned to Minneapolis as owner and manager in 1924, and Nick Allen managed the Saints to a showdown against first-place Indianapolis in the final week of the season, a five-game series in Lexington Park. Tony Faeth won three games of the series to clinch another pennant, and the Saints again squared off against Baltimore in the Little World Series. The best-five-of-nine series was a classic, stretching to ten games when the third contest was called because of darkness after 13 innings. Trailing 2–4–1, the Saints won the final three games to finally defeat Baltimore. Then the club traveled by train to Seattle to engage in the AA's first post-season series against the PCL champs since the controversial games between St. Paul and Vernon in 1919. After a rain delay of one day, Howard Merritt and the Saints won, 12–4. Rain set in again, and three days later the rest of the series was cancelled and the victorious Saints were given $175 apiece.

St. Paul dropped to third the next year, even though Sea Cap Christensen won the stolen base title (.325 with 49 steals), outfielder Cedric Durst led the league in doubles and triples (.348, 59 2B, 25 3B), and pitcher Walt Roettger hit so well (.350 in 75 games) that he soon would make the big leagues as an outfielder. In 1926 George Pipgras, a future New York Yankee star, led the AA in victories, innings and strikeouts (22–19, 312 IP, 156 K), and the next season second baseman Norm McMillen was the stolen base leader (.305 with 43 steals). In 1928 St. Paul recorded the most thefts in the league for the ninth time since 1917, and for the 13th time since the AA began play. The Saints would not win another stolen base title for more than two decades, but would record the best fielding percentage seven times from 1930 through 1937.

The 1923 Saints had become the only team in AA history to record 100 victories (111–57) without winning a pennant (Kansas City went 112–54). In 1929 St. Paul again won more than 100 games (102–64) only to lose the flag to a more powerful Kansas City club (111–56). The 1929 Saints featured the hitting of catcher-manager Bubbles Hargrave (.369), home run-RBI champ Dusty Cooke (.358, 153 R, 33 HR, 148 RBI), first baseman Oscar Roettger (.326), and future major league star Ben Chapman, who led the league in runs and total bases (.336, 31 HR, 162 R). The best pitchers were ERA titlist Archie Campbell (15–3, 2.79), victory leader Americo Polli (22–9), Huck Betts (21–13), and Slim Harriss (18–10). St. Paul was a close second the following year behind Harriss (18–13), Betts (17–12), victory leader Wilcy Moore (22–9), Roettger (.352), 39-year-old Bruno Haas (.374 in 82 games), catcher Robert Fenner (.391 in 98 games), outfielder George Davis (.366), and 19-year-old Lefty Gomez (8–4 in 17 games), down for a final tune-up before going on to a Hall of Fame career with the New York Yankees.

St. Paul returned to the throne room in 1931, leading the league in hitting (.311), home runs (167) and fielding, and outdistancing second-place Kansas City by 14 games. First sacker Oscar Roettger paced the batting barrage (.357), with ample help from stolen base champ Jack Saltzgaver (.340 with 26 steals), outfielders George Davis (.343 with 26 homers) and Ben Paschal (.336), and shortstop Joe Morrissey (.331 with 22 homers), while Huck Betts (22–13) and Slim Harriss (20–11) led a deep pitching staff. The

St. Paul produced the 1936 batting champ, Vern Washington (.390 — middle row, second from left) and the winningest pitcher, Lou Fette (25–8 — middle row, fourth from left).

— Courtesy Minnesota Historical Society

following year Ben Paschal (.325) twice went 6-for-6 and southpaw Russ Van Atta (22–17) tied for the lead in victories, but the Saints dropped to seventh place. Outfielder Bill Norman donned a Saints uniform in 1932 (.310 with 23 homers), and played in St. Paul again from 1934 through 1937; in five seasons he never hit below .300.

In 1936 St. Paul made the league playoffs behind victory and percentage titlist Lou Fette (25–8), outfielder Henry Steinbacher (.353, 49 2B), who led the AA in doubles and reeled off a 35-game hitting streak, and legendary minor league slugger Vernon Washington (.390 in 73 games). Washington began the season with the Chicago White Sox but was sent to St. Paul barely in time to qualify for the batting championship. The big Texan put in a solid season the next year (.311), then was felled by a broken right shoulder after a spectacular start in 1938 (.426).

Babe Ganzel took over the managerial post in 1938, and despite the loss of Washington produced St. Paul's eighth AA pennant. Second baseman Al Bejma (.326, 25 HR, 114 RBI), outfielder Bit McCulloch (.301 with a league-leading 41 doubles), and righthanders Vic Frasier (17–7) and Red Herring (16–6) sparked the Saints to the flag by a six-game lead over second-place Kansas

City, but the injury-riddled club lost to the Blues in the playoff finals. The Saints dropped to the second division the next year, even though third baseman Gil English became the last Saint to win an AA batting crown (.343).

English continued to hit well the next two years (.317 and .316), but the Saints remained in the second division, then dropped into the cellar in 1942 and 1943. The next two seasons, however, manager Ray Blades led the "Blademen" into the playoff finals. The best players on the 1944 club were outfielders John Marion (.345) and Glenn Chapman (.326), utilityman Joe Vitter (.273 in 140 games at second, third, short and in the outfield), and ERA champ Red Herring (8–5, 2.18, and a .378 batting average). Chapman again starred in 1945 (.308), along with Vitter, third baseman Leighton Kimball (.315 with 22 homers), and first sacker Paul Schoendienst (.315). The Blademen again reached the playoffs in 1946 behind first baseman John Douglas (.307), the all-purpose Vitter, and victory leader Harry Taylor (15–7).

Now affiliated with Brooklyn, St. Paul showcased 20-year-old Duke Snider in 1947, until the slugging outfielder (.316 with 12 homers and 46 RBIs in 66 games) was called up to the Dodgers. Walt Alston became manager in 1948 and immediately led the Saints to their first — and only — playoff title. John Douglas again played well (.303), and so did outfielders Robert Addis (.314) and Eric Tipton (.313, 28 HR, 115 RBI). Catcher Roy Campanella became the first black to play in the American Association, but he was called up to Brooklyn after a spectacular start (.325 with 13 homers and 39 RBIs in just 35 games). The Saints finished in third place, beat first-place Indianapolis in the playoff opener, then outlasted Columbus, four games to three, to win the finals.

The next year Alston guided St. Paul to pennant number nine. Although the Saints dropped the playoff opener, St. Paul fans were delighted that their club won an airtight pennant race by a mere one-half game over Indianapolis. The offense was led by Robert Addis (.348), stolen base champ Henry Schenz (.345, 17 HR, 30 SB), and third baseman Dan O'Connell (.314, 17 HR, 102 RBI). The pitching staff, which allowed the fewest runs in the league, starred reliever Clem Labine (12–6 in 64 appearances) and victory leader Phil Haugstad (22–7, and in 1947 he had been the leader in strikeouts and innings at 16–6 for St. Paul).

In 1950 Haugstad (16–11) and Labine (11–7) again helped

the Saints reach the playoffs. First baseman Lou Limmer (.277, 29 HR, 111 RBI) won the home run and RBI crowns, shortstop James Pendleton (.299, 19 3B) was the triples leader, and second sacker Jack Cassini (.276, 36 SB) was the stolen base king — although speedy outfielder Don Nicholas (.299 with 35 steals) would have won the title if he had come up earlier. In 1951 the Saints made it to the playoff finals behind Cassini (.305, 35 SB), Pendleton (.301, 21 HR), and a deep pitching staff: Labine (9–6, 2.62 ERA), Pat McGlothin (15–7), John Rutherford (15–8), and reliever Tub Epperly (13–4).

Jack Cassini won another stolen base crown in 1952 (.308, 35 SB) as the Saints made a fifth consecutive playoff appearance. Tub Epperly again manned the bullpen (9–4 in 57 appearances), but the 1952 Saints won with offense provided by third baseman Robert Wilson (.334, 17 HR, 117 RBI), and outfielders Sandy Amoros (.337), Dick Whitman (.333), Gino Cimoli (.310), and Bill Sharman (.294 with 16 homers). Sharman was a star guard in the NBA for 12 years (1950–61), but he also played minor league baseball for five seasons, including 1952 and 1955 (.292) in St. Paul. In 12 AA playoff appearances the Saints won it all just once, but from 1944 through 1952 St. Paul qualified for postseason play in eight of nine years.

In 1953 Jack Cassini again performed impressively (.324, 27 SB), and shortstop Don Zimmer (.300 with 23 homers and 63 RBIs in just 81 games) was voted Rookie of the Year. But the club finished in the second division in 1953 and for the following three years, even though the 1954 Saints led the league in homers (173). During this period there was a determined effort to bring big league baseball to the Twin Cities, and finally arrangements were made to construct a suitable stadium in Bloomington, a Minneapolis suburb. But the historic rivalry prevailed in St. Paul, and two weeks before work was initiated on Bloomington (later Metropolitan) Stadium, ground was broken at 1000 North Snelling Avenue on St. Paul's Midway Stadium.

When the Saints moved into their new $2 million home on April 25, 1957, more than 16,000 fans crowded into 10,000-seat Midway Stadium. The Saints responded with their first playoff appearance in six years. Sparked by strikeout leader Stan Williams (19–7 with 223 Ks in 246 IP), first baseman Norm Larker (.323), and outfielder Don Demeter (.309 with 28 homers), St. Paul downed first-place Wichita in the opener before losing to Denver in the finals.

The Saints sagged into the second division the next two years, but in 1960 St. Paul returned to the playoffs during the city's final season in the American Association. Danny Ozark was the manager, and he expertly utilized the talents of first baseman Gail Harris (.315 with 22 homers), infielder John Goryl (.306), outfielder Carl Warwick (.292 with 19 homers), and veteran righthander Art Fowler (13–10 and a 2.94 ERA, second best in the league). The star of the team was Jim Golden (20–9, 237 IP, 2.32 ERA), the league leader in victories, ERA and innings pitched, and the last pitcher to win 20 games in the American Association. Characteristically, the Saints lost in the playoff opener.

During the off-season Clark Griffith decided to move his American League club from the nation's capital to Minneapolis-St. Paul. The Minnesota Twins would play in The Met, and after 59 years and a record nine pennants the St. Paul Saints (and the Minneapolis Millers) ceased to exist. The American Association shrunk to six teams for 1961, while Midway Stadium, like Lexington Park and Nicollet Park before it, was razed. Even though three decades have passed, however, baseball people still remember with fond nostalgia the bittersweet rivalry between Minneapolis and St. Paul.

Year	Record	Pcg.	Finish
1902	72-66	.521	Third
1903	88-46	.657	First
1904	95-52	.646	First (lost Little World Series)
1905	75-78	.492	Fifth
1906	67-83	.447	Seventh
1907	59-95	.383	Eighth
1908	48-104	.316	Eighth
1909	80-83	.491	Fifth
1910	88-80	.524	Fourth
1911	79-85	.482	Fourth
1912	77-90	.461	Sixth
1913	75-87	.463	Fifth
1914	56-111	.331	Eighth
1915	90-63	.588	Second
1916	86-79	.521	Fourth
1917	88-66	.571	Second
1918	39-38	.506	Sixth
1919	94-60	.610	First
1920	115-49	.701	First (lost Little World Series)
1921	80-87	.479	Sixth

1922	107-60	.641	First (lost Little World Series)
1923	111-57	.661	Second
1924	95-70	.576	First (won Little World Series)
1925	91-75	.548	Third
1926	82-81	.503	Sixth
1927	90-78	.536	Fourth
1928	88-80	.524	Fourth
1929	102-64	.614	Second
1930	91-63	.591	Second
1931	104-63	.623	First (lost Little World Series)
1932	70-97	.419	Seventh
1933	78-75	.510	Fourth
1934	67-84	.444	Seventh
1935	75-78	.490	Fifth
1936	84-68	.553	Second (lost opener)
1937	67-87	.435	Seventh
1938	90-61	.596	First (won opener, lost finals)
1939	73-81	.474	Fifth
1940	69-79	.466	Fifth
1941	61-92	.399	Seventh
1942	57-97	.370	Eighth
1943	67-85	.441	Eighth
1944	85-66	.563	Fourth (won opener, lost finals)
1945	75-76	.497	Fourth (won opener, lost finals)
1946	80-71	.530	Third (lost opener)
1947	69-85	.454	Seventh
1948	86-68	.558	Third (won opener and finals, lost Jr. World Series)
1949	93-60	.608	First (lost opener)
1950	83-69	.546	Fourth (lost opener)
1951	85-66	.563	Second (won opener, lost finals)
1952	80-74	.519	Third (lost opener)
1953	72-82	.468	Sixth
1954	75-78	.490	Fifth
1955	75-78	.490	Sixth
1956	75-78	.490	Fifth
1957	82-72	.532	Fourth (won opener, lost finals)
1958	70-84	.455	Seventh
1959	81-81	.500	Fifth
1960	83-71	.539	Fourth

Toledo's first championship club.
— Courtesy Toledo Mud Hens

Toledo (Mud Hens)

The Toledo Mud Hens have immortalized one of the most picturesque nicknames in the history of professional baseball. Early clubs were called the Toledo Sox and various other sobriquets, but generations of baseball fans have embraced a unique designation. Before double-tiered Swayne Field opened in 1909, the best diamond in Toledo was located in the northeast section of town near the confluence of the Maumee River and Lake Erie. Abounding in nearby marshlands was a species of gallinule or coot referred to as "mud hens," and since the playing field often was wet and muddy, Toledo fans began calling the players Mud Hens. The name has made an indelible impression on the baseball world — even the eccentric character Klinger on the television series *M*A*S*H* wore a Mud Hens shirt.

Professional teams in Toledo predated the American Association by two decades and won pennants in the Northwestern League in 1883 and in the Inter-State League in 1896 and 1897. But as charter members of the AA, Toledo placed last during the league's first three seasons and became the first club in the league to lose 100 games (42–109 in 1904). Indeed, in 52 American Association seasons Toledo wound up in the cellar 13 times and next-to-last eight times, while recording a total of 37 second-division finishes. Toledo placed in the first division just 15 times, made only five playoff appearances, and won just two AA championships. But Toledo fans supported the Mud Hens with fierce loyalty, and Swayne Field became known as a tough park for visiting teams and umpires.

Catcher Red Kleinow played well enough during the first two AA seasons (.298 in 1902, .320 in 1903) to be promoted to a big league career that would last for eight years. After spending five seasons with four major league clubs, Charles "Eagle Eye" Hemphill went down to Toledo for 1905 and performed so impressively (.364 with 40 steals) that he went back to the big leagues for six more years. Although the 1905 club finished only in seventh place, Hemphill's teammates included stolen base champ George Moriarity (.295, 51 SB), who went on to a 13-year American League career, home run titlist Wyatt Lee (.301, 13 HR), and doubles leader Eugene DeMontreville (.290, 49 2B, 36 SB), an 11-year big league veteran.

The 1907 club finished a strong second behind stolen base champ Josh Clarke (.321, 54 SB) and righthanders Charles Chech (25–11) and Hi West (17–9), leading the AA in team hitting (.279), runs and stolen bases. In 1908 West (18–9) pitched the first no-hitter in AA history, and Toledo again paced the league in hitting (.264). Outfielder Charles "Piano Legs" Hickman, who logged a total of 12 seasons in the big leagues, was one of the circuit's most feared sluggers in 1909 (.284 and a league-leading 49 doubles and 261 total bases) and 1910 (.317 with a league-leading 15 triples). In 1910 southpaw Hank Robinson (16–12) twirled Toledo's second no-hitter, and in 1913 "Big Jim" Baskette *lost* a no-hitter to Minneapolis, 1–0.

Baskette pitched for Toledo several years (23–16 in 1911), and like fellow righthander Cy Falkenburg (25–8 in 1912) frequently spent time on the Cleveland mound corps during these seasons. Other players of the era also shuttled between Toledo and Cleveland, because coal magnate Charley Somers owned both clubs. In 1914 Somers decided to move his AA franchise to Cleveland, so that the minor leaguers could play in League Park while the Naps were on the road. The experiment of giving Cleveland fans a daily diet of baseball was devised to keep the Federal League out of the city, and lasted the two-year life of that controversial circuit. Swayne Field hosted a team in the Class C Southern Michigan League in 1914, then Toledo fans had to content themselves with semipro and amateur ball in 1915.

Toledo eagerly welcomed the Mud Hens back from Cleveland in 1916, even though the team soon settled again into the depths of the standings. The Mud Hens were last in 1917 and 1918, had the poorest batting average in each season (.248 and .221), and hit merely eight home runs in 1917, a low total even for the dead-ball era. But Mud Hen fans could cheer slugging first baseman Hamilton Hyatt, who led the league in doubles and walks in 1919 (.328, 36 2B, 97 W), and again in walks in 1920 (.317, 112 W). Right-hander Jim Middleton was the ace of the 1920 mound corps (26–14), while John Scott (20–20) and Claude Jonnard (22–19) led the league in innings worked in 1924 and 1925 respectively. In 1924 the greatest athlete of the early twentieth century, 35-year-old Jim Thorpe, played his next-to-last year of professional baseball in a Mud Hen uniform (.358 with 112 RBI). Outfielder William "Good Times" Lamar came down from Brooklyn in the middle of 1921 (.348 in 74 games), led the league in triples in 1922 (.352, 18 3B), won the 1923 batting crown (.391), then returned to the big leagues after a fine start in 1924 (.357 in 65 games). Two other fine outfielders, Fred Nicholson in 1923 (.306 with a league-leading 23 triples), 1924 (.306, 101 RBI) and 1925 (.309, 109 RBI), and rifle-armed Paul Strand in 1924 (.323) and 1925 (.300) were favorites at Swayne Field.

In 1926 veteran National League outfielder Casey Stengel made his managerial debut with Toledo. By this time the Mud Hens were a farm club of the New York Giants, whose longtime manager, John J. McGraw, was part owner of the Toledo franchise. Stengel had starred for McGraw in 1922 (.368) and 1923 (.339), and during Casey's first few seasons in Toledo he drew freely upon the Giants' stable of players (McGraw later sold the Mud Hens and Swayne Field to a group of Toledo businessmen). Stengel immediately lifted the Mud Hens into the first division behind the 1926 batting champ, outfielder Bevo LeBourveau (.385, 17 HR, 117 RBI), veteran American League outfielder Bobby Veach

(.362), and his own playing efforts as an outfielder and pinch hitter (.328 in 88 games).

In 1927 Stengel produced Toledo's first AA pennant, driving the Mud Hens to 10 straight victories to win the flag on the last day of the season, then trouncing Buffalo five games to one in the Little World Series. The Mud Hens had an explosive hitting attack (.312) led by LeBourveau (.346), RBI champ Veach (.363, 133 R, 145 RBI), first sacker Roy Grimes (.368, 128 R, 122 RBI), catcher John Heving (.356), Stengel's close friend and former Giant teammate, Irish Meusel (.354 in 47 games), and several other heavy hitters. Although the 38-year-old Stengel rarely inserted himself into the lineup (.176 in 18 games), he pinch hit in one crucial game in the bottom of the 11th with the bases loaded and two out. The count went to three-and-two, then Casey crashed a grand slam home run to win the game. This dramatic shot was the only homer Casey hit in Toledo.

During Stengel's final four years in Toledo, the Mud Hens finished in the first division just once, in 1930, when the club led the league in hitting (.315) and runs. But the Mud Hens boasted three consecutive batting champs, Bobby Veach in 1928 (.382), outfielders Art Ruble in 1929 (.376), and Bevo LeBourveau in 1930 (.380). In 1929, at the age of 40, Stengel made an impressive contribution, usually as a pinch hitter (.438 in 26 games), and he was a scrappy field general, engaging in at least three fights during the season and earning two suspensions. Stengel had invested in the franchise when the Mud Hens became community-owned, but by 1931 Depression difficulties and the second last-place finish in three seasons (67–100 in 1929 and 68–100 in 1931) caused the financial collapse of the club. The Toledo franchise went into receivership, and although Casey's friend, financier Allie Reuben, was appointed receiver, Stengel was discharged (he caught on with Brooklyn as a coach, and was named manager of the Dodgers in 1934).

The Mud Hens enjoyed a winning season in 1932, sparked by outfielder Mike Powers (.371), triples leader Odell Hale (.333, 22 3B, 110 RBIs), righthander Bill Bean (20–14), and shortstop Bill Knickerbocker (.336), who established an all-time AA record by pounding out 69 doubles. Infielder George Detore performed well in 1933 (.352), and so did Mike Powers (.336) and outfielder-first baseman Milt Galatzer (.351) the next year. Powers again starred in 1935 (.339), while new player-manager Fred Haney was the sto-

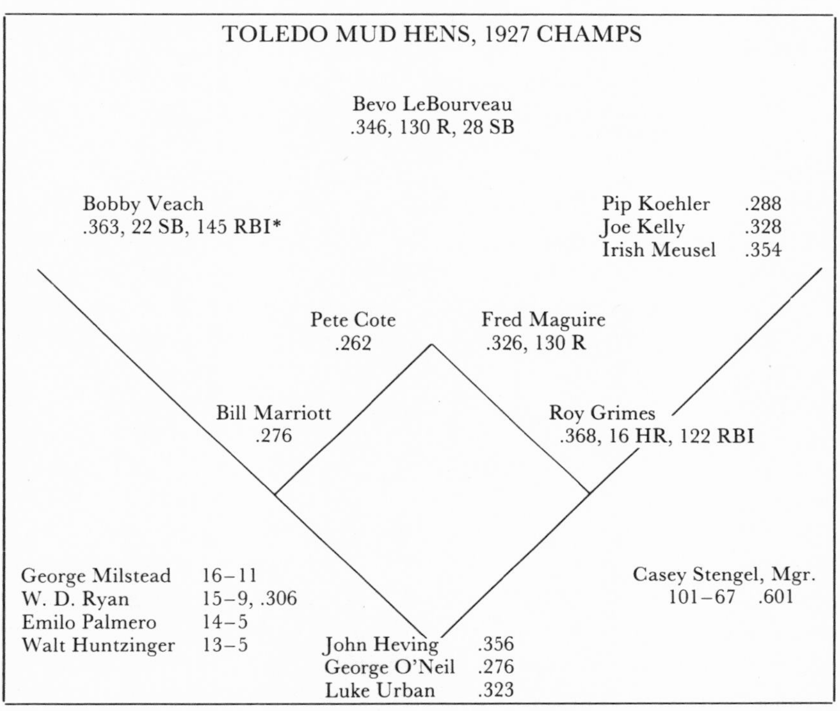

len base titlist (.321, 29 SB). Although the Mud Hens finished in the 1936 cellar, the next season Haney (.300 in 54 games) led the team to second place and Toledo's first playoff appearance. Longtime big league star Babe Herman (.324 lifetime) started 1937 with Detroit but went to Toledo in time to log 85 games in the outfield and lead the Mud Hens in batting (.348 with 79 RBIs). Other key hitters were outfielder Ed Coleman (.308, 25 HR, 123 RBI), and infielder-outfielder Roy Cullenbine (.308, 20 HR, 109 RBI). Southpaw Al Colen led the pitching staff (15–7, plus 30 games as an outfielder or pinch hitter). The major leagues' first relief ace, Firpo Marberry, worked in 13 games (7–2), while future American League standout Dizzy Trout took a regular turn throughout the season (14–16).

The following year the Mud Hens led the league in batting (.288) for the fourth (and last) time behind Ed Coleman (.332), fellow outfielders Chester Morgan (.357 in 71 games) and Homer Peel (.327 in 59 games), switch-hitter Roy Cullenbine (.309), triples leader Ben McCoy (.309, 16 3B), first baseman George Archie (.312 with 109 RBIs), and catcher Claud Linton (.314). In 1940 switch-hitter Johnny Lucadello (.334 with 102 RBIs) was a crowd-pleaser, and so was outfielder George "Red" McQuillen in 1940 (.333) and 1941 (.329). Pitcher-pinch hitter John "Footsie" Marcum also was effective in 1940 (13–12 and .323 in 73 games) and 1941 (17–7 and .358 in 77 games), while future Cardinals' star Harry Brecheen pitched impressively in 1941 (16–6).

During the next three seasons, 1942 through 1944, the Mud Hens made consecutive playoff appearances. Fred Haney returned as manager long enough to lead the Mud Hens to the 1942 finals, skillfully utilizing Toledo veteran John Marcum (14–16 and .299 in 62 games), infielder Robert Dillinger (.305), lefthander Archie "Happy" McKain (17–11), and second baseman James Bucher (.339 in 62 games). During the next two seasons, the Mud Hens' roster, like that of every other team in professional baseball, was in constant flux because of the war. Team leaders in 1943 were Bucher (.281 with a league-leading 35 doubles), outfielders Zeke Zarilla (.373 in 57 games), Tony Criscola (.317 in 86 games) and Harold Epps (.301 with a league-leading 13 triples), first baseman Phil Weintraub (.334), utility player Robert Boken (.333 in 54 games), and righthander Jack Kramer (8–2 with a 2.46 ERA in 10 games), who pitched the first AA no-hitter in the past eight seasons. The 1944 playoff club was rebuilt around outfielder-catcher Babe Martin (.350), outfielders Fred Reinhart (.327), Bill Burgo (.324) and George Corona (.308), catcher Joe Schultz (.315), southpaw Bill Seinsoth (16–11), and righthander Al LaMacchia (12–3).

A decade passed before Toledo made another playoff appearance, but in 1946 the Mud Hens won a rare home run title (101 homers) and righthander Fred Sanford led the league in victories, strikeouts, and innings (15–10, 230 IP, 154 K, 2.74 ERA). Local fans enjoyed the play of Pete Gray, the speedy, one-armed outfielder who had been a sensation with Memphis in 1943 and 1944, played with the St. Louis Browns in 1945 (.218), then was moved down to Toledo in 1946 (.250 in 48 games). Slugging first baseman Jerry Witte came back to baseball after three years in the service and donned a Toledo uniform in 1946. Witte led the league in homers (.312, 46 HR, 120 RBI) and was voted MVP and Rookie of the Year. He went up to the St. Louis Browns for the rest of the season, but was ineffective against big league pitching, and returned to Toledo late in 1947 (.279 with 13 homers and 46 RBIs in 55 games). Also returning to Toledo after playing with the Browns was Red McQuillen, who had a good year in 1947 (.310), then led the league in hitting and doubles the following season (.329, 37 2B, 90 RBI).

In 1949 the weak-hitting Mud Hens finished last, but on August 3 and 4 at Swayne Field, Hal White (10–8) and Walter Noble (8–8) set an AA record by holding Minneapolis hitless for 17 consecutive innings, and William Connelly (8–11, 6.17 ERA in 13 games) twirled a nine-inning no-hitter against Louisville. On June 25, 1950, righthander Marlin Stuart (9–3 with a 2.23 ERA in 13 games) pitched the second perfect game in league history, a nine-inning, 1–0 masterpiece over Louisville.

The 1952 Mud Hens staggered once more into last place, and poor attendance finally caused the franchise to fold. Since the American Association had opened play in 1902, the sole franchise shift had occurred when Toledo moved to Cleveland for 1914 and 1915, but on June 23, 1952, Toledo's club transferred to Charleston, West Virginia. The next season, however, brought major league ball to Milwaukee, and Toledo reentered the AA with a new franchise. Tommy Holmes opened the season as manager, but he was replaced on May 15 by George Selkirk, who directed the Mud Hens to their second AA pennant and who received the first Casey Stengel Award as Manager of the Year.

"Big Gene" Conley (at 6′8 he also was a fine NBA player) was named MVP and *The Sporting News* Minor League Player of the Year after winning a rare pitcher's Triple Crown (23–9, 211 K, 2.90 ERA). Switch-hitter Sam Jethroe led the league in runs and bases on balls (.309, 28 HR, 137 R, 109 W) and infielder Billy Klaus paced the AA in doubles (.275, 41 2B). Other productive hitters included outfielder Luis Marquez (.292, 37 SB) and lefthanded first baseman Harry Agganis (.281, 23 HR, 108 RBI), while the defense led the league in fielding percentage. The Mud Hens finished first by two games, beat Louisville, four games to three, in the playoff opener, but lost the finals to Kansas City in seven games.

The Mud Hens sagged into the second division the next two years, despite the performance of first basemen George Crowe, who led the league in RBIs, hits, doubles and total bases in 1954 (.334, 34 HR, 128 RBI), and Frank Torre in 1955 (.327). Despite community efforts to save the Mud Hens, the franchise was relocated to

Wichita. The Kroeger Company purchased Swayne Field and razed the historic old stadium to erect a new retail outlet.

But civic leader Ned Skeldon successfully pushed for the construction of a 10,000-seat stadium in 1963 and for the acquisition of an International League franchise two years later. Toledo had played in the IL in 1889, and local fans rejoiced at the return of the Mud Hens, who recorded a first-place finish in 1968. As a surge of baseball nostalgia increased throughout the country, the "Mud Hen" logo became more popular than ever — even the eccentric character Klinger (Jamie Farr) on *M*A*S*H* sported a Mud Hens jersey and cap. Lucas County Recreation Center and the Ohio Baseball Hall of Fame are adjacent to the ballpark, renamed Ned Skeldon Stadium in June 1988, just three months before Toledo's "Mr. Baseball" passed away.

Year	Record	Pcg.	Finish
1902	42-98	.300	Eighth
1903	48-91	.345	Eighth
1904	42-109	.272	Eighth
1905	61-92	.397	Seventh
1906	80-72	.529	Fourth
1907	88-66	.571	Second
1908	81-72	.530	Fourth
1909	80-86	.482	Sixth
1910	91-75	.548	Second
1911	78-86	.476	Sixth
1912	98-66	.598	Second
1913	69-98	.413	Sixth
1916	78-86	.476	Sixth
1917	57-95	.375	Eighth
1918	23-54	.299	Eighth
1919	59-91	.393	Seventh
1920	87-78	.524	Third
1921	80-88	.476	Seventh
1922	65-101	.392	Seventh
1923	54-114	.321	Eighth
1924	82-83	.497	Fifth
1925	77-90	.461	Sixth
1926	87-77	.530	Fourth
1927	101-67	.601	First (won Little World Series)
1928	79-88	.473	Sixth
1929	67-100	.402	Eighth
1930	88-66	.571	Third
1931	68-100	.402	Eighth
1932	87-80	.521	Fourth
1933	70-83	.458	Fifth

1934	68-84	.447	Sixth
1935	64-86	.427	Seventh
1936	59-92	.391	Eighth
1937	89-65	.578	Second (lost opener)
1938	79-74	.516	Fifth
1939	47-107	.305	Eighth
1940	59-90	.396	Seventh
1941	82-72	.532	Fifth
1942	78-73	.517	Fourth (won opener, lost finals)
1943	76-76	.500	Fourth (lost opener)
1944	95-58	.621	Second (lost opener)
1945	69-84	.451	Sixth
1946	69-84	.451	Sixth
1947	61-92	.399	Eighth
1948	61-91	.401	Seventh
1949	64-90	.416	Eighth
1950	65-87	.428	Seventh
1951	70-82	.481	Sixth
1952	46-107	.301	Eighth
1953	90-64	.584	First (won opener, lost finals)
1954	74-80	.481	Sixth
1955	81-73	.526	Fifth

Tulsa (Oilers)

"Let's . . . go . . . Tulsa!"

Andy Andrews, an Oilers fan for many years, became a fixture at Tulsa baseball games by slowly bellowing his familiar chant to the cheers of an expectant crowd. Professional baseball has been a going concern in Tulsa since 1905, when the oil-boom town of 4,000 fielded a team in the Missouri Valley League. The city's population reached 27,000 by 1920, 141,000 by 1930, and today the metropolitan area totals more than 500,000. Baseball has prospered along with the city.

The Tulsa Oilers played in the Oklahoma-Arkansas-Kansas League in 1907 and the Oklahoma-Kansas League the next year. The Oilers participated in the Western Association in 1910–1911, tried the Oklahoma State League in 1912, then returned to the Western Association from 1914 through 1917. In 1919 the Oilers joined the Western League, won five pennants, then became part of the Texas League from 1933 through 1965, reeling off 21 playoff appearances during the last 28 seasons.

Through the years the Oilers played in a number of ballparks, beginning with Athletic Park on West Archer. After a few seasons the diamond was moved to East Archer near First Street, then, a few years later, to South Main. When the Oilers joined the Western League in 1919, McNulty Park was built in 22 days at 10th and Elgin. A decade later McNulty Park was sold to commercial interests and demolished, which forced the Oilers to drop out of baseball in 1930. Playing on a diamond in front of the old Fairgrounds race track grandstand, the Oilers rejoined the Western League in 1931 and 1932. In 1934, after a year in the Texas League, the Oilers moved from their makeshift grandstand to a new wooden park just to the north. First called Tulsa County Stadium, the facility later was known as Texas League Park, then Oiler Park.

By the 1960s Tulsa's population growth and continued success in the Texas League fostered attendance exceeding 200,000 for three years in a row. Owner-president A. Ray Smith, who had bought the club in 1961, thus was encouraged to try Triple-A ball. The Arkansas Travelers of the Pacific Coast League, like Tulsa, were affiliates of the St. Louis Cardinals, but Little Rock felt out of place in the PCL. A franchise swap was arranged, with Little Rock moving into the Texas League and Tulsa going up to the PCL in 1966. Tulsa immediately won the Eastern Division crown, then won another title and the playoff championship in 1968.

The next year Tulsa was one of four PCL teams which joined the newly reorganized American Association, thus continuing a rivalry with Oklahoma City that had stimulated fan interest in the Western Association, Western League, Texas League, and PCL. The 1969 Oilers were managed by future Hall of Famer Warren Spahn to second place. Righthander Sal Campisi (13–2) led the AA in victories and winning percentage, and lefty Jerry Reuss matched his win total while claiming the strikeout crown (13–11 with 151 Ks). Catcher Ted Simmons, a switch-hitting 19-year-old who also played first, third and in the outfield for the Oilers, was voted AA Rookie of the Year (.317, 16 HR, 88 RBI).

The next year Simmons caught just 15 games (.373) before being called up permanently to the Cardinals. Outfielder Luis Melendez was the best hitter throughout the season (.306) as Spahn's club missed the Western Division crown by just half a game. Southpaw Fred Norman was brilliant in seven games (6–1 with 72 Ks in 62 IP), hurling a no-hitter against Indianapolis before being dealt to the Padres. Al Jutze fell short of the 1972 batting crown by one point (.324), but delivered the best fielding percentage of any catcher in the league.

Although the 1972 Oilers finished in last place, Tulsa leaped up to win Western Division and playoff titles the next two years. In 1973 outfielder Jim Dwyer won the batting crown (.387 in 87 games) and righthander Bob Forsch (12–12) pitched a no-hitter as the Oilers headed toward Tulsa's first division championship in the AA. Tulsa and Iowa, winners in the East, battled for seven games in the playoffs before the Oilers won the pennant. In what would prove to be the 49th and last Junior World Series, Pawtucket won over Tulsa, four games to one.

The Oilers successfully defended their titles the next year behind new manager Ken Boyer. First baseman Keith Hernandez, who played 31 games for the Oilers in 1973 (.333), won the 1974 batting crown (.351), while righthander Ray Bare, a reliever for the 1973 champs, was converted into a starter and responded with the 1974 ERA title (12–4, 2.34). Jim Dwyer returned for 36 games (.336) while catcher Marc Hill (.278) was voted AA Rookie of the Year, and outfielder Danny Godby (.344) finished second to Hernandez in the batting race.

The playoffs with Indianapolis opened with three games in Tulsa, and the Oilers won the first two. The Indians won the last game at Tulsa and the opener at Indianapolis to even the series, then took the lead with another victory in game five. In the sixth game the Indians held a 4–1 lead going into the ninth, but the Oilers rallied desperately for three runs, then won, 8–5, in the 15th. The next night brought a 3–1 Tulsa victory and a second consecutive playoff crown.

In 1975 Keith Hernandez was back for 85 games (.330) and Jim Dwyer played in 33 contests (.404). Third baseman Hector Cruz was voted Most Valuable Player after winning the home run and RBI crowns (.306, 29 HR, 116 RBI), while Richard Leon (.319) and Mike Easler (.313) also hit well. The next season Easler won the batting championship (.352 with 26 homers), and switch-hitting shortstop Garry Templeton (.321) was named AA Rookie of the Year.

Throughout the years, attendance was solid but not spectacular, in part because of decaying Oiler Park. A. Ray Smith, who annually absorbed the expense of repainting the ramshackle structure, was increasingly frustrated by the city's refusal to build a new stadium, and after the 1976 season he moved his club to New Orleans.

But construction executive Bill Rollings, a boyhood fan of the Oilers, and country music star Roy Clark purchased the Double-A Lafayette franchise and brought Texas League ball back to Tulsa. In 1981 the team finally moved into a new 7,300-seat facility located just east of old Oiler Park. Support for the Texas League Drillers has been strong, and Tulsa could readily accomplish another venture into Triple-A.

Year	Record	Pcg.	Finish
1969	79-61	.564	Second
1970	70-70	.500	Fifth
1971	64-76	.457	Seventh
1972	78-62	.557	Third
1973	68-67	.505	Third (won Western Division and finals, lost Junior World Series)
1974	76-58	.567	Second (won Western Division and finals)
1975	73-63	.537	Third
1976	65-70	.481	Fifth

Wichita (Braves, Aeros)

During the 1870s, Wichita was a rip-snorting Kansas cowtown, with roistering cowboys swaggering up and down Douglas Avenue and the Delano red-light district in search of recreation. But not all Wichita recreation in the 1870s was found in saloons, dance halls, gambling dens, and bagnios. The Ark Valley Boys and the Picked Nine competed against each other and teams from other communities on the baseball grounds at Second and Main across from the Occidental Hotel. Another diamond was laid out at Buffalo Bill Mathewson's cow pasture, located near present-day Central and Cleveland avenues, and a center for traveling circuses because of its proximity to the railroad tracks.

Baseball remained a popular pastime in Wichita after the Chisholm Trail closed, and the city's first professional team was entered in the Class C Western Association (1905–08). Wichita then served a long stint in the Class A Western League (1909–33). The Great Depression saw Wichita withdraw from organized baseball, but the city later returned to the Western League (1950–55). At various times Wichita clubs were called the Witches, Izzies, Aviators, Wolves, Oilers, and Indians.

Pro ball in Wichita was played first at Association Park, which had a covered wooden grandstand, bleachers down the left-field side, and a plank fence. Later the team moved into Island Park, on Ackerman Island in the Arkansas River just west of downtown. Because the river was a federal thoroughfare, Island Park was not subject to Sunday blue laws which prohibited baseball and other entertainments on the Sabbath. The ballpark was in the center of the half-mile-long island; shops were on the north side, and railroad tracks and a streetcar line crossed the south end. The Island Park grandstand burned down after the last game of the state semipro tournament in the summer of 1933. Wichita's Western League club moved to Muskogee for the rest of the season, but tournament organizer Hap Dumont (who changed the numbers on the Island Park scoreboard when he was a boy) talked the city into erecting a new ballpark by expanding the event into a large-scale national tournament.

The WPA built Lawrence Athletic Field, named after pioneer Robert Lawrence, on the west bank of the Arkansas River just south of the downtown area (and, at the same time, the WPA removed Ackerman Island as a navigation hazard). When the 1934 state tournament opened, 1,500 seats were ready at Lawrence Stadium. The first National Baseball Congress World Series was staged in 1935 with a seating capacity of 3,500 at the ballpark, and Satchel Paige, pitching for the Bismarck (North Dakota) Churchills, set an all-time record of 60 strikeouts in five games. Through the years Billy Martin, Tom Seaver, Dave Winfield, Ron Guidry, Chris Chambliss, Dave Kingman, and nearly 200 other future big leaguers have played in the tournament, which has attracted well over three million fans and legions of scouts. For decades Hap Dumont ran the tournament with promotional expertise, and after his death in 1971 the ballpark, renovated and expanded to 7,500 seats, was renamed Lawrence-Dumont Stadium.

The ballpark became the home of the Western League Indians when Wichita returned to pro ball in 1950. After Toledo dropped

Lawrence-Dumont Stadium opened in 1934.

— Photo by the author

out of the American Association following the 1955 season, Wichita felt ready to move up from Class A to Triple-A. Affiliated with Milwaukee, the first American Association Wichita club would be known as the Braves. The 1956 Braves were managed by former New York Yankee outfield star George Selkirk, but finished in seventh place.

Ben Geraghty took over the next year and led the Braves to the pennant. Outfielder Ray Shearer (.316, 29 HR, 109 RBI) sparked the offense, but the key to the first-place finish was a pitching staff that posted the league's best ERA (3.60). Righthander Carl Willey led the AA in victories and was voted Most Valuable Player (21–6), and he was ably backed by fastballer Joey Jay (17–10 with 199 Ks), veteran Red Murff (11–9), and lefty Juan Pizarro (4–0 in five starts). Although the Braves lost to St. Paul in the playoff opener, Geraghty was voted AA Manager of the Year.

Geraghty led the Braves to second place in 1958, but again dropped the opening round of playoffs. Carl Willey pitched a no-hitter but soon was called up (3–3, 2.70 ERA). Red Murff was sent to the bullpen with impressive results (11–5 with a 1.80 ERA in 51 games), and first baseman Earl Hersh won the RBI crown (.237,

17 HR, 98 RBI — the first time an AA RBI leader knocked in fewer than 100 runs). But despite success on the field, the Braves attracted only 101,000 fans, and Wichita pulled out of the American Association.

After an absence of more than a decade, professional baseball returned to the city due to the efforts of 17 civic-minded sports enthusiasts. As Wichita Professional Baseball, Inc., these investors purchased one of two American Association expansion franchises after the 1969 season. A working agreement with the Cleveland Indians was arranged, and 5,000 entries in a Name-the-Team contest labeled the new club the "Aeros."

In 1970 the Wichita Aeros finished in the cellar, but over 256,000 fans turned out to watch the performances of future big league stars, including the Aeros' own Chris Chambliss, who won the batting championship (.342) in his first year of pro ball. Although there was another losing season in 1971, attendance increased to more than 280,000 fans.

The following year Wichita led the league in attendance (276,451) by winning the Western Division with the best record in the AA. First baseman Pat Bourque (.279, 20 HR, 87 RBI) was voted MVP and righthander Joe Decker won the ERA crown (12–7, 170 Ks in 179 IP, and a 2.26 ERA). Other key performers included speedy outfielder Cleo James (.281 with 39 steals), shortstop Dave Rosello (.271), southpaw Larry Gura (11–4), and righty Bill Bonham (10–4). Once again Wichita was jinxed in the playoffs, suffering a three-game sweep at the hands of Evansville.

It proved to be Wichita's final playoff appearance in the American Association. The Aeros led the league in team hitting in 1973 behind Dave Rosello (.313), Pat Bourque (.347 with 35 runs and 42 RBIs in just 35 games), Tony LaRussa (.314) and switch-hitter Matt Alexander (.309). For the second year in a row the 1974 Aeros finished second in the West, as first baseman Pete LaCock won the MVP award (.327, 23 HR, 91 RBI) and outfielder-infielder Adrian Garrett took the home run crown (.280 with 26 homers and 83 RBIs in just 92 games).

But the Aeros began to lose on the field and at the gate, and last place in the West brought last place in the 1976 attendance race (124,107). By this time the original 17 investors had dwindled to one — Milton Glickman, who maintained his beloved Aeros as a civic service for a decade, despite losing money every year. Even as admissions sank, however, there were faithful superfans such as Helen Nichols, who attended Wichita ballgames from 1941 through the 1980s, and Christina Forster, who went to 951 Aero games from 1970 until 1984. Color at AA games was added by Captain Aero (Bill Talbot) who, attired in a flyer's cap, goggles and flowing scarf, frenetically attacked umpires and jeered opponents.

The 1977 Aeros, sparked by batting champ Jim Dwyer (.332 with 18 homers), infielder-outfielder Mike Adams (.321, 23 HR, 91 RBI), first base fielding leader Scot Thompson (.305), and righthander Dennis Lamp (11–4), missed the Western Division title by just one game. Scot Thompson had another good season in 1978 (.326), while outfielder Karl Pagel was voted Most Valuable Player of 1979 after winning the home run and RBI crowns (.316, 39 HR, 123 RBI).

During the 1980s, Wichita produced three consecutive batting champs and three consecutive MVPs. Mike Richardt won the batting title in 1981 (.354), followed by Roy Johnson in 1982 (.367) and Mike Stenhouse in 1983 (.355, 25 HR, 93 RBI). In 1983 Ken Phelps pounded his way to the home run and RBI crowns in one of the outstanding slugging performances of AA history (.333 with 46 homers and 141 RBIs in just 137 games), and was an overwhelming choice for Most Valuable Player. The 1983 MVP was batting champ Stenhouse, and in 1984 Alan Knicely kept the award in Wichita by leading the league in RBIs, hits, and total bases (.333, 33 HR, 126 RBI).

While Knicely helped the 1984 Aeros lead the AA in hitting, lefthander Tom Browning paced the league in strikeouts (12–10 with 160 Ks) and twirled a seven-inning no-hitter. But once again Wichita recorded the poorest attendance in the circuit (137,018), and Milton Glickman reluctantly agreed to sell the team to Bob Rich, Jr., of Buffalo. Glickman received about $1 million, approximately enough to cover his accumulated losses since 1976, while Rich moved the club to Buffalo.

The American Association did not completely leave Wichita. In 1971 innovative, progressive Joe Ryan left his position as general manager of the 89ers to assume the same post in Wichita. A year later, Ryan accepted the presidency of the AA, and he moved league headquarters from Oklahoma City to Wichita, where it remained for a decade and a half. In 1982 Ryan bought the National Baseball Congress, then obtained a lease on Lawrence-Dumont

Stadium, where he operated the AA offices until forced to resign because of ill health. By that time there was a new pro club in town; Larry Schmittou bought Beaumont's franchise in the Texas League and moved the Double-A club to Wichita. Today the Wichita Wranglers provide fans with quality baseball, while the National Baseball Congress World Series grows bigger every year.

Year	Record	Pcg.	Finish
1956	65-87	.428	Seventh
1957	93-61	.604	First (lost opener)
1958	83-71	.539	Second (lost opener)
1970	67-73	.479	Eighth
1971	66-74	.471	Sixth
1972	87-53	.621	First (won Western Division, lost finals)
1973	67-68	.496	Fourth
1974	67-68	.496	Fifth
1975	68-68	.500	Fifth
1976	56-79	.415	Seventh
1977	68-64	.515	Fourth
1978	58-77	.430	Eighth
1979	57-79	.419	Eighth
1980	61-74	.452	Sixth
1981	65-70	.481	Sixth
1982	70-67	.511	Fifth
1983	65-71	.478	Fifth
1984	78-77	.503	Fifth

American Association Records

ANNUAL STANDINGS

During 33 of the 84 seasons of American Association play, the team that compiled the best record over the regular schedule was declared champion. In 1933 and 1934 the clubs which had compiled the best record among the four easternmost and four westernmost cities in the league played a postseason series to determine the AA representative to the Junior World Series. Beginning in 1936, a total of 26 Shaughnessy playoffs were staged, with a Governors' Cup and a Junior World Series berth awarded to the victor. First in 1959, then from 1970 until the present, the AA was divided into Eastern and Western divisions. Nineteen times the division winners have played each other to determine the AA champion, and four times in the 1980s a split season resurrected a four-team playoff system. Composite standings year-by-year follow.

1902

Indianapolis	96-45	.681
Louisville	92-45	.671
St. Paul	72-66	.521
Kansas City	69-67	.507
Columbus	66-74	.471
Milwaukee	65-75	.464
Minneapolis	54-86	.385
Toledo	42-98	.330

1903

St. Paul	88-46	.657
Louisville	87-54	.617
Milwaukee	77-60	.562

Indianapolis	78-61	.561
Kansas City	69-66	.511
Columbus	56-84	.400
Minneapolis	50-91	.355
Toledo	48-91	.345

1904

St. Paul	95-52	.646
Columbus	88-61	.591
Milwaukee	89-63	.585
Minneapolis	78-67	.538
Louisville	77-70	.524
Indianapolis	69-85	.448
Kansas City	60-91	.387
Toledo	42-109	.272

1905

Columbus	102-53	.658
Milwaukee	90-61	.598
Minneapolis	90-64	.584
Louisville	76-76	.500
St. Paul	75-78	.492
Indianapolis	69-83	.454
Toledo	61-92	.397
Kansas City	45-102	.301

1906

Columbus	95-58	.622
Milwaukee	86-70	.552
Minneapolis	81-68	.544
Toledo	80-72	.529
Kansas City	72-83	.464
Louisville	73-79	.480
St. Paul	67-83	.447
Indianapolis	56-98	.383

1907

Columbus	90-64	.584
Toledo	88-66	.571
Minneapolis	80-74	.520
Kansas City	78-76	.510
Louisville	77-77	.500
Indianapolis	73-81	.473
Milwaukee	72-84	.460
St. Paul	59-95	.383

1908

Indianapolis	92-61	.601
Louisville	88-65	.575
Columbus	86-68	.558
Toledo	81-72	.530
Minneapolis	77-77	.500
Milwaukee	71-83	.461
Kansas City	70-83	.456
St. Paul	48-104	.316

1909

Louisville	93-75	.554
Milwaukee	90-77	.539
Minneapolis	88-79	.527
Indianapolis	83-85	.494
St. Paul	80-83	.491
Toledo	80-86	.482
Columbus	80-87	.479
Kansas City	71-93	.432

1910

Minneapolis	107-61	.637
Toledo	91-75	.548
Columbus	88-77	.533
St. Paul	88-80	.524
Kansas City	85-81	.512
Milwaukee	76-91	.455
Indianapolis	69-96	.418
Louisville	60-103	.368

1911

Minneapolis	99-66	.600
Kansas City	94-70	.573
Columbus	87-78	.527
St. Paul	79-85	.482
Milwaukee	79-87	.476
Toledo	78-86	.476
Indianapolis	78-88	.470
Louisville	67-101	.398

1912

Minneapolis	105-60	.636
Toledo	98-66	.598
Columbus	98-68	.590
Kansas City	85-82	.509
Milwaukee	78-85	.479
St. Paul	77-90	.461
Louisville	66-101	.395
Indianapolis	56-111	.335

1913

Milwaukee	100-67	.599
Minneapolis	97-70	.581
Louisville	94-72	.566

Columbus	93-74	.557
St. Paul	75-87	.463
Kansas City	69-98	.413
Toledo	69-98	.413
Indianapolis	68-99	.407

1914

Milwaukee	98-68	.590
Louisville	95-73	.565
Indianapolis	88-77	.533
Columbus	86-77	.528
Cleveland	82-81	.503
Kansas City	84-84	.500
Minneapolis	75-93	.446
St. Paul	56-111	.331

1915

Minneapolis	92-62	.597
St. Paul	90-63	.588
Indianapolis	81-70	.536
Louisville	78-72	.520
Kansas City	71-79	.473
Milwaukee	67-81	.453
Cleveland	67-82	.450
Columbus	54-91	.372

1916

Louisville	101-66	.605
Indianapolis	95-71	.572
Minneapolis	88-76	.537
St. Paul	86-79	.521
Kansas City	86-81	.515
Toledo	78-86	.476
Columbus	71-90	.441
Milwaukee	54-110	.329

1917

Indianapolis	90-63	.588
St. Paul	88-66	.571
Louisville	88-66	.571
Columbus	84-69	.549
Milwaukee	71-81	.467
Minneapolis	68-86	.442
Kansas City	66-86	.434
Toledo	57-95	.375

1918

Kansas City	44-30	.595
Columbus	41-34	.547
Indianapolis	41-34	.547
Louisville	43-36	.544
Milwaukee	38-35	.521
St. Paul	39-38	.506
Minneapolis	34-42	.447
Toledo	23-54	.299

1919

St. Paul	94-60	.610
Kansas City	86-65	.570
Louisville	86-67	.562
Indianapolis	85-68	.556
Minneapolis	72-82	.468
Columbus	70-84	.455
Toledo	59-91	.393
Milwaukee	58-93	.384

1920

St. Paul	115-49	.701
Louisville	88-79	.527
Toledo	87-79	.524
Minneapolis	85-79	.518
Indianapolis	83-83	.500
Milwaukee	78-88	.470
Columbus	66-99	.400
Kansas City	60-106	.361

1921

Louisville	98-70	.583
Minneapolis	92-73	.558
Kansas City	84-80	.512
Indianapolis	83-85	.494
Milwaukee	81-86	.485
St. Paul	80-87	.479
Toledo	80-88	.476
Columbus	67-96	.411

1922

St. Paul	107-60	.641
Minneapolis	92-75	.551
Kansas City	92-76	.548
Indianapolis	87-80	.521
Milwaukee	85-83	.506
Louisville	77-91	.458
Toledo	65-101	.392
Columbus	63-102	.382

1923

Kansas City	112-54	.675
St. Paul	111-57	.661
Louisville	94-77	.550

Columbus	79-89	.470
Milwaukee	75-91	.452
Minneapolis	74-92	.446
Indianapolis	72-94	.434
Toledo	54-114	.321

1924

St. Paul	95-70	.576
Indianapolis	92-73	.558
Louisville	90-75	.545
Milwaukee	83-83	.500
Toledo	82-83	.497
Minneapolis	77-89	.464
Columbus	75-92	.448
Kansas City	68-96	.415

1925

Louisville	106-61	.635
Indianapolis	92-74	.554
St. Paul	91-75	.548
Minneapolis	86-80	.518
Kansas City	80-87	.474
Toledo	77-90	.461
Milwaukee	74-94	.440
Columbus	61-106	.365

1926

Louisville	105-62	.629
Indianapolis	94-71	.570
Milwaukee	93-71	.567
Toledo	87-77	.530
Kansas City	87-78	.527
St. Paul	82-81	.503
Minneapolis	72-94	.434
Columbus	39-125	.238

1927

Toledo	101-67	.601
Milwaukee	99-69	.589
Kansas City	99-69	.589
St. Paul	90-78	.536
Minneapolis	88-80	.524
Indianapolis	70-98	.417
Louisville	65-103	.387
Columbus	60-108	.357

1928

Indianapolis	99-68	.593
Minneapolis	97-71	.577
Milwaukee	90-78	.536
St. Paul	88-80	.524
Kansas City	88-80	.524
Toledo	79-88	.473
Columbus	68-100	.405
Louisville	62-106	.369

1929

Kansas City	111-56	.665
St. Paul	102-64	.614
Minneapolis	89-87	.533
Indianapolis	78-89	.467
Louisville	75-90	.455
Columbus	75-91	.452
Milwaukee	69-98	.413
Toledo	67-100	.402

1930

Louisville	93-60	.607
St. Paul	91-63	.591
Toledo	88-66	.571
Minneapolis	77-76	.503
Kansas City	75-79	.487
Columbus	67-86	.438
Milwaukee	63-91	.409
Indianapolis	60-93	.393

1931

St. Paul	104-63	.623
Kansas City	90-77	.539
Indianapolis	86-80	.518
Columbus	84-82	.506
Milwaukee	83-85	.494
Minneapolis	80-88	.476
Louisville	74-94	.440
Toledo	68-100	.405

1932

Minneapolis	100-68	.595
Columbus	88-77	.533
Milwaukee	88-78	.530
Toledo	87-80	.521
Indianapolis	86-80	.518
Kansas City	81-86	.485
St. Paul	70-97	.419
Louisville	67-101	.399

1933

Columbus	101-51	.664
Minneapolis	86-67	.562
Indianapolis	82-72	.532

St. Paul	78-75	.510
Toledo	70-83	.458
Louisville	70-83	.458
Milwaukee	67-87	.435
Kansas City	57-93	.360

1934

Minneapolis	85-64	.570
Columbus	85-68	.556
Milwaukee	82-70	.539
Louisville	78-74	.513
Indianapolis	77-75	.507
Toledo	68-84	.447
St. Paul	67-84	.444
Kansas City	65-88	.425

1935

Minneapolis	91-63	.591
Indianapolis	85-67	.559
Kansas City	84-70	.545
Columbus	84-70	.545
St. Paul	75-78	.490
Milwaukee	75-79	.487
Toledo	64-86	.427
Louisville	52-97	.349

1936

Milwaukee	90-64	.584
St. Paul	84-68	.553
Kansas City	84-69	.549
Indianapolis	79-75	.513
Minneapolis	78-76	.506
Columbus	76-78	.494
Louisville	63-91	.409
Toledo	59-92	.391

1937

Columbus	90-64	.584
Toledo	89-65	.578
Minneapolis	87-67	.565
Milwaukee	80-73	.523
Kansas City	72-82	.468
Indianapolis	67-85	.441
St. Paul	67-87	.435
Louisville	62-91	.405

1938

St. Paul	90-61	.596
Kansas City	84-67	.556
Milwaukee	81-70	.536
Indianapolis	80-74	.519
Toledo	79-74	.516
Minneapolis	78-74	.513
Columbus	64-89	.418
Louisville	53-100	.346

1939

Kansas City	107-47	.695
Minneapolis	99-55	.643
Indianapolis	82-72	.532
Louisville	75-78	.490
St. Paul	73-81	.474
Milwaukee	70-83	.458
Columbus	62-82	.403
Toledo	47-107	.305

1940

Kansas City	95-57	.625
Columbus	90-60	.600
Minneapolis	86-59	.593
Louisville	75-75	.500
St. Paul	69-79	.466
Indianapolis	62-84	.425
Toledo	59-90	.396
Milwaukee	58-90	.392

1941

Columbus	95-58	.621
Louisville	87-66	.569
Kansas City	85-69	.552
Minneapolis	83-70	.542
Toledo	82-72	.532
Indianapolis	65-88	.425
St. Paul	61-92	.399
Milwaukee	55-98	.359

1942

Kansas City	84-69	.549
Milwaukee	81-69	.540
Columbus	82-72	.532
Toledo	78-73	.517
Louisville	78-76	.506
Indianapolis	76-78	.494
Minneapolis	76-78	.494
St. Paul	57-97	.370

1943

Milwaukee	90-61	.596
Indianapolis	85-67	.559
Columbus	84-67	.556

Toledo	76-76	.500
Louisville	70-81	.464
Minneapolis	67-84	.444
Kansas City	67-85	.441
St. Paul	67-85	.441

1944

Milwaukee	102-51	.667
Toledo	95-58	.621
Louisville	85-63	.574
St. Paul	85-66	.563
Columbus	85-67	.562
Indianapolis	57-93	.380
Minneapolis	54-97	.358
Kansas City	41-110	.272

1945

Milwaukee	93-61	.604
Indianapolis	90-63	.592
Louisville	84-70	.545
St. Paul	75-76	.497
Minneapolis	72-81	.471
Toledo	69-84	.451
Kansas City	65-86	.430
Columbus	63-90	.412

1946

Louisville	92-61	.601
Indianapolis	88-65	.575
St. Paul	80-71	.530
Minneapolis	76-75	.503
Milwaukee	70-78	.473
Toledo	69-84	.451
Kansas City	67-82	.450
Columbus	64-90	.416

1947

Kansas City	93-60	.608
Louisville	85-68	.556
Milwaukee	79-75	.513
Minneapolis	77-77	.500
Columbus	76-78	.494
Indianapolis	74-79	.484
St. Paul	69-85	.454
Toledo	61-92	.399

1948

Indianapolis	100-54	.649
Milwaukee	89-65	.578
St. Paul	86-68	.558
Columbus	81-73	.526
Minneapolis	77-77	.500
Kansas City	64-88	.421
Toledo	61-91	.401
Louisville	56-98	.364

1949

St. Paul	93-60	.608
Indianapolis	92-61	.604
Milwaukee	76-76	.500
Minneapolis	74-78	.487
Kansas City	71-80	.470
Louisville	70-83	.458
Columbus	70-83	.458
Toledo	64-90	.416

1950

Minneapolis	90-64	.584
Indianapolis	85-67	.559
Columbus	84-69	.549
St. Paul	83-69	.546
Louisville	82-71	.536
Milwaukee	68-85	.444
Toledo	65-87	.428
Kansas City	54-99	.353

1951

Milwaukee	94-57	.623
St. Paul	85-66	.563
Kansas City	81-70	.536
Louisville	80-73	.523
Minneapolis	77-75	.507
Toledo	70-82	.481
Indianapolis	68-84	.447
Columbus	53-101	.344

1952

Milwaukee	101-53	.656
Kansas City	89-65	.578
St. Paul	80-74	.519
Minneapolis	79-75	.513
Louisville	77-77	.500
Indianapolis	75-79	.487
Columbus	68-85	.444
Charleston-Toledo	46-107	.301

1953

Toledo	90-64	.584
Kansas City	88-66	.571
Louisville	84-70	.545

Indianapolis	82-72	.532
Minneapolis	76-78	.494
St. Paul	72-82	.468
Columbus	64-90	.416
Charleston	60-94	.390

1954

Indianapolis	95-57	.625
Louisville	85-68	.556
Minneapolis	78-73	.517
Columbus	77-76	.503
St. Paul	75-78	.490
Toledo	74-80	.481
Kansas City	68-85	.444
Charleston	59-94	.386

1955

Minneapolis	92-62	.597
Omaha	84-70	.545
Denver	83-71	.539
Louisville	83-71	.539
Toledo	81-73	.526
St. Paul	75-78	.490
Indianapolis	67-86	.438
Charleston	50-104	.325

1956

Indianapolis	92-62	.597
Denver	86-67	.562
Omaha	82-71	.536
Minneapolis	78-74	.513
St. Paul	75-78	.490
Charleston	74-79	.484
Wichita	65-87	.428
Louisville	59-93	.388

1957

Wichita	93-61	.604
Denver	90-64	.584
Minneapolis	85-69	.552
St. Paul	82-72	.532
Omaha	76-78	.494
Indianapolis	74-80	.481
Charleston	67-87	.435
Louisville	49-105	.318

1958

Charleston	89-62	.589
Wichita	83-71	.539
Minneapolis	82-71	.536
Denver	78-71	.523
Omaha	80-74	.519
Indianapolis	72-82	.468
St. Paul	70-84	.455
Louisville	56-95	.371

1959

EASTERN DIVISION		
Louisville	97-65	.599
Minneapolis	95-67	.586
Indianapolis	86-76	.531
St. Paul	81-81	.500
Charleston	77-84	.478
WESTERN DIVISION		
Omaha	83-78	.516
Fort Worth	81-81	.500
Denver	76-86	.469
Dallas	75-87	.463
Houston	58-104	.358

1960

Denver	88-66	.571
Louisville	85-68	.556
Houston	83-71	.539
St. Paul	83-71	.539
Minneapolis	82-72	.532
Charleston	65-88	.425
Indianapolis	65-89	.422
Dallas-Fort Worth	64-90	.416

1961

Indianapolis	86-64	.573
Louisville	80-70	.533
Denver	75-73	.507
Houston	73-77	.487
Dallas-Fort Worth	72-77	.483
Omaha	62-87	.416

1962

Indianapolis	89-58	.605
Omaha	79-68	.537
Denver	79-71	.527
Louisville	71-75	.486
Oklahoma City	66-81	.449
Dallas-Fort Worth	59-90	.396

1969

Omaha	85-55	.607
Tulsa	79-61	.564
Indianapolis	74-66	.529

Iowa	62-78	.443
Oklahoma City	62-78	.443
Denver	58-82	.414

1970

EASTERN DIVISION		
Omaha	73-65	.529
Iowa	70-68	.507
Indianapolis	71-69	.507
Evansville	67-71	.486
WESTERN DIVISION		
Denver	70-69	.504
Tulsa	70-70	.500
Oklahoma City	68-71	.489
Wichita	67-73	.479

1971

EASTERN DIVISION		
Indianapolis	84-55	.604
Iowa	71-69	.507
Omaha	69-70	.471
Evansville	60-78	.435
WESTERN DIVISION		
Denver	73-67	.521
Oklahoma City	71-69	.507
Wichita	66-74	.471
Tulsa	64-76	.457

1972

EASTERN DIVISION		
Evansville	83-57	.593
Omaha	71-69	.507
Iowa	62-78	.443
Indianapolis	61-79	.436
WESTERN DIVISION		
Wichita	87-53	.621
Tulsa	78-62	.557
Denver	61-79	.436
Oklahoma City	57-83	.407

1973

EASTERN DIVISION		
Iowa	83-53	.610
Indianapolis	74-62	.544
Evansville	66-70	.485
Omaha	62-73	.459
WESTERN DIVISION		
Tulsa	68-67	.505
Wichita	67-68	.496
Oklahoma City	61-74	.455
Denver	61-75	.449

1974

EASTERN DIVISION		
Indianapolis	78-57	.578
Iowa	74-62	.544
Evansville	68-67	.504
Omaha	54-82	.397
WESTERN DIVISION		
Tulsa	76-58	.567
Wichita	67-68	.496
Oklahoma City	62-73	.459
Denver	62-74	.455

1975

EASTERN DIVISION		
Evansville	77-59	.566
Indianapolis	71-64	.526
Omaha	67-69	.493
Iowa	56-79	.415
WESTERN DIVISION		
Denver	81-55	.596
Tulsa	73-63	.537
Wichita	68-68	.500
Oklahoma City	50-86	.368

1976

EASTERN DIVISION		
Omaha	78-58	.574
Iowa	68-68	.500
Indianapolis	62-73	.459
Evansville	55-81	.404
WESTERN DIVISION		
Denver	86-50	.632
Oklahoma City	72-63	.533
Tulsa	65-70	.481
Wichita	56-79	.415

1977

EASTERN DIVISION		
Omaha	76-59	.563
Indianapolis	72-64	.529
Evansville	65-68	.489
Iowa	61-75	.449
WESTERN DIVISION		
Denver	71-65	.522
Wichita	68-64	.515
Oklahoma City	70-66	.515
New Orleans	57-79	.419

1978

EASTERN DIVISION		
Indianapolis	78-57	.578
Evansville	78-53	.574
Springfield	70-66	.515
Iowa	66-70	.485
WESTERN DIVISION		
Omaha	66-69	.489
Denver	64-71	.474
Oklahoma City	62-74	.456
Wichita	58-77	.430

1979

EASTERN DIVISION		
Evansville	78-58	.574
Springfield	73-63	.537
Iowa	69-67	.507
Indianapolis	67-69	.493
WESTERN DIVISION		
Oklahoma City	72-63	.533
Omaha	65-71	.478
Denver	62-73	.459
Wichita	57-79	.419

1980

EASTERN DIVISION		
Springfield	75-61	.551
Evansville	61-74	.452
Iowa	59-77	.434
Indianapolis	58-77	.430
WESTERN DIVISION		
Denver	92-44	.676
Oklahoma City	70-65	.519
Omaha	66-70	.485
Wichita	61-74	.452

1981

EASTERN DIVISION		
Evansville	73-63	.537
Springfield	66-70	.485
Indianapolis	62-74	.456
Iowa	53-82	.393
WESTERN DIVISION		
Omaha	79-57	.581
Denver	76-60	.559
Oklahoma City	69-67	.507
Wichita	65-70	.4o1

1982

EASTERN DIVISION		
Indianapolis	75-61	.551
Iowa	73-62	.541
Louisville	73-62	.541
Evansville	68-65	.511
WESTERN DIVISION		
Omaha	71-66	.518
Wichita	70-67	.511
Denver	68-67	.504
Oklahoma City	43-91	.321

1983

EASTERN DIVISION		
Louisville	78-57	.578
Iowa	71-65	.522
Indianapolis	64-72	.471
Evansville	61-75	.449
WESTERN DIVISION		
Denver	73-61	.545
Oklahoma City	66-69	.489
Wichita	65-71	.478
Omaha	64-72	.471

1984

Indianapolis	91-63	.591
Iowa	80-74	.519
Denver	79-75	.513
Louisville	79-76	.510
Wichita	78-77	.503
Evansville	72-82	.468
Oklahoma City	70-84	.455
Omaha	68-86	.442

1985

EASTERN DIVISION		
Louisville	74-68	.521
Nashville	71-70	.504
Buffalo	66-76	.465
Indianapolis	61-81	.430
WESTERN DIVISION		
Oklahoma City	79-63	.556
Denver	77-65	.542
Omaha	73-69	.514
Iowa	66-70	.485

1986

EASTERN DIVISION		
Indianapolis	80-62	.563
Buffalo	71-71	.500

Nashville	68-74	.479
Louisville	64-78	.451
WESTERN DIVISION		
Denver	76-66	.535
Iowa	74-68	.521
Omaha	72-70	.507
Oklahoma City	63-79	.444

1987

Denver	79-61	.564
Louisville	78-62	.557
Indianapolis	74-64	.536
Oklahoma City	69-71	.493
Buffalo	66-74	.471
Iowa	64-74	.464
Omaha	64-76	.457
Nashville	64-76	.457

1988

EASTERN DIVISION		
Indianapolis	89-53	.627
Nashville	73-69	.514
Buffalo	72-70	.507
Louisville	63-79	.444
WESTERN DIVISION		
Omaha	81-61	.570
Iowa	78-64	.549
Denver	72-69	.511
Oklahoma City	67-74	.475

1989

EASTERN DIVISION		
Indianapolis	87-59	.596
Buffalo	80-62	.563
Nashville	74-72	.507
Louisville	71-74	.490
WESTERN DIVISION		
Omaha	74-72	.507
Denver	69-77	.473
Iowa	62-82	.431
Oklahoma City	59-86	.407

PLAYOFF RESULTS

1933 Columbus defeated Minneapolis 4 games to 2.

1934 Columbus defeated Minneapolis 5 games to 2.

1936 Indianapolis defeated St. Paul 4 games to 1. Milwaukee defeated Kansas City 4 games to 0. **FINALS:** Milwaukee defeated Indianapolis 4 games to 1.

1937 Columbus defeated Minneapolis 4 games to 2. Milwaukee defeated Toledo 4 games to 2. **FINALS:** Columbus defeated Milwaukee 4 games to 2.

1938 St. Paul defeated Milwaukee 4 games to 2. Kansas City defeated Indianapolis 4 games to 2. **FINALS:** Kansas City defeated St. Paul 4 games to 3.

1939 Louisville defeated Minneapolis 4 games to 1. Indianapolis defeated Kansas City 4 games to 1. **FINALS:** Louisville defeated Indianapolis 4 games to 1.

1940 Louisville defeated Columbus 4 games to 2. Kansas City defeated Minneapolis 4 games to 2. **FINALS:** Louisville defeated Kansas City 4 games to 2.

1941 Columbus defeated Kansas City 4 games to 2. Louisville defeated Minneapolis 4 games to 2. **FINALS:** Columbus defeated Louisville 4 games to 1.

1942 Columbus defeated Kansas City 4 games to 3. Toledo defeated Milwaukee 4 games to 2. **FINALS:** Columbus defeated Toledo 4 games to 0.

1943 Columbus defeated Milwaukee 3 games to 1. Indianapolis defeated Toledo 3 games to 2. **FINALS:** Columbus defeated Indianapolis 3 games to 0.

1944 Louisville defeated Milwaukee 4 games to 2. St. Paul defeated Toledo 4 games to 3. **FINALS:** Louisville defeated St. Paul 4 games to 0.

1945 Louisville defeated Milwaukee 4 games to 2. St. Paul defeated Indianapolis 4 games to 2. **FINALS:** Louisville defeated St. Paul 4 games to 2.

1946 Louisville defeated St. Paul 4 games to 1. Indianapolis defeated Minneapolis 4 games to 3. **FINALS:** Louisville defeated Indianapolis 4 games to 0.
1947 Milwaukee defeated Kansas City 4 games to 2. Louisville defeated Minneapolis 4 games to 3. **FINALS:** Milwaukee defeated Louisville 4 games to 3.
1948 St. Paul defeated Indianapolis 4 games to 2. Columbus defeated Milwaukee 4 games to 3. **FINALS:** St. Paul defeated Columbus 4 games to 3.
1949 Milwaukee defeated St. Paul 4 games to 3. Indianapolis defeated Minneapolis 4 games to 3. **FINALS:** Indianapolis defeated Milwaukee 4 games to 3.
1950 Columbus defeated Minneapolis 4 games to 2. Indianapolis defeated St. Paul 4 games to 0. **FINALS:** Columbus defeated Indianapolis 4 games to 3.
1951 Milwaukee defeated Kansas City 4 games to 1. St. Paul defeated Louisville 4 games to 1. **FINALS:** Milwaukee defeated St. Paul 4 games to 2.
1952 Milwaukee defeated St. Paul 4 games to 0. Kansas City defeated Minneapolis 4 games to 1. **FINALS:** Kansas City defeated Milwaukee 4 games to 3.
1953 Toledo defeated Louisville 4 games to 3. Kansas City defeated Indianapolis 4 games to 2. **FINALS:** Kansas City defeated Toledo 4 games to 3.
1954 Indianapolis defeated Milwaukee 4 games to 2. Louisville defeated Columbus 4 games to 3. **FINALS:** Louisville defeated Indianapolis 4 games to 1.
1955 Minneapolis defeated Denver 4 games to 0. Omaha defeated Louisville 4 games to 3. **FINALS:** Minneapolis defeated Omaha 4 games to 0.
1956 Indianapolis defeated Minneapolis 4 games to 3. Denver defeated Omaha 4 games to 2. **FINALS:** Indianapolis defeated Denver 4 games to 0.
1957 St. Paul defeated Wichita 4 games to 1. Denver defeated Minneapolis 4 games to 0. **FINALS:** Denver defeated St. Paul 4 games to 2.
1958 Denver defeated Charleston 4 games to 3. Minneapolis defeated Wichita 4 games to 2. **FINALS:** Minneapolis defeated Denver 4 games to 0.
1959 Ft. Worth defeated Louisville 4 games to 0. Minneapolis defeated Omaha 4 games to 2. **FINALS:** Minneapolis defeated Ft. Worth 4 games to 3.
1960 Denver defeated Houston 4 games to 3. Louisville defeated St. Paul 4 games to 2. **FINALS:** Louisville defeated Denver 4 games to 2.
1961 Houston defeated Indianapolis 4 games to 1. Louisville defeated Denver 4 games to 3. **FINALS:** Louisville defeated Houston 4 games to 2.
1962 Louisville defeated Indianapolis 3 games to 0. Denver defeated Omaha 3 games to 1. **FINALS:** Louisville defeated Denver 4 games to 2.
1970 Omaha defeated Denver 4 games to 1.
1971 Denver defeated Indianapolis 4 games to 3.
1972 Evansville defeated Wichita 3 games to 0.
1973 Tulsa defeated Iowa 4 games to 3.
1974 Tulsa defeated Indianapolis 4 games to 3.
1975 Evansville defeated Denver 4 games to 2.
1976 Denver defeated Omaha 4 games to 2.
1977 Denver defeated Omaha 4 games to 2.
1978 Omaha defeated Indianapolis 4 games to 1.
1979 Evansville defeated Oklahoma City 4 games to 2.
1980 Springfield defeated Denver 4 games to 1.
1981 Denver defeated Evansville 3 games to 1. Omaha defeated Springfield 3

games to 2. **FINALS:** Denver defeated Omaha 4 games to 0.

1982 Indianapolis defeated Omaha 4 games to 2.

1983 Denver defeated Iowa 3 games to 1. Louisville defeated Oklahoma City 3 games to 2. **FINALS:** Denver defeated Louisville 4 games to 0.

1984 Louisville defeated Wichita in a single game to determine fourth place. Louisville defeated Indianapolis 4 games to 2. Denver defeated Iowa 4 games to 1. **FINALS:** Louisville defeated Denver 4 games to 1.

1985 Louisville defeated Oklahoma City 4 games to 1.

1986 Indianapolis defeated Denver 4 games to 3.

1987 Denver defeated Oklahoma City 3 games to 2. Indianapolis defeated Louisville 3 games to 2. **FINALS:** Indianapolis defeated Denver 4 games to 1.

1988 Indianapolis defeated Omaha 3 games to 1.

1989 Indianapolis defeated Omaha 3 games to 2.

1990 Omaha defeated Nashville 3 games to 2.

1991 Denver defeated Buffalo 3 games to 2.

RESULTS: LITTLE WORLD SERIES JUNIOR WORLD SERIES

This postseason classic was called the Little World Series through 1931, after which it was officially designated the Junior World Series. On a few occasions the winners traveled west to play the champion of the Pacific Coast League. American Association champs also participated in the Kodak World Baseball Classic in 1972, the AAA World Series in 1983, and the Triple-A Classic in 1988 and 1989. The American Association champions won 27 of the 50 series, and Indianapolis has won both Triple-A Classics.

American Association team listed first; winner in CAPS; record in parentheses.

1904 St. Paul v. BUFFALO (2-1)
1906 Columbus v. BUFFALO (3-2)
1907 Columbus v. TORONTO (4-1)
1917 INDIANAPOLIS v. Toronto (4-1)
1920 St. Paul v. BALTIMORE (5-1)
1921 LOUISVILLE v. Baltimore (5-3)
1922 St. Paul v. BALTIMORE (5-2)
1923 KANSAS CITY v. Baltimore (5-4)
1924 ST. PAUL v. Baltimore (5-4-1)
1925 Louisville v. BALTIMORE (5-3)
1926 Louisville v. TORONTO (5-0)
1927 TOLEDO v. Buffalo (5-1)
1928 INDIANAPOLIS v. Rochester (5-1-1)
1929 KANSAS CITY v. Rochester (5-4)
1930 Louisville v. ROCHESTER (5-3)
1931 St. Paul v. ROCHESTER (5-3)
1932 Minneapolis v. NEWARK (4-2)
1933 COLUMBUS v. Buffalo (5-3)
1934 COLUMBUS v. Toronto (5-4)
1936 MILWAUKEE v. Buffalo (4-1)
1937 Columbus v. NEWARK (4-3)
1938 KANSAS CITY v. Newark (4-3)
1939 LOUISVILLE v. Rochester (4-3)
1940 Louisville v. NEWARK (4-2)
1941 COLUMBUS v. Montreal (4-2)
1942 COLUMBUS v. Syracuse (4-1)
1943 COLUMBUS v. Syracuse (4-1)
1944 Louisville v. BALTIMORE (4-2)
1945 LOUISVILLE v. Newark (4-2)
1946 Louisville v. MONTREAL (4-2)
1947 MILWAUKEE v. Syracuse (4-3)
1948 St. Paul v. MONTREAL (4-1)
1949 INDIANAPOLIS v. Montreal (4-2)
1950 COLUMBUS v. Montreal (4-2)
1951 MILWAUKEE v. Montreal (4-2)
1952 Kansas City v. ROCHESTER (4-3)
1953 Kansas City v. MONTREAL (4-1)
1954 LOUISVILLE v. Syracuse (4-2)
1955 MINNEAPOLIS v. Rochester (4-3)
1956 INDIANAPOLIS v. Rochester (4-0)
1957 DENVER v. Buffalo (4-1)
1958 MINNEAPOLIS v. Montreal (4-0)
1959 Minneapolis v. HAVANA (4-3)
1960 LOUISVILLE v. Toronto (4-2)

1961 Louisville v. BUFFALO (4-0)
1962 Louisville v. ATLANTA (4-3)
1970 Omaha v. SYRACUSE (4-1)
1971 Denver v. ROCHESTER (4-3)
1973 Tulsa v. PAWTUCKET (4-1)
1975 EVANSVILLE v. Tidewater (4-1)
1988 INDIANAPOLIS v. Rochester (4-2)
1989 INDIANAPOLIS v. Richmond (4-0)
1990 OMAHA v. Rochester (4-1)
1991 Columbus v. DENVER (4-1)

PRESIDENTS OF THE AMERICAN ASSOCIATION

1902-03 Thomas J. Hickey
1904- J. Ed Grillo
1905-09 Joseph D. O'Brien
1910-16 Thomas M. Chivington
1917-34 Thomas J. Hickey
1935-44 George M. Trautman
1945-47 H. Roy Hamey
1948-52 Bruce Dudley
1953-59 Edward S. Doherty
1960-62 James Burris
1969-71 Allie Reynolds
1972-87 Joe Ryan
1988-89 Ken Grandquist
1990-91 Randy Mobley
1991- Branch Rickey III

BATTING CHAMPIONS

1902	John Ganzel, Lou.	.370
1903	Phil Geier, St. Paul	.362
1904	George Stone, Mil.	.405
1905	Charles Hemphill, St. Paul	.364
1906	Billy Hallman, Lou.	.342
1907	Jake Beckley, KC	.365
1908	John Hayden, Ind.	.316
1909	Mike O'Neill, Minn.	.296
1910	Gavvy Cravath, Minn.	.326
1911	Gavvy Cravath, Minn.	.363
1912	Art Butler, St. Paul	.329
1913	Alex Chappelle, Mil.	.349
1914	Bill Hinchman, Col.	.366
1915	Jack Lelivelt, KC	.346
1916	Beals Becker, KC	.343
1917	Beals Becker, KC	.323
1918	Doc Johnson, Mil.	.374
1919	Tim Hendryx, Lou.	.368
1920	Joseph Rapp, St. Paul	.335
1921	Jay Kirke, Lou.	.386
1922	Glenn Myatt, Mil.	.370
1923	Bill Lamar, Tol.	.391
1924	Lester Bell, Mil.	.365
1925	Ed Murphy, Col.	.397
1926	Bevo Lebourveau, Tol.	.377
1927	Reb Russell, Ind.	.385
1928	Robert Veach, Tol.	.382
1929	Art Ruble, Tol.	.376
1930	Bevo Lebourveau, Tol.	.380
1931	Art Shires, Mil.	.385
1932	Art Ruble, Minn.	.376
1933	Frank Sigafoos, Ind.	.370
1934	Earl Webb, Mil.	.368
1935	John Cooney, Ind.	.371
1936	Vernon Washington, St. Paul	.390
1937	Enos Slaughter, Col.	.382
1938	Ted Williams, Minn.	.366
1939	Gil English, St. Paul	.343
1940	Ab Wright, Minn.	.369
1941	Lou Novikoff, Mil.	.370
1942	Eddie Stanky, Mil.	.342
1943	Grey Clarke, Mil.	.346
1944	John Wyrostek, Col.	.358
1945	Lew Flick, Mil.	.374
1946	Sibbi Sisti, Ind.	.343
1947	Heinz Becker, Mil.	.363
1948	Glenn McQuillen, Tol.	.329
1949	Tom Wright, Lou.	.368
1950	Bob Addis, Mil.	.323
1951	Harry Walker, Col.	.393
1952	Dave Pope, Ind.	.352
1953	Vic Power, KC	.349
1954	Hal Smith, Col.	.350
1955	Rance Pless, Minn.	.337
1956	Charles Peete, Omaha	.350
1957	Norm Siebern, Den.	.349
1958	Gordon Windhorn, Den.	.328
1959	Luis Marquez, Dallas	.345
1960	Larry Osborne, Den.	.342
1961	Don Wert, Den.	.328

1962	Tom McCraw, Ind.	.326
1969	Bernie Carbo, Ind.	.359
1970	Chris Chambliss, Wich.	.342
1971	Richie Scheinblum, Den.	.388
1972	Gene Locklear, Ind.	.325
1973	Jim Dwyer, Tul.	.387
1974	Keith Hernandez, Tul.	.351
1975	Lamar Johnson, Den.	.336
1976	Mike Easler, Tul.	.352
1977	Jim Dwyer, Wich.	.332
1978	Dane Iorg, Sprgfld.	.371
1979	Keith Smith, Sprgfld.	.350
1980	Tim Raines, Den.	.354
1981	Mike Richardt, Wich.	.354
1982	Roy Johnson, Wich.	.367
1983	Mike Stenhouse, Wich.	.355
1984	Tom Dunbar, Ok. City	.337
1985	Scott Madison, Nash.	.341
1986	Bruce Fields, Nash.	.368
1987	Dallas Williams, Ind.	.357
1988	Lavell Freeman, Den.	.318
1989	Junior Noboa, Ind.	.340
1990	Mark Ryal, Buff.	.334
1991	James Olander, Den.	.325

HOME RUN CHAMPIONS

1902	Smith, KC	10
1903	Mike Grady, KC	16
1904	Jim Jackson, St. Paul	13
1905	Wyatt Lee, Tol.	13
1906	Ed Green, Mil.	8
1907	Buck Freeman, Minn.	18
1908	Buck Freeman, Minn.	10
	Bert James, Col.	10
1909	Bert James, Col.	7
1910	Gavvy Cravath, Minn.	14
1911	Gavvy Cravath, Minn.	29
1912	Bert James, KC	10
1913	Joe Riggert, St. Paul	12
1914	Oscar Felsh, Mil.	19
1915	Bash Compton, KC	9
	Joe Riggert, St. Paul	9
1916	Beals Becker, KC	15
1917	Beals Becker, KC	15
1918	Joe Riggert, St. Paul	6
1919	Elmer Miller, St. Paul	15
1920	Bunny Brief, KC	23
1921	Bunny Brief, KC	42
1922	Bunny Brief, KC	40
1923	Carlton East, Minn.	31
1924	Elmer Smith, Lou.	28
1925	Bunny Brief, Mil.	37
1926	Bunny Brief, Mil.	26
1927	Frank Emmer, Minn.	32
1928	Spencer Harris, Minn.	32
1929	Dusty Cooke, St. Paul	33
1930	Nick Cullop, Minn.	54
1931	Cliff Crawford, Col.	28
1932	Joe Hauser, Minn.	49
1933	Joe Hauser, Minn.	69
1934	Russ Arlett, Minn.	41
1935	John Gill, Minn.	43
1936	John Winsett, Col.	50
1937	Roy Pfleger, Minn.	29
1938	Ted Williams, Minn.	43
1939	Vince DiMaggio, KC	46
1940	Ab Wright, Minn.	39
1941	Ab Wright, Minn.	26
1942	Willis Norman, Mil.	24
1943	Ted Norbert, Mil.	25
1944	Herb Barna, Minn.	24
1945	Herb Barna, Minn.	25
1946	Jerry Witte, Tol.	46
1947	Carden Gillenwater, Mil.	23
1948	Mike Natisin, Col.	30
1949	Charles Workman, Minn.	41
1950	Lou Limmer, St. Paul	29
1951	Hal Gilbert, Minn.	29
1952	Bill Skowron, KC	31
1953	George Wilson, Minn.	34
1954	Rocky Colavito, Ind.	38
1955	Marv Throneberry, Den.	36
1956	Marv Throneberry, Den.	42
1957	Marv Throneberry, Den.	40
1958	John Callison, Ind.	29
1959	Ron Jackson, Ind.	30
1960	Larry Osborne, Den.	34
1961	Cliff Cook, Ind.	32
1962	Leo Burke, Dal.-Ft. Worth	27
1969	Dan Walton, Ok. City	35
1970	Cotton Nash, Evans.	33
1971	Bill McNulty, Iowa	27

1972	Robert Hansen, Evans.	25
1973	Cliff Johnson, Den.	33
1974	Adrian Garrett, Wich.	26
1975	Hector Cruz, Tul.	29
1976	Roger Freed, Den.	42
1977	Frank Ortenzio, Den.	40
1978	Champ Summers, Ind.	34
1979	Karl Pagel, Wich.	39
1980	Randy Bass, Den.	37
1981	George Bjorkman, Sprgfld.	28
1982	Ken Phelps, Wich.	46
1983	Carmelo Martinez, Iowa	31
1984	Joe Hicks, Iowa	37
1985	Dave Hostetler, Ind.-Iowa	29
1986	Lloyd McClendon, Den.	24
1987	Brad Komminsk, Den.	32
1988	Van Snider, Nash.	23
1989	Greg Vaughn, Den.	26
1990	Juan Gonzalez, Nash.	29
1991	Dean Palmer, Ok. City	22

RBI LEADERS

1920	Bunny Brief, KC	120
1921	Bunny Brief, KC	191
1922	Bunny Brief, KC	151
1923.	Bunny Brief, KC	164
1924	Charley Dressen, St. Paul	151
1925	Bunny Brief, Mil.	175
1926	Pat Duncan, Minn.	123
1927	Robert Veach, Tol.	145
1928	Dud Branom, Lou.	128
1929	Dusty Cooke, St. Paul	148
1930	Nick Cullop, Minn.	152
1931	Cliff Crawford, Col.	154
1932	Babe Ganzel, Minn.	143
1933	Joe Hauser, Minn.	182
1934	Jack Kloza, Mil.	148
1935	John Gill, Minn.	154
1936	John Winsett, Col.	154
1937	Ralph Kress, Minn.	157
1938	Ted Williams, Minn.	142
1939	Vince DiMaggio, KC	136
1940	Ab Wright, Minn.	159
1941	Bert Haas, Col.	131
1942	John McCarthy, Ind.	113
1943	Ted Norbert, Mil.	117
1944	Nick Polly, Lou.	120
1945	Gene Nance, Mil.	106
1946	John McCarthy, Minn.	122
1947	Cliff Mapes, KC	117
1948	Les Fleming, Ind.	143
1949	Froilan Fernandez, Ind.	128
1950	Lou Limmer, St. Paul	111
1951	George Crowe, Mil.	119
1952	Bill Skowron, KC	134
1953	Wally Post, Ind.	120
1954	George Crowe, Tol.	128
1955	Marv Throneberry, Den.	117
1956	Marv Throneberry, Den.	145
1957	Marv Throneberry, Den.	124
1958	Earl Hersh, Wich.	98
1959	Ron Jackson, Ind.	99
1960	Larry Osborne, Den.	119
	Steve Boros, Den.	119
1961	Cliff Cook, Ind.	119
1962	Jim Koranda, Ind.	103
1969	Dan Walton, Ok. City	119
1970	Dick Scheinblum, Wich.	84
1971	Dick Scheinblum, Den.	108
1972	Roe Skidmore, Ind.	89
1973	Cliff Johnson, Den.	117
1974	Lamar Johnson, Iowa	96
1975	Hector Cruz, Tul.	116
1976	Roger Freed, Den.	102
1977	Frank Ortenzio, Den.	126
1978	Champ Summers, Ind.	124
1979	Karl Pagel, Wich.	123
1980	Randy Bass, Den.	143
1981	Dan Briggs, Den.	110
1982	Ken Phelps, Wich.	141
1983	James Adduci, Lou.	101
1984	Alan Knicely, Wich.	126
1985	Dave Hostetler, Ind.-Iowa	89
1986	Jim Lindeman, Lou.	96
1987	Wade Rowdon, Iowa	113
1988	Luis delos Santos, Omaha	87
	German Rivera, Den.	87
1989	Greg Vaughn, Den.	92
1990	Juan Gonzalez, Nash.	101
1991	Tim McIntosh, Den.	91

STOLEN BASE LEADERS

1902	Billy Hallman, Mil.	46
1903	Fox, Ind.	52
1904	Jim Jackson, St. Paul	59
1905	George Moriarty, Tol.	51
1906	Billy Hallman, Lou.	54
1907	Josh Clarke, Tol.	54
1908	Otto Williams, Ind.	38
1909	Warren Gill, Minn.	41
1910	Dave Altizer, Minn.	65
1911	Warren Gill, Minn.	55
1912	Dave Altizer, Minn.	68
1913	Bert Niehoff, Lou.	48
1914	Bash Compton, KC	58
1915	Joe Kelly, Ind.	61
1916	Jim Thorpe, Mil.	48
1917	Lee Dressen, St. Paul	55
1918	Joe Riggert, St. Paul	20
	Bob Bescher, Lou.	20
	Art Butler, St. Paul	20
1919	Lee Dressen, St. Paul	46
1920	Lee Dressen, St. Paul	50
1921	Doug Baird, Ind.	72
1922	Doug Baird, Ind.	29
1923	James Cooney, Mil.	60
1924	Johnny Neun, St. Paul	55
1925	Walt Christensen, St. Paul	49
1926	Lance Richbourg, Mil.	48
1927	Norm McMillan, St. Paul	43
1928	Fred Haney, Ind.	43
1929	Frank Emmer, Minn.	36
1930	Herman Layne, Lou.	40
1931	Jack Saltzgaver, St. Paul	26
1932	Evar Swanson, Col.	45
1933	James Adair, Lou.	33
1934	Melo Almada, KC	29
1935	Fred Haney, Tol.	29
1936	Don Gutteridge, Col.	36
	Bernie Uhalt, Mil.	36
1937	Lynn King, Col.	28
1938	Lynn King, Col.	30
1939	Pee Wee Reese, Lou.	35
1940	Phil Rizzuto, KC	35
1941	Herb Barna, Minn.	29
1942	George Myatt, Col.	32
1943	Herman Clifton, Minn.	16
1944	James Cookson, Minn.	47
1945	Frank Danneker, Minn.	50
1946	John Welaj, Lou.	37
1947	Charles Harrington, Col.	27
1948	Jack Cassini, Ind.	33
1949	Henry Schenz, St. Paul	30
1950	Jack Cassini, St. Paul	36
1951	Rudolph Rufer, Minn.	54
1952	Jack Cassini, St. Paul	35
1953	Donald Nicholas, Charl.	41
1954	Gale Wade, Ind.	24
1955	Leonard Johnston, Charl.	25
1956	Larry Raines, Ind.	22
1957	Curtis Roberts, Den.	23
1958	Wayne Terwilliger, Charl.	24
1959	Ellis Burton, Omaha	18
	Rod Kanehl, Hous.	18
1960	Dave Mann, Minn.	50
1961	Hiraldo Ruiz, Ind.	44
1962	Albert Weis, Ind.	31
1969	George Spriggs, Omaha	46
1970	George Spriggs, Omaha	29
1971	Wilbur Howard, Evans.	42
1972	Cleo James, Wich.	39
1973	Ken Griffey, Ind.	43
1974	Duane Kuiper, Ok. City	28
1975	Jerry Mumphrey, Tul.	44
1976	Richard Bosetti, Ok. City	42
1977	Willie Wilson, Omaha	74
1978	Lonnie Smith, Ok. City	66
1979	German Barranca, Omaha	75
1980	Tim Raines, Den.	77
1981	Robert Dernier, Ok. City	72
1982	Gary Redus, Ind.	54
1983	Tom Lawless, Ind.	46
1984	Vincent Coleman, Lou.	101
1985	Curtis Ford, Lou.	45
1986	Dwight Taylor, Omaha	67
1987	Gary Thurman, Omaha	58
1988	Lenny Harris, Nash.	45
1989	Alex Cole, Lou.	47
1990	Cedric Landrum, Iowa	46
1991	Jacob Brumfield, Oma.	36

PITCHERS
— MOST VICTORIES —

Year	Pitcher	Wins
1902	Ed Dunkle, Lou.	30
1903	Tom Walker, Lou.	26
1904	Charles Chech, St. Paul	27
1905	Gus Dorner, Col.	29
1906	Charles Berger, Col.	28
1907	George Upp, Col.	27
1908	Rube Marquard, Ind.	28
1909	Stony McGlynn, Mil.	27
1910	Tom Hughes, Minn.	31
1911	Roy Patterson, Minn.	24
1912	Fred Olmstead, Minn.	28
1913	Cy Slapnicka, Mil.	25
1914	Mel Gallia, KC	26
	George Northrup, Lou.	26
1915	Mutt Williams, Minn.	29
1916	Earl Yingling, Minn.	24
1917	Frank Davis, Lou.	25
	Grover Lowdermilk, Col.	25
1918	Dickie Kerr, Mil.	17
1919	Tiller Cavet, Ind.	28
1920	Charles Hall, St. Paul	27
1921	Adlai Bono, KC	25
	Dave Danforth, Col.	25
1922	Tom Sheehan, St. Paul	26
1923	Tom Sheehan, St. Paul	31
1924	Jesse Petty, Ind.	29
1925	Bill Burwell, Ind.	24
1926	George Pipgras, St. Paul	22
1927	Tom Sheehan, KC	26
1928	James Wingard, Mil.	24
1929	Americo Polli, St. Paul	22
1930	Wilcey Moore, St. Paul	22
1931	Frank Henry, Minn.	23
1932	Russ Van Atta, St. Paul	22
	Rosy Ryan, Minn.	22
1933	Paul Dean, Col.	22
1934	Wally Tauscher, Minn.	21
1935	Mike Ryba, Col.	20
1936	Lou Fette, St. Paul	25
1937	Max Macon, Col.	21
1938	Whitlow Wyatt, Mil.	23
1939	Herb Hash, Minn.	22
1940	Robert Logan, Ind.	18
	John Lindell, KC	18
1941	Murry Dickson, Col.	21
1942	Charles Wensloff, KC	21
1943	James Trexler, Ind.	19
1944	James Wilson, Lou.	19
	Earl Caldwell, Mil.	19
1945	Owen Sheetz, Mil.	19
1946	Fred Sanford, Tol.	15
	Harry Taylor, St. Paul	15
	Ewald Pyle, Mil.	15
1947	Clem Dreisewerd, Lou.	18
1948	Robert Malloy, Ind.	21
1949	Mel Queen, Ind.	22
	Phil Haugstad, St. Paul	22
1950	Harvey Haddix, Col.	18
1951	James Atkins, Lou.	18
1952	Edward Erautt, KC	21
1953	Gene Conley, Tol.	23
1954	Herb Score, Ind.	22
1955	Al Worthington, Minn.	19
1956	Curtis Barclay, Minn.	15
	Stan Pitula, Ind.	15
1957	Carlton Willey, Wich.	21
1958	John Gabler, Den.	19
1959	Georges Maranda, Lou.	18
	Don Nottebart, Lou.	18
1960	Jim Golden, St. Paul	20
1961	Don Rudolph, Ind.	18
1962	Nick Willhite, Omaha	18
1969	Sal Campisi, Tul.	13
	Jerry Reuss, Tul.	13
1970	Francisco Carlos, Den.	13
1971	Richard Estelle, Evans.	13
1972	Lloyd Gladden, Evans.	15
1973	Mark Littell, Omaha	16
1974	James Kern, Ok. City	17
1975	Steve Dunning, Den.	15
1976	Joe Keener, Den.	14
	John Montague, Ok. City	14
1977	Gary Lance, Omaha	16
1978	Sheldon Burnside, Evans.	14
	William Paschall, Omaha	14
1979	Dewey Robinson, Iowa	13
1980	Steve Ratzer, Den.	15
1981	Bryn Smith, Den.	15
1982	Ralph Citarella, Lou.	15
1983	Fernando Arroyo, Den.	14
1984	Reggie Patterson, Iowa	14
1985	Bill Long, Buff.	13
1986	Pete Filson, Buff.	14
1987	Bill Taylor, Ok. City	12

1988	Dave Johnson, Buff.	15		Jack Armstrong, Nash.	13
1989	Kevin Blankenship, Iowa	13	1990	Chris Hammond, Nash.	15
	Steve Fireovid, Omaha	13	1991	Richard Reed, Buff.	14

PITCHERS
— WINNING PERCENTAGE —

1902	Ed Dunkle, Lou.	30-10	.750
1903	Tom Walker, Lou.	26-7	.788
1904	Charles Chech, St. Paul	27-8	.771
1905	Gus Dorner, Col.	29-8	.784
1906	Pat Flaherty, Col.	23-9	.719
1907	George Upp, Col.	27-10	.730
1908	Lou Durham, Ind.-Lou.	19-7	.731
1909	Fred Olmstead, Minn.	24-12	.667
1910	Tom Hughes, Minn.	31-12	.721
1911	Rube Peters, Minn.	11-3	.786
1912	Hal Krause, Tol.	13-4	.760
1913	George McQuillen, Col.	12-4	.750
1914	Sam Jones, Clev.	10-4	.714
1915	Booth Hopper, Minn.	18-3	.857
1916	Paul Carter, Ind.	15-4	.789
1917	Frank Davis, Lou.	25-11	.694
1918	Dolph Luque, Lou.	11-2	.847
1919	Jesse Haines, KC	21-5	.808
1920	Sea Lion Hall, St. Paul	27-8	.771
1921	Ernest Koob, Lou.	22-9	.710
1922	Jimmy Zinn, KC	18-5	.783
1923	Jimmy Zinn, KC	27-6	.818
1924	Jesse Petty, Ind.	29-8	.874
1925	Ed Holley, Lou.	20-7	.741
1926	Nick Cullop, Lou.	20-8	.714
1927	Ossie Orwoll, Mil.	17-6	.739
1928	Ad Liska, Minn.	20-4	.833
1929	Arch Campbell, St. Paul	15-3	.833
1930	Ben Tincup, Lou.	14-3	.824
1931	Russ Van Atta, St. Paul	13-5	.722
1932	Roy Parmelee, Col.	14-1	.933
1933	Clarence Heise, Col.	17-5	.773
1934	Wally Tauscher, Minn.	21-7	.750
1935	Wilcey Moore, KC	15-5	.750
1936	Lou Fette, St. Paul	25-8	.758
1937	Bill McGee, Col.	17-7	.708
1938	Whitlow Wyatt, Mil.	23-7	.767
1939	Tom Reis, KC	17-4	.810
1940	Ernie White, Col.	13-4	.765
1941	John Grodzicki, Col.	19-5	.792
1942	Herb Karpel, KC	11-1	.917
1943	Jim Trexler, Ind.	19-7	.731

1944	Earl Caldwell, Mil.	19-5	.792
1945	James Wallace, Ind.	17-4	.810
1946	Earl Reid, Ind.	10-2	.833
1947	Steve Gerkin, Minn.	10-2	.833
1948	John Hutchings, Ind.	10-2	.833
1949	Royce Lint, Ind.	14-3	.824
1950	Dave Barnhill, Minn.	11-3	.786
1951	Ernie Johnson, Mil.	15-4	.789
1952	Don Liddle, Mil.	17-4	.810
1953	Melvin Wright, KC	13-2	.867
1954	Herb Score, Ind.	22-5	.815
1955	Hum Robinson, Tol.	14-4	.778
1956	Bud Daley, Ind.	11-1	.917
1957	Ryne Duren, Den.	13-2	.867
1958	Zack Monroe, Den.	10-2	.833
1959	Robert Hartman, Lou.	10-3	.769
1960	Don Nottebart, Lou.	13-5	.722
1961	Don Rudolph, Ind.	18-9	.667
1962	Al Worthington, Ind.	15-4	.789
1969	Sal Campisi, Tul.	13-2	.867
1970	Vida Blue, Iowa	12-3	.800
1971	Dave Hamilton, Iowa	12-4	.750
	Aurelio Monteagudo, Omaha	12-4	.750
1972	James Slaton, Evans.	11-2	.846
1973	Ken Frailing, Iowa	11-3	.786
	Gary Ryerson, Evans.	11-3	.786
1974	Wayne Granger, Iowa	10-3	.769
1975	Steve Grilli, Evans.	11-4	.733
	Pete Vuckovich, Den.	11-4	.733
1976	Gerald Cram, Omaha	11-3	.786
1977	Dennis Lamp, Wich.	11-4	.733
1978	Kip Young, Evans.	11-3	.786
1979	Gary Beare, Ok. City	12-1	.923
1980	Steve Ratzer, Den.	15-4	.789
1981	Bryn Smith, Den.	15-5	.750
1982	Jay Howell, Iowa	13-4	.765
1983	Fernando Arroyo, Den.	14-4	.778
1984	Joe Hesketh, Ind.	12-3	.800
1985	Freddie Toliver, Den.	11-3	.786
1986	Greg Maddux, Iowa	10-1	.909
1987	Tim Barrett, Ind.	10-1	.909
1988	Bob Sebra, Ind.	12-6	.667
	Bill Swaggerty, Omaha	10-5	.667
1989	Mark Gardner, Ind.	12-4	.750
	Urbano Lugo, Ind.	12-4	.750
1990	Chris Hammond, Nash.	15-1	.938
1991	Rick Reed, Buffalo		.778

PITCHERS
— MOST STRIKEOUTS —

Year	Player	SO
1902	No record	
1903	Claude Elliott, Mil.	226
1904	Clifton Curtis, Mil.	210
1905	Charles Berger, Col.	200
1906	Charles Berger, Col.	264
1907	Ambrose Puttman, Lou.	174
1908	Rube Marquard, Ind.	250
1909	Stony McGlynn, Mil.	183
1910	Tom Hughes, Minn.	222
1911	Martin O'Toole, St. Paul	199
1912	William Powell, KC	174
1913	Grover Lowdermilk, Lou.	197
1914	Grover Lowdermilk, Lou.	254
1915	Robert Steele, St. Paul	183
1916	Cy Falkenberg, Ind.	178
1917	Grover Lowdermilk, Col.	250
1918	Dick Kerr, Mil.	99
1919	Frank Davis, Lou.	165
1920	Dave Danforth, Col.	188
1921	Dave Danforth, Col.	204
1922	Joe Giard, Tol.	141
1923	Cliff Markle, St. Paul	184
1924	Rube Walberg, Mil.	175
1925	Robert McGraw, Minn.	141
1926	George Pipgras, St. Paul	156
1927	Pat Malone, Minn.	214
1928	Claude Jonnard, Mil.	150
1929	John Brillheart, Minn.	134
1930	Phil Weinert, Lou.	132
1931	Claude Jonnard, Mil.	130
1932	Paul Dean, Col.	169
1933	Paul Dean, Col.	222
1934	Stewart Bolen, Ind.	177
1935	Jack Tising, Lou.	230
1936	Clyde Hatter, Mil.	190
1937	Jack Tising, Lou.	174
1938	Whitlow Wyatt, Mil.	208
1939	Max Lanier, Col.	148
1940	Frank Melton, Col.	142
1941	Murry Dickson, Col.	153
1942	Harry Brecheen, Col.	156
1943	Elwin Roe, Col.	136
1944	James Wilson, Lou.	147
1945	Cliff Fannin, Tol.	126
1946	Fred Sanford, Tol.	154
1947	Phil Haugstad, St. Paul	145
1948	John McCall, Lou.	149
1949	Mel Queen, Ind.	178
1950	Harvey Haddix, Col.	160
1951	Robert Wiesler, KC	162
1952	Don Liddle, Mil.	159
1953	Gene Conley, Tol.	211
1954	Herb Score, Ind.	330
1955	Jerry Casale, Lou.	186
1956	Ted Abernathy, Lou.	212
1957	Stan Williams, St. Paul	223
1958	Robert Baylock, Omaha	193
1959	Robert Bruce, Charl.	177
1960	Dick Tomanek, DFW	172
1961	Charley Spell, Omaha	164
1962	Freddy Olivo, Lou.	151
1969	Jerry Reuss, Tul.	151
1970	Vida Blue, Iowa	165
1971	J. R. Richard, Ok. City	202
1972	Steve Busby, Omaha	221
1973	Lowell Palmer, Ok. City	203
1974	James Kern, Ok. City	220
1975	Steve Dunning, Den.	139
1976	Randy Lerch, Ok. City	152
1977	Larry Landreth, Den.	134
1978	Dan Warthen, Ok. City	144
1979	Bruce Berenyi, Ind.	136
1980	Bruce Berenyi, Ind.	121
1981	Dave LaPoint, Sprgfld.	129
1982	Michael Smithson, Den.	144
1983	Greg Harris, Ind.	146
1984	Tom Browning, Wich.	160
1985	Todd Worrell, Lou.	126
1986	Jack Lazorko, Nash.	119
1987	Sergio Valdez, Ind.	128
1988	Norm Charlton, Nash.	161
1989	Mark Gardner, Ind.	175
1990	Chris Hammond, Nash.	149
1991	Calvin Eldred, Den.	168

PITCHERS
— LOWEST EARNED RUN AVERAGE —

Year	Pitcher	ERA
1914	W. A. James, Clev.	2.35
1915	Earl Yingling, Minn.	2.17
1916	Paul Carter, Ind.	1.65
1917	Grover Lowdermilk, Col.	1.70
1918	George Merritt, St. Paul	1.50
	Gene Dale, Ind.	1.50
1919	Roy Wilkinson, Col.	2.09
1920	Charles Hall, St. Paul	2.06
1921	Dave Danforth, Col.	2.66
1922	Tom Sheehan, St. Paul	3.01
1923	Tom Sheehan, St. Paul	2.90
1924	Jesse Petty, Ind.	2.83
1925	Bill Burwell, Ind.	2.73
1926	Ernest Maun, Tol.	2.71
1927	Jimmy Zinn, KC	3.08
1928	Lefty Heimach, St. Paul	2.76
1929	Archie Campbell, St. Paul	2.79
1930	Hugh McQuillan, Tol.	3.33
1931	John Cooney, Tol.	2.49
1932	No record	
1933	Paul Dean, Col.	3.15
1934	Jim Elliott, Col.	3.27
1935	Clyde Hatter, Mil.	2.88
1936	Bill McGee, Col.	2.93
1937	Bill McGee, Col.	2.97
1938	Whitlow Wyatt, Mil.	2.37
1939	Marv Breuer, KC	2.28
1940	Ernest White, Col.	2.25
1941	Emerson Dickman, Lou.	1.94
1942	Harry Brecheen, Col.	2.09
1943	Jim Trexler, Ind.	2.14
1944	Arthur Herring, St. Paul	2.18
1945	James Wallace, Ind.	1.83
1946	Emerson Roser, Ind.	1.73
1947	Clem Dreisewerd, Lou.	2.15
1948	Ira Hutchinson, Col.	2.54
1949	Mel Queen, Ind.	2.57
1950	Harvey Haddix, Col.	2.70
1951	Ernie Johnson, Mil.	2.62
1952	Don Liddle, Mil.	2.70
1953	Gene Conley, Tol.	2.90
1954	Herb Score, Ind.	2.62
1955	Willard Schmidt, Omaha	2.56
1956	John Gray, Ind.	2.72
1957	Frank Barnes, Omaha	2.41
1958	Jerry Davie, Charl.	2.45
1959	Marion Fricano, Dallas	2.02
1960	Jim Golden, St. Paul	2.32
1961	Freddy Olivo, Lou.	2.66
1962	Conrad Grob, Lou.	2.86
1969	Ron Cook, Ok. City	3.11
1970	Ross Grimsley, Ind.	2.73
1971	J. R. Richard, Ok. City	2.45
1972	Joe Decker, Wich.	2.27
1973	Mark Littell, Omaha	2.51
1974	Ray Bare, Tul.	2.34
1975	Pat Zachry, Ind.	2.44
1976	Joe Henderson, Ind.	2.31
1977	John Kucek, Iowa	2.54
1978	John Kucek, Iowa	2.47
1979	Bruce Berenyi, Ind.	2.82
1980	Alan Olmsted, Sprgfld.	2.77
1981	Larry Pashnick, Evans.	2.89
1982	Jay Howell, Iowa	2.36
1983	Craig Eaton, Evans.	2.64
1984	Chris Welsh, Ind.	3.01
1985	Steve Farr, Omaha	2.02
1986	Pete Filson, Buff.	2.27
1987	Pascual Perez, Ind.	3.79
1988	Dorn Taylor, Buff.	2.14
1989	Rich Thompson, Ind.	2.06
1990	Chris Hammond, Nash.	2.17
1991	Richard Reed, Buff.	2.15

MOST VALUABLE PLAYERS

Through the years a "Most Valuable Player" sometimes was selected. In 1932, for example, 10 sportswriters were asked to determine an MVP by points. The points were "widely scattered" among 32 players, but Columbus first baseman Pat Crawford (.369, 30 HR, 140 RBI) was awarded the trophy. Another slugging first sacker, Rudy York of Milwaukee (.334, 21 3B, 37 HR, 148 RBI), was a more popular choice in 1936. Finally, in 1946, an official Most Valuable Player designation — now called the Mickey Mantle Award — was instituted:

1946 Jerry Witte, 1B, Tol.
1947 Steve Gerkin, P, Minn.
1948 Les Fleming, 1B, Ind.
1949 Froilan Fernandez, 3B, Ind.
1950 Ray Dandridge, 3B, Ind.
1951 Al Unser, C, Mil.
1952 Don Bollweg, 1B, KC
1953 Gene Conley, P, Tol.
1954 Herb Score, P, Ind.
1955 Rance Pless, 3B, Minn.
1956 Marv Throneberry, 1B, Den.
1957 Carlton Willey, P, Wich.
1958 Wayne Terwilliger, 2B, Charl.
1959 Bob Will, OF, Ft. Worth
1960 Steve Boros, 3B, Den.
1961 Cliff Cook, 3B, Ind.
1962 Jack Smith, P, Omaha
1969 Bernie Carbo, RF, Ind.
1970 George Spriggs, OF, Omaha
1971 Richard Scheinblum, OF, Den.
1972 Pat Bourgue, 1B, Wich.
1973 Cliff Johnson, DH, Den.
1974 Ralph LaCock, 1B, Wich.
1975 Hector Cruz, 3B, Tul.
1976 Roger Freed, 1B, Den.
1977 Frank Ortenzio, 1B, Den.
1978 Champ Summers, OF, Ind.
1979 Karl Pagel, OF, Wich.
1980 Randy Bass, 1B, Den.
1981 Manny Castillo, 3B, Omaha
1982 Ken Phelps, 1B, Wich.
1983 Mike Stenhouse, 1B, Wich.
1984 Alan Knicely, 1B, Wich.
1985 Steve Buechele, 3B, Ok. City
1986 Barry Larkin, SS, Den.
1987 Lance Johnson, OF, Lou.
1988 Luis De Los Santos, 1B, Omaha
1989 Greg Vaughn, OF, Den.
1990 Juan Gonzalez, OF, Ok. City
1991 Jim Olander, OF, Den.

THE SPORTING NEWS MINOR LEAGUE PLAYERS OF THE YEAR

1940 Phil Rizzuto, SS, KC
1946 Sibby Sisti, SS, Indianapolis
1952 Bill Skowron, 1B, KC
1953 Gene Conley, P, Toledo
1954 Herb Score, P, Indianapolis
1957 Norm Siebern, OF, Denver
1969 Dan Walton, OF, Okla. City
1975 Hector Cruz, 3B, Tulsa
1978 Champ Summers, OF, Indianapolis
1980 Tim Raines, 2B, Denver
1984 Alan Knicely, 1B, Wichita
1988 Gary Sheffield, 3B, Denver (Co-player with Sandy Alomar, Jr., of Las Vegas)

PITCHERS OF THE YEAR (ALLIE REYNOLDS AWARD)

1969 Sal Campisi, Tulsa
1970 Milt Wilcox, Indianapolis
1971 Garland Shifflet, Denver
1972 Lloyd Gladden, Evansville
1973 Mark Littell, Omaha
1974 James Kern, Okla. City
1975 Steve Dunning, Denver
1976 John Montague, Okla. City
1977 Jim Wright, Okla. City
1978 Dan Warthen, Okla. City
1979 Dewey Robinson, Iowa
1980 Steve Ratzer, Denver

1981 Bryn Smith, Denver
1982 Jay Howell, Iowa
1983 Rich Barnes, Denver
1984 Joe Hesketh, Indianapolis
1985 Mark Huismann, Omaha
1986 Pete Filson, Buffalo
1987 Pascual Perez, Indianapolis
1988 Bob Sebra, Indianapolis
1989 Mark Gardner, Indianapolis
1990 Chris Hammond, Nashville
1991 Rick Reed, Buffalo

MANAGERS OF THE YEAR (CASEY STENGEL AWARD)

1953 George Selkirk, Toledo
1954 Kerby Farrell, Indianapolis
1955 Bill Rigney, Minneapolis
1956 Kerby Farrell, Indianapolis
1957 Ben Geraghty, Wichita
1958 Gene Mauch, Minneapolis
1959 Gene Mauch, Minneapolis
1960 Bill Adair, Louisville
1961 Cot Deal, Indianapolis
1962 Luke Appling, Indianapolis
Danny Ozark, Omaha
1969 Jack McKeon, Omaha
1970 Jack McKeon, Omaha
1971 Vern Rapp, Indianaplois
1972 James Marshall, Wichita
1973 Joe Sparks, Iowa
1974 Vern Rapp, Indianapolis
1975 Fred Hatfield, Evansville
1976 Vern Rapp, Denver
1977 James Marshall, Denver
1978 Les Moss, Evansville
1979 Jim Leyland, Evansville
1980 Billy Gardner, Denver
1981 Joe Sparks, Omaha
1982 Jim Napier, Iowa
1983 Jim Fregosi, Louisville
1984 Buck Rodgers, Indianapolis
1985 Dave Oliver, Okla. City
1986 Joe Sparks, Indianapolis
1987 Joe Sparks, Indianapolis
1988 Joe Sparks, Indianapolis
1989 Tom Runnels, Indianapolis
1990 Sal Rende, Omaha
1991 Tony Muser, Denver

THE SPORTING NEWS MINOR LEAGUE MANAGERS OF THE YEAR

1936 Al Sothoron, Milwaukee
1939 Bill Meyer, Kansas City
1941 Burt Shotton, Columbus
1942 Eddie Dyer, Columbus
1943 Nick Cullop, Columbus
1947 Nick Cullop, Milwaukee
1950 Rollie Hemsley, Columbus
1951 Charley Grimm, Milwaukee
1954 Kerby Farrell, Indianapolis
1955 Bill Rigney, Minneapolis
1956 Kerby Farrell, Indianapolis
1957 Ben Geraghty, Wichita
1976 Vern Rapp, Denver
1978 Les Moss, Evansville
1980 Hal Lanier, Springfield
1982 George Scherger, Indianapolis
1984 Buck Rodgers, Indianapolis
1985 Jim Fregosi, Louisville
1988 Joe Sparks, Indianapolis

AMERICAN ASSOCIATION HALL OF FAMERS
(Hall of Famers Who Have Played, Managed, Or Umpired in the American Association)

Luke Appling (Mgr. — Indianapolis, 1962)
Dave Bancroft (Mgr. — Minneapolis, 1933)
Jake Beckley (KC, 1907–09)

Roger Bresnahan (Toledo, 1916–18; Mgr. and owner — Toledo, 1916–23)
Mordecai Brown (Columbus, 1917–18; Indianapolis, 1919)
Roy Campanella (St. Paul, 1948)
Jimmy Collins (Player-mgr. — Minneapolis, 1909)
Earle Combs (Louisville, 1922–23)
Jocko Conlon (Toledo, 1930; umpire, 1938–40)
Joe Cronin (KC, 1928)
Ray Dandridge (St. Paul, 1949–50)
Hugh Duffy (Mgr. — Milwaukee, 1912)
Red Faber (Minneapolis, 1911)
Elmer Flick (Toledo, 1911–12)
Whitey Ford (KC, 1950)
Bob Gibson (Omaha, 1957–59)
Lefty Gomez (St. Paul, 1930)
Burleigh Grimes (Mgr. — Louisville, 1936)
Jesse Haines (KC, 1919)
Gabby Hartnett (Player-mgr. — Indianapolis, 1942)
Billy Herman (Louisville, 1928–31; player-mgr. — Minn., 1948)
Miller Huggins (St. Paul, 1902–03)
Monte Irvin (Minneapolis, 1955)
George Kelly (Minneapolis, 1930–31)
Harmon Killebrew (Indianapolis, 1958)
Bill Klem (Umpire — 1904)
Nap Lajoie (Player-mgr. — Indianapolis, 1918)
Fred Lindstrom (Toledo, 1922–23)
Al Lopez (Toledo — 1948; mgr. — Toledo, 1948–50)
Mickey Mantle (KC, 1951)
Rube Marquard (Indianapolis, 1908)
Eddie Mathews (Milwaukee, 1951)
Willie Mays (Minneapolis, 1951)
Joe McCarthy (Toledo, 1908–11; Louisville, 1916–21; mgr. — Louisville, 1919–25)
Bill McKechnie (St. Paul, 1912–13; Minneapolis, 1921)
Roger Peckinpaugh (Mgr. — KC, 1934)
Ray Schalk (Milwaukee, 1911–12)
Al Simmons (Milwaukee, 1922–23)
Duke Snider (St. Paul, 1947)
Warren Spahn (Mgr. — Tulsa, 1967–68)
Casey Stengel (Player-mgr. — Toledo, 1926–31; mgr. — Milwaukee, 1944, and KC, 1945)
Bill Terry (Toledo, 1922–23)
Bert Tinker (Player-mgr. and president — Columbus, 1917–18)
Dazzy Vance (Columbus, 1916; Toledo, 1917)
Rube Waddell (Minneapolis, 1911–12)
Ed Walsh (Milwaukee, 1919)
Zack Wheat (Minneapolis, 1928)
Billy Williams (Fort Worth, 1959; Houston, 1960)
Ted Williams (Minneapolis, 1938)
Hack Wilson (Toledo, 1925)
Early Wynn (Mgr. — Evansville, 1970)

Carl Yastrzemski (Minneapolis, 1959–60)

LIFETIME RECORDS

BEST LIFETIME HITTING RECORDS

Years	Robert Logan	16
Games	Harry Clark	1,834
Average	Bevo LeBourveau	.360
Runs	Bunny Brief	1,342
Hits	Bunny Brief	2,196
Doubles	Bunny Brief	458
Triples	Joe Riggert	161
Home Runs	Bunny Brief	276
RBIs	Bunny Brief	1,451 +
Stolen Bases	Alex Reilly	330

BEST LIFETIME PITCHING RECORDS

Years	George Northrop	14
Games	Walt Tauscher	527
Victories	George Northrop	222
Losses	George Northrop	186
Strikeouts	George Northrop	1,176

SEASON RECORDS

INDIVIDUAL SEASON BATTING RECORDS

Average	George Stone (Milwaukee, 1904)	.405
Runs	Joe Mowry (Minneapolis, 1932)	175
Hits	Jay Kirke (Louisville, 1921)	282
Doubles	Bill Knickerbocker (Toledo, 1932)	69
Triples	Lance Richbourg (Milwaukee, 1928)	28
Home Runs	Joe Hauser (Minneapolis, 1933)	69
Total Bases	Joe Hauser (Minneapolis, 1933)	439
RBIs	Bunny Brief (Kansas City, 1921)	191
Hitting Streak	Eddie Marshall (Milwaukee, 1935)	43
(Games)	Howie Bedell (Louisville, 1961)	43
Consecutive Hits	Stan Bordagaray (Kansas City, 1940)	13
Stolen Bases	Vince Coleman (Louisville, 1944)	101
Walks	Nick Polly (Louisville, 1944)	147
Strikeouts	Jim McDaniel (Denver, 1961)	174
Fewest Strikeouts	Bill Conroy (Minneapolis, 1921)	4
	Richard Ferrell (Columbus, 1928)	4

INDIVIDUAL SEASON PITCHING RECORDS

Games	George Spencer (Charleston, 1959)	85
Victories	Tom Hughes (Minneapolis, 1910)	31
	Tom Hughes (St.Paul, 1923)	31
Losses	E. G. Erickson (Minneapolis, 1923)	25
Winning Pcg.	Roy Parmelee (Columbus, 1932, 14-1)	.933
Lowest ERA	Paul Carter (Indianapolis, 1916)	1.65
Most Innings	Stony McGlynn (Milwaukee, 1909)	446
Shutouts	Stony McGlynn (Milwaukee, 1909)	14
Consecutive Wins	Charley Hall (St. Paul, 1915)	16
Strikeouts	Herb Score (Indianapolis, 1954)	330
Walks	Harry Weaver (Indianapolis, 1922)	173
Most HBP	Frank Schnieberg (Milwaukee, 1907)	34
Most Wild Pitches	Roy Parmelee (Minneapolis, 1938)	22
	Wayne Simpson (Indianapolis, 1969)	22

CENTURY CLUB

	Winners			**Losers**	
1920	St. Paul	115-49	1926	Columbus	39-125
1923	Kansas City	112-54	1923	Toledo	54-114
1929	Kansas City	111-56	1912	Indianapolis	56-111
1923	St. Paul	111-57	1914	St. Paul	56-111
1922	St. Paul	107-60	1944	Kansas City	41-110
1910	Minneapolis	107-61	1916	Milwaukee	54-110
1939	Kansas City	107-47	1904	Toledo	42-109
1925	Louisville	106-61	1927	Columbus	60-108
1926	Louisville	105-62	1952	Charleston-Toledo	46-107
1931	St. Paul	104-63	1939	Toledo	47-107
1929	St. Paul	102-64	1920	Kansas City	60-106
1944	Milwaukee	102-51	1925	Columbus	61-106
1905	Columbus	102-53	1928	Louisville	62-106
1933	Columbus	101-52	1957	Louisville	49-105
1952	Milwaukee	101-53	1908	St. Paul	48-104
1916	Louisville	101-66	1955	Charleston	50-104
1927	Toledo	101-67	1959	Houston	58-104
1948	Indianapolis	100-67	1910	Louisville	60-103
1913	Milwaukee	100-67	1927	Louisville	64-103
1932	Minneapolis	100-68	1905	Kansas City	45-102
			1922	Columbus	63-102
			1951	Columbus	53-101
			1922	Toledo	65-101
			1912	Louisville	66-101
			1911	Louisville	67-101
			1932	Louisville	67-101
			1938	Louisville	53-100
			1929	Toledo	67-100
			1931	Toledo	68-100
			1928	Columbus	68-100

1990 Wrapup Features Triple Crown Pitcher

The American Association opened the '90s with a Triple Crown pitching performance by Nashville southpaw Chris Hammond. The 23-year-old Hammond, who starred for Double-A Chattanooga in 1988 (16–5 with a 1.72 ERA), was brilliant in his second year at the Triple-A level. Hammond led the 1990 AA in victories, winning percentage, strikeouts, ERA and shutouts (15–1, .938, 149 Ks in 149 IP, 2.17 ERA, 3 shutouts). The league's best reliever was Louisville righthander Mike Perez, who recorded 31 saves in 57 appearances. Omaha lefty Gene Walter twirled a nine-inning no-hitter in the first game of a July 13 doubleheader.

The home run and RBI champ was Oklahoma City outfielder Juan Gonzalez (.258, 29 HR, 101 RBI), who was named Most Valuable Player, Rookie of the Year, All-Star MVP, and recipient of the "Star of Stars" Award. On May 9 Louisville left fielder Bernard Gilkey set an AA record by collecting three hits — two singles and a homer — during a 16-run third inning as the Redbirds pounded Nashville, 18–4; Louisville sent 21 men to the plate and collected 14 hits (but the previous night the Sounds had blasted out a 17–5 victory over the Redbirds).

Buffalo outfielder-first baseman Mark Ryal (.334) won the batting title with a 2-for-4 performance in a single-game playoff with Nashville for the Eastern Division crown. Ryal did not have enough at-bats to qualify, and it appeared that Omaha outfielder Gary Thurman (.331) would be the batting champ. But when the playoff game became necessary, Ryal had an opportunity to collect the four at-bats he needed. Ryal lined an RBI double in the first inning, collected two more official at-bats, then came up again when the game went into extra innings and singled in the 10th to clinch the crown.

The playoff was forced when division leader Buffalo lost at Indianapolis on the last day of the season, while Nashville won at Louisville, which left the Bisons and Sounds deadlocked with identical 85–61 records. Buffalo had a head-to-head edge over Nashville during the regular season and was awarded the home field advantage. For the third year in a row, the Bisons had attracted over one million fans, and despite only 19 hours notice, a crowd of more than 16,000 surged into Pilot Field on a Tuesday night to see the September 4 showdown. Ironically, the two franchises had played dead-even ball (63–63) since entering the American Association in 1985, and the opposing managers, Terry Collins of Buffalo and Pete Mackanin of Nashville, had once met in a single-game playoff in the Venezuelan winter league (Collins' team won in 14 innings). The two teams battled for five hours and 18 innings before Mackanin's Sounds finally prevailed, 4–3.

Western Division winner Omaha, managed by Sal Rende, outlasted Nashville, three games to two, for the AA championship, then went on to win the Triple-A Alliance Classic over IL titlist Rochester, 4–2.

Bibliography

Books

The library of the Baseball Hall of Fame in Cooperstown supplied photocopied sections from the annual baseball guides which provide information essential to a project of this nature. The guides I studied were: *Reach's Official American League Guide* (1902–1904); *The Reach Official American League Guide* (1905–1925); *Reach Official American League Base Ball Guide* (1926–1938); *Spalding-Reach Official Base Ball Guide* (1939–1940); *Official Baseball Record Book* (1941); *Baseball Guide and Record Book* (1942–1961); *Official Baseball Guide* (1962–1988). Other books containing pertinent information included:

Allen, Maury. *You Could Look It Up, The Life of Casey Stengel.* New York: Times Books, 1979.

Alou, Felipe, with Herm Weiskopf. *Felipe Alou . . . My Life and Baseball.* Waco, Texas: Word Books, 1967.

American Association Sketch and Record Book 1989. Published by the American Association, 1989.

Anderson, Harry H., and Frederick I. Olson. *Milwaukee: At the Gathering of the Waters.* Milwaukee: The Milwaukee County Historical Society, n.d.

Brewers 1947 Sketch Book. Milwaukee: Milwaukee Brewers Baseball Club, 1947.

Bruce, Janet. *The Kansas City Monarchs, Champions of Black Baseball.* Lawrence: University Press of Kansas, 1985.

Buege, Bob. *The Milwaukee Braves, A Baseball Eulogy.* Milwaukee: Douglas American Sports Publications, 1988.

Campanella, Roy. *It's Good To Be Alive.* Boston: Little, Brown and Company, 1959.

Creamer, Robert W. *Stengel, His Life and Times.* New York: Dell Publishing Co., Inc., 1984.

Dolson, Frank. *Beating the Bushes, Life in the Minor Leagues.* South Bend, Indiana: Icarus Press, 1982.

The Dream Lives On. Published by the Buffalo Bisons, 1988.

Durso, Joseph. *Casey, The Life and Legend of Charles Dillon Stengel*. Englewood Cliffs, New Jersey: Prentice-Hall, Inc., 1967.

Dustin, Dorothy Devereux. *Omaha and Douglas County, A Panoramic History*. Woodland Hills, California: Windsor Publications, Inc., 1980.

Egerton, John. *Nashville, The Faces of Two Centuries, 1780–1980*. Nashville: PlusMedia Incorporated, 1979.

Etkin, Jack. *Innings Ago*. Kansas City, Missouri: Normandy Square Publications, 1987.

Fidrych, Mark, and Tom Clark. *No Big Deal*. Philadelphia and New York: J. B. Lippincott Company, 1977.

Ford, Whitey, with Phil Pepe. *Slick*. New York: William Morrow and Company, Inc., 1987.

Foster, Mark S. *The Denver Bears, From Sandlots to Sellouts*. Boulder, Colorado: Pruett Publishing Company, 1983.

Goldstein, Richard. *Spartan Seasons — How Baseball Survived the Second World War*. New York: Macmillan Publishing Company, 1985.

Guidry, Ron, and Peter Golenbock. *Guidry*. Englewood Cliffs, N.J.: Prentice-Hall, Inc., 1980.

Herzog, Whitey, and Kevin Horrigan. *White Rat, A Life in Baseball*. New York: Harper and Row, Publishers, 1987.

Hornsby, Rogers, and Bill Surface. *My War With Baseball*. New York: Coward-McCann, Inc., 1962.

Inside the Astrodome. Houston: Houston Sports Association, Inc., 1965.

Kane, Lucile M., and Alan Ominsky. *Twin Cities: A Pictorial History of Saint Paul and Minneapolis*. St. Paul: Minnesota Historical Society Press, 1983.

Kiersh, Edward. *Where Have You Gone, Vince DiMaggio?* New York: Bantam Books, 1983.

Kunz, Virginia Brainard. *St. Paul, Saga of an American City*. Woodland Hills, California: Windsor Publications, Inc., 1977.

Lewis, Franklin. *The Cleveland Indians*. New York: G. P. Putnam's Sons, 1949.

Long, R. M. *Wichita Century, A Pictorial History of Wichita, Kansas, 1870-1970*. Wichita: The Wichita Historical Museum Association, Inc., 1969.

MacFarlane, Paul, ed. *Daguerreotypes of Great Stars of Baseball*. St. Louis: The Sporting News Publishing Co., 1981.

MacLean, Norman, ed. *Who's Who In Baseball 1989*. New York: Who's Who In Baseball Magazine Co., Inc., 1989.

Mantle, Mickey, with Herb Gluck. *The Mick*. Garden City, New York: Doubleday and Company, Inc., 1985.

Martin, Billy, and Peter Golenbock. *Number 1*. New York: Dell Publishing Co., Inc., 1981.

Mays, Willie, with Lou Sahadi. *Say Hey, The Autobiography of Willie Mays*.

New York: Simon and Schuster, Inc., 1988.

McComb, David G. *Houston, the Bayou City*. Austin: University of Texas Press, 1969.

McRaven, Henry. *Nashville, "Athens of the South."* Chapel Hill: Scheer and Jervis, 1949.

Mehl, Ernest. *The Kansas City Athletics*. New York: Henry Holt and Company, 1956.

Obojski, Robert. *Bush League, A History of Minor League Baseball*. New York: Macmillan Publishing Co., Inc., 1975.

O'Connor, Richard. *Wild Bill Hickok*. New York: Doubleday and Co., Inc., 1959.

Okkonen, Marc. *The Federal League of 1914–1915, Baseball's Third Major League*. Garrett Park, Maryland: Society for American Baseball Research, Inc., 1989.

Overfield, Joseph M. *The 100 Seasons of Buffalo Baseball*. Kenmore, N.Y.: Partners' Press, 1985.

Petree, Patrick K. *Old Times to the Goodtimes, The History of Oklahoma City Baseball*. Oklahoma City: Oklahoma City 89ers, n.d.

Reddick, David B., and Kim M. Rogers. *The Magic of Indians' Baseball: 1887–1987*. Indianapolis: Indians, Inc., 1988.

Reichler, Joseph L., ed. *The Baseball Encyclopedia*. New York: Macmillan Publishing Company, 1988.

Reidenbaugh, Lowell. *Take Me Out to the Ball Park*. St. Louis: The Sporting News Publishing Co., 1983.

Ritter, Lawrence S. *The Glory of Their Times*. New York: William Morrow and Company, Inc., 1984.

Rorrer, George, and Stan Denny. *Redbirds: Thanks A Million*. Louisville, Kentucky: The Courier-Journal and The Louisville Times, 1983.

Ryan, Bob. *Wait Till I Make the Show: Baseball in the Minor Leagues*. Boston: Little, Brown and Company, 1974.

Schumacher, Max, and Cliff Rubenstein. *Indianapolis Indians, 25th Anniversary of Community Ownership, 1956–1980, Record Book*. Indianapolis: Indians, Inc., 1980.

Society for American Baseball Research. *Minor League Baseball Stars*. Vol. I. Manhattan, Kansas: Ag Press, Inc., 1984.

Society for American Baseball Research. *Minor League Baseball Stars*. Vol. II. Manhattan, Kansas: Ag Press, Inc., 1985.

Somers, Dale A. *The Rise of Sports in New Orleans, 1850–1900*. Baton Rouge: LSU Press, 1972.

Thornley, Stew. *On To Nicollett, The Glory and Fame of the Minneapolis Millers*. Minneapolis: Nodin Press, 1988.

Turkin, Hy, and S. C. Thompson. *The Official Encyclopedia of Baseball*. New York: A. S. Barnes and Company, 1956.

Veeck, Bill, with Ed Linn. *The Hustler's Handbook*. New York: G. P. Putnam's Sons, 1965.

Veeck, Bill, with Ed Linn. *Veeck — As in Wreck, The Autobiography of Bill Veeck*. Evanston, Illinois: Holtzman Press, Inc., 1962.

Walton, Ed. *The Rookies*. New York: Stein and Day, 1982.

Westlake, Charles W. *Columbus Baseball History*. Columbus: Pfeifer Printing Company, 1981.

Williams, Ted, with John Underwood. *My Turn at Bat, The Story of My Life*. New York: Pocket Books, 1970.

Articles

Bebar, Richard. "Take that, Peter Ueberroth." *Forbes* (February 9, 1987), 36–38.

Brady, Erik. "Buffalo rates No. 1 in field of expansion." *USA Today* (April 14, 1988).

Briley, Ron. "The Times Were A-Changin': Baseball As a Symbol of American Values in Transition, 1963–1964." *The Baseball Research Journal* (1988), 54–60.

Carlson, Chuck. "Beating the Bushes." *Baseball America* (August 15, 1984), 19.

Edmond, George. "Take Me Out To The Old Saints & Millers Games." *The Grand Gazette,* Vol I, No. 8 (May 1974), 1, 12–13.

Garrity, John. "The Newest Look Is Old." *Sports Illustrated* (October 12, 1987).

Gergen, Joe. "The Triple-A Difference: Grass Instead of Glitz." *The Sporting News* (July 25, 1988), 7.

Green, Paul. "Joe Hauser." *Sports Collectors Digest* (April 21, 1989), 202–204.

Hayes, Gordon, with Noury Mulligan. "1924's 'Prime Underdogs' And Their Two-Title Victory." *Ramsey County History,* Vol. 10, No. 1 (Spring 1973), 14–20.

Hendrickson, Robert. "How Pete Gray Defied the Odds." *Baseball Digest* (May 1971), 226–228.

Justice, Richard. "Buffalo Makes Major League Effort." *The Washington Post* (September 5, 1988).

Murphy, J. M. "Napoleon Lajoie, Modern Baseball's First Superstar." *The National Pastime* (Spring 1988), 7–79.

"The 1932 A.L. Batting Champs." *Oldtyme Baseball News* (July 1, 1988), 1 and 7.

Ringolsby, Tracy. "The Road to Success." *Baseball America* (November 15, 1983), 5.

Rudolph, Barbara. "Bonanza in the Bushes." *Time* (August 1, 1988).

Scher, Jon. "The graying of Triple A." *Baseball America* (October 10, 1989), 18.

———. "In Buffalo, they feel like a Million." *Baseball America* (July 10, 1988), 18–19.

Tomlinson, Gerald. "A Minor-League Legend: Buzz Arlett, the 'Mightiest Oak'." *The Baseball Research Journal* (1988), 13–16.

Van Fleet, Bill. "The Cats Is Back." *Fort Worth Press* (April 1964), 16–19, 50.

Wagner, Bill. "The League That Never Was." *The Baseball Research Journal* (1987), 18–21.

Newspapers

Baseball America (1986–89).
Buffalo *Bison Gram* (1989).
Columbus *Anchors Aweigh* (1988–89).
Dallas *Morning News* (1887–1958, 1960, 1965–71).
Des Moines *Register* (1937, 1946, 1950, 1981–83).
Evansville *Press* (1975, 1977–79, 1984).
Fort Worth *Press* (1925, 1950, 1957, 1959, 1968).
Fort Worth *Star-Telegram* (1949, 1950, 1970, 1980).
Houston *Chronicle* (1963, 1968, 1976).
Houston *Post* (1936, 1952, 1966, 1978, 1979).
Louisville *Courier-Journal* (1943, 1944, 1949, 1950, 1955, 1956, 1957, 1958, 1964, 1967, 1969, 1971, 1980, 1982, 1983, 1984, 1985, 1987).
Milwaukee *Brewer News* (1943–46).
Milwaukee *Sentinel* (1979).
Nashville *Banner* (1867, 1967, 1970, 1971, 1978, 1986).
Oklahoma City *Times* (1940).
Omaha *World-Herald* (1954, 1960, 1968, 1969, 1970, 1971, 1975, 1982, 1984, 1985, 1986).
The Sporting News (1986–89).
Tulsa *World* (1965, 1967, 1969, 1971, 1976, 1977, 1983).
Wichita *Eagle-Beacon* (1957, 1961, 1970, 1977, 1979, 1980, 1982, 1984).

Local Baseball Files

Buffalo Public Library
Fort Worth Public Library
Houston Public Library
Iowa State Historical Museum, Des Moines
Kansas City, Kansas, Public Library
Kansas City, Missouri, Public Library
Louisville Public Library
Milwaukee Public Library
Minnesota State Historical Society, St. Paul
The Nashville Room, The Public Library of Nashville and Davidson County

Metropolitan Library System, Oklahoma City
Omaha Public Library
St. Paul Public Library
Toledo Public Library
Tulsa Public Library
Wichita Public Library

Miscellaneous

Brewers Official Score Card Magazine (1943–45, 1949–52).
Milwaukee Brewers Official Score Card (1905, 1911, 1913, 1914, 1917). On file at Milwaukee Public Library.
Vitter, Joe. Scrapbooks. Carthage, Texas.
Wallace, Carl M. Scrapbooks. Evansville, Indiana.
York, Mariana. Scrapbooks. Hubbard, Texas.

Index

C